Cases in Qualitative Research

Research Reports for Discussion and Evaluation

Andrea K. Milinki

Pyrczak Publishing

P.O. Box 39731 • Los Angeles, CA 90039

Scanning services provided by Kenneth Ornburn.

Cover design by Robert Kibler and Larry Nichols.

Editorial assistance provided by Cheryl Alcorn, Elaine Fuess, Sharon Young, and Randall R. Bruce.

Printed in the United States of America.

10 9 8 7 6 5 4 3 2 1   DOC   04 03 02 01 00 99 98 99

ISBN 1-884585-17-5

Table of Contents

Continued →

Topic B: Evaluating Alcohol and Drug Abuse Education

Qualitative Case

Quantitative Case

Appendices

Introduction

The cases in this book illustrate a wide variety of methods for conducting qualitative research. All were drawn from recent issues of journals in the social and behavioral sciences, including education.

Underlying this book is the assumption that it is essential to read and critique the research of others in order to become a skilled researcher. In a classroom setting, this is best accomplished by having all students read the same article(s) for homework and come to class ready to discuss them. The questions at the end of each article are designed to stimulate such discussions.

Organization of This Book

This book is divided into three sections. In the first section are eight examples of qualitative research—each with its own blend of methods and approaches. The second section presents four examples in which researchers rely primarily on qualitative methods, but supplement them with quantitative methods for certain aspects of their research. Finally, the third section consists of two pairs of articles. Each pair is on the same general research topic, but one member of each pair is qualitative while the other is quantitative. This section provides stimulus material for students to use in comparing and contrasting the two methods of research, and the questions at the end of the second member of each pair (the quantitative article) explicitly ask students to make such comparisons.

The Appendices

The three appendices provide various perspectives on the evaluation of qualitative research. Some of the questions at the end of each qualitative article are based on Appendix A, so this appendix is a good place for beginning students to start. After reading one or two cases, the other two appendices should be read. They provide material that will help in identifying additional criteria for the evaluation of qualitative research and illustrate that there are varying views on its evaluation.

On Evaluating Qualitative Research

The evaluation of qualitative research is difficult because the methods are diverse both in their nature and execution. The questions at the end of each qualitative report in this book are meant only to prod and stimulate classroom discussions. Keep in mind that a qualitative research report may be deficient on most of the questions and still be judged to make an important overall contribution to their fields. Trying to quantify the evaluation of qualitative research by adding up points earned on specific evaluation questions would run counter to the rich tradition that qualitative researchers follow. As Margarete Sandelowski aptly put it, "The skilled critic of qualitative work is able to move beyond the rigid application of absolute standards to choose the criteria most fitting to a work and to separate fatal from merely surface errors in evaluating a work."[1]

---

[1] Sandelowski, M. (1997). "To be of use": Enhancing the utility of qualitative research. *Nursing Outlook, 45,* 125–132 (p. 129).

A Word of Welcome

If you are new to qualitative research, welcome! It's a fascinating and diverse field. Those who practice its craft study some of the most interesting and important issues in the social and behavioral sciences. I believe you will find that the articles in this collection live up to this tradition.

Andrea K. Milinki
Editor

Case 1

Turning Points in the Lives of Young Inner-City Men Forgoing Destructive Criminal Behaviors: A Qualitative Study

MARGARET HUGHES
San Diego State University

ABSTRACT. This article explores the lives of inner-city African American and Latino American young men previously involved in trajectories of destructive behavior, including violence, illegal drug marketing, and other crimes, who had made positive behavioral changes and were now contributing to their community's well-being. In-depth interviews with 20 young men examined their life courses from the time of their earliest memories. Personal and environmental transitions that contributed to their decisions to change were uncovered. Maturation was a significant factor in their transition experiences; however, findings indicated four other significant factors: respect and concern for children; fear of physical harm, incarceration, or both; contemplation time; and support and modeling. Implications for social services providers, policymakers, and youth program staff are discussed.

From *Social Work Research*, 22, 143–151. Copyright © 1998 by the National Association of Social Workers, Inc. Reprinted with permission.

Youths and young adults represent the largest population of property and violent crime arrests in the United States. The 1993 crime statistics show that ju-
5 veniles younger than 18 years accounted for 41 percent of arrests for all serious crimes, of which 18 percent were for murder and nonnegligent manslaughter and 20 percent were for aggravated assault. Young adults ages 18 to 24 accounted for 26 percent of arrests for all serious crimes, of which 41 percent were for murder and
10 nonnegligent manslaughter and 27 percent were for aggravated assault. These arrest rates are alarmingly disproportionate for African Americans and Latinos (U.S. Bureau of the Census, 1996). The arrest rates should alert researchers to the critical need to find so-
15 lutions to these problems.

The majority of research has focused on the causes of criminal behavior. However, understanding the causal factors of crime is only half of the solution; the other half is to understand what makes young men
20 forgo crime. Examining life courses of individuals has uncovered important information about how attitudinal and behavioral changes develop. Elder (1985) defined the life course as a pathway differentiated by age: "Movement through the age-graded life course in each
25 [institutional] sphere may correspond with social expectations or depart markedly from them" (p. 30). The concepts of trajectories and transitions are unifying themes. A *trajectory* is defined as "a lifeline or career, a pathway over the life span. The pathway may be psy-
30 chological...or social. Worklife, marriage, and parenthood represent multiple, interlocking social trajectories" (pp. 17–18). A pathway of criminal activity would also be considered a trajectory. *Transitions* or "changes in state are embedded in trajectories; the lat-
35 ter give meaning and shape to the transition experience" (p. 18). Whether a transition is present or absent may be reflected in the choices made by the individual. First significant job, committed relationship, and childbirth are examples of transitions. Several studies have
40 used the life course perspective in an effort to understand how transitions affect a trajectory of crime (Caspi, Elder, & Herbener, 1990; Laub & Sampson, 1993; Loeber & Stouthamer-Loeber, 1996; Macmillan, 1995).

45 Sampson and Laub's (1993) secondary data analysis of Glueck and Glueck's (1950, 1968) longitudinal study of 500 delinquents and 500 controls found evidence that "childhood pathways to crime and conformity over the life course are significantly influenced by
50 adult social bonds" (p. 243). The authors emphasized "the quality and strength of social ties more than the occurrence or timing of life events" (p. 246). Strong marital attachment and job stability were two transitions related to desistance from crime. These transi-
55 tions are proposed as informal social bonds and forms of social capital that can facilitate positive change in behavior despite deviant trajectories from early childhood. Macmillan (1995) studied the changes three life course transitions (marriage, living at home, and labor
60 force participation) had on crime rates among youths and young adults ages 15 to 24. Using a time series analysis of Canadian property crimes, Macmillan found significantly lower crime rates for youths and young adults in his sample who were married, lived at home,
65 or were employed.

The uniform crime reports show a positive correlation between age and desistance from crime. Shover and Thompson (1992) offered several explanations as to why deviance desists with age, including loss of interest, ability to understand consequences of a criminal lifestyle, degree of payoff, disenchantment with a criminal lifestyle, and fear of consequences. The "differential expectations" influence individuals engaged in a criminal lifestyle to desist. These explanations suggest an age of maturation at which individuals reach a cognitive developmental stage that acts as a transition from a criminal trajectory. Gove (1985) suggested the age-criminal desistance correlation is influenced, in part, by normative, socially structured transitions (for example, marriage and childbirth). The adolescent and early adult years are ages when anomie, or normlessness, is most apt to occur, in part because of a lack of socially structured roles and uncertainty about the future. Gove argued that "if social roles change and life takes on structure and meaning, then deviance should decline accordingly" (p. 126).

Loeber and LeBlanc (1990) argued for a developmental approach—developmental criminology—to the study of delinquency. One focus of this approach is "the identification of explicative or causal factors which predate behavioral development and have an impact on its course" (Loeber & Stouthamer-Loeber, 1996, p. 13). This approach can also be used to study desistance from delinquency by identifying factors that affect decisions to turn from delinquency. This article describes a study that explored the lives of previously delinquent young men to uncover factors that facilitated their decisions to desist from criminal activity.

The Study

This study contributes to the literature by focusing on African American and Latino American young men who are desisting from crime after long criminal histories; one white young man who grew up in a predominantly African American community and who associated solely with African American youths was interviewed and used as a comparison. The study used primary data collection methods. One limitation of the study was its reliance on self-reported histories. Longitudinal panel studies like Glueck and Glueck's are ideal because they increase reliability; however, such studies are rare because of time, money, and attrition. Some findings in this study matched transitions leading to desistance found in other studies, that is, marriage, childbirth, and labor force participation (Macmillan, 1995; Sampson & Laub, 1993). However, variations of these transitions as well as transitions not previously noted in literature were found.

Participants

Twenty young adult, inner-city men made up the sample population in this exploratory study. Demographics of the participants were diverse, particularly with respect to age, ethnicity, education, and city of residence. There were nine (45 percent) African Americans, three (15 percent) Mexican Americans, four (20 percent) Puerto Ricans, three (15 percent) Jamaicans, and one (5 percent) white young man who grew up in an inner-city community with a predominantly African American and Latino population. The participants ranged in age from 18 to 27. Throughout most of their adolescent years, they resided in Boston, New York, San Francisco, Philadelphia, and Chicago. Only two participants were married; however, seven (35 percent) had children. Two other participants considered themselves fathers but were not the biological parent. Their educational backgrounds were less than high school, seven (35 percent); high school graduate, four (20 percent); GED, three (15 percent); trade school in addition to high school, three (15 percent); and some college, three (15 percent).

Criteria

The following criteria were used to choose the sample: male between the ages of 18 and 28, history of destructive behavior (that is, individual and group participation in violent acts, property crimes, other crimes against people, illegal drug marketing, and illegal drug use), evidence of efforts to make positive life changes (for example, legal employment; participation in programs emphasizing positive change; and self-reports indicating they no longer participated in acts of violence, illegal drug marketing and use, and other criminal activities), and evidence of positive involvement in the community (for example, mentoring for other youths at risk of engaging in destructive behaviors, volunteering with organizations promoting community improvement, volunteering with recreational programs for youths, and speaking against destructive behaviors in schools and other centers serving youths).

Data Collection

Data collection began with open selection by convenience. I selected the initial group of participants (five) from an intervention program I had worked with as a volunteer mentor for the preceding two years. Through information obtained from the program staff as well as personal knowledge from direct contact with some of the young men, I determined that each participant met the criteria for the study.

Intervention program directors, community leaders, and pastors identified the remaining participants using the study's criteria. Nine participants were part of a residential program that accepted young men from across the United States. Three participants were identified by pastors of local churches, and three were identified by community leaders.

I collected data over a two-year period. I conducted in-depth interviews with each participant, each lasting approximately 90 minutes. I contacted sixteen participants a second time, either by phone or in person, for a shorter interview; four participants had moved and could not be contacted. I used data from the second

interviews to validate interpretations and information, to obtain any missing information, and to include the sample as active participants in the study's analysis. In addition, I made ethnographic observations of some
180 participants from the first group over the two-year period.

Interviews took place in offices or the participants' homes with no other people present. The interviews began by my verifying that each participant met the
185 criteria. Then I collected demographic data (age, ethnicity, marital and parental status, education level attained, employment status, and place of residence). The remainder of the first interviews focused on open-ended, topical questions concerning experiences with
190 family, school, law enforcement and criminal justice, significant people, intervention programs, community, street group affiliation (if applicable), and significant life events. I chose these topics to ensure that the participants covered significant life stages and agents
195 contributing to their socialization. I asked the participants to detail those periods and events related to their decisions to make positive changes in their life course.

Data Analysis

I transcribed each taped interview verbatim. I then used the computer program, Qualitative Solutions and
200 Research, Nonnumerical Unstructured Data Indexing, Searching, and Theorizing 3.0 (1994) to manage and analyze the interviews. Analytic conclusions can be formulated by coding and then categorizing similar statements of experiences from data.
205 When examining the outcomes of individuals using Elder's Life Course Dynamics model (Elder, 1985), it is important to consider the trajectories taken by other agents who influence the individual's life. It is also important to examine the "connections between widely
210 separated events and transitions, as in the relation between young adulthood and old age" (Elder, 1985, p. 34). A list of codes was predetermined that described phenomena related to me during the interviews and during my previous work as a mentor. The list con-
215 tained codes describing influential agents in the participants' lives (family, school, church, law enforcement, employers, peers, and role models), developmental periods (childhood, adolescence, and young adulthood), and phenomena connected to the onset of
220 trajectories of criminal activity and desistance from crime. I subsequently read each transcript and categorized passages using these codes. The coded passages were analyzed to determine which were related to participants' decisions to make positive changes in their
225 behaviors. These passages were grouped and recategorized as factors facilitating positive change. Conclusions were drawn from these factors (Strauss & Corbin, 1990).

Findings

Conclusions drawn from the categorized passages
230 indicated four significant factors: (1) respect and con-

cern for children, (2) fear of physical harm or incarceration, (3) contemplation time, and (4) support and modeling. These factors are reported in summary form.

Respect and Concern for Children

The many crises faced, the all too frequent need to
235 self-nurture because of absent parents, perilous environments requiring development of survival techniques, and a shortage of characteristics of a healthy childhood (for example, play, laughter, wonderment, pleasurable experiences, and feelings of security, love,
240 and worth) give rise to an atypical childhood for many poor youths in the inner cities. Data revealed that these unhealthy childhood experiences were typical for participants throughout their juvenile and adolescent years. Perhaps because of their unhealthy experiences,
245 these young men sensed the critical importance of a healthy childhood. Participants revealed the development of a deep-seated respect and concern for children. They alluded to experiences involving children as playing a role in their decision to change.
250 Six participants indicated that love for their own children was a factor leading to their decision to change. Ronnie stated that a traumatic incident involving his son led to his decision to change: "I robbed this dude one day, and I was high, and I had my son.
255 He might have been like six months. He ran up on me with a gun, and he said, 'I won't kill you right now because your son's in the carriage, but next time I see you man, it ain't no tellin' what I'll do.' So after that, I was like man I can't do this anymore. I can't do this.
260 My son could a got hurt. You know bullets don't have no name."

The incident also evoked memories of his childhood pain from an absent father. He stated,

> Sometimes I feel like I'ma die not knowing who my fa-
265 > ther is. So do I wanna go on not letting my kids know? It's like a vicious cycle; it's going on and on and on. Now somebody's gonna have to change that. And you know, I'm steppin' off the merry-go-round. I mean this is in my whole family, the lifestyle…I feel like I'm a young man.
270 > I got a lot to live for. I'm steppin' off the merry-go-round. I'm going to make things happen. You know, things ain't happening when you keep going around in circles. That's what I want to do for mine.

George stated, "What's workin' for me now, and
275 what will work for me in the long run, I have a son. Without a doubt, I don't want him to grow up and I don't be around." A similar statement was made by Michael: "But pretty much now, I'm just tryin' to establish with my daughter. I'd say that was the number
280 one reason, other than me just wanting to get out of it [drug dealing and drug abuse], the number one motive to do the right thing." Other participants made statements indicating their own children gave them a feeling of worth. Daniel stated,

285 > Sometimes I look back at all the things I've done, and I be like, I knew there was some kind of plan that God had

3

for me, and when I first moved up here, I said, "Look, I know I've been through a war." I been shot and stabbed and beat down and all this. I said, "You gotta have something better. You gotta have something better." I guess this is it, and I got a little girl. I'm tryin', a black man trying to get custody of his child. I could never see myself saying, wow!, I'm really trying to get custody of a child, you know. But the good thing about it is that I'm able to do it.

For one respondent, observing the dangerous situation his drug marketing exposed a child to influenced him to change. John recounted:

I went into a house one day. This dude owed me my money. So me and my boy Earl, my boy James, we went into this house. And then I never got my money, but I went in the house. I saw the condition of the house. It was disgusting. It was like it had never been cleaned for the past two years and a crib over in the corner with a little baby in the crib in this nasty, filthy, stinky house. And I just stood there, and I couldn't believe that this had happened. It was a crack house. Everyone in that house was usin'. That was one of our biggest buyers. And I saw. I was so devastated just to see what the drugs had done. I mean I really started to feel for them. Before, I would just be a heartless person with no conscience. I had no conscience. Oh yeah, just to see that little baby. The baby had sores all over his body. He was in the crib and no one was taking care of him. You could tell he had gone to the bathroom in his diaper. Ahhhh! And no one was taking care of the child. So I made it a point, and I just called DSS [Department of Social Services]. I told 'em there was a baby in that house and no one was taking care of him. DSS checked on the baby, checked on the apartment. By me being able to do something like that, I just couldn't go on. I just couldn't.

Three other participants stated it bothered them when they realized children were being affected by their drug marketing. They felt that parents using Aid to Families with Dependent Children money to buy drugs was wrong and that they were neglecting their children by getting high.

Fear of Physical Harm, Incarceration, or Both

Participants reported that the longer they remained active in the street life, the greater the probability of their being physically harmed. They attributed this increased danger to an increase in the number of peer enemies and new competition in the drug market trying to take over their established territory.

John explained about the time limits as well as the dangers of the drug business for young men like him:

It was knuckled up in spots. It got to the point when we were blowing people away when I got 19, and I had two more years left in the streets. 'Cause it's known that you're only large [real successful] in the streets for six years. If you work you figure if you get into the game at six years, you work for two or three years, then you get some money. And then, if you're smart you invest your money in more drugs and have people buying and selling for you. That's how you get large. You have a total of six years 'cause that crop of young boys is comin' up. And

that's where the violence started comin' into play. Everybody wants to knock this dude off, knock this dude off and get his territory. Get what he had. You either get what you want and realize you have enough to get out or you can stay there, fight for your territory, and eventually die. I know a lot of guys who eventually died 'cause they gunna stay and fight for their territory. That's why there's so many young people in jail for killing someone. Chances are, they shot someone older than them 'cause they want what they had.

Vicente recounted being shot by a competitor while making a drug deal. He described being double-crossed by the other person in the deal. He emphasized the need to always be on the alert. "I did business with him before, you see. So I didn't expect that, but I always brought along a gun because you know things happen. Expect the unexpected, and this was what happened." Other participants talked about times when drug deals went bad and they felt their lives were endangered.

Data revealed that participants reached a point at which the fear of physical harm, particularly death, had a significant influence on their leaving the street life. Allen stated, "If you gonna be true to it, you wanta be on the streets, you should be true to it. But I don't think I want to be true to the streets. There ain't nothin' out there but jail or death. I got too much life to live." Laron recounted what it was like once he tried to make a positive change: "Man, I been carrying a weapon ever since. Since this year, I ain't had a gun on me. I ain't had a gun on me, not a piece on me since this fall, this whole '94 year. This is my first shot ever from '86 to now. This is my first year that I didn't have a gun. As a matter of fact, I got shot at the most this year out of my whole life. That's why I came to [this program]."

Although the street life, especially in connection with drug dealing, was perceived by respondents to have gotten more dangerous as they got older, other factors influenced their fear. Eighty percent of these young men recounted experiences of being shot or stabbed. In some cases, these experiences had occurred more than once. Many had had critical injuries. The longer they continued in the street life, the more enemies they gained, and, as a result, the more they felt their lives were in danger. Second, all but one participant stated he had been incarcerated more than once as a juvenile and some as an adult. They stated that it was not a big deal as a juvenile because they received short sentences, but that as adults they would receive longer, harsher sentences. Most of those who had served sentences as adults, which ranged from one to three years, indicated their experiences were unbearable and that they were afraid of having to serve any more time. Some circumstances of their incarceration that they felt made it unbearable included sexual assaults, physical assaults, and unlivable prison conditions.

Contemplation Time

A significant factor in their decisions to change destructive behaviors was occasions when participants had time away from their chaotic environments to contemplate their lives. Eleven participants indicated that during this time they were able to understand more clearly the progression their lives had taken and what circumstances led to that progression. They also indicated realizing that only they could change their life course. The critical aspect of this factor is the time away from those environments that foster destructive behaviors, not the site where contemplation occurs.

The nine participants who made changes in their behavior while participating in the previously mentioned residential program underwent a very intensive and disciplined regime. They were not permitted to leave the facility for an initial three-month period except during program-supervised outings. The staff worked on instilling new values and building self-esteem and self-worth. The participants involved in this program all described it as hard because of the regimentation and consistency of expectations of them. They also commented that they were forced to live 24 hours a day, seven days a week with what they termed bad attitudes. Although they encountered bad attitudes in the streets, at the facility they were unable to deal with these attitudes in a manner counterproductive to the program's purpose. Although support was an additional significant factor in this program (see Support and Modeling section), participants indicated by their statements that the contemplation time the program offered them was a separate influence.

Devon stated his initial reason for coming to this program was the $5,000 stipend it offered at the end of three years. He had no desire to change his street life behavior before coming to the program. He recounted, "I wanted the $5,000 that I heard they was supposed to give you. But then after awhile, I was like, I'm liable to stay 'cause I need a change. Let me see, let me mess with myself a little bit. Let me see what'll happen on the other side of the fence. So I tried, and I like it."

Relocation allowed other participants the opportunity to contemplate and decide to make changes. Jay recounted several experiences of short incarcerations in detention facilities and jail and indicated that his behavior worsened after these confinements. However, at the age of 18, he left his neighborhood environment where he had engaged in illegal drug marketing and armed robberies. It was during this period of time that he began to experience changes in his behavior and way of thinking. He stated, "I came to Boston. I came here and spent the summer here and got away from Philadelphia for the rest of the summer. I ended up going to Nantucket where I went to school, and I ended up like just removing myself from Philadelphia. And then, from then, that's when I started doing some of my growing, and I started re-examining some of my values. And I was like, what's going on in my life?"

Gilberto indicated he began thinking about change after a period he spent in Mexico. He went to live in Mexico to escape problems with the law. Recounting what occurred on returning, he stated, "This was the summer when I had barely came back from Mexico. And after that I was trying to get out of it [participating in destructive behaviors]. I was working at the letter company which was real good. I was working there and then I was going to school at night."

Four participants made the decision to change their behavior while incarcerated. They indicated that it gave them time to think about where their lives were going. Allen clearly described this experience: "When I got arrested the last time, and I had a lot of time to think in jail. That's when we usually do it. And I was just thinking. I was like just sayin', 'What if?' Well being behind bars, my freedom is worth more than this. And I just want to change my life. And I just thought about it."

Ricardo expressed deep feelings about his two-year prison experience, stating, "Honestly, I didn't think I could make it in prison. Prison wasn't for me. Prison was not what changed me. What it was, I had [realized] that I was wrong. Prison was that, yo, you need to chill. But you could have stuck me anywhere for a week and same thing. I didn't need to do that." Ricardo also spoke about the significance of getting out of his chaotic environment. He stated,

I go to church to get down on my knees an' thank God for my life. And to me church is the most peaceful thing in the world. People never realize that you can go to church and stop the whole world from affecting you. No one ever realizes that you can stop the whole world. 'Cause you don't hear nothin'. You don't hear brothers swearing. You don't hear brothers killin' each other. You don't hear ambulances. You don't hear cops. You just hear yourself.

None of those who had been incarcerated indicated that the harsh treatment gave rise to thoughts of change. Instead they mentioned feelings of anger and hatred because of such treatment. It was at those times in prison when they were alone to think without the mind-cluttering, punitive conditions that they thought of change.

Support and Modeling

All 20 participants associated the support of a consistently dedicated person with their ability to make changes in their lives, although none felt that this alone was the influential change factor. The kinds of support participants described as influential in their decisions to change included unconditional acceptance of them, particularly at times of relapse into destructive behavioral patterns; availability on a consistent basis when they needed advice, counseling, or just someone to talk to; involvement with them in activities that were recreational and gave a feeling of "family"; assistance with job training and placement or educational attainment; and instillation of self-worth and self-esteem.

The most commonly reported quality of effective support people was genuine concern and caring. Gilberto described one woman whom he felt especially influenced him to change: "She's been working for about three years, and it's only her by herself. It's just one lady. And what's weird is that her sons and daughters are never been in gangs, never been in problems, but she's still working in the community. 'Cause usually what happens, a mother gets involved after her son gets killed and stuff like that. And this lady doesn't have nothin' like that."

Another participant, Jesus, also mentioned this same woman as an influential support person. He stated, "She's the one that got me in this program [the residential program] 'cause she knew me and my friend, and she knew that we could make something better of our life than being gang bangers."

Several support people reported by participants as influential in their decisions to change were females. In addition to the woman described by Gilberto and Jesus, two young men from the program that I was a mentor for reported female mentors were a factor in their decisions to change. Five participants indicated that they experienced their greatest support from an intimate female. They talked about feeling, particularly in childhood and early adolescence, that no one really cared for or loved them. They stated that females whom they dated were only with them for material gain (clothes, jewelry, and entertainment they bought for them). Gilberto described the supportive feeling his girlfriend gave him: "My girlfriend showed me that she did care, so then I figured there is someone out there that cares. She totally changed my life around, showed me that there actually are people who care." Jerome identified his wife, a girlfriend at the time, as the person who most influenced him to get out of the street life and return to school. Vicente described a time when he felt that he had relapsed by hanging around with an old friend and connecting the friend with a drug dealer. He said that he later cried because he felt he had let down all those who had helped him. It was his girlfriend who was most supportive at this time. He stated, "That's right, and my girl was the one that supported me so much in this, 'cause she gave me a lot of counseling, personal counseling you know. And she pointed out all the things that I've achieved and all the people that supported me and started naming things and names. I was like, I can't do this, and that was why I got my act together. I have to straighten up. And now I'm like more serious." Other participants talked about the importance of intimate females who supported them and who they felt genuinely loved them.

Data indicate that the important aspect of support is its consistency. These young men have typically experienced interactions with people earlier in their lives that resulted in their perception that adults cannot be counted on. This feeling of not being able to trust was very apparent to me as a mentor. The young men I worked with required long-term evidence of my sincerity and commitment before an indication of trust

evolved.

David's experiences with individuals he felt were very instrumental in his desire to change showed the importance of the support's being consistent and unconditional. David experienced a relapse in his effort to change because of the traumatic loss of his grandmother, who had raised him. This relapse unfortunately ended in years of incarceration. Yet, as he recounted, the support people continued to be there for him throughout his prison term and after his release. David presently works as a mentor in a program assisting other young men like himself. He is also in a premed program.

One particularly striking finding was that seven participants reported that seeing a change in the behavior of their previously drug- and alcohol-addicted parents motivated them to change their own lives. Allen reported that seeing his mother become active in the community had a big influence on him. This finding indicates the resilience, the parental attachment, and the power of positive role modeling, despite severe childhood abuse. Only one of the seven participants indicated that his parent made a conscious effort to encourage positive behavior changes in his life.

Conclusion

The notion that young men like the participants in this study are a lost generation is far too terminal. Findings from this study indicate survival, strength, and determination among the sample population. The findings suggest that young men moving along a trajectory or pathway of criminal activity can make transitions to pathways of desistance from crime. The turning points for the sample participants were facilitated by four significant factors: respect and concern for children, fear of physical harm or incarceration, contemplation time, and support and modeling.

Respect and concern for children appeared to be the most significant factor, because it is the only one that is an unselfish motive. The data indicated that these young men experienced great difficulty in caring for and trusting others. Given their early childhood experiences of abuse, it is no wonder. Children may represent a safe population for these participants—a population they view as less likely to disappoint them. Social workers can use this factor as a healing tool with similar young men. Connecting troubled young men with programs that give them the opportunity to help troubled children can develop their feelings of worth. Also, social workers can make an effort to develop meaningful relationships and contacts among troubled young men and their children. They can advocate for policy changes so that visitation programs for incarcerated fathers can take place in secured, children-centered sections of prisons where fathers can spend quality time with their children.

The high percentage of participants from the study active in intervention programs suggests that these pro-

grams are effective arenas for addressing aspects of young men's lives, indicated by the sample as facilitating their decisions to change. Intervention programs can promote the powerful bond young men reported
635 feeling for their children through focus groups, such as the Men as Teachers group formed by Fagan and Stevenson (1995), which allows open discussion about issues of parenthood, counseling to assist young parents in overcoming the social and personal forces that act as
640 barriers to good parenting practices, and modeling of positive parent-child relationships by mentors who are parents. Fostering functional, cooperative male-female relationships, particularly those in which children are present, is another area in which intervention programs
645 could place emphasis. Including significant females in focus group discussions and counseling sessions when topics address such issues as parenting, social and environmental stressors, and relationship stressors may build the kind of supportive male-female bonds re-
650 ported by the participants as influential in their decisions to change. These strong bonds could be a preventive measure against raising another generation of children that engages in destructive behaviors.

The fear of physical harm and incarceration was re-
655 ported by some participants as influential in their decisions to change their destructive behavioral patterns. However, participants also reported that time away from their chaotic and often dangerous environments, either in residential programs in their own communities
660 or in other locations, had the same effect. Programs that offer a residential component need to be evaluated to assess whether the residential component makes a significant difference in outcome. If this component is found to be an effective intervention, courts, as an al-
665 ternative to imprisonment, could offer placement in residential programs to offenders as a last step before imprisonment, especially for first time and nonviolent offenders.

Further research that continues to explore and test
670 factors leading to positive changes in behavior is of utmost importance. Findings from such research will be useful to program directors, social services providers, and policymakers. The population of young men attempting to desist from previous delinquent behav-
675 iors is also more accessible to researchers as this study's findings seem to indicate, because this population participates in community assistance programs.

Human capital investments we as a society make in these young men will determine the future stability of
680 our inner cities. Participants in this study demonstrate the success of such investments as they return to their communities to give back. They become social capital where little is found.

References

Caspi, A., Elder, G., & Herbener, E. (1990). Childhood personality and the prediction of life course patterns. In L. Robins & M. Rutter (Eds.), *Straight and devious pathways from childhood to adulthood* (pp. 13–35). Cambridge, England: Cambridge University Press.

Elder, G. (1985). *Life course dynamics.* Ithaca, NY: Cornell University Press.

Fagan, J., & Stevenson, H. (1995). Men as teachers: A self-help program on parenting for African American men. *Social Work with Groups, 17,* 29–42.

Glueck, S., & Glueck, E. (1950). *Unraveling juvenile delinquency.* New York: Commonwealth Fund.

Glueck, S., & Glueck, E. (1968). *Delinquents and nondelinquents in perspective.* Cambridge, MA: Harvard University Press.

Gove, W. (1985). The effect of age and gender on deviant behavior: A biopsychosocial perspective. In A. S. Rossi (Ed.), *Gender and the life course* (pp. 115–144). New York: Aldine de Gruyter.

Laub, J., & Sampson, R. J. (1993). Turning points in the life course: Why change matters to the study of crime. *Criminology, 31,* 301–325.

Loeber, R., & LeBlanc, M. (1990). Toward a developmental criminology. In N. Morris & M. Tonry (Eds.), *Crime and justice* (pp. 375–473). Chicago: University of Chicago Press.

Loeber, R., & Stouthamer-Loeber, M. (1996). The development of offending. *Criminal Justice and Behavior, 23,* 12–24.

Macmillan, R. (1995). Changes in the structure of life courses and the decline of social capital in Canadian society: A time series analysis of property crime rates. *Canadian Journal of Sociology, 20,* 51–79.

Qualitative Solutions and Research, Non-numerical Unstructured Data Indexing, Searching, and Theorizing 3.0 [Computer software]. (1994). Victoria, Australia: La Trobe University, Bundoora.

Sampson, R., & Laub, J. (1993). *Crime in the making: Pathways and turning points through life.* Cambridge, MA: Harvard University Press.

Shover, N., & Thompson, C. (1992). Age differential expectations and crime desistance: *Criminology, 30,* 89–104.

Strauss, A., & Corbin, J. (1990). *Basics of qualitative research.* Newbury Park, CA: Sage Publications.

U.S. Bureau of the Census. (1996). *Statistical abstract of the United States: 1996* (116th ed.). Washington, DC: U.S. Government Printing Office.

About the Author: Margaret Hughes, PhD, is assistant professor, School of Social Work, San Diego State University, 5500 Campanile Drive, San Diego, CA 92182-4119. E-mail: mhughes2@mail.sdsu.edu

Note: This article is based on a doctoral dissertation (UMI Microfilm No. 9537820). A related publication can be found in *Smith College Studies in Social Work, 67*(3).

Exercise for Case 1

1. Introduction

A. Is the problem area for the research clearly described? Explain.

B. Has the researcher convinced you that the problem area is important? Explain.

C. To what extent does the literature presented in the introduction help you understand the problem? Is the literature used to put the problem in context? Explain.

D. Does the researcher indicate how this study is different from and/or similar to earlier ones reported in the literature?

E. Does the researcher reveal her personal perspectives on the problem area, including any possible biases? Explain.

2. Methods

A. Are the demographics of the participants (i.e., background characteristics such as age, race, and so on) described in sufficient detail? Explain.

B. Considering the problem area for the research, do you think that appropriate participants were selected? If you had been conducting the study, would you have selected the same type(s) of participants? Would you have used the same number of participants? Explain.

C. Which strategies listed in Table 1 on page 161 of this book were employed by the researcher? Are they described in sufficient detail? Explain.

D. In addition to those you named in response to question 2C, has the researcher used any additional strategies to help assure the validity of the study? If yes, what are they? Are they described in sufficient detail? Explain.

3. Analysis and Results

A. Are the steps taken in the analysis described in sufficient detail? Explain.

B. Are the results clearly organized? Explain.

C. Are the results discussed in terms of a theory or theories (either theories that emerged from this study or previously existing ones)? Explain.

D. Were the direct quotations of the participants' statements, if any, judiciously selected? Do they help you understand the results? Explain.

E. Are there other ways the results could have been organized and interpreted? Explain.

4. Conclusions/Implications

A. Are the researcher's concluding remarks appro-

priate? Do they flow logically from the material presented earlier?

B. Does the researcher describe any implications? If yes, are they appropriate? Are there other implications that are not discussed by the researcher? Explain.

5. Ethical Considerations

A. In your opinion, could this research have caused physical or psychological harm to the participants? If yes, did the researcher take adequate measures to ameliorate the potential for harm? Explain.

B. If you had conducted this research, would you have obtained written, informed consent from the participants before conducting the study? Explain. Does this research report indicate that the researcher obtained such consent?

6. Overall Evaluation

A. Throughout the article, are all specialized terms and jargon defined to your satisfaction? Explain.

B. Briefly describe your overall evaluation of the research report, noting any special strengths and weaknesses.

C. If you had been a reviewer for the journal in which this report was published, would you have recommended publication of the report? If yes, would you have recommended that it be published "as is" or modified before publication? Explain. If no, what is the primary reason why you would recommend not publishing it?

Case 2

Always Single and Single Again Women:
A Qualitative Study

KAREN GAIL LEWIS
Silver Spring, MD

SIDNEY MOON
Purdue University

ABSTRACT. What is it like to be a single woman to-day? Are the experiences of women who have always been single different from those who find themselves single again after having been married? How can family therapists promote the development of single women both individually and relationally? The purpose of this phenomenological, multiple-case study was to investigate perceptions of being single among heterosexual single women between the ages of 30 and 65. Nine focus group interviews and a semistructured, mailed questionnaire were used to collect the data. Constant comparative analyses were used to develop the findings. The findings were organized around the most salient theme that emerged from the analyses: single women have unresolved or unrecognized ambivalences about being single. This overarching theme was supported by three subassertions: (a) single women are aware of both the advantages and the drawbacks of being single; (b) single women are ambivalent about the reasons for their singleness; (c) although content with being single, many women simultaneously experience feelings of loss and grief. Implications for the clinical practice of family therapy and future research on single women are discussed.

From *Journal of Marital and Family Therapy, 23,* 115–134.

Single women are living on the cusp of change (Anderson & Stewart, 1994). Stereotypes of spinsters and old maids are outmoded, but there are few new descriptions of the single woman. Anderson and Stewart (1994) note that the media dichotomously depicts single women as "pathetic leftovers from the marriage market," unhappy and desperate, or "power-obsessed barracudas bent only on greedily acquiring the empty rewards of money and fame" (p. 14). Even the popular Cathy cartoon reflects the dual images of stigma and glamorization (Lewis, 1994). Schwartzberg, Berliner, and Jacob (1995), in *Single in a Married World,* have started looking at where adult singlehood fits into the life cycle framework. However, more work is needed to develop a complete understanding of the single life style.

The field of family therapy has not kept abreast of the changing lives of single women. Both in clinical practice and in research, there is a significant gap in understanding one of the fastest growing life-stage populations. As a result, there has been a persistent call by family therapists for more research on issues relevant for single women (Sprenkle, 1993, 1994; Sprenkle & Lyness, 1995). The study presented here is one step toward filling that gap. The purpose of the study was to understand the experience of being a single woman in midlife (ages 30–65) from the perspective of women themselves and to investigate their perceptions of familial influences on their images of themselves as single women. Qualitative methods were utilized because the area of investigation was new and the focus of the study exploratory and phenomenological (Boss, Dahl, & Kaplan, in press; Moon, Dillon, & Sprenkle, 1990). This paper presents the most salient themes from the study and discusses clinical implications of the research.

Literature Review

A computer search was made of Psych Lit and Sociofile from 1974 to 1995. There were slightly more than 300 entries in the two databases on "single women." Most of the articles were on very specific subpopulations, such as mentally disturbed low income single mothers (Sands, 1995). Many of the articles dealing with the social and adjustment issues of being single used college women as subjects (Sarch, 1993; Tanfer & Cubbins, 1992). Other articles showed up only because single women were part of the sample (Shore, McCoy, Toonen, & Kuntz, 1988); these papers offered little information of significance to family therapists about single women's issues. One professional journal devoted a special issue to "Spinsterhood" (Watkins, 1984), but the information is somewhat dated since it was published 12 years ago.

No articles were found for "single women" with the subcategories of "family therapy" or "supervision." However, three subcategories of studies relevant to family therapy were identified: life cycle and life transitions, therapy, and married versus single. The research on these issues is reviewed below.

Life Cycle and Life Transitions

There is a growing interest in the effect of chronological development on single women, transitioning into the 30s (Kaslow, 1992), into their 30s and 40s (Nadelson, 1989), into the 50s (Niemela & Lento, 1993), older women who have returned to singlehood by choice or not (Chasteen, 1994; Walters, Carter, Papp, & Silverstein, 1988), and older women whose families expected them to choose a single life (Allen, 1989).

There is also an interest in the stress related to the importance of career and career satisfaction for single women (Anderson & Stewart, 1994; Fong & Amatea, 1992; Schwartzberg et al., 1995). One study looked at previously married women's stress in returning to a single life, particularly in regard to their decisions about housing, transportation, and leisure activities (Chasteen, 1994). The issue of ambivalence was considered in the literature only in terms of older women wanting to become mothers (Siegel, 1995).

A hand search yielded three other important references, two ground-breaking books and one book chapter. Anderson and Stewart (1994) present an image of today's successful single women. They interviewed about 90 always single (AS) and single again (SA) women who were "upbeat, positive, and satisfied" (p.17) with themselves and their lives. Although single and living alone, many of these women were in committed relationships. Those who were not were comfortable with their singleness yet aware of how a man might add to (not define) the quality of their lives. Schwartzberg et al. (1995) offer the first major attempt at a life cycle framework with a place for single adults. Their model has five stages: Not yet married; The thirties: Entering the "Twilight Zone" of singlehood; Midlife (40s to mid-50s); Later life (50s to when physical health fails); Elderly (between failing health and death). In addition, they present a clinical application for each life stage and for gay and lesbian singles. Lewis (1994) offers eight developmental tasks for a healthy adjustment to adult singlehood. These include grounding, emotional intimacy, daily needs, mutual empowerment and nurturance, sexual feelings, grieving lost childhood dreams, making peace with parents, and preparing for old age.

Therapy

In the last decade a little attention has been given to the unique therapy needs of single women. Bankoff (1994) did a comparison of reasons for treatment for women at different life stages. Her results indicate that among all women, single mothers and women who lack life roles such as wife, worker, or student are the most emotionally vulnerable. Rucker (1993) looked at how single women's need for intimacy impacts their working with a male analyst. Therapists are consistently warned not to pathologize women's reasons for their singleness (Lewis, 1994; Papp, 1988; Schwartzberg et al., 1995).

Married versus Single

A few studies have compared married and single women on various adjustment dimensions. One study found that single men and women are more likely either to be socially isolated or to have a very active social network than married people (Seccombe & Ishii-Kuntz, 1994). Married women seem to have better physical health than unmarried women, perhaps because they tend to have more financial resources (Hahn, 1993). One study found that married women experience as high a stress level as single mothers in juggling work and family since husbands do not share much of the home responsibilities (Googins & Burden, 1987). An opposite finding was that single mothers had significantly higher levels of stress than married mothers (Fong & Amatea, 1992). Several studies have suggested that both married and single women can have full, contented lives (Anderson & Stewart, 1994; Lewis, 1994; Schwartzberg et al., 1995). And there was a special issue of a professional journal devoted to the differences in sexuality for married and single women (Caplan, 1985).

One interesting study found that the television image of single women has changed considerably in the last 30 years. There is an increase in the number of shows about single women and an increase in the status of the (Caucasian) women. This change, however, is more a statement about economics (what will sell) than about advocacy for singleness as a life stage (Atkin, 1991).

Evolving Image of Single Women

Prior to the 1960s, there was a definite stigma attached to being a single woman. The question was not "if" but "when" a woman would marry. A study conducted in the 1950s showed that women remained single primarily for negative reasons, for example, hating men or feeling ugly (Kuhn, 1955). In the 1960s, Helen Gurley Brown (1962/1983), although not generally recognized as a feminist, urged women to be more assertive, own their competence, and keep their options to marry or not. Her work supported the tone ushered in by the sexual revolution, changing the image of the single woman. By the 1970s, there were positive reasons for remaining single, such as more opportunity for personal development and increased freedom (Lowenstein, 1981; Stein, 1976).

In the beginning of the 1980s, Nadelson and Notman (1981) concluded that there were many reasons women did not marry, but a general theme was that being a wife was seen as a subordinate role. Peterson's (1982) study of single women (ages 20–78) concurred, adding that remaining single was a "form of withdrawal and boycott" (p. 259). During the later 1980s, feminist literature suggested that many women were choosing to remain single (Hicks & Anderson, 1989; Nadelson, 1989; Nadelson & Notman, 1981; Walters et al., 1988). The 1990s have been graced with a new study (Anderson & Stewart, 1994) of successful single women who are leading full and contented lives. Almost all of the women in this study said that having a man would be, as a chapter title put it, the icing on the cake, not the whole cake. The 1990s also opened an exploration of adult singlehood as a separate life stage. As previously mentioned, Schwartzberg et al. (1995) have divided this period into five stages of development, each with its emotional processes, and Lewis (1994) has identified eight developmental tasks for adult singlehood.

The Importance of This Subject for Family Therapists

The field of family therapy is lagging behind in understanding singleness as an adult life stage and its impact on extended families (Sprenkle, 1993, 1994; Sprenkle & Lyness, 1995). Family therapists need to recognize that the term *single* includes a heterogeneous group of women who face different issues in different phases of their lives (Schwartzberg et al., 1995).

Family therapists need to understand the issues of singleness in order to help single adults accomplish the developmental tasks of singleness (Lewis, 1994; Schwartzberg et al., 1995). They also need to understand singleness in order to provide balanced treatment for adults who are involved in relationship decision making. Family therapists often work with young and midlife adults considering a first marriage, divorce, or remarriage. Since most decisions about coupling or uncoupling involve movement out of or into singleness, it is vital for therapists who specialize in relationships to be knowledgeable about the unique issues, the ambivalences, and the advantages and disadvantages of single living across the life span.

It is important for family therapists to understand the ways that singleness interacts with relationship networks, especially friendship and extended family networks. Single adults have reported that their friendship networks are as important to them as family members are to most married adults but find that their friendships are not valued by others the way family relationships are (Schwartzberg et al., 1995). Family therapists also need to be aware of the unique family-of-origin issues common to single women. Single women at midlife have reported feeling intense pressure from their family of origin to marry and/or parental disparagement of achievements outside of marriage (Anderson & Stewart, 1994).

Finally, many of the developmental tasks for single women, such as "creating new rules" (Schwartzberg et al., 1995), "accepting the ambiguity," and "acknowledging sexual feelings" (Lewis, 1994), require women to challenge familial and cultural stereotypes. This study was designed to begin to fill the gap in the family therapy literature on single women and to suggest ways that family therapists can promote both individual and relationship development among single women across the life span.

Methods

The study was designed in two phases. In the first phase, open-ended questions were explored with single women (*n* = 37) in focus groups using ethnographic (Spradley, 1979), focus group (Piercy & Nickerson, in press), and phenomenological (Boss et al., in press) interviewing techniques. In the second phase, the findings from the interviews were used to guide the development of a structured questionnaire that was administered to 39 additional single women. Triangulation was achieved by using different participants for the two stages and group interview methodology in one stage and a mailed questionnaire in the second stage. The assertions generated from the data analyses reflect common themes that were voiced by single women in both phases of the study.

Role of the Researchers

The first author has a master's in social work and an EdD in counseling psychology. She is a clinical member of AAMFT and an approved supervisor. She has over 28 years experience as both a family and a group therapist. She became interested in the subject of single women from two perspectives. As a clinician, she had noted dramatic changes in the ways her single heterosexual women clients spoke about men over the past two decades. Her single female clients, from a wide range of ages, ethnic backgrounds, and economic situations, were raising similar questions and concerns about their inability to establish gratifying romantic relationships. In addition, as a woman who has always been single herself (now 51 years old), she was struck by the parallels between what she was hearing from clients and what seemed like a sequence of issues she had tackled and/or continues to tackle in her own life. She felt that the time was ripe to conduct a study exploring the women's perspectives on their singleness.

The second author has a PhD in educational psychology and is a clinical member of AAMFT. She has 6 years of experience as a family therapist and 10 years of experience as a single again woman and single parent. She was interested in working on the project because she was aware that singles have been neglected in the family therapy literature (Sprenkle, 1993, 1994; Sprenkle & Lyness, 1995), and she felt that the study had the potential to help clinicians work more effectively with single women and their families.

The first author designed the study, conducted all of the group interviews, designed the survey form, and did the preliminary data analysis. The second author joined the project after the data had been collected as a co-analyst, peer debriefer and co-author of the research report. The second author was asked to participate in the project both because of her expertise in qualitative research methods and because of her interest in single women. Both researchers began their work on this project with positive experiences of their single lives and positive perceptions of singleness. They shared the belief that both singleness and single parent families tend to be stereotyped and misunderstood. To counteract these positive biases, they made an effort to pay particular attention to the disadvantages and negative statements expressed by the participants.

Phase One

Participants. To begin the study, the first author placed an ad in a metropolitan newspaper with a circulation of 855,171 stating that she was looking for single women between the ages of 30 and 65 who would be willing to participate in a research study on the experience of being a single woman. Two hundred and fifteen women responded. The first 80 women who responded to the ad were asked to participate in a small group interview; 68 of them agreed to do so. The remainder were told that the first phase was filled and asked to participate in the second phase. Nine focus group interviews were conducted in the first phase. Of the 68 women who were scheduled for a group interview, 37 (54%) actually participated. Participants in the groups were matched on one or two theoretically important characteristics such as type of singleness. All other characteristics were allowed to vary randomly in each group. Demographic characteristics of the women in each group are shown in Table 1. There were four groups of women who had always been single (Groups 2, 6, 7, 8), three groups of women who were single again following death or divorce (Groups 1, 4, 5), one group that was formed primarily on the basis of age (Group 3), and another on ethnicity (Group 9). Group 3 included AS and SA women with and without children; Group 9 included AS African Americans with and without children.

Group interviews. All of the interviews followed a similar format and were videotaped. Each of the nine group interviews lasted 3–4 hours and was guided by a semistructured interview protocol. The protocol was revised after each group session to reflect the themes that had emerged. For example, if a question did not seem to be clear to the participants, it was clarified prior to the next focus group interview. If a new issue arose in a group discussion, a question related to that issue was added to the interview protocol and the questionnaire.

Prior to each interview, the participants were given demographic and permission forms to complete. The demographic information collected included ethnic background of their parents; religion in childhood and currently; socio-economic status during their childhood and within the past year; living situation; age at time of first and consecutive marriages; their height and that of each husband; and questions about their preferences related to marriage, their family's reaction to their singleness, and their self-identified category of singleness.

The interviews began with an explanation of the purpose of the study and an open-ended question such as "What does it mean to you to be single?" An effort was made to give each woman a chance to be heard as well as to encourage the participants to discuss the topics among themselves. As the groups continued, less time was spent on topics that seemed to have reached theoretical saturation and more time on new issues or underdeveloped topics.

All of the group interview sessions were transcribed. They were then read holistically by the first author, noting themes, interesting quotes, and so forth, on the transcript itself. Then the marked transcripts were read a second time in order to compare across individuals and groups. The themes that emerged from this analysis were used to develop a structured questionnaire for the second phase of the study.

Phase Two

Participants. Eighty-three questionnaires were sent out. Thirty-nine were returned in time to be included in the study, a response rate of 46.99%. A few women who had originally agreed to participate called to say that they could not complete the questionnaire because it made them feel too emotional or depressed.

Questionnaire. Two parallel versions of the questionnaire were developed, one for SAs and one for ASs. Each questionnaire had 10 sections. The first section contained demographic items on SES, occupation, education level, and category of singleness. The substantive portion of the questionnaire was divided into nine categories: being single (23 items), men (30 items), nurturing (8 items), daily life (13 items), peer networks (14 items), sex (10 items), grief (12 items), old age (11 items), and therapy (9 items). These categories had emerged as important themes in the lives of single women during the group interviews. Initial versions of the questionnaire were piloted with four single colleagues (2 AS and 2 SA women), revised, and prepared for distribution.

Completed questionnaires were returned by 21 AS women and 18 SA women. Respondents were encouraged to write explanations of their responses and comments on separate sheets of paper. Most (79%) did so. Their comments ranged in length from 0 to 22 pages with an average of 5.07 pages. The ASs tended to write more ($X = 6.4$ pages) than the SAs ($X = 3.5$ pages).

Data analysis. The questionnaires were numbered so that responses could be traced back to specific individuals. Then cross-case analyses were conducted separately for the SA and AS respondents. Responses to the closed items were tallied. Comments and responses to open-ended items were identified by respondent number and listed together verbatim on separate sheets of paper so they could be easily compared across cases. Then a theoretical memo (Strauss & Corbin, 1990) was written summarizing the responses to all of the items in each of the 10 sections for both ASs and SAs. When all of the sections had been summarized, assertions were developed that captured the general themes that had emerged from both phases of the study. These assertions were then taken back to the data for further clarification and refinement in a recur-

12

Table 1
Number of Participants in the Interview Groups and Demographics of Each Group

	#1	#2	Singleness	Children	Relationships	Age	Ethnicity
Group 1	5	5	SA	No	None	37–44	White
Group 2	9	6	AS	No	None	30–35	1 Asian 5 White
Group 3	8	5	4SA/1AS	3 Yes 3 No	Mixed	> 58	White
Group 4	9	5	SA	4 Yes 1 No	None	< 48	White
Group 5	7	4	SA	Yes	Dating	> 49	White
Group 6	6	4	AS	No	Committed	31–46	3 White 1 Black
Group 7	8	6	AS	No	Dating	31–48	White
Group 8	8	4	AS	No	Dating	32–55	White
Group 9	8	3	SA	No	Mixed	30–36	Black

#1 = The number of women who agreed to participate in the group
#2 = The number of women who actually participated in the group
SA = Single again following death or divorce
AS = Always single; never married

395 sive, analytic process that continued until the researchers were satisfied that a parsimonious set of assertions, well-supported by the data, had been developed. In the final stages of the data analysis, the researchers used selective coding techniques (Strauss & Corbin, 1990)
400 to identify and explicate the dominant storyline in the single women's focus group conversations and questionnaire responses.

In order to maintain narrative flow in reporting the findings, specific words are used to represent numbers
405 of participants. The words used and the number of participants represented by them are reproduced below:

Overwhelming	=	more than two thirds
Most	=	two thirds to one half
Some	=	one half to one third
Few	=	less than one third

Issues of reliability, and validity. Some qualitative research is context-bound description. Such research usually flows from in-depth, single case studies (Moon
410 & Trepper, in press). The findings from such studies are generally characterized by thick, narrative description and are judged by criteria of credibility and trustworthiness (Lincoln & Guba, 1985). Other qualitative research, such as this study, uses multiple cases, trian-
415 gulation, and a variety of analytic techniques to develop generalizable theory (Miles & Huberman, 1994; Moon & Trepper, in press; Rafuls & Moon, in press; Strauss & Corbin, 1990). The findings from multiple-case studies are usually reported as theoretical proposi-
420 tions or as grounded theory and are judged by qualitative standards of reliability and validity.

The present study was a multiple-case phenomenological study conducted for the purpose of developing theoretical assertions about the experiences of mid-
425 life, single women. The reliability and validity of the study were enhanced by the use of a two-phase re-

search design, triangulation of data sources and methods, criterion-based selection procedures, the large number of participants, the voluminous amounts of
430 data collected, immersion in the data by the first author, constant-comparative data analysis, and peer debriefing.

The sample was heterogeneous with respect to several important demographic variables such as age, type
435 of singleness, and dating/relationship status—enhancing the robustness of the assertions generated. However, the sample was fairly homogeneous with respect to other theoretically important variables. Most of the women were white, urban, middle class, professionals,
440 and all were heterosexual. These demographic similarities limit the generalizability of the study and should be kept in mind when reading and interpreting the findings.

Findings

Many themes emerged from the questionnaire and
445 the focus groups. However, there was one overriding issue that seems highly significant for family therapists: *single women have unresolved or unrecognized ambivalences about being single.* This assertion was supported by three subassertions: (a) women are aware
450 of both the advantages and the drawbacks of being single, (b) women are ambivalent about the reasons for their singleness, and (c) although content with being single, many women simultaneously experience feelings of loss and grief.

Women Are Aware of Both the Advantages and the Drawbacks of Being Single

455 Every woman in the focus groups and all but two of the questionnaire participants, ASs and SAs, felt that there were advantages to being single. The advantages can be generalized as freedom from caretaking a man; freedom for doing what they want, when they want,

how they want; and freedom from having to answer to others in terms of time, decisions, and behaviors.

The words and phrases most frequently used to describe the advantages of being single were "I do what I want when I want," "freedom," "independence," and "making my own decisions." One woman added, "Taking pride in accomplishments and investments that have been accumulated over the years of being alone; having friends that care for you as a person and not as part of a couple; the solitude." The women were also very clear about the advantages of not having to give up parts of themselves, of being able to resist what Anderson and Stewart (1994) call the "urge to merge" that often causes women in relationships to lose competent parts of themselves.

They identified many things that contributed to making life as a single woman meaningful. Primary were their interpersonal relationships with family and friends, closely followed by their work. Some of the other comments included "helping others gives meaning to my life." "Beautiful days and nights…and flowers." One SA mother said it was "The little successes…my boys helping without being asked, spending time picking strawberries, laughing with my friends at dinner, looking in the mirror and seeing an intelligent, attractive, very nice lady smile back." In general, there were few differences between the ASs and the SAs when discussing the advantages of being single. However, the AS women seemed somewhat more likely to struggle with the question of the meaningfulness of their lives.

The women identified a much wider range of drawbacks to being single, with no specific differences between ASs and SAs. Divorced women, though, expressed little ambivalence about being single again. This may have been because they were contrasting their single life with their previous unhappy marriage. The most frequently mentioned drawbacks to not being married or remarried were the absence of being special to a man, the absence of touch, the absence of children, the lack of ready companionship and someone for sharing interests, and sadness about growing old alone. One woman made some of the generalizations concrete when she said that one drawback was not having "someone to help with back buttons." Another drawback was the concern about how others would perceive them if they talked about the parts of being single they did not like. Therefore, they often did not share these feelings. "It hurts more to talk about being single. [Instead,] I appear [to others] to be strong and in control." Or, as another woman said, "Others don't understand. I don't want to appear desperate."

The AS and SA women expressed a significant difference in what they heard from others about their being single. The SAs felt they were likely to be envied; the ASs overwhelmingly felt that others pitied them, saw them as failures, or blamed them for their singleness. More than a few ASs said, "It is better to be divorced than never married."

When asked their perceptions of family members' reactions to their being single, there was no difference in regard to their mothers. Slightly more than half of ASs and SAs felt that their mothers were worried or concerned. However, twice as many of the SAs believed that their fathers were worried about them. (Although the women were asked about their siblings' reactions, no clear trends emerged from the analysis of their responses.) Of significance, perhaps, is that slightly more than half of the women's children were content.

The responses indicated an overlap between the advantages and the drawbacks of being single. For example, the freedom of not having to consult another around major decisions is clearly linked to the drawback of not having anyone with whom to share the responsibility of these decisions. In the second focus group, a mid-30-year-old AS woman described the interplay as follows:

I'm free to do a lot of self-disclosure. I'm free to work on me; I have energy to figure out who I am, where I'm going, without also having to work on a relationship…. The drawbacks, though, are that…part of me will only grow and develop within a relationship; that part of me will never be developed"

Women Are Ambivalent About the Reasons for Their Singleness

Ambivalence about reasons for singleness was related to locus of control, with women seemingly unaware that they switched between internalizing and externalizing the blame. The focus groups offered an opportunity to explore this ambivalence in depth. When asked why they were single or not remarried, every one of the women initially responded in terms of self-blame. Through their group discussion, however, they fleshed out a much more complex explanation.

For example, in one AS group, all of the women's first responses related to why they were not emotionally ready for a relationship. Yet when they talked among themselves, they probed beyond that initial response and concluded that although women were becoming more assertive and wanting more emotional responsiveness in men, men were still looking for women "to take care of them" or "to be like their mothers." All of these women complained that there were few appropriate potential men for them. One AS said, "I am more choosy now"; another added, "I have more discretion in my choice of men now [than when younger]." Then, as if they had never had the above conversation, the group switched back to taking responsibility for their singleness by identifying what was wrong with them as explanations for why men were not interested in them.

When the researcher pointed out this switch and the women were encouraged to explore the contradiction in their explanations, they raised the issue of control.

They discovered that if they could identify a problem within themselves (they most often mentioned weight, intimacy, co-dependency, and low self-esteem), they felt they had a goal. They could fix the problem (lose weight, work on intimacy, stop being co-dependent, improve self-esteem) and then be able to find a partner. As one SA in her 40s said, "Well, I'd rather think I'm single [because of] my weight. Then I can do something about it."

The majority of the divorced women did not blame themselves for the breakup of their marriage but did blame themselves for not finding another partner. In an SA group, a woman saw how she had blamed herself, then gave good explanations for why the man was not appropriate for her, then switched back to blaming herself. When this was pointed out, she said, "If asked again, I think I'd say the same thing again." Those women who saw this pattern were clear that giving up self-blame was difficult because, in part, it meant giving up the control to make the situation better—to find a man.

Because of these complex responses in the group interviews, the questionnaire was designed to gain a broader understanding of how women understood their singleness. There were 12 questions addressing the reasons women believed they were single and their feelings about being single. For example, the women were asked, "Are you single by choice?" "How do you understand your being single?" "Do you believe you will ever marry?" "How will you feel if you never marry?" "Do you envision yourself still being interested in marriage in old age?" There was no consistency among their answers.

A striking example of ambivalence about reasons for being single was demonstrated by the responses to the question, "Are you single by choice?" The questionnaire responses were almost equally divided between "yes" and "no," with more SAs responding "yes." However, the comments explaining these responses were almost identical. "Yes, I am single by choice because I have not met anyone I want to marry." "No, I am not single by choice because I have not yet met anyone I want to marry." One AS, aware of the contradiction, bridged the two with, "Yes and no. I would rather not be single. However, I am not willing to date or marry just anyone to avoid being single."

On the questionnaire, half of the women said they wished to be married and half said they did not, with more SAs answering in the negative. When asked if they expected to marry before old age, again it was about half and half. However, the half that believed they would never marry came from both sides of the prior questions about marriage. When asked if they were averse to marrying, only two said yes.

Self-blaming explanations for being single, in the questionnaire data, fell primarily into four categories: physical (big bust, overweight, fainting spells); personality (shyness, independence or dependence, lack of

social skills, excessive or lack of competency); psychological (selfishness, low self-esteem, demandingness, vulnerability, sexually abused as child, co-dependent); and cognitive (too much or too little intelligence, learning disability). Although they all knew married women who had similar problems, they explained that those women must have had less serious problems, been more patient, less choosy, or more willing to compromise.

Contributing to their self-blame, especially for the ASs, were others' comments about their singleness, for example, "You're so smart/pretty, I'm surprised you haven't found a man yet"; "You're smart, you've taken the career route" "You're too fussy"; "You're not giving him a chance." Whether they understood these comments to be positive or negative, the women did not appreciate them. However they chose to respond, they were left feeling defensive, angry, or guilty. Some of the women's reactions included, "No matter what I say, it only makes it worse." "I feel exasperated. Why should I have to defend myself?" "[I feel] hypocritical since I pretend it doesn't bother me."

At the same time that they blamed themselves, an overwhelming majority of women also wrote comments that laid blame on men. ASs and SAs, regardless of their age, complained that the men they were meeting were not able to deal with their intelligence, competence, assertiveness, accomplishments (etc.). Here are two typical comments: "I've been told I'm too assertive. I'm direct and honest. Men are put off by that." "It scares them. Guys don't want women who are smarter than they, unless they are looking for a mother." And using almost the identical words, women in their 30s through 60s said, "I'm intelligent, have a responsible job, and money. This makes me inappropriate for 95% of the men I meet."

What was most striking was that the women who held themselves *and* men accountable for their singleness did not seem aware that they held both views. At different times they gave full (or primary) responsibility for their singleness to themselves or to the men—without reference to the alternative explanation.

Although Content With Being Single, Many Women Simultaneously Experience Feelings of Loss and Grief

On the questionnaire, the women's degree of grief about not being a mother seemed directly related to their position as AS or SA. Twenty-five of the ASs were child free and only 5 of them were content without children. The others felt varying degrees of disappointment and loss. Of the nine SAs who were child free, five were content without children. Although most of the women (ASs and SAs) said they did not believe it was necessary to wait for marriage before parenting, only two (both ASs) had actually elected to adopt. Before giving up on children or making a decision to be a single parent, the women seemed to be waiting until some magic age, most often 40. One AS woman in her late 30s said, "I used to think I would wait until 30 before thinking about having a child by myself; as I get older, I keep pushing [the age] back."

690 Another area of loss was related to the issue of searching for a man. An overwhelming majority of the ASs responding to the questionnaire felt they had lost a lot by investing so much time and energy in their earlier years focusing on men. "I didn't appreciate my world [when I was younger.]" "I lost learning who I 695 am, developing myself." "I lost a lot of time." However, they also recognized that there had been gains in the search: wisdom and experience, independence, toughness, and knowing what is important in a relationship.

700 Currently, only a few women said they were wasting time when they were not looking for a man (*n* = 8). However, many described an internal struggle around this. Below are similar comments from two very different single women.

705 I try to do things that I like doing, that may provide an opportunity for meeting men. But I don't feel I have wasted time if I don't meet anyone because it was something I wanted to do anyway. Well, now that I think about it, I do feel like I'm wasting time when I clean house or 710 spend time alone doing things at home that have to be done, however, when I could be [out] meeting people. (42-year-old SA)

I think I should move to an apartment where hopefully there would be men my age or play golf or take up danc-715 ing or go to Elder Hostel. This isn't so urgent a feeling as it was in the past, though. (64 year-old AS).

In the questionnaire, most women said they would not do anything different with their lives if they knew for sure they would never marry or remarry. However, 720 in the focus groups, although most of the women's first responses were no, they would not do anything different, as a result of the group discussion, almost all of them concluded that it would have an impact. The typical effects would be to change jobs or go back to 725 school—both for more enjoyment and for more income. They also said there would be relief in knowing they would not marry because although they would be sad, at least they would know for sure.

This is directly related to another major loss—the 730 lack of assurance about the future. Singlehood can be experienced as an ambiguous loss (Boss, 1991), for at no point do women know for sure if they will marry in the future. As long as there is hope of marriage, there is the pain of the ambiguity. As so many women, ASs 735 and long time SAs, said, "It'd be easier if I just knew for sure, then I could adjust fine." They could grieve the loss of their dreams and move on. Without this clarity, there is no closure. As one woman said, "If I knew for sure I would never meet a man, I could get on 740 with my life. Without that, it becomes my life."

Discussion

The study suggests that single women are keenly aware of both the many advantages and the drawbacks of being in a committed relationship with a man. Is 745 their ambivalence any different, though, than the ambivalence married women may experience about being married? Without research on this question, there is only speculation, but both the findings of the study and the literature review suggest that many single women 750 still experience social pressure to be married, whereas married women have no similar pressure to be single. Furthermore, married women can decide to change their marital status, as divorced SAs have done. Although married women may have fears about their finances, their ability to live independently, their children's welfare, or being single, they still have more 755 control over their decision to change their status than single women do. The women in this study felt that while they did have control over *looking* for an appropriate partner, they had none over *finding* one.

760 Women's ambivalences about being single have implications for both family therapy clinical practice and research. If, as this study suggests, women's ambivalence about their singleness is often unrecognized and/or unresolved, family therapists need to be alerted 765 to the subtleties of women's dichotomous feelings and to the impact that family perceptions of their singleness have on their lives. And since so little research has been done on single women, this study opens many avenues for further exploration. The discussion below 770 focuses on the clinical and research implications of the study.

Clinical Implications

Therapists working with single women need to listen for overt as well as more subtle ambivalent feelings about being single. Although not an issue for all single 775 women, it may be important to help many single women recognize and/or resolve their contradictory feelings about being single. A frequent contradiction in the study revolved around identity as a single woman. Therapists need to help women clarify whether they are 780 articulating their public or private beliefs, their conscious or unconscious beliefs. That is, some women may say what they believe is socially and politically correct or what will counter the family's pessimism about being single, while not mentioning other feelings 785 they may be having, such as being lonely for a relationship. This is different from those women who say one thing without any conscious awareness that their behaviors demonstrate something very different. Therapists need to appreciate the multiplicity and complexity 790 of a woman's feelings about being single.

Therapists need to be careful not to participate inadvertently in a woman's self-blame. Therapists may perpetuate the stigma of being single by seeing a woman's singleness as a sign of her inability to estab-795 lish intimacy. Although a single woman *may* have problems with intimacy, talking *first* about the pathology perpetuates self-blame and stereotypes, and it may re-create blaming comments she hears from her parents and extended family. In this light, therapists need to use caution when they look for and hence find "personal neurosis" in a single woman's childhood and psyche (Papp, 1988, p. 377). If, as the study suggests, women assume blame in hopes of taking control, therapists need carefully to question women's self-blaming comments. Do these comments, in part, assist women in not seeing the problems a man is presenting in the relationship?

On the other hand, therapists may perpetuate the glamorization of the single life by reiterating the advantages of being single and the reality that a woman can live a successful productive life without a man. It is important to assess each client in terms of her own comfort level with her singleness. While some women may need help focusing on positive aspects of being single, others may need permission to acknowledge their grief or disappointment. What is most useful is validating their reality, helping them explore other perspectives about being single, and acknowledging for them that being heterosexual without a man can be difficult and lonely for those wanting a partner.

A third way therapists may avoid perpetuating a woman's self-blame is by taking seriously her complaints about the lack of emotionally available men (Lewis, 1994). Hite's (1989) study of 2,000 married women found a similar dissatisfaction with men. Women in this study of single women were clear that they want marriage only if the man is willing to take equal responsibility for the concrete and emotional components of the relationship. Without this mutuality (Jordan, 1991), they claimed to prefer remaining single.

Therapists need to consider many possible explanations for a single woman's depression. There are several possible explanations for how depression can be related to singleness. One explanation for a single woman's depression could be unresolved grief. She may have spent many childhood hours thinking about her wedding dress, about how her future husband's last name sounds with her first name, about who should be in her bridal party, about the children she would have one day, and so on. When grief work does not relieve a woman's depression about being single, therapists might describe the concept of singleness as an ambiguous loss. Giving a more accurate label to the feeling may help assuage some of the depression.

Another explanation could be that the emphasis a woman has placed on men has detoured her from thinking about developing herself or what else might give meaning to her life. So her depression may be related to this lack of personal growth and the lack of meaningfulness in life. The depression might also be related to her sense of failure at an important job (finding a man). Devoting much time and energy to a project only to have it continually fail is often a valid cause for depression.

The depression also might be related to a woman's attempted solution to her singleness. As some women in the study said, adopting a self-blaming explanation for their singleness allows them to identify a problem that they can then attempt to fix.

Little is known about any connection between depression and the lack of physical contact for single women. We do know that for infants, touch deprivation can lead to depression and failure to thrive (Spitz, 1945, 1946). However, there is no research about the effect of touch deprivation on unpartnered single women. This study did not ask specifically about it, but many women made comments such as "I miss his touch," "I miss cuddling more than intercourse," "I realized the only person I had touched all week was the doorman." Lack of physical contact was almost always listed as one of the drawbacks of being single. Therefore, it seems possible that some of the depression single women experience, especially those without children or close friendships, may be related to touch deprivation.

Therapists need to help single women recognize underutilized resources. Many single women are knowledgeable about resources for enjoying a satisfying single life (Anderson & Stewart, 1994; Peterson, 1982; Walters et al., 1988). Therapists need to assess the resources their clients already have and open new avenues of resources—ones the women may not have considered. These resources may be less directly related to finding men than to providing more satisfaction in their single lives—for however long they are single.

One type of resources that may be added are rituals. Rituals provide structure and validation for a life (Wolin & Bennett, 1984). However, most rituals are based around married life, for example engagement, weddings, christenings, anniversaries (Imber-Black & Roberts, 1992). Since single women have few models for life-affirming rituals, therapists can help women establish their own. For example, some women in the study had regular summer or holiday vacations with friends. Other possible rituals might be to celebrate a job promotion, a new home, the annual birthday. They can also be used to create a positive bridge between work and home and to enhance meal times (Imber-Black & Roberts, 1992).

Another avenue is an assessment of a woman's close friendship network. Many women think about emotional intimacy only in terms of their sexual partners. However, this study supports others (Eichenbaum & Orbach, 1987; Hite, 1989; Pogrebin, 1987) that claim women can get their emotional needs met from the important women in their lives. Therefore, therapists can talk with women about how well they are nurturing these friendships. Are they expecting less from a close friend than from a lover? Do they take their good friends for granted? Do they invest as much energy into their close women friends as they do their lovers? Are these close friendships gratifying or growing stale?

Therapists need to help women assess how they fare with the eight developmental tasks for adult singles. Lewis (1994) described eight nonsequential developmental tasks for moving through adult singlehood (Table 2). If a woman has succeeded at these developmental tasks, she has a home that reflects who she is and "belongs" to her; she has friends who enhance her personal and professional growth and who meet her social and intimacy needs. She recognizes her basic daily needs at work and at home, has established rituals that enhance her life, uses her free time in enriching and empowering ways. She has made an active decision (not a de facto one) about children. She has found ways to nurture others and let others nurture her, being aware of the difference between mutual nurturance and unilateral caretaking.

She acknowledges her sexual feelings and has found enhancing ways to deal with them when not in a sexual relationship. She has accepted the ambiguity of being single, has grieved her lost childhood dreams, and avoids absorbing, as if her own, others' grief about her singleness. She has made peace with her parents, teaching them how to treat her as an adult single, accepting the positives from them and avoiding the unhealthy and conflictual aspects from them. She has financially and emotionally prepared for old age—even though she may hope never to be old and single.

This list of tasks can be used with single women to help validate how well they are doing in establishing a fulfilling life without a man. It is also useful in helping women who are stuck. Often, going over the list can pinpoint unrecognized areas that may be causing the depression, for example, lack of professional or financial success or loneliness.

Future Research Implications

This study was an exploratory examination of the perceptions that single women have of their singleness. Like most exploratory studies, it has limitations. Minority, rural, lower class, poor, and homosexual women are underrepresented. The questionnaire sample may be biased due to the low response rate, a possibility that is reinforced by the fact that some of the nonrespondents told the researcher that they were upset by the questionnaire. This suggests that they may have been less comfortable with being single than those who chose to respond.

However, the study has strengths as well. It included women from several age groups and both major categories of singleness. It utilized accepted qualitative methods for enhancing reliability and validity, such as triangulation and constant comparative analysis, and included a fairly large number of participants for a multiple-case study.

One of the most important functions of exploratory studies is to raise questions for future research. Since the topic of single women is so uncharted, dozens of avenues for future research were suggested by this study. We have chosen to focus on five areas that we feel are particularly relevant to family therapists.

Table 2

Nonsequential Developmental Tasks for Adult Singlehood

1. *Grounding*
   in the home
   in the neighborhood
   in a career
   in finances
   in a social life
2. *Friendships*
   having close female friends
   pruning close friendships, keeping them compatible with personal and professional growth
   making new friendships
3. *Basic Needs*
   for daily contact
   for security
   for touch
   for rituals
   for enhanced use of free time
4. *Sexual Feelings*
   acknowledging them
   numbing them
   transitioning between
5. *Children and Other Forms of Nurturance*
   making a decision about children
   nurturing self
   nurturing others
   being nurtured by others
6. *Grieving*
   accepting the ambiguity
   grieving lost dreams
   separating a single woman's grief from her family's grief
7. *Making Peace with the Parents*
   teaching them to treat the single woman as an adult
   resolving old issues or finding a tolerable place for them
   accepting the positive traits/styles/rituals and rejecting the rest
8. *Old Age*
   having a positive image of the single self in old age
   preparing financially for old age
   maintaining friendships in old age
   considering living options for old age
   preparing for death, e.g., will, burial

Phenomenological methods can help researchers clarify the thoughts, experiences, and feelings of single women in a variety of contexts. Based on our experiences with group interviewing and open-ended questionnaires, it seems that future research on single women would benefit from phenomenological methods that allow participants' voices to be heard, addressing gaps in our knowledge about women and their experiences that concern feminist family therapists (Avis & Turner, in press). Individual, in-depth interviews provide deeper understanding of the perspectives of particular women and allow exploration of the complexity of women's feelings about their singleness. Phenomenological methods can help researchers distinguish between women's public and private views of their singleness and between their conscious and unconscious feelings about themselves. Such research might also target women in transition from marriage to singleness or singleness to marriage in order to explore the changing perceptions of self and others that occur during these transitions. Similarly, phenomenologists might explore single women's perceptions of therapy, therapists, and effective therapeutic interventions. And finally, phenomenological research is helpful for examining how others, particularly extended family members, perceive single adults.

Researchers can clarify the differences between different types of single women and between single women and single men. What are the differences between ASs and SAs (divorced and widowed) in different age categories (e.g., under 30 years, between 30 and 65 years, over 65 years) and across specific issues? Are there significant differences between women who are not dating at all, casually dating, or in a committed relationship? Is there a difference between women who have been single or single again for many years and those who have been single again for only a few years? Are there differences for women from different racial, ethnic, socio-economic class backgrounds; from happily married, unhappily married, or divorced parents? Are there any differences between single (unpartnered) women who are heterosexual or homosexual? Do lesbians feel they carry a double stigma; are they freed from the internal mandate to be mated? What about single men? Their gender socialization clearly differs from that of single women. Are their experiences of singleness also different from those of women?

Researchers can clarify the differences between single women and married women. What differences exist in the personal, professional, and/or leisure goals of single and married women? How do the stressors and resources in the lives of single women compare to those of married women? Are women who claim to prefer remaining single opposed to a life partner or only to marriage? Is there any merit to the suggestion made by some single women that being single makes it easier to focus on personal growth while being married makes it easier to focus on relationships? Can women focus on both, regardless of whether they are married or single?

How do these two groups of women use their weekends and free time? The data from the focus groups of this study suggested that some women believed their free time would be more fulfilling if they were married. What are the implications of any differences that exist for therapists working with married women who are considering divorce or single women who are considering marriage? How might therapists help married women realize more of the benefits of singleness—freedom, independence, personal growth, and autonomy?

Researchers can investigate the role of rituals in the lives of single women. Wolin and Bennett (1984) say rituals are necessary for providing life structure; therefore, we need to know more about the ways that rituals structure the lives and transitions of single women. This research concurs with the work of Imber-Black and Roberts (1992), who note that traditional, societal rituals are lacking for single women. Therefore, future research might investigate the ways that therapists could help single women create rituals for the important events (e.g., job promotion) and transitions (e.g., first purchased home) in their lives.

Researchers can investigate single women in therapy. What therapeutic approaches and techniques work best with which types of single women? How is family therapy different when a family is headed by a single female than when a family is headed by a single male or a couple? How might family therapists help a single woman decide whether to adopt a child? What issues are important for therapists to address when married women are considering a transition back to singleness or single women are considering a transition into a relationship? How might friendships be dealt with in family therapy with single women? What other relational issues are relevant to therapy with single women?

In conclusion, this study provides family therapists with a glimpse at the complex inner lives of single women and the ambivalent feelings that they have about their singleness in a social context that tends either to stigmatize or to glamorize the single life. Adult singleness is a life stage that everyone experiences for varying durations at varying times. We hope that this study will encourage family therapists to focus more of their clinical, theoretical, and research resources on developing an understanding of the single life and its impact on relationships and families.

References

Allen, K. (1989). *Single women/family ties: Life histories of older women.* Newbury Park, CA: Sage.

Anderson, C., & Stewart, S., with Dimidjian, S. (1994). *Flying solo: Single women in midlife.* New York: W. W. Norton.

Atkin, D. (1991). The evolution of television series addressing single women, 1966–1990. *Journal of Broadcasting and Electronic Media, 35,* 517–523.

Avis, J. M., & Turner, J. (in press). Feminist lenses in family therapy research: Gender politics and science. In D. H. Sprenkle & S. M. Moon (Eds.), *Family therapy research: A handbook of methods.* New York: Guilford.

Bankoff, E. (1994). Women in psychotherapy: Their life circumstances and treatment needs. *Psychotherapy, 31,* 610–619.

Boss, P. (1991). Ambiguous loss. In F. Walsh & M. McGoldrick (Eds.), *Living beyond loss: Death in the family* (pp. 164–175). New York: W. W. Norton.

Boss, P., Dahl, C., & Kaplan, L. (in press). The use of phenomenology for family therapy research: The search for meaning. In D. H. Sprenkle & S. M. Moon (Eds.), *Family therapy research: A handbook of methods*. New York: Guilford.

Brown, H. G. (1983). *Sex and the single girl*. New York: Avon. (Original work published 1962)

Caplan, P. (1985). Single life and married life. *International Journal of Women's Studies* [Special issue: Feminist psychology: Single life and married life and women's sexuality], *8*(1), 6–11.

Chasteen, A. (1994). The world around me: The environment and single women. *Sex Roles, 31*(5–6), 309–328.

Eichenbaum, L., & Orbach, S. (1987). *Between women*. New York: Viking.

Fong, M., & Amatea, E. (1992). Stress and single professional women: An exploration of causal factors. *Journal of Mental Health Counseling, 14*(1), 20–29.

Googins, B., & Burden, D. (1987). Vulnerability of working parents: Balancing work and home roles. *Social Work, 32*(4), 295–299.

Hahn, B. (1993). Marital status and women's health: The effect of economic marital acquisitions. *Journal of Marriage and the Family, 55*, 495–504.

Hicks, S., & Anderson, C. (1989). Women on their own. In M. McGoldrick, C. Anderson, & F. Walsh (Eds.), *Women in families* (pp. 309–334). New York: W. W. Norton.

Hite, S. (1989). *Women and love*. New York: Knopf.

Imber-Black, E., & Roberts, J. (Eds.). (1992). *Rituals for our times*. New York: Harper Collins.

Jordan, J. (1991). The meaning of mutuality. In J. Jordan, A. Kaplan, J. B. Miller, I. Stiver, & J. Surrey (Eds.), *Women's growth in connection: Writings from the Stone Center* (pp. 81–96). New York: Guilford.

Kaslow, F. (1992). Thirty-what and not married. In B. Wainrib (Ed.), *Gender issues across the life cycle* (pp. 77–94). New York: Springer.

Kuhn, M. (1955). How mates are sorted. In H. Becker & R. Hill (Eds.), *Family, marriage and parenthood* (pp. 246–275). Boston, MA: DC Heath & Co.

Lewis, K. G. (1994). Heterosexual women through the life cycle. In M. Mirkin (Ed.), *Women in context: Toward a feminist reconstruction of psychotherapy* (pp. 170–187). New York: Guilford.

Lincoln, Y., & Guba, E. (1985). *Naturalistic inquiry*. Beverly Hills, CA: Sage.

Lowenstein, S. (1981). A study of satisfactions and stresses of single women in midlife. *Sex Roles, 7*, 1127–1141.

Miles, M. B., & Huberman, A. M. (1994). *Qualitative data analysts: An expanded sourcebook* (2nd ed.). Thousand Oaks, CA: Sage.

Moon, S. M., & Trepper, T. S. (in press). Case study research. In D. H. Sprenkle & S. M. Moon (Eds.), *Family therapy research: A handbook of methods*. New York: Guilford.

Moon, S. M., Dillon, D. R., & Sprenkle, D. H. (1990). Family therapy and qualitative research. *Journal of Marital and Family Therapy, 16*, 357–373.

Nadelson, C. (1989). Issues in the analyses of single women in their thirties and forties. In J. Oldham & R. Liebert (Eds.), *The middle years: New psychoanalytic perspectives* (pp. 105–122). New Haven, CT: Yale University Press.

Nadelson, C., & Notman, M. (1981). To marry or not to marry: A choice. *American Journal of Psychiatry, 138*, 1352–1356.

Niemela, P., & Lento, R. (1993). The significance of the 50th birthday for women's individuation. *Women and Therapy, 14*(1–2), 117–127.

Papp, P. (1988). Single women: Early and middle years. In M. Walters, B. Carter, P. Papp, & O. Silverstein (Eds.), *The invisible web: Gender patterns in family relationships* (pp. 371–389). New York: Guilford.

Peterson, N. (1982). *The ever single woman: Life without marriage*. New York: Quill.

Piercy, F., & Nickerson, V. (in press). Focus groups in family therapy research. In D. H. Sprenkle & S. M. Moon (Eds.), *Family therapy research: A handbook of methods*. New York. Guilford.

Pogrebin, L. C. (1987). *Among friends*. New York: McGraw-Hill.

Rafuls, S. E., & Moon, S. M. (in press). Grounded theory. In D. H. Sprenkle & S. M. Moon (Eds.), *Family therapy research: A handbook of methods*. New York: Guilford.

Rucker, N. (1993). Cupid's misses: Relational vicissitudes in the analyses of single women. *Psychoanalytic Psychology, 20*, 377–391.

Sands, R. G. (1995). The parenting experience of low-income single women with serious mental disorders. *Families in Society, 76*(2), 86–96.

Sarch, A. (1993). Single women's use of the telephone in dating relationships with men. *Journal of Communication, 43*(2), 128–144.

Schwartzberg, N., Berliner, K., & Jacob, D. (1995). *Single in a married world: A life cycle framework for working with the unmarried adult*. New York: W. W. Norton.

Seccombe, K., & Ishii-Kuntz, M. (1994). Gender and social relationships among the never-married. *Sex Roles, 30*, 585–603.

Shore, E., McCoy, M., Toonen, L., & Kuntz, E. (1988). Arrests of women for driving under the influence. *Journal of Studies on Alcohol, 49*(1), 7–10.

Siegel, J. (1995). Looking for Mr. Right? Older single women who become mothers. *Journal of Family Issues, 16*(2), 194–211.

Spitz, R. (1945). Hospitalism. *Psychoanalytic Study of the Child, 1*, 53–74.

Spitz, R. (1946). Hospitalism: A follow-up report. *Psychoanalytic Study of the Child, 2*, 113–117.

Spradley, J. P. (1979). *The ethnographic interview*. New York: Holt, Rinehart, & Winston.

Sprenkle, D. H. (1993). [Editor's report]. *Journal of Marital and Family Therapy, 19*, 107–110

Sprenkle, D. H. (1994). [Editor's report]. *Journal of Marital and Family Therapy, 20*, 107–111.

Sprenkle, D. H., & Lyness, K. P. (1995). [Editor's report]. *Journal of Marital and Family Therapy, 20*, 107–110.

Stein, P. (1976). *Single in America*. Englewood Cliffs, NJ: Prentice Hall.

Strauss, A., & Corbin, J. (1990). *Basics of qualitative research: Grounded theory procedures and techniques*. Newbury Park, CA: Sage.

Tanfer, K., & Cubbins, L. (1992). Coital frequency among single women: Normative constraints and situational opportunities. *Journal of Sex Research, 29*(2), 221–250.

Walters, M., Carter, E., Papp, P., & Silverstein, O. (Eds.). (1988). *The invisible web: Gender patterns in family relationships*. New York: Guilford.

Watkins, S. (Ed.). (1984). Spinsterhood [Special issue]. *Journal of Family History, 9*.

Wolin, S., & Bennett, L. (1984). Family rituals. *Family Process, 23*, 401–420.

About the Authors: Karen Gail Lewis, EdD, is in private practice, 1109 Spring Street, Suite 803, Silver Spring, MD 20910. Sidney Moon, PhD, is an Assistant Professor, Department of Educational Studies, Purdue University, West Lafayette, IN 47907-1446.

Acknowledgments: The authors wish to thank Joanne Kipnis, MSW, and Shirley Salmon, MSW, for their assistance with the videotaping of the focus groups and transcribing the tapes. We also give a special thanks to the women who participated in the study.

Exercise for Case 2

1. Introduction

A. Is the problem area for the research clearly described? Explain.

B. Have the researchers convinced you that the problem area is important? Explain.

C. To what extent does the literature presented in the introduction help you understand the problem? Is the literature used to put the problem in context? Explain.

D. Do the researchers indicate how this study is different from and/or similar to earlier ones reported in the literature?

E. Do the researchers reveal their personal perspectives on the problem area, including any possible biases? Explain.

2. Methods

A. Are the demographics of the participants (i.e., background characteristics such as age, race, and so on) described in sufficient detail? Explain.

B. Considering the problem area for the research, do you think that appropriate participants were selected? If you had been conducting the study, would you have selected the same type(s) of participants? Would you have used the same number of participants? Explain.

C. Which strategies listed in Table 1 on page 161 of this book were employed by the researchers? Are they described in sufficient detail? Explain.

D. In addition to those you named in response to question 2C, have the researchers used any additional strategies to help assure the validity of the study? If yes, what are they? Are they described in sufficient detail? Explain.

3. Analysis and Results

A. Are the steps taken in the analysis described in sufficient detail? Explain.

B. Are the results clearly organized? Explain.

C. Are the results discussed in terms of a theory or theories (either theories that emerged from this study or previously existing ones)? Explain.

D. Were the direct quotations of the participants' statements, if any, judiciously selected? Do they help you understand the results? Explain.

E. Are there other ways the results could have been organized and interpreted? Explain.

4. Conclusions/Implications

A. Are the researchers' concluding remarks appropriate? Do they flow logically from the material presented earlier?

B. Do the researchers describe any implications? If yes, are they appropriate? Are there other implications that are not discussed by the researchers? Explain.

5. Ethical Considerations

A. In your opinion, could this research have caused physical or psychological harm to the participants? If yes, did the researchers take adequate measures to ameliorate the potential for harm? Explain.

B. If you had conducted this research, would you have obtained written, informed consent from the participants before conducting the study? Explain. Does this research report indicate that the researchers obtained such consent?

6. Overall Evaluation

A. Throughout the article, are all specialized terms and jargon defined to your satisfaction? Explain.

B. Briefly describe your overall evaluation of the research report, noting any special strengths and weaknesses.

C. If you had been a reviewer for the journal in which this report was published, would you have recommended publication of the report? If yes, would you have recommended that it be published "as is" or modified before publication? Explain. If no, what is the primary reason why you would recommend not publishing it?

Collaborative Teaching of a Social Studies Methods Course: Intimidation and Change

JOANN HOHENBRINK
Ohio Dominican College

MARILYN JOHNSTON
The Ohio State University

LISA WESTHOVEN
Worthington School District, Ohio

From *Journal of Teacher Education*, *48*, 293–300. Copyright ©
1997 by Corwin Press, Inc. Reprinted with permission of Corwin Press, Inc.

In this article, we describe our initial apprehensions, difficulties of working across our differences, and changes in our understandings and teaching practice as we collaboratively taught a social studies methods course.

We began with stereotypes of each other implied by our university/school and professor/graduate student/classroom teacher roles. After 4 years of working together, we have come to understand our positions, knowledge, and expertise in different ways and as a result have changed our teaching.

We began our co-teaching experience as members of a Professional Development School (PDS) project. In this PDS, university faculty, graduate associates, school principals, and classroom teachers work closely to construct and evaluate the redesign of the university's elementary teacher education programs. One important aspect of this collaboration is co-teaching the methods courses for the Master of Education certification students in the program. Classroom teachers, doctoral students, and university professors make shared decisions about course syllabi, assignments, and evaluation to bring theory and practice into a productive dialogue.

Despite initial support for co-teaching the methods courses, both university faculty and classroom teachers were reluctant. Classroom teachers were uncertain about working with university faculty, about the time necessary for planning, and especially about leaving their classrooms for half a day each week. University faculty were hesitant to relinquish their autonomy and worried about the time required to team teach.

These hesitancies resulted in less concern about teachers' expertise in the subject area and more on their willingness to participate. Rather than participating in a formal selection process, faculty and teachers were asked to volunteer; decisions about which teachers would teach with which faculty were left to informal negotiations.

This article focuses on the co-teaching of a social studies methods course. We do not include practical descriptions of how we organized the social studies course, the students' evaluations of the course, or assessment of student learning. This is not to deny the importance of student outcomes that we discuss in other work in progress, but to situate this study within the literature on collaborative work and professional development.

Studies of teachers' professional development supported our interest in looking at our own learning and development. Traditionally evaluation of change initiatives have considered classroom instruction and student performance more than the teachers who managed the learning environments. Attention to teachers' growth and development has been slow in coming, particularly studies that include self-study and reflection.

Recently, researchers have been using case studies, collaborative methodologies, narrative forms, and feminist theories to look at the complexities and perspectives of teachers (Miller, 1990; Witherell & Noddings, 1991). Action research is enjoying a resurgence, and teachers are increasingly studying and publishing reports on their own teaching and beliefs (Bricher, Hawk, & Tingley, 1993; Nalle, 1993; Paley, 1989). Journals are increasingly including collaborative studies by teachers or between teachers and researchers (Gitlin, 1992; Hunsaker & Johnston, 1992). Greene (1988) argues that *stories—and myths, and diaries, and histories—give shape and expression to what would otherwise be untold about 'our lives'* (p. x). Multiple forms of expression help to reveal the complexities of personal lives as they are reflected in professional lives and development. These studies point to the value of teachers considering their own thinking and teaching as sites for reflection, inquiry, and change.

The authors (Lisa Westhoven, a classroom teacher; JoAnn Hohenbrink, a graduate teaching associate; and Marilyn Johnston, a professor) co-taught a two-quarter course for 2 years (1991–1993). Marilyn and Lisa co-taught the same course the following year, 1993–1994, and again in 1995–1996. JoAnn did her dissertation study on change in the first year of co-teaching (data collected 1991–1992). We extended what we learned in

85 the first year through continued conversations and self-reflection during the subsequent 3 years.

The changes we describe did not come easily. We were initially uncomfortable working together. Lisa and JoAnn felt intimidated; Marilyn was unclear how 90 to bring others into *her* class. We began the course using Marilyn's syllabus and reading materials because co-teaching arrangements were approved by the school district and university just before the quarter began. We had no time before class started to plan the course col-95 laboratively or to talk about our apprehensions and differences.

We spent much time talking and planning through-out our co-teaching experience. Marilyn found plan-ning took much more time than would have been re-100 quired had she taught alone. Lisa had to plan for her substitute teacher as well as the methods course. We tried to deal directly with feelings of intimidation and imposition, which required building trusting relation-ships to support handling sensitive issues and criti-105 cisms. Our attempts were necessarily partial. We could pursue only those things of which we were aware; we left undisturbed other issues and silences. We are nev-ertheless convinced that co-teaching has rich potential for prompting self-reflection for both university and 110 school-based participants. It led us to significant changes in our understandings and teaching practices and, most important, brought the limitations of the tra-ditional separate roles of schools and universities in teacher education into stark relief.

Methodology

115 We used several theoretical positions in our re-search. First, we used interpretive/hermeneutic theories (Gadamer, 1984; Ricoeur, 1981; van Manen, 1990) to inform our interest in understandings. We were par-ticularly interested in how our individual understand-120 ings about teaching and learning, and about schools and universities, influenced our ability to collaborate. We were also curious to trace our construction of indi-vidual as well as shared meanings that might emerge from this experience.

125 Second, we depended on poststructural feminist theorists (Davies & Harré, 1990; Harding, 1986; Hara-way, 1986; Lather, 1991; Weedon, 1987) to think about issues of language, positionings, and voice. Like inter-pretive theorists, poststructural feminists are interested 130 in the discursive and historical construction of mean-ing. Feminists, in addition, pay attention to the personal and political character of the self and the social context within which issues of power and control are ever pres-ent. In particular, we were interested in how our insti-135 tutional contexts and socialization made interpretations of each others' meanings difficult. Our commitment to separate texts written to represent our different voices and perspectives is also supported, as well as problem-atized (Lather, 1991, p. 43), in feminist work.

140 We used audiotaped conversations over a period of 3 years (some 50 conversations), journal writing from 4 years, and the individual and group interviews con-ducted for the dissertation study as our major data sources. Periodically, we examined the data to look for 145 themes and changes in our understandings. These analyses became the focus of further conversations that in turn were data to be examined at a later point in time. This article is the collaborative result of 5 years of working and writing together.

Three Voices in a Dialogue

150 We write in three voices in order to capture our in-dividual perspectives. We address the two themes of intimidation and change emerging from our study. The first theme addresses our beginning assumptions about knowledge that led to intimidation and apprehension. 155 In the beginning, we assumed that university knowl-edge is more important than school knowledge and valued theoretical/research knowledge over practical knowledge. From our present perspective, we would argue that such distinctions are not helpful because 160 they mask both teachers' theories and professors' prac-tical knowledge. The second theme, change in teach-ing, describes our evolving understandings and teach-ing practices.

Whose Knowledge Counts?

We struggled continually with assumptions about 165 the different knowledge bases that we carried into our co-teaching experience. These assumptions, at times, led to feelings of intimidation and fears of imposition. These feelings are reflected in some of our journal en-tries during the first two quarters we worked together.

170   Lisa: I am very excited, very nervous, and very ap-prehensive—I am entering a world I know little about. What am I hoping to be able to offer? Social studies is not an area I would call my strength!! The conversations at Bernies [the deli where we had our morning planning 175 meetings] are quite intimidating. The other three [profes-sor and two doctoral students] sit there and discuss things I've never heard of—'postmodern,' 'hermeneutic'—and they throw around authors' names. I could have been lis-tening to a conversation in Japanese. That's when I 180 think—What am I doing here? (10-1-91)

JoAnn: I really am intimidated by Marilyn and how she thinks and how differently we come at things. She has had more interactions with the topics we are teach-ing—she has used them in classes before. I see her strug-185 gling with not taking control of what has to be done. It must be frustrating for someone who has too much to do to take 2+ hours to plan something she has done so of-ten…. Instead of backing away and thinking I may look stupid, I really need to take some responsibility so things 190 can be accomplished. (10-10-91)

Marilyn: JoAnn did the discussion of one of the as-signed readings today and seemed uncomfortable. I've wondered whether I should leave when she's doing her part sometimes just to give her some space. She said she 195 doesn't feel comfortable sometimes because it's about social studies and I'm her advisor. Maybe she's trying to

200 do things in the way I would, but it's not how she would do it on her own. She runs a discussion in a very open way, asking students to respond to other students' ideas without focusing the questions. It made me think how much I try to get students to think through an issue (i.e., my issue) in a way that may not be responsive to their interests. I need to think about this. (1-13-92)

205 JoAnn: My part of class today was the assigned reading. I wanted students to be involved in discussion. Because of the time frame, I couldn't (or didn't feel I had time) to do the outline of the article. I was uncomfortable with Marilyn being there. I was in Marilyn's graduate social studies seminar and we worked on the same reading.

210 I didn't want to put her on the spot, but I wanted her to talk about how she thought the example in the article was realistic. I remember her doing that in the seminar. I was uncomfortable not telling the students what I thought because I thought Marilyn expected that of me. It's not

215 what I would do in my own class. Sometimes I just feel soooo wishy/washy. (11-13-91)

Marilyn: At this evening's planning session we had a difficult time talking about how much this is my class and how much ownership I should have or want. JoAnn

220 clearly brings a level of expertise in social studies, but we have different perspectives about the goals. Lisa brings classroom expertise, but in ways that don't get well integrated into what we are doing in class. Maybe it's because she's teaching social studies in a different way than

225 is espoused in class. Does this mean imposition of my way or university perspectives over what teachers typically do in their classrooms? Is this what co-teaching is all about? I keep asking myself how much of the course and my perspective I am willing to give away. (11-16-91)

230 Lisa: Doing small groups in class again makes me a little nervous especially when Marilyn asks if we need to generate questions together. Is that because she wants us all to do the same kind of thing, or is it that she isn't sure I understand the gist of what is to be covered? I hope she

235 doesn't think that I won't move the conversation along and challenge their thinking. I don't really think that is the case. I think she would say something if she felt that way. (2-2-92)

JoAnn: I like what we planned for class. I like the

240 book, 'White Teacher,' and I think having students reflect on their classroom experience will be good. Again Marilyn is handling the discussion of the reading. But, again, it's her topic. I'm glad we're using the video from Marilyn teaching in Lisa's classroom. (3-2-92)

245 Lisa: Next I think I need to write about Marilyn's visit to teach in my room. At first I worried about what her first impressions of my room would be. Once she got there, I worried about what she would think of my kids. What would she think about the way I handle my kids?

250 Her lesson went very well especially for not knowing the kids. It made me feel good because I thought she asked the same kinds of questions I ask them. I think the lesson went similar to the way it would have gone if I had known how to do it. I guess I thought she would have

255 every child sitting on the edge of his/her seat and they would all be wrapped around her finger. (3-6-92)

Marilyn: I've puzzled a bit about why it's the eighth week of the quarter and I'm just getting out to Lisa's classroom to do some teaching. It's clear from our dis-

260 cussions that coming to her classroom bothers her. I get

set up as the authority and therefore a critical eye. But then, I feel like I'm under scrutiny having co-teachers in my class. I often wonder what they think, what doesn't make sense, how my biases appear to them. There's

265 rarely any negotiation that suggests I'm doing it wrong and that it ought to be more like how Lisa is teaching. There are differences between my philosophy and Lisa's, but it always seems like she's changing to accommodate my point of view rather than the other way around. Is this

270 imposition from the power of one knowledge base over the other? (3-6-92)

Joint Reflections on "Whose Knowledge Counts?"

Our worries as we started our co-teaching experience were clear. Lisa was apprehensive about entering the university world with its new vocabularies and ex-

275 pectations. Her strength as a teacher was not in social studies; in fact, she did not like social studies much at all. She had signed up to teach language arts, but at the last minute, the professor decided not to take a co-teacher, and Lisa joined us. JoAnn was *intimidated* by

280 Marilyn because she was her adviser. In addition, they had differences of opinion about what should occur in a social studies methods course. She was also apprehensive about looking uninformed if she did things more to her liking. Marilyn was committed to co-teaching in

285 principle but unsure about how to keep some integrity to what she wanted in the course and still share the decision making. Underlying all of this was the assumption that the university knowledge exemplified in Marilyn's attitudes and purposes had higher value than

290 what a graduate student or teacher might bring to the course.

Throughout the two quarters of co-teaching, we worried about what each of us thought about each other. We talked a lot about issues of power and role

295 and the ways they interfered with making our work together more genuinely collaborative. We made decisions to work in ways that would push against the stereotypic expectations we held for each other and that students held as well. We decided never to let Marilyn

300 begin class so that students would see Lisa and JoAnn as equally in charge of the announcements, assignments, and evaluation issues discussed at the beginning of each class. We tried to share different aspects of the class and defy expectations when we could. Rather

305 than Marilyn leading discussions about the readings, we shared this responsibility. Rather than Lisa doing all the talking about a videotape of her classroom, we discussed it ahead of time and shared in the class discussions. We divided different sections of each class ses-

310 sion so that each of us had equal responsibility for setting up activities or beginning discussions. We set time periods for each section so that Marilyn's tendency to go on and on about something would not infringe on what Lisa and JoAnn had prepared to do in class. These

315 arrangements were symbolically important to us even if the students did not always recognize them.

It was easy, however, to fall back into stereotypic

power relations and role definitions. Lisa countered this by pushing hard for her fair share and for a sense of equality. We nicknamed her our *watchdog of hierarchy*. It was extremely helpful that she was willing to say when she thought that Marilyn and JoAnn were usurping more than their share of time. Marilyn and JoAnn tried also to do their share of asking questions about procedures and responsibilities. We were continually amazed at how easy it was to fall back into familiar patterns and expectations. The hours we spent the first year talking into a tape recorder for JoAnn's dissertation helped us to continually keep these issues in front of us.

Changes in Understanding Teaching

Change occurred for each of us as a result of this co-teaching experience. We have made changes in our teaching and readjusted our goals for teaching the social studies methods course. Although change occurred for all of us, the character of the change was different. How we changed is related to the problems and demands of our institutional contexts and our backgrounds and personalities. These influences are reflected in our separate accounts of change written after a second year of co-teaching together.

Lisa: I could probably fill a book if I were to describe all the changes that have taken place in my classroom and in myself since becoming a part of the co-teaching team. I have questioned my whole approach to teaching. Because change demands time, thought, planning, and risk taking, I have only begun to make the changes I want. I have gone from being a very traditional teacher who was very teacher centered, and moved to a classroom where children are more involved in their own learning. I now focus less on facts and more on critical thinking, inquiry, and process. I make fewer classroom decisions without first having a conversation with the class in order to have a better understanding of students' wants and needs. For example, at the beginning of this school year instead of having the room setup when students walked in, we discussed the physical arrangement of our classroom and what makes one way work better than the next. Students were involved in the decision about the room. I was wondering lately what the kids think about our community-building time, so I asked them to write about it:

Jeff: I learned we can work things out as a group and the teacher doesn't make all the decisions by herself.

Jane: What you can learn is how to solve problems.

Mary: I think it is worthwhile because it helps you think about your problems and we solve class problems together. Working together is better than working alone.

I was pleased to find that this kind of classroom is making a difference in their thinking. Their responses have encouraged me to plan more group cooperative work and less individual isolated work. These changes have not always been easy and I find myself much more unsure about what I'm doing than when I was the teacher and this is what we're going to do. I'm never sure if I am giving too much input and therefore having too much influence. I'm also not sure exactly when to step in and be

'the teacher.' These emerging ideas, like shared classroom ownership and openness to children's input, make my job less predictable and more ambiguous. In many ways I feel like a first year teacher again; I have more questions than answers.

JoAnn: When I think about how I have changed based on my co-teaching experience, I reflect especially on my attitudes and beliefs. First, I would say that I thought of teaching as a one-person job and of myself as the one who has the knowledge that students need to learn. This was based on my own experience in elementary school and college. How could it be any different? What I found out is that it could be very different. I experienced a classroom situation that was filled with ideas. I became aware of the socio-cultural nature of learning as I co-taught with others whom I knew and respected. I was continually aware of how much I was learning from our conversations both in class and during planning. In turn, I realized that the students in our class were also learning from one another, and us from them. Was it because there were more 'teachers' with ideas that students felt they could share their ideas as well? We used cooperative learning groups to generate ideas. We encouraged students to speak from their own perspectives, and to value other points of view. Co-teaching was definitely not a hierarchical experience of teaching and learning for me.

Because of my co-teaching, I have taken a much different view of my teaching now that I am a college professor on my own. Instead of having college students focus on me as a teacher, I have students sit in a way that they can see and talk with each other. I try to encourage them to take an active part in class believing now that there are always as many teachers and learners as there are participants in the room.

Through this experience, I came to understand how isolating teaching is and the problems isolation can create. Only by doing the teaching differently was I able to understand better my previous experiences. I also experienced how this isolation kept me from seeing different options. For example, I used to think that each student should be assigned an individual field placement. Now I see the importance of students working in pairs in their fieldwork because of the social learning that takes place as they discuss their experiences together.

Co-teaching challenged me to think about how others see issues and teaching. Seeing other perspectives has helped me to examine my own, and, as a consequence, I have changed my mind about some things and expanded my thinking about others. I have not adopted someone else's perspective, but rather used their ideas to extend my own thinking and teaching practice.

Marilyn: Initially, I thought I could best facilitate collaborative teaching by helping my co-teachers become more like me and my becoming more like them. I thought if I gently shared what I knew with them and spent time in classrooms with them, we could both benefit. I knew the practical examples I used in my courses needed updating, but I wasn't sure that I had anything particularly new to learn. I had been a classroom teacher for 15 years. I always thought my courses were practical because I brought in lots of classroom activities. I thought that Lisa could offer fresh examples because she was in a classroom every day and by being around her and her classroom I could gather some 'fresh' examples as well. I

440 knew I would change in some ways because I'm always looking for new ideas and like a good debate about issues. Nevertheless, deep in my heart, I thought Lisa and JoAnn had more to gain from this experience than I did. Lisa kept asking me how I was changing. She was full of

445 stories about how her classroom was changing and was convinced that a test of genuine collaboration would be that I was also changing. It was clear that the course was different. There were three of us contributing, we expressed our different points of view, and we handled

450 class situations and student questions in different ways. I could see the students were benefiting from this diversity. This was not the kind of change Lisa was looking for. It took a while for me to see the impact co-teaching was having on my own understandings. Rather than thinking

455 we would all become the same, I came to see how much we were learning from our differences. It was from the differences that I was learning about my own ideas. Rather than imparting knowledge that I assumed others needed, their questions were helping me to think better

460 about my own conceptions of social studies. Many times my commitment to a particular point of view came into question as Lisa and JoAnn asked questions. Sometimes the questions came from Lisa's immediate classroom context; sometimes the questions were more abstract.

465 Lisa and JoAnn were more sophisticated with issues than the preservice students in our classes and so their questions pushed harder at the core of my beliefs. I saw much more clearly how complicated some of these ideas are and the ways in which they can be easily misunderstood.

470 For example, I used to rant and rave about the shortcomings of textbooks for social studies instruction. Lisa and JoAnn helped me to see the ways in which I made students feel guilty about using them especially as first year teachers. That was not what I intended. As they helped

475 me to see the consequences of my position, I could work on ways to make my point, but not debilitate new teachers. We now talk about textbooks as 'springboards' rather than 'platforms.' The students have benefited and so have I.

480 The question of whose knowledge counts gradually disappeared; rather the conversations became three people working together to understand better what we were trying to do together. Whether it was a theoretical or practical issue became a useless distinction. We

485 were working to understand each other and our different ideas. Each of us at times had questions that helped us understand something new. We eventually trusted each other enough to take risks, expose our ignorance, and test our ideas before they were well formed. It was

490 exciting rather than intimidating. We worked hard to understand that we each had different/helpful things to offer in the conversation.

Joint Reflections on Change

As Lisa and Marilyn begin a third year of co-teaching, things again changed considerably in the

495 course. It seemed less important to work against typical expectations. Marilyn started class if it made sense for her to do so. Lisa discussed a videotape from her classroom because she best knew what had happened. We no longer felt it necessary to put time limits on sections

500 of class designated to a particular person. Rather, we decided who would be responsible for moving from one topic to another and let the flow of the class determine the time spent on a particular issue.

The major change in the course, however, was not

505 as obvious as these changes in course structure. It concerned our growing appreciation for each other's knowledge and expertise. This moved us beyond an appreciation for differences that developed during the first year. Appreciating another person's knowledge

510 and expertise came to mean seeing a potential for others to contribute to our own thinking and our shared project. This involved an acknowledgment that we needed another's ideas and expertise, that there will be times when their ideas will be better than our own, and

515 that they will legitimately claim the right to their fair share of authority and decision making. Intimidation is less likely when both parties respect the other's knowledge and expertise, especially in the context of a trusting relationship. In such a context, challenge becomes

520 a way to learn rather than a means to intimidation; differences of opinion provide options rather than conflict.

Appreciating each other's knowledge and expertise took time. We needed to know about each other's in-

525 stitutional contexts and background. We needed to understand each other's commitments and concerns. We needed to build some shared understandings. What we have come to share is as important and valuable as our differences. For example, Lisa has recently come to

530 understand how the differences in expectations in schools and universities influence how people talk to each other.

Lisa: It took awhile but I have come to recognize that in different contexts (my school and the university) dif-

535 ferent types of discourses are used. At the university, multiple perspectives, divergent thinking, and the questioning of ideas are encouraged. Schools typically socialize teachers to accept ideas, ask questions only to clarify, and keep quiet when we disagree with the per-

540 ceived majority. When teachers act at school in the same manner as university-based teachers do at their institutions, they are thought to be negative or 'trouble makers.'

With different expectations inherent in our separate institutional contexts, it is no wonder that university-

545 and school-based practitioners have difficulty talking to each other. We are used to different ways of dealing with ideas and conflicts. In our co-teaching, we needed to understand these different norms and positionings (Davies & Harré, 1990) and how they influenced our

550 interactions as we worked together.

Change came slowly. We may be slow learners, but I think not. There are many barriers to be overcome, many understandings that must be constructed, and levels of trust that must be nurtured. Expecting imme-

555 diate changes in minds or institutional structures seems to us to be naive. Collaboration across the significant differences of schools and universities is challenging,

and change for us took commitment, empathy, and good will.

Conclusion

560   In the beginning of our co-teaching experience, we could do little more than articulate our differences. Although we started in contradictory positions, we have influenced each other's thinking and have found new ways to help students negotiate the differences
565 between what research says and the realities of classrooms. But, of course, we have not resolved all potential conflicts. And the possibility of intimidation from university folks and passive resistance from school participants is as likely as not. Working together does
570 not guarantee better feelings or avoid all intimidation. There are issues of role, beliefs, and personality that must be considered and taken into account. None of this is easy, but when it works, it can be very rewarding.

575   Most school-based and university-based educators acknowledge, along with the popular press and national commissions reports (Carnegie Forum, 1986; Holmes Group, 1990), that the lack of cooperation between schools and universities is counterproductive. How to
580 work against the stereotypes and hierarchies that interfere with more genuinely collaborative relationships is unclear. How to resolve the differences in purposes and institutional rewards is uncharted territory. How to construct situations where we learn to appreciate our
585 different expertise and work toward common goals presents a clear challenge. We found the weekly interactions and joint decision making of a co-teaching situation to be a rich context to discuss and surmount some of these challenges.

References

Bricher, R., Hawk, M., & Tingley, J. (1993). Cross-age tutoring for at-risk students. *Teaching and Change*, *1*(1), 82–90.

Carnegie Forum on Education and the Economy. (1986). *A nation prepared: Teachers for the 21st century*. New York: Author.

Davies, B., & Harré, R. (1990). Positioning: The discursive production of selves. *Journal for the Theory of Social Behavior*, *20*(1), 43–63.

Gadamer, H. (1984). *Truth and method* (G. Barden, & J. Cummings, Trans.). New York: Crossroad.

Gitlin, A. (1992). *Teachers' voices for school change: An introduction to educative research*. London: Routledge.

Greene, M. (1988). Forward. In C. Witherell & N. Noddings (Eds.), *Stories lives tell* (pp. i–xi). New York: Teachers College Press.

Haraway, D. (1986). Situated knowledges: The science question in feminism and the privilege of partial perspectives. *Feminist Studies*, *14*(3), 575–599.

Harding, S. (1986). *The science question in feminism*. Ithaca, NY: Cornell University Press.

Holmes Group. (1990). *Tomorrow's schools: Principles for the design of professional development schools*. East Lansing, MI: Author.

Hunsaker, L., & Johnston, M. (1992). Teacher under construction: A collaborative case study of teacher change. *American Educational Research Journal*, *29*(2), 350–372.

Lather, P. (1991). *Getting smart*. New York: Routledge.

Miller, J. (1990). *Creating spaces and finding voices: Teachers collaborating for empowerment*. Albany: State University of New York Press.

Nalle, K. (1993). Democratic processing of children's classroom concerns. *Teaching and Change*, *1*(1), 91–97.

Paley, V. (1989). *White teacher*. Cambridge: Harvard University Press.

Ricoeur, P. (1981). *Hermeneutics and the human sciences: Essays on language, action, and interpretation* (J. B. Thompson, Trans.). Cambridge: Cambridge University Press.

van Manen, M. (1990). *Researching lived experience: Human science for an action sensitive pedagogy*. Albany: State University of New York Press.

Weedon, C. (1987). *Feminist practice and post-structuralist theory*. London: Basil Blackwell.

Witherell, C., & Noddings, N. (1991). *Stories lives tell: Narrative and dialogue in education*. New York: Teachers College Press.

About the Authors: JoAnn Hohenbrink is assistant professor at the Ohio Dominican College, Columbus. Her specializations include teacher education and social studies education.

Marilyn Johnston is associate professor at The Ohio State University, Columbus. Her specializations include school/university collaboration, collaborative research, and social studies/social foundations.

Lisa Westhoven is a teacher and clinical educator at Worthington School District, Ohio. Her specializations include classroom research and social studies.

Exercise for Case 3

1. Introduction

A. Is the problem area for the research clearly described? Explain.

B. Have the researchers convinced you that the problem area is important? Explain.

C. To what extent does the literature presented in the introduction help you understand the problem? Is the literature used to put the problem in context? Explain.

D. Do the researchers indicate how this study is different from and/or similar to earlier ones reported in the literature?

E. Do the researchers reveal their personal perspectives on the problem area, including any possible biases? Explain.

2. Methods

A. Are the demographics of the participants (i.e., background characteristics such as age, race, and so on) described in sufficient detail? Explain.

B. Considering the problem area for the research, do you think that appropriate participants were selected? If you had been conducting the study, would you have selected the same type(s) of participants? Would you have used the same number of participants? Explain.

C. Which strategies listed in Table 1 on page 161 of this book were employed by the researchers? Are they described in sufficient detail? Explain.

D. In addition to those you named in response to question 2C, have the researchers used any additional strategies to help assure the validity of the study? If yes, what are they? Are they described in sufficient detail? Explain.

3. Analysis and Results

A. Are the steps taken in the analysis described in sufficient detail? Explain.

B. Are the results clearly organized? Explain.

C. Are the results discussed in terms of a theory or theories (either theories that emerged from this study or previously existing ones)? Explain.

D. Were the direct quotations of the participants' statements, if any, judiciously selected? Do they help you understand the results? Explain.

E. Are there other ways the results could have been organized and interpreted? Explain.

4. Conclusions/Implications

A. Are the researchers' concluding remarks appropriate? Do they flow logically from the material presented earlier?

B. Do the researchers describe any implications? If yes, are they appropriate? Are there other implications that are not discussed by the researchers? Explain.

5. Ethical Considerations

A. In your opinion, could this research have caused physical or psychological harm to the participants? If yes, did the researchers take adequate measures to ameliorate the potential for harm? Explain.

B. If you had conducted this research, would you have obtained written, informed consent from the participants before conducting the study? Explain. Does this research report indicate that the researchers obtained such consent?

6. Overall Evaluation

A. Throughout the article, are all specialized terms and jargon defined to your satisfaction? Explain.

B. Briefly describe your overall evaluation of the research report, noting any special strengths and weaknesses.

C. If you had been a reviewer for the journal in which this report was published, would you have recommended publication of the report? If yes, would you have recommended that it be published "as is" or modified before publication? Explain. If no, what is the primary reason why you would recommend not publishing it?

Case 4

The Impact of Homelessness and Shelter Life on Family Relationships

ELIZABETH W. LINDSEY
University of North Carolina at Greensboro

ABSTRACT. This study explored mothers' perceptions of how homelessness and shelter life affected family relationships. Participants reported increased closeness and heightened quality and quantity of interaction with their children, but a disruption in their roles as disciplinarians and providers/caretakers. Factors which mothers perceived to affect relationships were shelter conditions (rules and interactions with staff and residents), the mother's emotional state, and the child's emotional state, temperament, and behavior. Implications for practice are suggested.

From *Family Relations*, *47*, 243–252. Copyright © 1998 by the National Council on Family Relations. Reprinted with permission.

Members of homeless families currently comprise approximately a third of the U.S. homeless population, and homeless children comprise the fastest growing segment of the homeless population (McChesney,
5 1995; Reyes & Waxman, 1989; U.S. Department of Housing & Urban Development, 1994). The vast majority (80–85%) of these families are headed by single mothers. The first wave of family homelessness that began in the 1980s has been attributed to federal cuts in
10 housing programs, loss of privately owned low-income housing stock, the failure of public assistance benefits to keep pace with inflation, increased rate of divorce, and failure of courts to enforce child support orders. At the same time, structural changes in the U.S. economy
15 resulted in loss of higher paying jobs that were replaced by lower paying service sector jobs (Rossi, 1994). Recent changes in welfare programs threaten to create a second wave of family homelessness. With public assistance no longer an entitlement and benefits
20 limited to 2–5 years (depending on the state), it is likely that the numbers of homeless families will increase, especially when the economy takes its next downturn and recent hires lose their jobs. Both service providers and formerly homeless mothers have asserted
25 the pivotal role public assistance has played in helping homeless families emerge from homelessness (Lindsey, 1997; 1998). Without this safety net, families will find it harder to emerge from homelessness, and the length of time families are homeless is likely to
30 increase. In addition, the absence of benefits may well precipitate some families into homelessness who would otherwise have managed to maintain their own residences.

Despite the fact that family homelessness has been
35 increasing for over 15 years we still know very little about the impact of homelessness on family relationships. Research has focused primarily on precipitants of family homelessness (Bassuk & Rosenberg, 1988; McChesney, 1990; Weitzman, Knickman, & Shinn,
40 1990), characteristics of homeless family members (Bassuk, 1990; Johnson, 1989; Mills & Ota, 1989), and the effect of homelessness on mothers and children (Hall & Maza, 1990; Rafferty & Shinn, 1991). Much less is known about how homelessness affects the fam-
45 ily itself, especially from the parents' point of view.

Family shelters have been built, existing shelters have been opened to families, and transitional housing programs have been initiated, often with very little attention paid to the unique issues presented by fami-
50 lies. When shelters that previously served single men and/or women have been opened to families, frequently the same rules have been applied to families as to singles, regardless of how inappropriate or how destructive they are to family relationships. For example, for-
55 merly homeless mothers have reported having to leave shelters each day, with their preschool age children, at 7:00 a.m. and not being allowed to return until 5:00 p.m., regardless of the weather (Lindsey, 1997). Many women have left their children with relatives or placed
60 them in foster care rather than take them into a shelter (Liebow, 1993).

The purpose of this study is to explore mothers' perceptions of how homelessness and shelter life affect relationships in mother-headed families. The percep-
65 tions of these mothers can provide valuable information for shelter staff and other service providers about how to maintain the integrity of family relationships as parents attempt to resolve their housing crises.

Literature Review

Before reviewing the literature on family relation-
70 ships, it is important to recognize certain qualities and characteristics of homeless mothers and children that can affect their relationships.

Homeless Mothers and Children

The average homeless female head of household is in her late twenties and has two or three children, gen-
75 erally of preschool age (McChesney, 1990). African American families are overrepresented in the population of homeless families, as they are among the poverty population in general (McChesney, 1995). Many homeless mothers have not graduated from high
80 school, have very inconsistent work histories, and are much more likely to rely on public assistance than on earned income to support their families (Burt & Cohen, 1989; Goodman, 1991). One-third to one-half of these families become homeless because mothers are fleeing
85 abusive relationships (Homeless Information Exchange, 1994). Other events associated with family homelessness include job loss, eviction or inability to pay rent, and conflict with family or friends with whom the family is living prior to becoming homeless
90 (Weitzman et al., 1990).

While psychiatric or substance abuse problems are not a major cause of homelessness among families (Burt & Cohen, 1989), there is evidence that the conditions of poverty and homelessness have a "consistent
95 negative effect on mothers' day-to-day mental health" (McChesney, 1990, p. 437), and high rates of depression and personality disorders have been documented (Bassuk & Rosenberg, 1988; Bassuk, Rubin, & Lauriat, 1986; Goodman, 1991). Goodman, Saxe, and Harvey
100 (1991) have characterized the condition of homelessness itself as a psychological trauma that is a risk factor for emotional disorder.

Many homeless women have had extremely traumatic childhoods and/or adult relationships (Browne,
105 1993). They are more likely than housed low-income women to have: lived in foster care, a group home, or institution; run away from home; been physically or sexually abused; and lived on the street or other public place. They also tend to have small social networks
110 that they turn to and exhaust before entering shelters (Shinn, Knickman, & Weitzman, 1991).

The average age of children in homeless families is 6 years, with a majority of children being of preschool age (Burt & Cohen, 1989; Dail, 1990). These children
115 are at grave risk for various health, developmental, and psychological problems including depression, anxiety, and serious behavior problems (Bassuk, 1990; Bassuk et al., 1986; Molnar, Rath, & Klein, 1990; Wright, 1990). These children are often absent from school and
120 demonstrate poor academic performance (Rafferty & Rollins, 1989).

Despite the challenges homeless mothers face, they possess strengths as well. For example, Dail (1990) reported "surprisingly good overall psychosocial
125 status" (p. 298) among a sample of homeless mothers, and Wagner and Menke (1991) noted no significant difference in the types of coping behaviors used by homeless and housed poor mothers. Banyard (1995) reported specific coping strategies that homeless moth-
130 ers use, including doing something to confront the problem directly, getting social support, having patience and enduring, and positive thinking. In a study of homeless and formerly homeless mothers, Montgomery (1994) found such personal strengths as pride,
135 a positive orientation, clarity of focus, determination, and a moral structure these women used to guide their lives. Participation in a community, commitment to personal relationships (especially with their children), religious beliefs, and finding purpose in helping others
140 were valuable coping resources for these mothers. It is also important to note that women who enter shelters with their children have managed to maintain enough stability to avoid having the children placed into foster care. Thus, while mothers who are homeless with their
145 children may have difficulty fulfilling some aspects of their roles as parents, many are able to keep their families intact and find ways to cope with the stress of homelessness and conditions that precipitate homelessness.

Relationships Within Homeless Families

150 Based on an observational study of parent-child relations in an Atlanta shelter, Boxil and Beaty (1990) noted "the overarching theme/concept that emerged was the difficulty mothers and their children as family units face in establishing and maintaining *ordered*
155 *mother/child relationships*" (p. 53–54). Three dynamics that affect family relationships were noted: (a) public mothering; (b) the unraveling of the mother role; and (c) the mothers' experience of being externally controlled by shelter rules. Public mothering refers to
160 the fact that family interactions are often observed by other residents and staff. Thus, parents find their decisions and actions judged by others, and frequently their mothering is "influenced and often directed by the presence and needs of other mothers" (p. 58). In fami-
165 lies with both teenage girls and younger children, researchers observed "unraveling" of the parental role as the older girls took on parental responsibilities for younger children. Rather than seeing this dynamic as an abdication of responsibility by the mothers, the
170 authors saw this as an attempt by older children to "soothe" their mothers and noted that "in an unkind and often assaulting world, mothers were comforted by their children's special acts of assistance and caring" (p. 59). The third dynamic that seemed to affect family
175 relationships was the mothers' experience of being externally controlled by shelter rules and characteristics of group living. Mothers no longer had control over daily family routines such as when and what their children ate, when they went to bed, or when they
180 bathed and felt as though they had lost their roles as "provider, family leader, organizer and standard setter" (p. 60) while living in the shelter. This finding has been supported by later research which indicates that many homeless mothers experience "difficulties and frustra-
185 tion in child caretaking and in the parent-child relation-

ship because of the stress of homelessness and shelter rules that exacerbated already diminished parental authority" (Thrasher & Mowbray, 1995, p. 97). Boxil and Beaty (1990) concluded that homelessness and shelter living creates "out-of-order" mother/child relationships.

Hausman and Hammen (1993) asserted that, for many families, relationships during periods of homelessness are not merely "out-of-order...but, rather, instances in which the pillars of successful parenting...are fractured" (p. 361). These authors see homelessness as a "double crisis: the disruptive and traumatizing experience of losing a home as well as impediments to a parent's ability to function as a consistent and supportive caregiver" (p. 358). Hausman and Hammen describe three factors which can disrupt parent-child relationships: (a) the environment, which sets resource constraints and generates stressors; (b) the mother's own level of psychological distress; and (c) the child's temperament and behavior. The reciprocal interactions of highly distressed mothers with highly distressed children who are acting out may lead to serious consequences for parent-child relationships. These authors note that "virtually all the high risk conditions that have been studied for their negative impact on mothers and children come together in the situation of homelessness" (p. 365). Hausman and Hammen drew on the literature on effective parenting and perceptions gathered from human service professionals serving homeless families, but did not include perceptions of homeless parents in the development of their schema.

Other studies have also noted difficulties in parent-child relationships in homeless families. Molnar et al. (1990) reported a high degree of ambivalence in homeless preschoolers' relationships with their mothers and a high prevalence of depression among homeless mothers; they also discussed the risk that sustained parental depression creates for children. Homeless mothers tend to report significantly higher levels of intrafamily strain than housed poor or low-income mothers, citing such difficulties as emotional problems among family members, increased arguing between parents and children, and an increase in the number of family problems that are not resolved (Wagner & Menke, 1991). In one study, 52% of homeless mothers reported that "child problems" were a frequent source of stress for them (second only to housing problems) (Banyard, 1995). Higher rates of child abuse and neglect have been reported for homeless families than for low-income housed families (Alperstein, Rappaport, & Flanigan, 1988).

Most research into the impact of homelessness on family relationships has relied on observations of researchers and service providers and data from psychological or psychiatric tests, from which researchers have derived implications for parent-child relationships. Although some of these studies involved homeless mothers, they were not directly focused on moth-

ers' perceptions of the impact of homelessness and shelter life on their family relationships. If family-friendly services are to be developed, it is imperative that parents' experiences be taken into account. This study extends the existing research by systematically studying mothers' perceptions of the effect of homelessness and shelter life on family relations.

Methodology

The idea for the present study emerged during an earlier qualitative study of the process of restabilization among homeless families in Georgia (Lindsey, 1996; 1997). Family relationships were not the focus of the original study, but during interviews almost all of the participants began talking about the impact of homelessness on their family relationships. The research question for this study emerged directly from conversations with participants in the restabilization study.

Because the purpose of the current study is to explore mothers' perceptions of the impact of homelessness and shelter life on their relationships with their children, the qualitative research paradigm was selected as most appropriate. Qualitative methodology is particularly useful in studying families because of the emphasis on meanings, interpretations, interactions, and subjective experiences of family members (Daly, 1992; Gilgun, 1992). The theoretical underpinnings of the qualitative research paradigm in family research are phenomenology and symbolic interactionism. Phenomenology attempts to "understand the meaning of events and interactions...and the subjective aspects of people's behavior" (Bogdan & Bicklen, 1992, p. 34). Symbolic interactionism asserts that "human experience is mediated by interpretation.... Objects, people, situations, and events do not possess their own meaning, rather meaning is conferred on them" (Bogdan & Bicklen, 1992, p. 36). Thus, to understand how homelessness and shelter life might impact family relations, it is important to explore the subjective experience of families within the context of homelessness and how mothers interpret and make meaning of that experience.

The current study involved secondary analysis of data from the Georgia restabilization study (Lindsey, 1996; 1997) and analysis of new data collected during a follow-up study in North Carolina. Specific questions regarding family relationships were added to the interview guide for the follow-up study. Therefore, the present study comprises two phases: (1) the original research conducted with 10 Georgia women in 1993–94 and (2) the follow-up research, conducted with 7 North Carolina women in 1994–95.

Sample Selection

Phase 1. A purposeful sample, consisting of formerly homeless female heads of household that were currently stably rehoused with their children, was chosen for Phase 1. The criteria of successful restabilization was selected because the thrust of the original research was to discover how mothers were able to successfully restabilize their families after periods of homelessness. The specific strategy used was criterion sampling. Key informants who worked in homeless shelters in three small Georgia towns were asked to nominate formerly homeless mothers who they perceived to have been particularly successful in stably rehousing their families. The sites were limited to nonmetropolitan areas, as the experience of homeless families in such areas has not been well studied. Two shelters cooperating with the study primarily served women and children while the third shelter served all homeless people.

To be included in the study, nominated participants had to meet the following criteria: (a) They must have stayed in a shelter with at least one of their children; (b) at least one of the children who stayed in the shelter must have been under the age of 18 during the episode of homelessness; (c) the family must have been in a stable living situation for at least 6 months prior to the interview (i.e., the family did not experience an episode of homelessness during that period). If the family had moved during the past 6 months, it must have been to improve their living situation, not because of an inability to pay rent or eviction; and (d) participants had to be mentally capable of participating in the interview and articulating their experience.

Several potential participants who were known to have psychiatric illnesses or who appeared to the researcher to have limited mental capacities during telephone conversations were excluded from the sample.

One of the women included in the Phase 1 sample did not meet criterion (c), having only been stably rehoused for 4 months. I decided to include her in the sample because later contact with this woman confirmed that she was still employed and living in the same residence nine months after leaving the shelter.

The sample size was determined by the criterion of redundancy, that is, interviewing stopped when additional interviews ceased to generate new data (Lincoln & Guba, 1985). In Phase 1, redundancy began appearing rather soon in the data analysis. After the sixth interview was conducted and analyzed, only minor modifications were made to the findings. Subsequent interviews validated the findings. The total number of participants for Phase 1 was 10 (6 African American and 4 White).

Phase 2. The process and criteria for sample selection were similar for Phase 2. Participants were nominated by staff from four shelters in three North Carolina towns that reflected a more urban demographic profile than the Georgia towns. In addition to studying family relations, a second major purpose of Phase 2 was to validate findings regarding the process of restabilization that had emerged during the original study. By interviewing respondents in another state and in a more urban area, I hoped to establish a basis for generalizing the findings beyond the original sample and

geographic area. Two of the shelters that cooperated with Phase 2 served all homeless populations while the other two were battered women's shelters.

Again, a purposeful sample was selected, and participants had to meet the same criteria as specified for Phase 1. The sample size was determined by the principle of redundancy, resulting in a sample of seven participants (6 African Americans and 1 White).

Thus, in terms of the racial composition of the entire sample (Phases 1 and 2), of the 17 participants, 12 (71%) were African American and 5 (29%) were White. While I was interested in assuring that both White and African American mothers were included in the sample, there was no attempt to sample in direct proportion to the racial makeup of homeless families in either geographic area. Nevertheless, the racial make up of this sample was not dissimilar from that of the population of homeless families in general, in which African Americans are overrepresented (McChesney, 1995).

A note about the sample representativeness and generalizability of findings within the qualitative research paradigm is in order. Within the qualitative paradigm, generalizability is conceptualized as "transferability" or the extent to which "findings fit into contexts outside of the study situation that are determined by the degree of similarity or goodness of fit between the two contexts" (Krefting, 1991, p. 216). It is the researcher's responsibility to provide enough "rich, thick description" (Geertz, 1973) to persuade the reader of the validity of the findings and to enable readers to decide the extent to which these findings are transferable to other situations of interest. Use of a nominated sample has been suggested as one strategy to enhance the applicability or transferability of qualitative findings (Krefting, 1991). In this study, participants were nominated by key informants who were in a position to know whether the participants met the criteria of the study and the extent to which potential participants were typical or atypical of homeless female heads of household.

Data Collection

Phase 1. Phase 1 data came from the initial restabilization study (Lindsey, 1996; 1997). Data was gathered through in-depth interviews that lasted from one and a half to two hours. I conducted all of the interviews which usually took place in participants' homes (one interview was conducted in my office and another in a hotel room). Participants were informed of the purpose of the project, asked to give informed consent, and were paid $25. The semi-structured interview guide used primarily open-ended questions, and the interviews were conversational in nature rather than conforming to a rigid order or wording of questions. Main topic areas included: demographic information, family composition and history, homeless episode(s) and precipitants, experience of homelessness, process of restabilization, role as mother (this area of inquiry was added as the importance of the issue emerged during initial interviews), and current living situation. In addition, a genogram (McGoldrick & Gerson, 1989) was developed to identify family structure, relationships, and nodal events in the life of the family. Interviews were audiotaped and transcribed in their entirety. Summaries of the interviews were prepared and sent, along with the genograms, to participants to review for accuracy.

Phase 2. The Phase 1 interview guide was modified to add questions regarding family relationships during times of homelessness. These questions emerged during the Phase 1 data analysis, as described above. For example, participants in Phase 2 were asked, "What was it like for you to try to be a mother to your children while you were without a home?" "What was it like trying to parent your children in a shelter?" "Do you think this time in your lives had an effect on your family relationships? If so, how?" and, when appropriate, "How did the experience of being homeless affect relationships among your children?" After asking such open-ended questions, I described the findings regarding family relations from the secondary analysis of Phase 1 data and asked participants to reflect on the extent to which their experiences were similar to or different from those described by Georgia participants. A student assistant and I conducted the interviews, which were audiotaped, transcribed, and checked for accuracy. Participants received copies of interview summaries and genograms to review for accuracy.

Data Analysis

Phase 1. Data from Phase 1 was analyzed first, using elements of the constant comparative method (Strauss & Corbin, 1990). It was not possible to create the interplay of data collection and analysis which is a hallmark of the constant comparative method because this was a secondary analysis of data which had been conducted during the original study of the restabilization process of homeless families. However, I did conduct open coding in relation to the question of interest to this current study: What are homeless mothers' perceptions of how homelessness and shelter life affect their family relationships? Specifically, I read through each of the 10 transcripts from the Georgia study with this question in mind, looking for themes, commonalities, and distinctions. As the findings emerged, I developed a set of initial conceptual categories which were very specific, based on open coding of the first several interviews. This initial set of categories expanded as additional interviews were analyzed and new information emerged. The initial categories were modified to create a schema (set of higher level categories which encompassed the more specific initial categories) that I then used to reanalyze each transcript to assure that data had not been lost in the process of expanding the original categories as data analysis proceeded. At this

point, I also began coding specific interview segments as exemplars for each category. Only minor modifications to the conceptual categories were made during this process. Finally, I used the *Ethnograph* (Seidel, Kjolseth, & Seymour, 1988) computer software package to code interview segments and organize data according to conceptual categories and subcategories.

Phase 2. Phase 1 data was used to conceptualize questions that were added to the Phase 2 interview guide regarding family relations. Phase 2 data was analyzed by using the conceptual categories that emerged during Phase 1. That is, I read through the transcripts and coded interview segments according to the coding schema based on the findings of Phase 1. At the same time, I looked for evidence that existing categories did not adequately describe the experiences reported by Phase 2 participants. Phase 1 conceptual categories were for the most part adequate to encompass the Phase 2 data, and only one minor change was made to the schema (see the Findings section and Table 1). Again, I used the *Ethnograph* (Seidel et al., 1988) computer program to code and organize interview segments for purposes of study and retrieval.

Table 1

Dimensions of Family Relationships Affected by Homelessness and Shelter Life

Quality of parent-child relations
Emotional closeness
Quality and quantity of interaction
Parental role
Disciplinarian
Provider/caretaker
Role reversal[a]

[a]This subcategory emerged in Phase 1 but was not supported in Phase 2.

Participant Characteristics

Participants ranged in age from 19 to 52 years. The families had stayed in shelters an average of 3 months, with a range of from 2 weeks to 8 months. An average of 2 children (range 1–5) had stayed in shelters with their mothers, with an average age of 7½ years (range 6 months–16 years). Some of these families had been homeless more than once, but the interviews focused primarily on their last episode of homelessness. The primary reasons these families became homeless were: job loss (2), leaving abusive partners/spouses (4), mother's substance abuse (3), substance abuse of mother's partner/spouse (2), conflict with mother's family of origin (4), and eviction due to nonpayment of rent or conflicts with landlords (2). At the time of the interview, participants had been out of the shelter an average of 19 months (range 4 months–4 years). Pseudonyms are used in reference to all participants.

Findings

Two sets of findings emerged from Phase 1: (a) di-

510 mensions of family relationships that were affected by homelessness and shelter stay and (b) factors that affected those relationships. These findings were largely validated by data from Phase 2, with only one exception as described below and in Table 1.

Dimensions of Family Relationships Affected by Homelessness and Shelter Life

515 Mothers perceived that two specific aspects of family relationships were affected by homelessness and living in a shelter: (a) the quality of parent-child relations and (b) the parental role (see Table 1). Although participants were asked specifically about sibling rela-

520 tionships, they perceived very little if any impact on relations among their children. However, they all (except for the one participant who was in a shelter with an infant only) experienced a significant impact on their own relationships with their children.

Quality of Parent-Child Relations

525 Mothers found that two aspects of their relationships with their children seemed to be affected by the experience of homelessness and shelter life: emotional closeness and the quality and quantity of their interactions. Almost all the mothers reported that relationships

530 with their children became closer while they were living in the shelter. For instance, Beth noted the impact of living in the close proximity of a shelter family room: "I think it brought [us] closer together. You're cramped in a room smaller than this.... And we

535 talked." Mandy said of her preschool age son, "We're closer...because there were not many children that would come through that was his age. He only had me." Jean also noted that she and her young son "became friends moreso.... It might have actually im-

540 proved [our relationship] on the friendship level instead of a parent-child thing."

This closeness seemed to develop because of the amount of time they spent together and because they perceived themselves as banding together in a time of

545 crisis. Although most mothers did report increased closeness in their relationships with their children, the almost constant interaction required by shelter life became a burden for some of the women. Ann and Lois reflected on their sense of being overwhelmed by the

550 shelter requirement that children always be with their parents, regardless of age:

> The kids is supposed to be with you at all times. [Even] at 15, they supposed to be with you at all times.... You're supposed to know where your kid is at all times, but it's
555 very hard to do,...to keep your child 24-7 when you're here.

> The only time I really got peace was at night, cause we had to be in bed by 9:30. And that's the only time I got peace and quiet because sometimes I would ask [the
560 shelter staff] just to let me sit downstairs by myself.

Several mothers noted that, upon leaving the shelter, relationships with their children eroded. Conflicts

that had remained unspoken during the period of shelter stay emerged. For example Beth said,

565 > When we moved out of the shelter [family relationships] were strained at first. I think it's because we were so cramped and the rules had changed so much that everybody wanted to spread their wings, crow a little.... It was difficult at first.

570 Thus, while mothers' overall perception was that they and their children became closer, they also noted how difficult it was for them and the children to be constantly in each other's company. Sometimes conflicts erupted once the family moved into its own

575 home, perhaps reflecting some children's ability to suppress their emotions during the housing crisis, but a need to express those emotions once the crisis was resolved.

Parental Role

All of the mothers (except the one who had the in-

580 fant only) found it difficult to parent their children while living in a shelter. Specifically, it was hard for them to be disciplinarians and to fulfill the provider/caretaker role because they were not able to meet their children's basic needs for shelter, food, safety,

585 and emotional nurturance. Mothers tended to attribute disciplinary problems to shelter rules that prohibited corporal punishment and to the interference of other residents, a dynamic that will be explored in the next section. Regarding the overall parental role and care-

590 taking functions, mothers often reported feeling inadequate. For instance, Ellie, whose family had stayed in several shelters and had finally gotten stabilized, found her family once again in a shelter. She said:

> All we had accomplished, we turned around and lost it
595 once we went to the shelter, cause they was frightened. And they looked for me to fight all their battles for them. So they got where they trusted me more, but...they got wherein that I had to do everything for them.

Katrina and her children were only in a shelter for
600 about a month, but still she felt

> like I was just doing them wrong. It was like I was letting them down. All I could do for them, I did: make sure they didn't get hurt; make sure they got food. It was hurting me, like I was doing them wrong, cause they hadn't ever
605 had that experience, and I hadn't either.

Three of the parents from Phase 1 indicated that, at times, their children seemed to be taking on a parental role, a phenomenon observed by Boxil and Beaty (1990). During Phase 2, participants were asked di-

610 rectly whether they had observed role reversal or caretaking of them by their children during the housing crisis. Only two of the participants responded affirmatively, but they were not talking about the children taking on parental roles with other children, as Boxil

615 and Beaty (1990) found. Instead, mothers tended to perceive mutual support among themselves and their children, rather than perceiving that their children were

taking care of them or younger children. For instance, Susan, said, "I think we probably helped each other. Who knows where I would have been if I hadn't 've had her, I mean emotionally. I may never have come out of it." Tammy also denied observing any role reversal with her 15-year-old daughter, but saw their support as mutual, what family members do for each other:

> No. I don't think that happened, but I can understand that.... It's like you saw an [inkling] of that right here when my daughter saw me crying [during the interview]. She came out and she hugged me. Yeah, we've actually had to depend upon one another.... I can remember when my mother was upset and I'd do the same thing. It's just part of caring about the people that you love.

Factors that Affect Family Relationships During Homelessness and Shelter Stay

The participants believed that three main factors influenced their family relationships while they were living in a shelter: conditions of shelter life; their own emotional state; and their children's emotional state, temperament, and behavior (see Table 2). Conditions of shelter life were also perceived to influence mothers' and children's emotional states as well as the family relationships.

Shelter conditions. All of the mothers complained that shelter conditions such as certain shelter rules and behavioral expectations hurt family relationships. Homeless shelters usually held families to the same rules they had for singles. Mothers objected strongly to requirements that they and their children leave the shelter during the day, regardless of weather. Other problematic rules and regulations involved curfews, rigid mealtimes and no access to kitchen facilities, and the requirement that children always be with their parents in the shelter. Residents and staff were not always understanding of children's normal activity level or misbehavior. Shelters designed for women and children tended to be more family-friendly, although they usually had rules against male children over a certain age (as young as 8) staying in the shelter, which meant that some boys had to stay with friends, relatives, or at another shelter. The following quotes illustrate ways in which these rules created problems for families:

> It was a very difficult situation, because it didn't make any difference how cold it was or whether it was rain or shine, you had to be gone...had to find a place to go during the day.... How can this mother go out and look for a job or even look for a place to live when she's got three kids, and it's raining, or it's cold?

> We had to eat the main meal at 4:00...[and you] couldn't bring any food in there.... Little boys eat all the time, and they don't eat their main meal of the day at 4:00, 4:30 in the evening.

> [My son] was more or less suffocated because you couldn't really be a child.... You could sit there and play with their toys, look at their books, and watch TV up to a point, but just to get wild, like a child likes to do, you

couldn't do it.... [Shelter staff expected children to] act like adults.... Basically, they were to be seen and not heard.

Table 2
Factors that Affect Family Relationships During Homelessness and Shelter Stay

Shelter conditions
Rules
Family members' interactions with staff and other residents
Mothers' emotional state
Frustration, impatience with children
Emotional unavailability due to stress
Children's emotional state, temperament, and behavior
Reactions to mother's emotional state
Degree of disruption in the child's life
Child's temperament and/or behavior

Probably the most troublesome aspect of shelter life to mothers was prohibition against any type of corporal punishment in the shelters (Rossi, 1994, notes that 66.5% of shelters have this rule). Parents were expected to make their children behave but were not allowed to use their main form of discipline. At times, shelter staff corrected the mothers in front of their children, undermining their parental authority. For instance, Ellie was very angry at how a staff member informed her she could not spank her children:

> Maybe if he had of took me to myself and told me [about the no spanking rule]...instead of saying it in front of the child, then they probably wouldn't have got as far out of hand as they did...that undermined me.

Ann talked about how children would use the no spanking rule against their parents:

> If [staff] found out that you hit your child, they would call social services on you. What happened was the kids knowed that, so therefore, they try your patience. They know, "Mama can't hit us in here." ...Sometimes it's very hard to discipline them and you know your child and how far you can go, but once that child find your place, your game, they'll play you every time.

Delores had a solution for her discipline problem with her daughter, one that other mothers used as well: "She thought I couldn't whip her, but I would actually take her out in the parking lot off the premises and just tear her up. So I knew how to work that, too. I wasn't just going to allow her [to misbehave]."

Although several of the shelters offered or required parenting classes to teach nonviolent disciplinary approaches, participants' reactions to what they learned varied. One mother said, "I really enjoyed the parenting classes. They kind of helped, just the group. I liked being in a place with women that understood me, that were going through the same thing." However, it was unclear whether the techniques she learned were useful in disciplining her children. Toni did not find the par-

715 enting skills she was taught to be very helpful: "I learned things, but I don't know, maybe it's just me. My kids just don't abide by time out and stuff. They just don't. So I just spank them every now and then."

720 Interactions with other residents and shelter staff also contributed to family difficulties. Some mothers found that other residents interfered with their parenting. This seemed primarily to involve either telling children what to do or "spoiling" them. For example, Beth said, "[My daughter] didn't like that there was 725 other people trying to boss her around. Marie was not a very good person for taking authority from anybody but me." Jean said,

> The people that are…in the shelter are sorry to see a child there, and so it took me awhile to get Aaron unspoiled 730 after leaving there because everybody was always overriding your authority…. So that we had a bit of an attitude problem, not from having been homeless and being in the shelter, but from having people interfere with your authority in raising your child…. guests and, sometimes 735 the staff as well.

Tammy also noted the impact that disciplining children in front of other residents had on parents, similar to what Boxil and Beaty (1990) called the phenomenon of public mothering.

740 I think that some times the women that had children were maybe a little critical of some of the other women that had children, as far as, if someone was acting like a good mother or not a good mother or lost their temper. I think that they felt that they were being watched, observed, and 745 judged accordingly.

Sometimes mothers found that their children were in danger from other residents who were "angry and hostile." Ellie threatened to fight a resident to protect her daughter:

750 One of them was getting fresh with my oldest girl, kept on trying to feel them, or talk about how good she supposed to look and all this stuff…. A lot of times [my kids] were missing out on eating the way they should because we'd wait till everybody else done eat…. It was 755 more violent there.

The sanitary conditions in shelters were also of concern to some mothers, as Toni indicated: "There's some nasty people in there. You wear your bedroom shoes in the shower. You hold your children when you 760 place them in there, you don't let them crawl on the floor. It's things you can do to avoid nastiness."

Although there were many complaints about negative effects of rules, conditions, and interactions with other residents on children and parent-child relations, 765 some mothers appreciated certain rules and aspects of shelter life that they saw as necessary for harmonious communal living. For instance, two mothers said,

> They have a bedtime for the children, 8:00…. And if you can't get them in the bed, they require that you put them 770 in the room if you can, and keep them occupied until they're sleepy. Which, you know, they need those rules

with that many people.

> It was a clean environment…. [The director] let me bring my TV, my VCR, my Nintendo, cause these are things 775 my children weren't used to being without…. And it was hard enough…. You were in a loving, caring environment. They had their rules, but everybody has rules, but it was home. It smelt good, it looked good. I didn't want to leave.

780 Similarly, relationships with residents and with staff were often seen in a positive light. Denise's 14-year-old son "got along with everyone. I think he liked it because of the guys that was there. They were all older than he was, but they all like took him under their 785 wing." Ellie also noted that one of the shelter staff took a special interest in her son, and they "would play ball in the evening…. I could just sit back and just see how happy my kids were. And it was all coming from these people that was strangers to us." Ellie went on to note 790 that, "I was closer to people in the shelter, even though people was going and coming, and the staff, than I was with my own family."

Mothers' emotional state. The mothers' emotional state also affected family relationships. Since mothers 795 rarely enter shelters with their children until they have exhausted other resources, it is not surprising that they report being depressed, full of despair, and impatient with their children once they come into a shelter. Several mothers talked about how their own stress level 800 made it very difficult for them to deal with their children. For example, Mandy and Ann said,

> I started getting really stressful…. I come from a very dysfunctional, abusive family, and it was starting to cycle, and I had to break it…. My stress level had reached 805 its breaking point with [my son] one night, and I went, BAM [she "back-handed" him].

> For the first month…when both our emotions got together it was very traumatizing, and I found myself hollering at them or I found myself getting a little bit an-810 gry…. Sometimes I got upset at myself and took it out on them, and it shouldn't have been that way, but it did.

Other mothers did not take their frustrations out on the children in such harsh ways, but they described such high levels of stress and emotionality that it is 815 questionable how emotionally available they could have been to their children. For instance Beth said, "I wanted to kill myself. I wanted to die. I wanted somebody to take away the humiliation and the pain away…. It was too hard for the girls; it was too hard 820 for me." Susan described herself as being

> in a daze…. I really didn't know where to turn. My nerves were gone. I couldn't sleep. I was about afraid to close my eyes, and I didn't feel safe when I first got there…. I had a 3-year-old, and I was like panicking, "What am I 825 going to do?"

Jean, who had stayed in several homeless shelters, supported this researcher inference regarding emotional unavailability when she observed,

830 the children need about the same thing as the woman does. And that's reassurance and knowing that everything is going to be okay. And if you can get the mom settled down, she's the best one to settle the kids down, and she can't do that as long as she's upset and scared and worried.

835 *Children's emotional state, temperament, and behavior.* Mothers believed that their children's emotional state, temperament, and behavior also affected their relationships. Children's emotional state seemed to be influenced strongly by the mother's own emotional state, whether the child had any existing behavioral or emotional difficulties, and the extent to which their lives have been disrupted prior to shelter entry and by living in the shelter.

If mothers were themselves highly distressed, their 845 children tended to pick up on that and acted out themselves. As Jean observed in the above quote, when mothers calmed down and got their own emotions under control, often they noticed their children calming down, and their role as parent became easier. For instance, Ellie said, "I learned that once I get me happy, [the children] will be happy, too." Susan echoed her sentiments: "If you're not happy, your children are not going to be happy. And if you're not in frame of mind to help yourself, then they're in trouble because you 855 can't help them."

The extent to which children's lives were disrupted also affected their emotions and behaviors, and, as a result, their interactions with their parents. Age seemed to play a significant part in the extent of life disruption, 860 with older children's lives tending to be more disrupted by homelessness and shelter life than those of younger children. For example, older children tended to be embarrassed about living in a shelter, leading to stress in the parent-child relationship as parents often felt guilty 865 about what their children were having to go through. Older children also presented more challenges for their parents in terms of discipline and maintaining a normal routine of daily life. For instance, older children who had to change schools and leave behind friends were 870 often angry at their mothers and acted out. Tammy found that her daughter "was going through a tough time emotionally, too.... She had to leave her friends when we left her dad.... We couldn't go there because I was afraid...he'd see me." Sissy's daughter reflected 875 the feelings of many adolescents: "She had a problem with staying there.... She thought it was degrading, embarrassing." Lois noted how disruptive shelter life was to her oldest son:

My 12-year-old, oh gosh! He was so depressed. His atti-
880 tude changed. His personality changed, and I had to learn how to deal with that. And it was so tough because he had always been such a sweet child...but his attitude became rotten. He was fed up with the rules.... He couldn't play with the kids down the block because we was at the
885 shelter. He had no friends.... And he said, "I love my brothers and sisters. And I love playing with them,

Mama, but I need somebody my age."

Ann noted a difference between how her two sons handled living in the shelter:

890 My 10-year-old, he wasn't too bad, but my 15-year-old was. I had to make sure that his feelings wouldn't get hurt too bad. He didn't want to stay here. He would rather walk all the way to school instead of catching the bus out here because kids would tease him.... My youngest son
895 did, too, but he would punch them. I know it isn't being nice. This is how he would get his anger out.

Children with emotional or behavioral problems or who had experienced traumatic events such as being abused themselves or witnessing their mother's abuse, 900 often acted out in shelters. Betty, whose daughter had been physically abused by her father, found out how difficult it was to deal with children's emotional problems in the shelter:

They say after a child's been abused, once they are in a
905 safe place they have to act out, they just completely show off.... When we got to the shelter...I wasn't equipped to handle it.... I was afraid I was going to hurt her because she was just that bad.... It was like she was just compelled to do the opposite of what I tell her to do, every-
910 thing, and to beat up on her brother.... And I thought I was going to lose it.... Once I started going to Mental Health, it helped a lot.

Mandy's son had a particularly difficult time fitting into shelter life:

915 It was tough on him, it was real tough on him. My son's ADD, and there he had to be quiet and still, play quietly in the bedrooms, no running around. And you could only play in the backyard where you couldn't be seen by traffic.

920 Children who were younger, more sociable, did not have already existing behavioral or emotional problems, and had not had traumatic experiences themselves tended to adapt to shelter life more easily and posed fewer problems for their mothers in terms of 925 discipline and caretaking. For some children, the safety and security of the shelter was a vast improvement over the instability of their lives before coming into the shelter. A number of younger children liked the feelings of safety and security and the attention they received from residents and staff and did not want to 930 leave. Kate said that, after leaving the shelter, her two sons "used to ask me, 'When are we going back?' They liked it, the playing, and they liked the people." Susan thought that "it's probably a smaller child that would finally realize, 'Well, I'm safe here, and my mama is 935 going to be okay.'"

Discussion

This exploratory study used qualitative methodology to understand and describe mothers' perceptions of the impact of homelessness and shelter life on family 940 relationships. The mothers perceived that the dimensions of family relations that were most effected were quality of parent-child relations and their own fulfillment of the parental role. They believed that shelter conditions, their own emotional state, and their children's emotional state, temperament, and behavior most influenced these relationships. These findings are consistent with those of previous studies that used other methodologies and data sources.

The participants in this study confirm some of the phenomena reported by Boxil and Beaty (1990), especially the difficulty in maintaining parent-child relations due to the public nature of parenting in shelters and interference from other residents and shelter staff. However, the extent to which there is "unraveling" of the parental role or "soothing" of parents by older children as described by Boxil and Beaty remains unclear. It is possible that children are more likely to try to take care of their parents in certain types of situations (e.g., when mother has a substance abuse problem or a physical disability). It is also likely that some mothers may be reluctant to recognize the possibility that some role reversal may occur. However, some of the behaviors that professionals may see as role reversal or parental caretaking may be defined by mothers as family members helping each other out during times of crisis. As long as children are not being exploited or expected to take on roles which are harmful, it may be that the mutual support parents and children give each other during their housing crisis strengthens their family bonds.

The participants in this study highlighted two issues that have not received much attention in earlier research. The first issue is the sense of becoming closer to their children while living in the shelters and, the second is the intensity and depth of their feelings about shelter rules that prohibit corporal punishment. Despite the stresses and strains of homelessness and shelter life, almost all of the participants reported increased emotional closeness with their children during this time. They attributed this phenomenon to the amount of time they had to spend with their children, the fact that they slept in the same room, often in the same bed, and to the fact that all they had was each other. At times, the constant presence of children was a burden, especially when mothers had to take their young children out of shelters during the day while they looked for work and housing or kept appointments at social service agencies. However, for the most part their children were a source of comfort, and several mothers indicated they got to know their children in new ways. For some families, the parent-child relationship may grow stronger during periods of shelter stay, and that closeness may extend after the family moves into a home of their own. There is also evidence that, in some families, these relationships may become conflictual after leaving the shelter, as children finally feel safe enough to express emotions they have contained while living in the shelter.

The factors mothers identified as having an impact on their relationships with their children parallel the categories developed by Hausman and Hammen (1993) based on their review of literature and their study of perceptions of service providers: (a) the environment of the shelter, including rules, conditions, and interpersonal interactions; (b) mother's level of psychological distress; and (c) children's emotional state and temperament (which this study indicates is affected by the extent of disruption of the child's life, existence of previous emotional or behavioral problems, and their mother's emotional state). The fact that such similar categories of factors emerged in the two studies from different data sources (service providers and mothers) provides strong support for the validity and reliability of these factors.

Mothers were almost uniformly unhappy about the shelter rule against corporal punishment. While the purpose of this rule is to reduce violence within families and help parents learn alternative discipline techniques, mothers perceived these rules as undermining their parental authority and often find ways around them. Many of these mothers do not know any other way to discipline their children. They often felt caught in a bind because if their children acted out, the family was in danger of being ejected from the shelter. Parenting classes helped some mothers learn new ways to manage their children, but it may be unrealistic to expect women in the throes of crisis to learn and use new parenting techniques. No spanking rules do not necessarily prevent corporal punishment since some mothers just take their children away from the shelter to administer discipline.

Implications for Shelters Serving Homeless Families

Since this was a qualitative research project using a small nonrandom sample, implications for practice must be offered with caution. The nature of the sample must also be considered: these women had all been judged by key informants to have been particularly successful in restabilizing their families. Their experiences may not be typical of mothers who are not as successful in achieving stability after homeless episodes. Furthermore, these implications are based on mothers' perceptions only; it is likely that service providers have other perceptions which must be taken into account in developing and operating shelter programs. Nonetheless, the fact that the study involved participants from seven different shelters in two different states over two different time periods adds credibility to the findings. In addition, findings from Phase 2 of the study supported almost all of the Phase 1 findings, and the findings are largely consistent with previous research. Although we have much left to learn about how family relationships are affected by homelessness, the knowledge gained from this study, combined with findings of previous studies suggest the following implications for practice in shelters which house homeless families:

1.   Parents should have as much authority and control

as possible regarding such daily matters as bedtimes, bath times, and eating arrangements. Requiring families to leave shelters during the day and that mothers supervise their preschool age children 24 hours a day while they are also trying to look for work and/or housing actually exacerbate parent-child conflicts. Shelter staff should look for ways to better support parents, including provision of day care, having shelters accessible to families during the day, and making kitchen facilities available.

2. Punitive approaches toward parents who rely on corporal punishment do not necessarily prevent parents from spanking. Shelter staff need to find ways, in addition to parenting classes, to help parents learn and use nonviolent disciplinary practices. Zeifert and Brown (1991) offer some excellent ideas about how service providers can serve as parental consultants regarding discipline.

3. Service providers should be particularly aware of emotional needs of parents and children. Children's emotional and behavioral reactions to being homeless may be largely mediated by their mothers' emotional states. If shelter staff and other service providers can help mothers resolve their emotional crises, they will be more effective in fulfilling their parental roles and taking care of their children's emotional needs. Counseling with these women should focus on the mother's strengths, accomplishments, and ability to be successful in restabilizing their families. Support groups among homeless mothers could also be a valuable resource.

4. Mothers perceived that some types of interactions had positive effects on their families. For example, when residents or staff "take children under their wing," or play with them, both children and mothers benefit. These findings have implications beyond the provision of formal counseling services, indicating that how staff interact on a daily basis with residents can have a large positive impact on family members. Shelter staff should examine their day-to-day interactions with mothers and children to determine ways in which they support or detract from mothers' attempts to maintain family integrity. They can also look for ways to promote constructive interactions among shelter residents so that shelters are safe and warm places for families to live.

5. Policies that prevent boys over a certain age from staying with their families should be changed. Whenever possible, children who are still under parental authority, regardless of age, should be allowed to stay with the family unless specific problems arise with an individual situation. If it is necessary to impose some type of age restrictions, preteen boys should certainly be able to stay with their families in shelters.

References

Alperstein, G., Rappaport, C., & Flanigan, J. M. (1988). Health problems of homeless children in New York City. *American Journal of Public Health, 78*, 1232–1233.

Banyard, V. L. (1995). Taking another route: Daily survival narratives from mothers who are homeless. *American Journal of Community Psychology, 23*, 871–891.

Bassuk, E. L. (1990). Who are the homeless families? Characteristics of shelter mothers and children. *Community Mental Health Journal, 26*(5), 425–433.

Bassuk, E. L., & Rosenberg, L. (1988). Why does family homelessness occur? A case-control study. *American Journal of Public Health, 78*(7), 783–788.

Bassuk, E. L., Rubin, L., & Lauriat, A. S. (1986). Characteristics of sheltered homeless families. *American Journal of Public Health, 76*(9), 1097–1101.

Bogdan, R. C., & Biklen, S. K. (1992). *Qualitative research for education* (2nd ed.). Boston: Allyn & Bacon.

Boxil, N. A., & Beaty, A. L. (1990). Mother/child interaction among homeless women and their children in a public night shelter in Atlanta, Georgia. *Child and Youth Services, 14*(1), 49–64.

Browne, A. (1993). Family violence and homelessness: The relevance of trauma histories in the lives of homeless women. *American Journal of Orthopsychiatry, 63*(3), 370–384.

Burt, M. R., & Cohen, B. E. (1989). Differences among homeless single women, women with children, and single men. *Social Problems, 36*(5), 508–524.

Dail, P. W. (1990). The psychosocial context of homeless mothers with young children: Program and policy implications. *Child Welfare, 69*(4), 291–308.

Daly, K. (1992). The fit between qualitative research and characteristics of families. In J. Gilgun, K. Daly, & G. Handel (Eds.), *Qualitative methods in family research* (pp. 3–11). Newbury Park, CA: Sage.

Geertz, C. (1973). *The interpretation of culture.* New York: Basic Books.

Gilgun, J. (1992). Definitions, methodologies, and methods in qualitative family research. In J. Gilgun, K. Daly, & G. Handel (Eds.), *Qualitative methods in family research* (pp. 22–39). Newbury Park, CA: Sage.

Goodman, L. (1991). The prevalence of abuse among homeless and housed poor mothers: A comparison study. *American Journal of Orthopsychiatry, 61*(4), 489–500.

Goodman, L., Saxe, L., & Harvey, M. (1991). Homelessness as psychological trauma. *American Psychologist, 46*(11), 1219–1225.

Hall, J. A., & Maza, P. L. (1990). No fixed address: The effects of homelessness on families and children. *Child and Youth Services, 14*(1), 35–47.

Hausman, B., & Hammen, C. (1993). Parenting homeless families: The double crisis. *American Journal of Orthopsychiatry, 63*(3), 358–369.

Homeless Information Exchange. (1994). *Domestic violence—A leading cause of homelessness* (Fact Sheet #10). Washington, DC: National Coalition for the Homeless.

Johnson, A. K. (1989). Female-headed homeless families: A comparative profile. *Affilia, 4*(4), 23–39.

Krefting, L. (1991). Rigor in qualitative research: The assessment of trustworthiness. *American Journal of Occupational Therapy, 45*(3), 531–541.

Liebow, E. (1993). *Tell them who I am.* Detroit: Free Press.

Lincoln, Y. S., & Guba, E. G. (1985). *Naturalistic inquiry.* Beverly Hills: Sage.

Lindsey, E. W. (1996). Mothers' perceptions of factors influencing the process of restabilization among homeless families. *Families in Society, 77*(4), 203–215.

Lindsey, E. W. (1997). The process of restabilization for mother-headed homeless families: How social workers can help. *Journal of Family Social Work, 2*(3), 49–72.

Lindsey, E. W. (1998). Service providers' perceptions of factors that help or hinder homeless families. *Families in Society, 79*(2), 160–172.

McChesney, K. Y. (1990). Family homelessness: A systemic problem. *Journal of Social Issues, 46*(4), 191–205.

McChesney, K. Y. (1995). A review of the empirical literature on contemporary urban homeless families. *Social Service Review, 69*(3), 429–460.

McGoldrick, M., & Gerson, R. (1989). Genograms and the family life cycle. In B. Carter & M. McGolderick (Eds.), *The changing family life cycle* (2nd ed., pp.164–187). Boston: Allyn & Bacon.

Mills, C., & Ota, H. (1989). Homeless women with minor children in the Detroit metropolitan area. *Social Work, 34*(6), 485–489.

Molnar, J. M., Rath, W. R., & Klein, T. P. (1990). Constantly compromised: The impact of homelessness on children. *Journal of Social Issues, 46*(4), 109–124.

Montgomery, C. (1994). Swimming upstream: The strengths of women who survive homelessness. *Advances in Nursing Science, 16*(3), 34–45.

Rafferty, Y., & Rollins, N. (1989). *Learning in limbo: The educational deprivation of homeless children.* New York: Advocates for Children of New York.

Rafferty, Y., & Shinn, M. (1991). The impact of homelessness on children. *American Psychologist, 46*(11), 1170–1179.

Reyes, L. M., & Waxman, L. D. (1989). *A status report on hunger and homelessness in America's cities: 1988.* Washington, DC: U.S. Conference of Mayors.

Rossi, P. H. (1994). Troubling families: Family homelessness in America.

American Behavioral Scientist, 37(3), 342–395.

Seidel, J., Kjolseth, R., & Seymour, E. (1988). *The Ethnograph* (Version 3.0). Corvallis, OR: Qualis Research Associates.

Shinn, M., Knickman, J. R., & Weitzman, B. C. (1991). Social relationships and vulnerability to becoming homeless among poor families. *American Psychologist, 46*(11), 1180–1187.

Strauss, A., & Corbin, J. (1990). *Basics of qualitative research: Grounded theory procedures and techniques.* Newbury Park, CA: Sage.

Thrasher, S. P., & Mowbray, C. T. (1995). A strengths perspective: An ethnographic study of homeless women with children. *Health and Social Work, 29*, 93–101.

U.S. Department of Housing and Urban Development. (1994). *Priority: Home! The federal plan to break the cycle of homelessness.* Washington, DC.

Wagner, J., & Menke, E. M. (1991). Stressors and coping behaviors of homeless, poor, and low-income mothers. *Journal of Community Health Nursing, 8*(2), 75–84.

Weitzman, B. C., Knickman, J. R., & Shinn, M. (1990). Pathways to homelessness among New York city families. *Journal of Social Issues, 46*(4), 125–140.

Wright, J. D. (1990). Homelessness is not healthy for children and other living things. *Child and Youth Services, 14*(1), 65–88.

Ziefert, M., & Brown, K.S. (1991). Skill building for effective intervention with homeless families. *Families in Society, 72*(4), 212–219.

Note: Research supported in part by The University of North Carolina at Greensboro School of Human Environmental Sciences Foundation. Paper based on a presentation given at the annual conference of the National Council on Family Relations, Minneapolis, MN, November 1994.

About the Author: Elizabeth W. Lindsey received the Ph.D. in Child and Family Development and M.S.W. from the University of Georgia. She teaches social work practice and research at the University of North Carolina at Greensboro.

Address correspondence to: Elizabeth W. Lindsey, Department of Social Work, The University of North Carolina at Greensboro, P.O. Box 26170, Greensboro, NC 27402-6170; (336) 334-5225; FAX (336) 334-5210; e-mail: Betsy_ Lindsey@uncg.edu

Exercise for Case 4

1. Introduction

A. Is the problem area for the research clearly described? Explain.

B. Has the researcher convinced you that the problem area is important? Explain.

C. To what extent does the literature presented in the introduction help you understand the problem? Is the literature used to put the problem in context? Explain.

D. Does the researcher indicate how this study is different from and/or similar to earlier ones reported in the literature?

E. Does the researcher reveal her personal perspectives on the problem area, including any possible biases? Explain.

2. Methods

A. Are the demographics of the participants (i.e., background characteristics such as age, race, and so on) described in sufficient detail? Explain.

B. Considering the problem area for the research, do you think that appropriate participants were selected? If you had been conducting the study, would you have selected the same type(s) of participants? Would you have used the same number of participants? Explain.

C. Which strategies listed in Table 1 on page 161 of this book were employed by the researcher? Are they described in sufficient detail? Explain.

D. In addition to those you named in response to question 2C, has the researcher used any additional strategies to help assure the validity of the study? If yes, what are they? Are they described in sufficient detail? Explain.

3. Analysis and Results

A. Are the steps taken in the analysis described in sufficient detail? Explain.

B. Are the results clearly organized? Explain.

C. Are the results discussed in terms of a theory or theories (either theories that emerged from this study or previously existing ones)? Explain.

D. Were the direct quotations of the participants' statements, if any, judiciously selected? Do they help you understand the results? Explain.

E. Are there other ways the results could have been organized and interpreted? Explain.

4. Conclusions/Implications

A. Are the researcher's concluding remarks appropriate? Do they flow logically from the material presented earlier?

B. Does the researcher describe any implications? If yes, are they appropriate? Are there other implications that are not discussed by the researcher? Explain.

5. Ethical Considerations

A. In your opinion, could this research have caused physical or psychological harm to the participants? If yes, did the researcher take adequate measures to ameliorate the potential for harm? Explain.

B. If you had conducted this research, would you have obtained written, informed consent from the participants before conducting the study? Explain. Does this research report indicate that the researcher obtained such consent?

6. Overall Evaluation

A. Throughout the article, are all specialized terms and jargon defined to your satisfaction? Explain.

B. Briefly describe your overall evaluation of the research report, noting any special strengths and weaknesses.

C. If you had been a reviewer for the journal in which this report was published, would you have recommended publication of the report? If yes, would you have recommended that it be published "as is" or modified before publication? Explain. If no, what is the primary reason why you would recommend not publishing it?

Student Perceptions of the Influence of Race on Professor Credibility

KATHERINE GRACE HENDRIX
University of Memphis

From *Journal of Black Studies, 28*, 738–763. Copyright © 1998 by Sage Publications, Inc. Reprinted with permission.

Teacher communication is sometimes referred to as the interface between knowing and teaching. Two major instructional goals include the acquisition of knowledge and the ability to transfer the knowledge learned in one context to new situations. The behavior of teachers can result in positive classroom outcomes because teachers can serve as catalysts who motivate students to achieve the cognitive and self-esteem goals associated with an academic environment (Brophy, 1979). Two factors influence a teacher's ability to affect the self-concepts of students: (a) credibility and (b) self-esteem. Teacher credibility is formed in "the minds of students," and teacher self-esteem is personal and internal (Bassett & Smythe, 1979, p. 179). The credibility construct, when applied to teachers, has been defined by McCroskey, Holdridge, and Toomb (1974) as consisting of five dimensions: character, sociability, composure, extroversion, and competence.

The communication discipline has devoted much attention to identifying speaker characteristics associated with credibility (O'Keefe, 1991). These studies, however, have typically focused on public speaking or public figures with whom the audience possessed limited, if any, direct contact. Of 99 studies with the term *credibility* in the title, only 5 examined ways in which teachers established, maintained, and lost credibility, or the effect of teacher credibility on learning (Beatty & Behnke, 1980; Beatty & Zahn, 1990; Frymier & Thompson, 1992; McCroskey et al., 1974; McGlone & Anderson, 1973). None of the 5 teacher credibility studies employed a qualitative method despite the complexity of the classroom as evidenced by educational research within Shulman's (1986) classroom ecology paradigm.[1] Thus, the depth and texture normally associated with qualitative approaches were missing.

In addition to the absence of extensive research exploring teacher credibility, communication and education researchers have overlooked the classroom experiences of teachers and professors of color. In particular, the experience of being a member of a subordinate minority (Fordham & Ogbu, 1986) functioning as a professional within a predominantly White educational environment has escaped the interest of the White social scientist (Foster, 1990; Weinberg, 1977). Yet, Black teachers and professors do exist.

Black teachers have contributed to the education of children and adolescents in the United States for 2 centuries. With the onset of desegregation, most Black teachers and principals were dismissed or demoted at the same time Black students were being enrolled in previously all-White schools (Coffin, 1980; Smith & Smith, 1973). According to Banks (1986), parents in the Northern cities were often as violently opposed to desegregation as their Southern counterparts. White flight to the suburbs was another means of avoiding desegregation under the guise of desiring neighborhood schools. At present, public schools in the United States (a) are becoming increasingly non-White and poor and (b) are segregating a disproportionate number of White students from the rest of the student body by assigning them to academically gifted courses (Delpit, 1995; Ladson-Billings, 1994).

At the collegiate level prior to 1900, teaching positions for Blacks were confined to land grant colleges rather than to privately supported institutions. Only two Blacks, besides Dr. W.E.B. DuBois, held teaching po-

---

[1] The credibility literature review spans the 80-year period from 1915 to 1996. The following journals were reviewed by the author from inception through 1996: *Association for Communication Administration Bulletin, Central States Speech Journal, Communication Education, Communication Monographs, Communication Quarterly, Critical Studies in Mass Communication, Human Communication Research, Journal of Communication, Philosophy and Rhetoric, Southern Communication Journal, Quarterly Journal of Speech,* and the *Western Journal of Speech Communication.* The researcher recognizes that the term *ethos* or the terms representing the specific dimensions of credibility (e.g., integrity and trustworthiness) will undoubtedly reveal more studies. I chose to narrow the literature review to a manageable group of 99 studies by reading the research with the term *credibility* used in the title. Another useful summary of credibility research can be found in O'Keefe's (1991) text, *Persuasion: Theory and Research.*

sitions within predominantly white colleges prior to 1900 (Moss, 1958). According to Guess (1989), a U.S. Equal Opportunity Commission Report revealed that in 1985, 90% of the full-time faculty was White, whereas only 4.1% was Black. The number of Black professors has only increased slightly over the past two decades. *The Chronicle of Higher Education* (Magner, 1996) reported that Black faculty represented 4.4% of the senior faculty members at U.S. institutions and 5.4% of the new faculty hires.

Given the (a) restricted interactions between Black teacher/professors and White students, (b) negative tenor of race relations within the United States (Guess, 1989; "For the Record," 1996; Frisby, l994), and (c) continued expression of alienation by Black faculty (Cook, 1990; Lopez, 1991), it is logical to speculate that a classroom of predominantly White students may present particular challenges to building credibility and acceptance (and promoting student learning) for the Black teacher and professor.

Black teachers and professors are expected to motivate students and to cultivate learning while also instilling a sense of appropriate and inappropriate behavior; yet, the classroom experiences of these educators have not been carefully analoged. In view of the gaps in the extant literature regarding the (a) way teachers establish, maintain, and lose credibility; (b) classroom experience of Black teachers and professors; and (c) extensive reliance on quantitative research methods to identify and assess the impact of credibility, I developed four research questions to investigate the credibility of Black and White professors teaching at a predominantly White postsecondary institution (see Hendrix, 1994, 1997).

The investigation, grounded in a review of the literature as well as my professional experience, addressed four research questions relative to student and professor perceptions regarding how (a) credibility is communicated in the classroom and (b) race influences student perceptions of professor credibility.[2] This article details the research methods I used to investigate the credibility of six male professors and provides a

brief overview of the students' definitions of professor credibility. However, the focal point of this article is not what was revealed in response to the original four research questions but, rather, what Black and White student participants revealed about credibility beyond direct responses to the research questions.

This article explores the underlying motivations leading students to look and listen for particular cues when enrolled in courses taught by Black professors.

Research Methods

Research Site

Nonparticipant observation occurred in six undergraduate courses at a large 4-year research institution in the Northwest reflecting a predominantly White student enrollment. The university was selected as the site of the investigation because the percentage of Black faculty and Black student enrollment was consistently small. The fall 1993 student enrollment at this research institution was as follows: Native American Indian, 1.1%; Black, 3.2%; Hispanic, 3.3%; Asian, 16.1%; and White, 76.3%. Thus, out of a student body of 34,000, only 3.2% (1,088) of the students were Black. Yet, according to the 1990 federal census records, 10.1 % of the metropolitan area's residents were Black. Black faculty represented 1.5% (60) of the 3,986 faculty, whereas White faculty represented 89.6% (3,573).

Professor Participants

The participants in this study represented a "purposeful rather than random" sample (Miles & Huberman, 1984, p. 36). Six professors (two in Phase 1, four in Phase 2) were selected using the following criteria: (a) race, (b) gender, (c) age, (d) teaching experience, and (e) departmental affiliation. My goal was to obtain the participation of male dyads reflecting professors who worked in the same division and possessed comparable years of teaching experience at the collegiate level. However, three of the professors would be Black and three would be White.

This study reflected the beginning stage in a series of planned investigations on this topic. Thus, it was important to keep the level of complexity to a minimum. The study findings and their interpretation would have been complicated by the use of both male and female professors—especially considering the small number of professor participants. Using all male professors allows the study to be replicated at a future date with all female professors and, thereby, will allow for a comparison between the data sets. Thus, the criteria were developed to keep constant those variables that might otherwise account for differences (Nisbett & Ross, 1980) in perceived credibility (e.g., gender).

Dyads (using fictitious names) were created that consisted of two professors teaching in the same division within a particular college of the university. The three dyads represented the social sciences (Professors Bryan and Wyatt), performing arts (Professors Bell and Wilson), and an undergraduate professional program

---

[2] The four research questions were originally worded as follows:

RQ1:   What verbal and nonverbal communication cues do professors believe lead their students to perceive them as credible?

RQ2:   What verbal and nonverbal communication cues exhibited by professors lead students to perceive their professors as credible?

RQ3:   When the professor's race is not the same as the majority of the students' in the class, what verbal and nonverbal cues does the professor view as leading to student perceptions of credibility?

RQ4:   When the professor's race is not the same as the majority of the students' in the class, what verbal and nonverbal cues do the students view as leading to perceptions of credibility?

(Professors Blair and Webb). Professors Blair and
Webb taught within a structured undergraduate professional program. The program admitted approximately
50 competitively selected undergraduate students each
year into a structured series of courses taught over a 2-
year period. The professional program prepared students for immediate entrance into the job market, and
students moved through the curriculum sequence as a
class. The remaining professors taught undergraduate
courses with enrollments ranging from 100 to 400.

Student Participants

A total of 28 students enrolled in one of six courses
under observation participated in this study. Data were
gathered from 9 students in Phase 1 and 19 students in
Phase 2. In Phase 1, on the 3rd week of the quarter, a
Professor Credibility Survey (see the appendix) was
disseminated in the classes taught by Professors Bryan
and Wyatt. Student volunteers (those providing identifying information allowing for follow-up contact) were
separated by class standing (i.e., sophomore, junior,
etc.), race, and major (in the same field as the professor
or in another field). Student interviewees were then
randomly selected from a volunteer pool within each
category. In the second phase of data collection, the
selection procedures were adapted. Due to the limited
number of students who volunteered to make themselves available for in-person interviews, data collection in the second phase was adjusted to ensure a diverse pool. Because of the small number of students of
color who volunteered, all were accepted. The students
who were selected from the volunteer pool and assigned fictitious names are summarized in Table 1.

Data Collection Procedures

Three different methods were used in this study: (a)
nonparticipant observation (Spradley, 1979, 1980), (b)
semistructured interviews (Ginsburg, Jacobs, & Lopez,
1992) of students and professors, and (c) open-ended
questionnaires. Findings were triangulated across these
three methods (Erickson, 1986; Mathison, 1988).

Nonparticipant observation schedule. In Phase 1,
observations occurred on a daily basis during the 1st
week of the quarter. Observations of one class period
were also made during the 2nd, 3rd, 5th, 7th, and 10th
weeks of the quarter. In the study's second phase, the
communicative behavior of four professors and their
interaction with students were noted during 7 weeks in
a 10-week quarter.

Semi-structured student interviews. Student interviews occurred several weeks after the distribution of
an open-ended survey during class time (see the appendix). Student interviews that assessed the credibility
of their professors were critical because the students
were the target audience for the professors' efforts.

One interview was conducted with each of the 28
student participants. Most interviews occurred during
Weeks 6 and 7 in the quarter and typically lasted close
to 60 minutes. Interviews were generally conducted in

the researcher's office. When a student arrived, the
person was greeted and left alone for several minutes to
review the Student Consent Form. The time alone was
also designed to give each student a personal glimpse
by seeing my space within the office, family photos,
books, and so forth as well as those of my office mates.
The artifacts functioned as one means of self-
disclosure. My ultimate goal was to allow self-
disclosure before (artifacts) and during the interview to
build trust and elicit honest answers from both the students of color and White students.

Professor credibility survey. The term *credibility*
was first used during Week 3 when the researcher addressed each professor's class to explain the research
project, distribute the Professor Credibility Survey
document to each student, and to persuade students to
provide identifying information that would allow for
follow-up appointments and interviews. In each case,
the professor left the room.

Once at the front of the room, I introduced myself
and explained my objective of investigating how professors communicate to build, maintain, and even lose
credibility. I then explained that the triangulated design
called for input from professors, students, and me. An
overlay of Page 1 of the survey was placed on the
overhead and the following three options were discussed: (a) do not complete the survey; (b) complete
only the demographic and open-ended questions but
leave Section B (name and phone number) blank; and
(c) complete all sections of the survey, including identifying information.

Data Analysis

Student interviews. Most of the student interviews
were conducted in my office. Students were asked to
comment on their responses on the Professor Credibility Survey as well as additional questions. I listened to
the participant responses and took handwritten notes
while also audio recording the interview. When analyzing the data from student interviews, the audio recording was played while handwriting the student
comments verbatim. The verbatim transcript was cross-
checked against the written information provided by
the student on the Professor Credibility Survey and the
researcher's notes taken during the actual interview.

The transcription from each interview was reread
with marginal and reflective researcher comments jot-
ted in the left margin along with location of the comment on the audiotape. Key phrases or words within
the transcript were occasionally circled or underlined.
Marginal comments included noted areas of similarity
with other respondents—including the professor participants. Matrices were then constructed to visually
display the student's oral and written responses to the
questions posed on the Professor Credibility Survey
(see the appendix). In addition, student responses to a
particular set of questions and my general impression
of each interview were also reduced and placed within

275 the matrix. Examples of interview questions include: (a) Why are you enrolled in this course? (b) Have you ever taken a class from a Black professor or teacher? and (c) Do you typically assess the credibility of your professors?

Table 1
Student Interviewees

Fictitious Name	Race/Ethnicity and Gender	Year in School
Professor Bryan		
Allan	White male	Freshman
Carrie	Native American female	Senior
Jay	Pacific Islander male	Freshman
Marie	White female	Junior
Steve	Black male	Senior
Professor Wyatt		
Antoinnette	Black female	Sophomore
Bill	White male	Junior
Mark	Black male	Junior
Patricia	White female	Junior
Professor Wilson		
Martin	White male	Freshman
John	White male	Sophomore
Walter	White male	Junior
Pete	Black male	Junior
Kandy	White female	Freshman
Brenda	White female	Junior
Darlene	White female	Senior
Professor Bell		
Carl	White male	Freshman
Gary	White male	Sophomore
Brent	White male	Senior
Frances	Black female	Freshman
Sabrina	White female	Junior
Robin	White female	Junior
Cantrel	White female	Senior
Professor Blair		
Anthony	White male	Senior
Harriet	Asian female	Senior
Professor Webb		
Nathan	White male	Fifth year
Kramer	White male	Senior
Dorothy	White female	Senior

280 The visual display was constructed in a series of stages. Stage 1 entailed the construction of a checklist matrix that allowed quick comparisons between the male/female and White/non-White students within one particular professor's class. As the data analysis pro-
285 ceeded (Stage 2), the checklist matrix grew class-by-class to allow an across class comparison of student responses. When the data from each of the six professor participants were added to the checklist matrix, it transformed into a role-ordered matrix as well as a
290 checklist, which allowed multiple comparisons across professors and students. In Stage 4, the final stage, the matrix became a checklist by role over time as the visual display could be viewed as Phase 1 (Professors

Bryan and Wyatt) in contrast with the Phase 2 profes-
295 sors (Bell, Wilson, Blair, and Webb).

During the process of visually creating a grid of participant responses, interviews were listened to or reread to ensure that key points and depth were not lost during the process of reducing the data to fit in the ma-
300 trix. In sum, professor and student interviews were transcribed from audiotapes with the characteristics associated with credibility and the influence of race given particular attention. Who (gender, race, class) perceived what (Hymes, 1972) was transferred from
305 narrative form into matrices to examine possible relationships.

Professor credibility survey. I balanced the potential for providing socially desirable answers by contrasting the survey and interview responses of three
310 groups of student participants. The responses of the students actually interviewed were compared and contrasted with those provided by volunteers who were not interviewed and nonvolunteers who completed the survey (but did not provide their names and phone num-
315 bers), all of whom were enrolled in the same course. Every student survey was read and coded then reread and coded again at another time in the quarter. Key words, themes, and perceived components of credibility associated with each survey question were noted
320 across gender and race. Tallies of responses (e.g., yes, no, probably) were also compiled depending on the nature of the survey question to which students responded.

Results: Defining Credibility

When defining professor credibility in general,
325 without reference to a particular person, the student participants in this study defined credibility in two ways: (a) being knowledgeable or (b) being knowledgeable and a good teacher. For the second group of students, to say that a professor was credible was sim-
330 ply a confirmation of the person's knowledge of the subject matter (whether from academic or field experience) without attesting to his/her teaching ability.

However, in either case, knowledge was a critical foundation from which to build an image of being an
335 effective teacher. Knowledge could be obtained both academically and experientially. Experiential knowledge was particularly important to the students enrolled in the professional program courses. The difference, however, between a good professor and a poor one was
340 not necessarily the presence versus the absence of knowledge. The critical difference was the ability to translate one's knowledge into statements and explanations easily understood by the students enrolled in one's course.

345 Subject matter knowledge was consistently listed as one of the top three components of professor credibility across all six classes. Work experience and good teaching techniques were listed as two of the top three components of professor credibility by students in four

350 of the six classes. In addition, the ability to understand a professor's comments and explanations was listed as one of the top four components of credibility by students in four of the six classes (Hendrix, 1997).

Race And Credibility

Students' responses to Research Question 4 (RQ4)
355 (see Note 2) actually revealed their underlying motivations that led them to look and listen for particular cues when a professor's race differed from the majority of the students' in a class. The nature of the institutional enrollment patterns focused this question on students of
360 the Black professors. However, all interviewees were asked how they would assess the credibility of a Black professor.

When responding, the student interviewees provided answers that can be categorized as follows: (a)
365 applying more stringent credibility standards to professors depending on a combination of professor race and subject matter, (b) the belief that Black professors worked harder than White professors to earn their educational and professional status, and (c) the presence of
370 favorable/fair attitudes toward Black professors once credibility had been established.

Applying more stringent credibility criteria to professors depending on race and subject matter. The majority of the students who were interviewed (19)
375 indicated that race alone would not automatically establish a professor's credibility in the classroom. Unlike Patricia, who believed she would rate Black professors higher on credibility scales because she had not had the exposure, most of these student interviewees
380 indicated they would typically use the same standards when assessing the credibility of both Black and White professors. And these students usually repeated the same criteria they had listed on the Professor Credibility Survey in response to Question 2—What does it
385 mean to say a professor is credible? For instance, Carl mentioned that he based his assessment on the individual's educational background (as listed in the college catalog), classroom presence, and knowledge, whereas Dorothy said credibility assessment depended on "how
390 they set it up. How I get a feel for what I need to do." However, one of the students, Cantrel, did note, "I think the White male has an advantage over everybody else just because of our bias in the culture. For me, I'm more sensitive to whether it's a man or a woman."

395 Even though the majority of the students indicated race alone would not automatically establish credibility and that they would not personally apply a different set of standards to their Black professors, the discussions regarding race and class subject matter revealed when
400 credibility might be more readily questioned. Antoinnette spoke of, even as a Black person, struggling with not assigning negative stereotypes to Black professors teaching courses without an ethnic/racial component in them. The tendency to find credence in the comments
405 of Black professors speaking about Blacks or subjects typically connected with Blacks (e.g., crime) was also reflected in the comments of seven other students. Student interviewees admitted they assigned more credibility to Blacks teaching "ethnic" courses or believed
410 other students—in particular, Whites—would do so. For example, three of Professor Bell's students (Cantrel, Gary, and Frances) believed other students would perceive him differently if he were teaching a course with classical content only. As Cantrel talked, she
415 stated the belief that for herself (and others), "the more removed from cultural identity, the more you have to figure out the fit...[like fitting] a square peg into a round hole." Thus, Professor Bell would have a more difficult time establishing his credibility if his Black-
420 ness could not be somehow linked to the subject and attributed as providing him with a unique understanding of the subject.

Two other students indicated they personally would assign more credibility to a Black professor teaching
425 English (Brent) or ethnic studies courses (Sabrina). Brent explained that he would judge all of his professors based on how "they handle themself *[sic]* in front of the class...whether they are well-versed in the subject matter and how they articulate [their points]."
430 However, he went on to say a Black professor who was able to teach standard English, given the distinctions between Black dialects and standard English, would be given "an extra plus."

Sabrina indicated that a White person teaching an
435 ethnic studies course could be viewed as credible if he or she met her criteria of believability, truth, and experience. However, even a White person with experience living with particular minorities could only present a marginalized view—"They can only get so close"—
440 versus obtaining the perspective of an actual member of the community. Sabrina went on to say, "I'd want a minority perspective...[but] I don't think I'd typify any other subject like that."

Finally, one of the Black student interviewees, Pete,
445 introduced his expectations regarding White professors. Pete indicated he expected "more liberalism" from his professors depending on their disciplinary area. Thus, he did not speak of assigning more credibility to professors of color teaching race-related
450 courses; rather, he spoke of a different system of dividing curriculum. Pete believed professors teaching courses in the social sciences would likely be more liberal and well-rounded in their world outlook than those in the hard sciences or disciplinary areas, such as
455 math.

Although students stated they would not automatically favor one race over another, some of their discourse revealed that Black professors had to work harder to establish their credibility. Carrie and Mark
460 (both people of color) were very aware that the qualifications of Black professors were often questioned by their White classmates. During their interviews, both students spoke of overheard comments and conversa-

tions in class as well as open challenges to the authority of Black professors during class lectures. And Professor Bryan's student, Allan, noted that he tried to "embrace differences," yet he also mentioned that given his homogeneous upbringing, the physical appearance of his professors did have an impact. Allan was unable to clearly delineate whether the impact was a bias in favor of his professors of color or a bias in favor of those professors of his same race.

In addition to scrutiny from White students, three Black interviewees noted their own critical review of Black professors. Even though Antoinnette was Black, she revealed that she constantly fought the negative stereotypes (e.g., Blacks cannot do math) she had learned from American society when making judgments about her Black professors. A second student, Pete, said Black professors would not begin with an automatic advantage and, in fact, would be judged harder than his White professors. Pete indicated he had greater expectations of his Black professors and, as a result, would be more stringent in his evaluation of their capabilities and ability to meet his needs as a student.

Thus, ironically with these two students, negative stereotypes about the intelligence and academic preparation of Black professors coexisted with a positive belief that Blacks must be quite accomplished individuals to be employed as professors because they must work harder than Whites to achieve professor status. The view that Black professors must work harder was held predominantly by the students of color.

The belief that Black professors work harder to earn their academic positions. In Phase 1, all five of the students of color believed Black professors had to work harder to earn their academic degrees and to become employed at predominantly White educational institutions. Black professors were believed to deserve more respect because they experienced a "tougher" time earning their position and must "work twice as hard." Jay, a freshman of Pacific Islander descent, said he did not give professors of any particular race an automatic advantage. However, he acknowledged that his professors were judged "not just by sight" but, rather, by "what [they have] been through." Jay indicated he perceived "colored" persons, like Professor Bryan, as being more aggressive in their studies to reach the same status as their White counterparts.

Pete agreed with his counterparts and, as a result, indicated he was usually very impressed when he met Black professors—especially given Pete's more stringent expectations of them. Two White students, Brent and Robin, also noted their belief that Black professors face many more academic and workplace challenges than do White professors. Robin, interestingly, combined race and age as a criterion for a professor's credibility. She believed older Black professors and older female professors to have "really been ahead" of their time to become successful prior to the passage of fairly recent antidiscriminatory legislation.

Favorable/fair attitudes toward Black professors once credibility has been established. These students indicated a desire to be exposed to Black professors based on positive experiences with Black professors, previous exposure to Blacks in general, the desire to rectify limited or no exposure to Blacks in the past, and the desire to increase their comfort level (as Black students) at a predominantly White institution.

Gary said he usually would give anyone a "fair shake" based on their personality and knowledge and would begin to form judgments about a professor's credibility after the first week. Gary indicated Professor Bell was his first Black professor and had "set a precedent" in his mind because he was definitely credible and a good teacher. The first exposure to a Black professor setting a precedent—a standard of expected performance—was also reflected in Walter's comments. Walter had been exposed to three Black professors during his community college education and noted that he realized, as we talked, that his criteria for assessing credibility were drawn from experiences with his Black female drama teacher. His criteria for judging credibility included (a) believability (reliability of the lecture material, clear explanations, and an ability to answer questions) and (b) approachability ("humanity").

As noted earlier, Cantrel indicated she had worked with Blacks and Asians but had not experienced Blacks within her inner-circle of friends. Cantrel openly admitted that she was concerned that her daughter did not mingle with people of color because she did not see her mother doing so. Allan, Marie, and Patricia (all White students like Cantrel) indicated a desire for exposure to a less homogeneous environment. One way of achieving this was to expose oneself to Black professors. Thus, these students were in agreement with Professor Bryan, who during his interviews, stated the importance of his presence for the benefit of White students as well as students of color.

Steve expected both Black and White professors to be knowledgeable; however, he gave the judgments he made about the capabilities of Black professors greater weight. This decision was based on the tougher time he perceived Black professors to have experienced while earning higher degrees in an Anglicized educational environment.

A number of the student interviewees—Gary, Brent, Robin, Martin, Walter, and Kramer—had previous exposure to Blacks. The implication from the interviews is that they possessed less bias against Blacks in general due to having Black friends and role models. Brent said his "Black friends [gave] a more understandable, straightforward answer [than his White friends]" when he had problems and, thus, he expected the same would be true of his Black professors in the way they handle their classes—they would be more easily understood. Robin said, "White professors I

580 don't really think much of.... They're common." She went on to say she also understood that among Black people, including professors, "there are wonderful ones [pause], crappy ones [pause].... They're just people like everybody else." In other words, Robin believed
585 she was capable of making fair assessments because undue stereotypes (positive or negative) were not applied to Blacks because she had been exposed to a range of personalities. The same was true of her counterparts Gary, Brent, Martin, Walter, and Kramer.
590 Martin, Anthony, Kramer, and Robin all indicated they would welcome a Black professor because they believed he or she would present a different worldview. Two Black student interviewees, Pete and Frances, indicated that being in the presence of Black professors
595 increased their comfort level. These students represented 3.2% of the student body and stood out in obvious contrast to the number of White students enrolled at this research institution. The comfort level of Black students in a predominantly White environment (and of
600 new Black professors in the same environment) was an area of concern that was acknowledged by all three Black professor participants during their interviews—Professors Bryan, Bell, and Blair.

Discussion

The findings associated with student motivations
605 are summarized here along with a discussion of (a) phenomena reflected in recurring patterns of the data, (b) study limitations, and (c) reflections from an outsider within.

Summary

The findings in this article evolved from a general
610 discussion of verbal and nonverbal cues to internalized factors students consider to assess credibility. These factors contributed to situations where particular verbal (e.g., the use of standard English) and nonverbal cues (e.g., age) were emphasized. Most of the students who
615 were interviewed did not personally believe any professor had an automatic advantage in establishing credibility based on race, yet they simultaneously discussed a different set of criteria for evaluating the credibility of their Black professors teaching particular
620 subjects. When doing so, one of the students articulated her belief that there was a "cultural" or "societal" norm that would automatically favor the White, male professor before he even spoke.

Several of the students acknowledged that it may be
625 more difficult for Black professors to establish their credibility in subject areas that were not linked to their race—for example, ethnic studies versus electrical engineering. Several noted that even though they would use the same criteria for a Black and a White professor
630 teaching math and science, they believed their White counterparts would use more rigorous standards before assessing a Black professor as being credible.

Students typically seemed interested in Black professors because they were accustomed to Blacks (had

635 friends, role models, or Black teachers/professors) or because they were tired of a homogeneous, White upbringing and desired exposure to differing worldviews. Finally, students (especially students of color) acknowledged their belief that Black professors must
640 work harder to achieve academically and perform successfully as professionals within Anglicized educational systems.

Recurring Phenomena

Researcher status and influence. Common experiences between the student interviewees and me (more
645 specifically, being persons of color and/or women) made the interview process enjoyable and comfortable. My race and gender attracted most of the students to volunteer for the interview as well as for the opportunity to share their thoughts regarding appropriate
650 teaching pedagogy. Two White males (one in Phase 1, one in Phase 2) can best be described as curious rather than attracted to any of my characteristics or the research topic. One possible explanation is that these two students may have been curious about my ability to
655 design a research project and to conduct interviews professionally.

The professors (or their research assistants) could have been asked to explain and distribute the survey, or a written statement could have been attached in the
660 form of a cover letter; however, I believed it was critical that I appear personally in front of the students. To generate interest in the research and in volunteering for interviews, it was critical that the students see and hear me. The students needed to see my gender, age, cloth-
665 ing, and my brown skin. The students needed to hear my voice tone, volume, articulation, speech pattern, and my sense of humor. Showing myself to the students was consistent with Allen, Heckel, and Garcia's (1980) belief that new Black researchers "must chart an
670 insightful course for those who will follow" (p. 770). For this researcher, that means using a combination of my formal academic training and my daily life experiences.

Student self-protection of identity. None of the stu-
675 dent participants sat near, waved at, or approached me before, during, or after the class. A student interviewee would occasionally smile but it was a ritualistic salutatory greeting that they executed with others entering the class as well. Most students appeared comfortable
680 and forthright in my office. Yet if a student and I completed an interview and walked together to a course designated for observation, it was common for the student to sit in a different location rather than sitting next to me or even in the same row. Students protected their
685 identity as study participants from their classmates and professors and communicated nonverbally that they expected me to do so as well.

Study Limitations

The absence of interviews over time. Extra credit could not be offered to student participants because no

690 other extra credit was offered by these professors, therefore making it impossible to camouflage the activity. Given that students were not being compensated, their time commitment to the study was minimized. Thus, I requested one interview from each student par-
695 ticipant rather than two. I balanced the potential for providing socially desirable answers by contrasting the survey and interview responses of the interviewees with those provided by volunteers and nonvolunteers enrolled in the same class.

700 *The nature of the data collection site.* This research was conducted in a geographic area in the United States where 10.1% of the population in the metropolitan area was Black, whereas only 1.5% of the faculty, and 3.2% of the student body were Black. The
705 tolerance of racial differences and exposure to Blacks in one's community may vary in other geographic areas.

Reflections From An Outsider Within

I approached this study from the particular vantage point of what Collins (1991) refers to as *the outsider*
710 *within.* I was a Black female investigating cases in a predominantly White educational institution. Before concluding, a few reflections are noted here to provide a glimpse into the psyche of an outsider within and to suggest the direction of future research.

715 First, most of the 28 student interviewees were positively disposed toward the six professors in this study. The students viewed their professors as knowledgeable and, in most cases, as good teachers. These student interviewees likely reflect a minority perspec-
720 tive rather than that of the majority. It is critical to acknowledge and give credence to the Black professors' beliefs that generally White students (and even some Black students) assess them according to a more stringent standard (Hendrix, 1994). In addition, we should
725 remember the organizational communication research of Foeman and Pressley (1987), which revealed that Black employees possessed a heightened awareness of the influence of race on their interactions with their White peers. The positive orientation of White student
730 interviewees in this research is likely atypical of many Whites in the classroom.

Second, White confederates were not used to assist in the interview process. In my view, the use of White confederates denies (a) the commonplace position of
735 underlying racial tension in everyday interaction within the United States settlement; (b) creates a second-order, contrived reality; (c) eliminates an opportunity for Black researchers to refine disciplined subjectivity in such a communicative event; and (d) diminishes the
740 importance of the reality associated with Black/White encounters. According to Allen et al. (1980), "the journey outside the fishbowl for neophyte black researchers will be fraught with obstacles and pitfalls, for it is they who must chart an insightful course for those who will
745 follow" (p. 770).

Third and finally, most of the student interviewees were attracted not only to the research topic (classroom communication and professor credibility) but to me, as the researcher, as well. Students came to participate in
750 the study and to (a) commiserate with another woman they admired somewhat for my level of academic accomplishment, (b) commiserate with another person of color within the oasis of my office, and (c) seek advice about how to approach a Black classmate and/or make
755 Black friends on campus.

When the interview progressed to a discussion about the credibility of Black professors, some White students also chose to discuss their ideas about race relations in general, noting that they appreciated the
760 opportunity to talk out loud with someone. They apparently viewed me as a safe person and my office as a nonthreatening environment.

As a researcher, I was aware of the need to balance my roles and their corresponding responsibilities. It
765 was necessary to anticipate what roles I would perform (researcher, person of color, confidant, advisor, etc.), what behavior each role entailed, and how the roles could be executed without sacrificing the integrity of the research. As noted by Allen et al. (1980), I was
770 charting a course while conducting this research. And in my effort to chart a course through unexplored territory, I consciously chose to be guided by both my (a) formal academic training and (b) intuitive sense of human interaction between and among races (gained from
775 my daily lived experience as a Black woman in America).

A parallel can easily be drawn between the multiple roles of this Black female researching in a predominantly White (and male) academic environment and the
780 three Black male professors teaching within the same environment; even though the professors were male, we all functioned as outsiders within, performing our requisite tasks and recognizing additional responsibilities and obligations as well.

Conclusion

785 According to Rose (1966), universities reflect the ills of society rather than serving as agents for change. Although many classroom studies have been conducted over the past 40 years that assess teachers' effectiveness in the classroom, few have investigated how
790 teachers establish and maintain their credibility and even fewer have addressed the experiences of Black teachers and professors. Instructional communication and education literature are incomplete as the classroom perspective and pedagogical knowledge of Black
795 professors and teachers has often been overlooked.

Research findings indicate that (a) perceived source competence is the most consistent predictor of the selective exposure of receivers, and (b) highly ego-involved receivers are less likely to change attitudes
800 and assign positive credibility ratings (Tucker, 1971; Wheeless, 1974a, 1974b). A research curiosity should

naturally arise regarding parallel behavior on the part of highly prejudiced students. In other words, if highly ego-involved receivers are less likely to change atti-
805 tudes and assign positive credibility ratings, can similar behavior be expected from highly prejudiced students in the classroom of Black professors? In my study, students revealed that the competence of Black professors was more likely to be questioned depending, in
810 part, on the subject matter they taught.

Given the results of this study and the selective exposure research, it is likely that the classroom experiences of Black teachers and professors do not completely parallel those of their White counterparts, yet
815 they are expected to motivate and teach students as well as meet promotional requirements (e.g., tenure). Considering the pivotal role of teachers and professors within the educational system and the differing student perceptions and expectations of professors based on
820 race, as reflected in the findings of this study, it is imperative that additional research be conducted. We must add to our body of knowledge by incorporating the educational experiences of teachers and professors of color (male and female) and the perspectives and
825 experiences of their students.

We must also investigate academe as an organization and research racial communication patterns (Foeman & Pressley, 1987). The key to addressing some of the critical issues associated with credibility and race
830 undoubtedly lay with the students who chose to remain silent in this study. This knowledge may increase the (a) successful classroom and career experiences for professors of color; (b) cognitive, behavioral, and affective development of students; and (c) the level of
835 interracial understanding and respect between Black and White inhabitants of the United States.

Appendix[3]

Professor Credibility Survey

Section A

Gender (circle one):   Male   Female

Major:
Year in School
(circle one):   Freshman   Sophomore   Junior

                       Senior   Other

Race/Ethnicity
(circle one):   Black/   Asian   Hispanic
                       African   American   American
                       American

                       American   White/   Pacific
                       Indian   Anglo   Islander
                                    American

                       International (country)

---

[3] The original document was two pages printed back-to-back to allow for writing space. Question 3 under Section C did not appear on the survey in Study 1.

If you are willing to participate in a 1-hour interview with me regarding your impressions of this class and the professor, please complete BOTH Sections B and C. Your name will NOT be used in my final report, and the professor will NOT know you spoke with me. If you are not interested in the 1-hour interview, leave Section B blank and complete Section C.

Section B

Name: _____
Phone Number: _____
Convenient Times to Call: _____

Section C

1.   Is the professor credible? Please discuss why or why not.
2.   What does it mean to say a professor is credible?
3.   What verbal and nonverbal communicative cues does the professor exhibit to convey credibility?
4.   What other words are the same as or similar to *credible*?
5.   What was your first impression of the professor on the very first day of class? Why?

References

Allen, S. S., Heckel, R. V., & Garcia, S. J. (1980). The Black researcher: A view from inside the goldfish bowl. *American Psychologist, 35*(8), 767–771.

Banks, J. A. (1986). Race, ethnicity, and schooling in the United States. In J. A. Banks & J. Lynch (Eds.), *Multicultural education in western societies* (pp. 30–50). New York: Holt, Rinehart, & Winston.

Bassett, R. E., & Smythe, M. (1979). *Communication and instruction.* New York: Harper and Row.

Beatty, M. J., & Behnke, R. R. (1980). Teacher credibility as a function of verbal content and paralinguistic cues. *Communication Quarterly, 9*(1), 55–59.

Beatty, M. J., & Zahn, C. J. (1990). Are student ratings of communication instructors due to "easy" grading practices? An analysis of teacher credibility and student reported performance levels. *Communication Education, 39*, 275–282.

Brophy, J. E. (1979). Teacher behavior and its effects. *Journal of Educational Psychology, 71*, 733–750.

Coffin, G. (1980). The Black principal—the vanishing American. *Professional Psychology, 11*(5), 39–44.

Collins, P. H. (1991). Learning from the outsider within: The sociological significance of Black feminist thought. In M. M. Fonow & J. A. Cook (Eds.), *Beyond methodology: Feminist scholarship as lived research* (pp. 35–59). Bloomington: Indiana University Press.

Cook, D. A. (1990). Alienation of Black college students on White campuses: University-centered and student-centered interventions. *Educational Considerations, 18*, 19–22.

Delpit, L. (1995). *Other people's children: Cultural conflict in the classroom.* New York: New Press.

Erickson, F. (1986). Qualitative methods in research on teaching. In M. C. Wittrock (Ed.), *Handbook of research on teaching* (pp. 119–161). New York: Macmillan.

Foeman, A. K., & Pressley, G. (1987). Ethnic culture and corporate culture: Using Black styles in organizations. *Communication Quarterly, 35*(4), 293–307.

Fordham, S., & Ogbu, J. U. (1986). Black students' school success: Coping with the "burden of 'acting White.' " *The Urban Review, 18*(3), 176–206.

For the record. (1996, November). *Klanwatch Intelligence Report: A Project of the Southern Poverty Law Center, 84*, 21–31.

Foster, M. (1990). The politics of race: Through the eyes of African-American teachers. *Journal of Education, 172*(3), 123–141.

Frisby, M. K. (1994, March). Weathering the storm: Ron Brown's nightmarish year at the commerce department. *Emerge*, pp. 46–50.

Frymier, A. B., & Thompson, C. A. (1992). Perceived affinity-seeking in relation to perceived teacher credibility. *Communication Education, 41*(4), 388–399.

Ginsburg, H. P., Jacobs, S. F., & Lopez, L. S. (1992). Assessing mathematical thinking and learning potential. In H. P. Ginsburg, R. B. Davis, & C. Maher (Eds.) *Schools, math, and the world of reality* (pp. 237–262). Boston: Allyn & Bacon.

Guess, J. M. (1989). Race: The challenge of the 90s. *Crisis, 96*, 28–30, 32–33.

Hendrix, K. G. (1994). *Is the classroom really like 'To Sir, With Love?' Case studies of professor credibility and race.* Unpublished doctoral dissertation, University of Washington.

Hendrix, K. G. (1997). Student perceptions of verbal and nonverbal cues leading to images of Black and White professor credibility. *The Howard Journal of Communication, 8,* 251–274.

Hymes, D. (1972). Models of the interaction of language and social life. In J. J. Gumperz & D. Hymes (Eds.), *Directions in sociolinguistics: Ethnography of communication* (pp. 35–71). New York: Holt, Rinehart, & Winston.

Ladson-Billings, G. (1994). *The dreamkeepers: Successful teachers of African American children.* San Francisco, CA: Jossey-Bass.

Lopez, T. R. (1991). *Some African-American and Hispanic voices from the University of Toledo: A monograph* (ERIC Document Reproduction Service No. ED 328153). Toledo, OH: University of Toledo.

Magner, D. K. (1996, February 2). The new generation: Study shows proportions of female and minority professors are growing. *The Chronicle of Higher Education,* pp. A17–A18.

Mathison, S. (1988). Why triangulate? *Educational Research, 17,* 5–12.

McCroskey, J. C., Holdridge, W., & Toomb, J. K. (1974). An instrument for measuring the source credibility of basic speech communication instructors. *The Speech Teacher, 23,* 26–33.

McGlone, E. L., & Anderson, L. J. (1973). The dimensions of teacher credibility. *The Speech Teacher, 22,* 196–200.

Miles, M. B., & Huberman, A. M. (1984). *Qualitative data analysis: A sourcebook of new methods.* Newbury Park: Sage.

Moss, J. A. (1958). Negro teachers in predominantly White colleges. *Journal of Negro Education, 27*(4), 451–462.

Nisbett, R., & Ross, L. (1980). *Human inference: Strategies and shortcomings of social judgment.* Englewood Cliffs, NJ: Prentice Hall.

O'Keefe, D. J. (1991). *Persuasion: Theory and research* (3rd ed.). Newbury Park, CA: Sage.

Rose, H. M. (1966). An appraisal of the Negro educator's situation in the academic marketplace. *Journal of Negro Education, 35*(1), 18–26.

Shulman, L. S. (1986). Paradigms and research programs in the study of teaching: A contemporary perspective. In M. C. Wittrock (Ed.), *Handbook of research on teaching* (pp. 3–36). New York: Macmillan.

Smith, J. W., & Smith, B. M. (1973). For Black educators: Integration brings the axe. *The Urban Review, 6*(3), 7–12.

Spradley, J. P. (1979). *The ethnographic interview.* New York: Holt, Rinehart, and Winston.

Spradley, J. P. (1980). *Participant observation.* New York: Holt, Rinehart, & Winston.

Tucker, R. K. (1971). Reliability of semantic differential scales: The role of factor analysts. *Western Speech, 35,* 185–190.

Weinberg, M. (1977). *A chance to learn: The history of race and education in the United States.* Cambridge, UK: Cambridge University Press.

Wheeless, L. R. (1974a). The relationship of attitude and credibility to comprehensive and selective exposure. *Western Speech, 33*(2), 88–97.

Wheeless, L. R. (1974b). The effect of attitude, credibility, and homophily on selective exposure to information. *Speech Monographs, 41*(4), 329–338.

About the Author: Katherine Grace Hendrix is an assistant professor and the basic communication director in the Department of Communication at the University of Memphis. She is responsible for training the graduate teaching assistants (GTAs) and part-time faculty in that department. She earned her Ph.D. from the University of Washington in Seattle, Washington. Her current research interests focus on the experiences of professors and GTAs of color at predominantly White postsecondary institutions.

Exercise for Case 5

1. Introduction

A. Is the problem area for the research clearly described? Explain.

B. Has the researcher convinced you that the problem area is important? Explain.

C. To what extent does the literature presented in the introduction help you understand the problem? Is the literature used to put the problem in context? Explain.

D. Does the researcher indicate how this study is different from and/or similar to earlier ones reported in the literature?

E. Does the researcher reveal her personal perspectives on the problem area, including any possible biases? Explain.

2. Methods

A. Are the demographics of the participants (i.e., background characteristics such as age, race, and so on) described in sufficient detail? Explain.

B. Considering the problem area for the research, do you think that appropriate participants were selected? If you had been conducting the study, would you have selected the same type(s) of participants? Would you have used the same number of participants? Explain.

C. Which strategies listed in Table 1 on page 161 of this book were employed by the researcher? Are they described in sufficient detail? Explain.

D. In addition to those you named in response to question 2C, has the researcher used any additional strategies to help assure the validity of the study? If yes, what are they? Are they described in sufficient detail? Explain.

3. Analysis and Results

A. Are the steps taken in the analysis described in sufficient detail? Explain.

B. Are the results clearly organized? Explain.

C. Are the results discussed in terms of a theory or theories (either theories that emerged from this study or previously existing ones)? Explain.

D. Were the direct quotations of the participants' statements, if any, judiciously selected? Do they help you understand the results? Explain.

E. Are there other ways the results could have been organized and interpreted? Explain.

4. Conclusions/Implications

A. Are the researcher's concluding remarks appropriate? Do they flow logically from the material presented earlier?

B. Does the researcher describe any implications? If yes, are they appropriate? Are there other implications that are not discussed by the researcher? Explain.

5. Ethical Considerations

A. In your opinion, could this research have caused physical or psychological harm to the participants? If yes, did the researcher take adequate measures to ameliorate the potential for harm? Explain.

B. If you had conducted this research, would you have obtained written, informed consent from the participants before conducting the study? Explain. Does this research report indicate that the researcher obtained such consent?

6. Overall Evaluation

A. Throughout the article, are all specialized terms and jargon defined to your satisfaction? Explain.

B. Briefly describe your overall evaluation of the research report, noting any special strengths and weaknesses.

C. If you had been a reviewer for the journal in which this report was published, would you have recommended publication of the report? If yes, would you have recommended that it be published "as is" or modified before publication? Explain. If no, what is the primary reason why you would recommend not publishing it?

Case 6

Psychotherapy Process Variables Associated With the Retrieval of Memories of Childhood Sexual Abuse: A Qualitative Study

ALISA PHELPS
University at Albany,
State University of New York

MYRNA L. FRIEDLANDER
University at Albany,
State University of New York

CAROLYN ZERBE ENNS
Cornell College

ABSTRACT. This study investigated, from the client's perspective, how the therapeutic process is associated with the retrieval of sexual abuse memories in psychotherapy. A qualitative analysis was applied to the transcripts of semistructured interviews of 11 adult women who identified themselves as victims of childhood sexual abuse and as retrieving memories of abuse during ongoing or past psychotherapy. Results are reported as themes or codes that represent participants' perspectives about the therapeutic process. Noteworthy codes are organized within the categories of (a) the therapeutic relationship, (b) therapeutic effects, (c) therapist characteristics, and (d) therapy techniques.

From *Journal of Counseling Psychology, 44,* 321–332. Copyright © 1997 by the American Psychological Association, Inc. Reprinted with permission.

In recent years, a great deal of controversy has focused on the nature of client memories of child sexual abuse and the manner in which psychotherapy is related to the retrieval of such memories (Alpert et al.,
5   1996; Enns, McNeilly, Corkery, & Gilbert, 1995). Critics charge that therapists have contributed to the creation of false memories through the use of leading questions or suggestive techniques such as hypnosis and age regression methods (e.g., Lindsay & Read,
10 1994; Loftus, 1993; Ofshe & Watters, 1994; Yapko, 1994). The existing research literature relevant to this issue has focused on the extent to which delayed memory for child sexual abuse exists (e.g., Briere & Conte, 1993; Cameron, 1994; Elliott & Briere, 1995; Feld-
15 man-Summers & Pope, 1994; Herman & Schatzow, 1987; Loftus, Polonsky, & Fullilove, 1994; Williams, 1994) and on the nature of techniques that psychotherapists use when working with potential sexual abuse survivors with delayed memory for abuse (Po-
20 lusny & Follette, 1996; Poole, Lindsay, Memon, & Bull, 1995).

Both areas of study have relied primarily on retrospective self-reports. Surveys of self-identified survivors of child sexual abuse have found that between
25 19% (Loftus et al., 1994) and 59% (Briere & Conte,

1993) of respondents indicated that they had forgotten abuse or did not remember abuse for some period of time. Most studies based on self-reports have found that between 28% and 42% of survivors of child sexual
30 abuse revealed delayed memory of that abuse (Cameron, 1994; Elliott & Briere, 1995; Feldman-Summers & Pope, 1994; Herman & Schatzow, 1987). Surveys of psychologists (Polusny & Follette, 1996; Poole et al., 1995) have inquired about the degree to which they
35 ever used various techniques for the purposes of memory recovery. Findings reveal a lack of agreement regarding the appropriateness of techniques that are potentially suggestive. Furthermore, roughly one quarter of psychologists have reported using one or more tech-
40 niques such as journal writing, guided imagery, and dream interpretation with clients who had no specific memories of child sexual abuse (Polusny & Follette, 1996; Poole et al., 1995).

The literature provides little information about the
45 actual experience of clients in therapy and the factors related to the retrieval of partially or completely forgotten memories of child sexual abuse. More specifically, little research attention has been given to the influence of the therapeutic relationship on any aspect
50 of the treatment of childhood sexual abuse survivors (Saakvitne, 1990). Beutler and Hill (1992), in an article addressing research needs in the area of treatment of adult survivors of child sexual abuse, specifically highlighted the importance of examining the therapeu-
55 tic process from the client's perspective. They noted that clients' experiences of their therapists' behaviors are often more highly correlated with outcome than are independent ratings of therapist behaviors (Gurman, 1977). Beutler and Hill (1992) emphasized the need for
60 research on the therapeutic alliance because many adult survivors of sexual abuse tend to mistrust others.

In light of a current climate that is highly critical of therapists, an absence of professional guidelines for working with survivors of child sexual abuse, and a
65 lack of research about the actual practices of therapists, it has sometimes been difficult for counseling psychologists to proceed with confidence in their work

with clients who report a history of child sexual abuse. Furthermore, current controversies about memories for
70   child sexual abuse exemplify a widening gap between scientists and practitioners (Alpert et al., 1996). Counseling psychologists are uniquely prepared to transcend the divisive nature of this debate by bringing a scientist-practitioner perspective to this controversy and
75   providing suggestions for practice that are embedded in research. The present research provides an initial step toward this end, one that will help therapists practice in this area with greater confidence and help researchers identify themes to study in greater depth. Our purpose
80   in the study was to investigate, from the client's perspective, aspects of the psychotherapy relationship that are associated with the access of sexual abuse memories and the impact of such access on the client's well-being.

85   Given the absence of empirical data on this topic, the clinical literature on treatment recommendations provided a point of departure for this study. A review of the literature on psychotherapy with child sexual abuse survivors revealed seven aspects of the thera-
90   peutic relationship that appear to be important in working with these adult clients. The seven factors include (a) a therapeutic relationship of safety and trust (e.g., Briere, 1989, 1992; Cornell & Olio, 1991, 1992; Courtois, 1988, 1992; Dominiak, 1992; Herman,
95   1992); (b) client control of as much of the therapeutic process as possible, or therapist-client collaboration (e.g., Courtois, 1988; Herman, 1992; Meiselman, 1990); (c) emotional availability of the therapist (e.g., Cornell & Olio, 1991; Dominiak, 1992; Olio & Cor-
100   nell, 1993); (d) therapist assistance with managing the emotional intensity of memories, including intrusive emotions, emotional numbing, and denial (e.g., Briere, 1989, 1992; Cornell & Olio, 1991, 1992; Courtois, 1988, 1992; Herman, 1992; Olio & Cornell, 1993); (e)
105   therapist willingness to help the client deal with dissociated or unintegrated aspects of the self, such as the client's childlike emotional self (e.g., Briere, 1989; Davies & Frawley, 1994); (f) therapist validation of the client's experience and willingness to explore trau-
110   matic material (e.g., Courtois, 1988; Herman, 1992; Olio & Cornell, 1993); and (g) therapist openness to the possibility of abuse but avoidance of suggestive therapeutic techniques (Briere, 1992; Courtois, 1992; Herman, 1992). The final theme is controversial be-
115   cause of its relationship to recent debates about the veracity of delayed memories of child sexual abuse. In order to avoid underestimating or overestimating the likelihood that a client has been abused, therapists are encouraged to include questions about trauma and child
120   sexual abuse within a comprehensive, holistic assessment that explores a wide range of experiences that may be related to a client's presenting problems (Herman, 1992; Polusny & Follette, 1996; Pruitt & Kappius, 1992).
125   Our purpose in this study was twofold: (a) to as-

sess, from the client's perspective, the relevance of aspects of the therapeutic relationship identified in the literature and (b) to develop a greater understanding of therapists' behaviors and attitudes that are associated
130   with the self-reported accessing of forgotten traumatic memories. Thus, in the study we tested theory as well as attempted to discover new theory. In the latter aspect of the investigation we relied on grounded theory (Strauss & Corbin, 1990) to derive interpretations from
135   concrete observations. We used a qualitative research method to examine the therapeutic experiences of women who identified themselves as child sexual abuse survivors. A semistructured interview was developed and informed in part by the seven factors
140   identified in the literature review. Qualitative analysis of the 11 narratives involved identifying codes and themes generated by participants and the comparison of these themes with the existing literature.

Method

Participants

Participants were 11 Caucasian women who resided
145   in a northeastern city and its vicinity; they were recruited through fliers that were distributed in various locations. These women, who ranged in age from 31 to 59 years and whose mean age was 41.7 years, identified themselves as having been sexually abused as
150   children. Approximately one half ($n = 5$) of the women were married, and about one half were single or divorced ($n = 6$). In terms of occupation, 4 worked in social services; of the remaining 7, 2 were teachers, 1 was a graduate student, 1 was a nurse, and 1 was an
155   artist. The age at which abuse occurred ranged from infancy to 18 years. Seventy-five percent indicated having been abused by a family member, and 25% indicated being abused by non-family-members. McCracken (1988) recommended the following guide-
160   lines for the selection of qualitative research participants: They should be strangers, few in number, and represent some contrasts with regard to background and demographic characteristics. Consistent with these suggestions, our participants were strangers and varied
165   on factors such as current age and occupation, type of abuse experienced, age at which the abuse occurred, age at which memories were recovered, and type of relationship to the perpetrator of the abuse.

Individuals with continuous memories of sexual
170   abuse were not included in the study. All participants reported partial or no memory of abuse for a period of time and began to retrieve memories prior to therapy or during treatment. Five participants reported having some memories before seeking professional help, and 6
175   indicated retrieving their first memories of abuse during psychotherapy. The number of years individuals participated in therapy ranged from 2 to 10; the mean length of psychotherapy was 3.7 years. Three women were in psychotherapy at the time of the study, and 8
180   had terminated therapy. Five women had worked non-

concurrently with more than one therapist, and the majority (*n* = 8) had seen women therapists.

Participants were asked to rate their therapists on an 11-point scale, with 0 being the least helpful and 10 being the most helpful. The 11 participants worked with a total of 16 therapists. Therapist ratings ranged from 4 to 10; the overall mean rating of the 16 therapists was 8.91. The mean rating for the 8 participants who had terminated treatment was 8.8, and the mean rating for the 3 participants currently in treatment was 9.7. One participant cited a significantly negative experience with the first of her two therapists (rated as 4) and indicated having deteriorated during treatment.

Procedure

Data collection. A sample of self-selected individuals was recruited through fliers that were distributed in a northeastern city and the surrounding area. Fliers were made available at a conference on sexual abuse and posted on bulletin boards in women's organizations, grocery stores, a laundromat, and the waiting room of a community mental health center. An advertisement also appeared in a newspaper in a northeastern city. The flier sought women volunteers "who suffered sexual abuse as a child and who recovered memories of abuse in individual therapy" and indicated that participation would involve a private interview about "your therapy experience, not your personal history."

Volunteers contacted Alisa Phelps by phone. Each of the women who responded to the fliers agreed to become a participant and completed the interview. Interviews were conduced at a community women's center, and the duration of the interviews was generally between 1½ to 2 hr. The longest interview was 3 hr, and the shortest interview lasted approximately 1 hr.

Research was conducted according to the ethical principles for research involving human participants (American Psychological Association [APA], 1987). Participants completed a form indicating their consent to participate in an audiotaped interview that would be transcribed by a professional secretary. They were further informed that other professionals would read the interview transcripts and that excerpts would appear anonymously in published form.

Participants were informed that the content of their memories would not be a focus of the interviews and that all personal information would be confidential. They were instructed not to disclose the names of their therapists but were also told that they were free to discuss the project with their therapists. A list of referrals to therapists was provided to participants in the event that the study aroused distress or discomfort that participants were not comfortable processing with their own therapists. Finally, participants were informed that they were free to withdraw their participation at any time during the course of the study. They were reminded of this option in the follow-up letter requesting feedback about the preliminary results.

Consistent with McCracken's (1988) suggestions, the semistructured interview questions were informed by a literature review that focused on the qualities of the therapeutic relationship that are important for psychotherapy with child sexual abuse survivors. Our own experiences also shaped questions. We designed the questions to be as open-ended and nondirective as possible with the exception of one question ("How helpful do you think your therapy was in general?") that requested participants to rate on a 0–10 scale the value of each therapeutic experience. In general, questions were constructed to provide some consistency of structure to the interview while also allowing each participant to describe her experience in her own words (McCracken, 1988). Alisa Phelps made slight modifications in the interview protocol as the study progressed when there were indications that changes would yield more informative data. This practice is consistent with Miles and Huberman's (1994) proposal that instrumentation be iterative in nature. In other words, an interview with one informant may lead to a restructuring of the interviewer's perspective and the modification of instrumentation for subsequent interviews.

The interview protocol was pilot tested on the first 3 individuals who volunteered, but these data were not included in the analysis. Following the pilot interviews, we reviewed the interview protocol, as recommended by Taylor and Bogdan (1984). As a result of this review, we restated several of the original questions or phrased them in a more open-ended fashion in order to facilitate the effective gathering of information. Follow-up questions that could be used to gain more specific information and questions regarding additional demographic data were also incorporated into the existing interview protocol. Examples of questions in the final protocol included the following:

> What were the major problems you worked on in therapy?
> How did the issue of sexual abuse originally come up in your therapy?
> How did your feelings and thoughts about your therapist and the work you did together change over time, if at all?
> Please describe any highlights of your treatment that led you to gain key insights or experience new personal growth.
> How did your emerging memories affect your ability to function?

As noted earlier, follow-up questions were used when applicable. For example, if the participant indicated that the topic of sexual abuse was initiated by the therapist, the interviewer asked, "What was your response when your therapist suggested abuse?" If the participant indicated that memories emerged during a session, the interviewer asked, "How did your therapist respond when memories came up during your sessions?" If memories surfaced outside of therapy, a follow-up question was "How did you cope when you

295 retrieved memories outside of sessions?"

In general, participants were asked to describe how their therapists inquired about and responded to memories and what therapists did or said that was helpful or hindering. Participants were also asked about the de-
300 gree to which they had influenced the nature of the therapeutic process, how they coped with memories as they were retrieved, and what they viewed as the outcome of their work with traumatic memories. Neither the content nor the veridicality of the memories was a
305 focus of the interview.

All interviews were conducted by Alisa Phelps. At the time of data collection, she was a 32-year-old doctoral candidate in counseling psychology with 3 years of supervised clinical experience. She had in-depth
310 knowledge of the treatment and research literatures on psychotherapy with survivors of child sexual abuse and intended to specialize in the treatment of childhood abuse. Prior to collecting data, she had treated only one individual in psychotherapy who retrieved sexual abuse
315 memories during the course of therapy.

All three of us are Caucasian. Myrna L. Friedlander and Carolyn Zerbe Enns, 49 and 45 years old, respectively, are licensed counseling psychologists who work primarily as psychology professors. Myrna L. Fried-
320 lander has a part-time independent practice, and Carolyn Zerbe Enns maintains a part-time counseling appointment at a state university. All three of us have had experience working therapeutically with sexual abuse survivors and other women from a feminist perspec-
325 tive.

Alisa Phelps and Myrna L. Friedlander are psychodynamic-systemic in orientation, and Carolyn Zerbe Enns describes her approach as feminist. All three of us believe that most retrieved memories of sexual abuse
330 are valid when they emerge in a non-suggestive therapeutic climate and that a cautious therapeutic approach is essential when working in this area. Furthermore, the recovery of memory in psychotherapy is a complex, inexact, reconstructive process, and its primary purpose
335 is to help clients make sense of the past for the purpose of creating productive future choices. We agree with the final report of the APA Working Group on Investigation of Memories of Childhood Abuse (Alpert et al., 1996), which stated:

340   In short, a responsible path for therapists to pursue is one
        in which clients are empowered to be the authority about
        their own lives and reality, where the emphasis is on re-
        covery and function, and where memories of trauma are
        viewed within the context of what one might tentatively
345   assume to be a post-traumatic response (p. 7).

Data analysis. Interviews were audiotaped and transcribed verbatim by a professional secretary and then checked for accuracy by Alisa Phelps, who listened to the tapes while simultaneously reading the
350 transcripts. Consistent with McCracken's (1988) recommendations, Alisa Phelps and four coders (see be-

low) read and reread the transcripts, highlighting themes relevant to the psychotherapy relationship and memory retrieval and identifying logical relationships.
355 Through pattern coding (Miles & Huberman, 1994), the volume of verbal data was reduced into units that were meaningful as well as parsimonious (Stiles, 1993) and that suggested themes or patterns. In general, pattern codes are "explanatory or inferential
360 codes, ones that identify an emergent theme, pattern, or explanation" (Miles & Huberman, 1984, p. 67). Miles and Huberman (1994) identified four main areas that are typically represented by pattern codes: themes, theoretical constructs, relationships, and causes or ex-
365 planations.

For this study, we defined a code as a phrase that described the participant's perspective on the therapeutic process, including (a) the client-therapist relationship or interaction (e.g., "client processes feelings
370 about therapist with therapist"), (b) the client's thoughts, feelings, and behaviors toward the therapist (e.g., "client trusts therapist"), (c) the therapist's thoughts, feelings, and behaviors toward the client (e.g., "therapist modulates intensity and/or pace of
375 treatment"), and (d) the behaviors, feelings, and thoughts the client engaged in as a result of treatment (e.g., "client self-soothes not using therapist"). All descriptions of the process were included in the pattern coding regardless of their valence, that is, their nega-
380 tive or positive perspectives on the therapy experience.

Transcripts were coded by four individuals: Alisa Phelps, two female counseling psychology graduate students at the internship level, and one male licensed psychologist with four years of postgraduate experi-
385 ence. Five transcripts, selected randomly, were coded by two judges and Alisa Phelps, whereas the remaining six transcripts were coded by one individual and Alisa Phelps. In the transcripts coded by three judges, codes were retained for further consideration when at least
390 two judges of transcripts coded the same section of the transcript similarly. In the case of transcripts coded by two individuals, codes were retained only when both individuals coded the same section of the transcript similarly. This process resulted in some codes that
395 were highly similar. Where there were similarities but the wording was not exactly identical (e.g., "client feels listened to," and "client feels listened to and respected by therapist"), we combined the codes.

Next, the codes that emerged from this first pass
400 through the data were sorted into categories, areas, and subareas by a new panel of four judges, two of whom had served as coders. The new panel consisted of two male and two female graduate students at the internship level. (Alisa Phelps was not a part of this panel.)
405 Judges were unaware of the purpose of the study or the results of the literature review. The codes were placed on cards, which the judges sorted into categories that they perceived as expressing similar ideas. The judges then formed a hierarchy of relevant categories and sub-

410 categories.

After all codes were sorted into categories, the transcript from which each code was taken was identified. A code was determined to be "noteworthy," that is, worthy of further attention, if it was repeated in at least
415 6 of the 11 transcripts (i.e., 55%). Noteworthy codes and their thematic categories represent the major results of the research. Consistent with the principles of grounded theory (Glaser & Strauss, 1967; Strauss & Corbin, 1990), we supported noteworthy codes by text
420 passages from the narratives to illustrate the themes that emerged from the interview data. Codes that appeared in at least four or five transcripts represent minor themes found in the study.

Memo writing (Miles & Huberman, 1994) was an-
425 other form of data reduction used in this study. Through the use of memos, Alisa Phelps synthesized various pieces of data in a sentence, paragraph, or several pages. Memos were written by Alisa Phelps and were used to help develop concepts from the data, to
430 refine and expand on codes, to demonstrate interrelationships between main categories, and in general to construct a more integrated overview. Memos were dated, given a title that illustrated key concepts, and anchored to specific sections of narratives.

435 After we identified the codes and thematic categories, we recontacted the participants by mail for feedback. Participants were asked to react in writing to each code and to indicate how important it was to or how accurately it described their own experience of
440 retrieving traumatic memories in outpatient psychotherapy, regardless of whether they had personally discussed the issue in their interview with the investigator. Our purpose in obtaining this feedback was to confirm or disconfirm the importance of each noteworthy code.

445 We instituted a number of safeguards to decrease bias in the analysis of the data. In order to increase the reliability and validity of this study, we observed standards proposed by Stiles (1993). The principle of trustworthiness focuses on the repeatability of obser-
450 vations. In order to establish trustworthiness, we examined the consistency of themes across transcripts and compared these themes with observations that appear within the clinical literature. Statements about our theoretical orientation and expectations, an important
455 consideration in qualitative research, served as another source of reliability. Reliability was also enhanced when we tested our theories or interpretations with the experiences and interpretations of participants. We partially established validity by examining the coher-
460 ence and internal consistency of our interpretations and observations. For example, a theme of safety would be considered consistent with a theme of trust but inconsistent with a theme of therapist unpredictability. Through the use of triangulation (Yin, 1994), we used
465 multiple sources of evidence. Two panels, one of coders and one of judges, independently coded interview data and developed categories from the obtained codes.

Although Alisa Phelps served as a coder, codes were retained for further consideration only if they were in
470 agreement with the code phrases of two or three other coders. Furthermore, an independent panel of judges, not including Alisa Phelps, sorted the codes. Both coders (other than Alisa Phelps) and judges were unaware of the results of the literature review or the purpose of
475 the present study. We also applied the principle of consensus through the comparison of researchers' findings and interpretations with the clinical literature of sexual abuse. Finally, we sought testimonial validity by asking participants to indicate whether the interpretations de-
480 rived from the transcripts were consistent with their experience (see Results section).

Results

Problems Addressed in Therapy

Participants reported the following problems and issues addressed in therapy: identifying, expressing, and resolving feelings ($n = 5$); learning interpersonal
485 trust and intimacy or dealing with the loss of a relationship ($n = 5$); sexuality or sexual identity work ($n = 4$); drug and food addictions ($n = 3$); dealing with abusers and family members ($n = 3$); and dissociative identity disorder ($n = 1$). Finally, severe anxiety or depression,
490 issues of self-esteem, problems in the identification of needs, deficits in self-care, dissociation, difficulties coping with sexual abuse memories, identity problems, existential issues, and sleeping difficulties were mentioned by 1 or 2 participants each.

Qualitative Results

495 We identified a total of 180 codes in the transcripts. Fifteen codes emerged as noteworthy, appearing in at least 6 transcripts. Of the 15 codes, 14 were described by participants as helpful and 1 as hindering. An additional 6 codes were repeated in 4 or 5 transcripts. The
500 second panel of judges sorted the 180 codes into three major areas and a number of subareas: therapeutic variables (relationship and effects), therapist variables (characteristics and techniques), and outside variables. Noteworthy, or major, codes were located in all areas
505 and subareas except outside variables (e.g., "client utilizes support system"). Within each subarea were several categories. The categories with one or more noteworthy codes (i.e., codes appearing in at least 6 different transcripts) are listed in Table 1, as are minor
510 themes, which are listed below the noteworthy codes.

Within the subarea of therapeutic relationship were two categories, safety-and-trust and valued-and-respected, with two noteworthy codes each. In the safety-and-trust category were the codes "client trusts
515 therapist" and "client feels safe." The valued-and-respected category was represented by the noteworthy codes "client-therapist bond" and "client feels listened to." The codes and illustrative excerpts from the transcripts are listed below:

520 Client trusts therapist (11 transcripts, 100%):

57

The fact that I've been able to trust her...implicitly...has made a huge difference in my being able to...remember and therefore heal from...the memories and from the abuse.... So, um, [my therapist] has been nothing but kind to me and...validating and supportive so...I have felt safe with her. I've felt that she won't hurt me, just about from the very beginning.

I totally, totally trust her with...telling her anything.

Client feels safe (8 transcripts, 73%):

It was extremely safe which is, I think, part of why I was able to do the work I was able to do with her because she was extremely safe.

I felt safe. I felt his caring and his soft-spoken ways as comforting.... I felt a tremendous amount of warmth and support.

Client-therapist bond (6 transcripts, 55%):

I was very aware of her...deep concern and love for me as a therapist and as a person.

I became very attached to her very quickly, I mean to the point, I guess it's called the process of transference or something and she um...she became my surrogate mother.

Client feels listened to (6 transcripts, 55%):

I think in general it was just so helpful to have her there to listen. Somebody who listens and believes.

One of the things that she does that it looks so funny when I watch her do it with my fellow group members, but it means the world to me when she does it to me...say that I come in and I'm recounting a memory dream. After...every one or two sentences she'll almost repeat back word for word just what I said to her.... I feel so heard when she says back to me what I'm saying to her. But I love that, I love when she does it.

Within the subarea of therapeutic effects were two categories: affective-intrapersonal and interpersonal-affective. (No noteworthy codes were located in any of the behavioral or cognitive categories in this subarea.) The noteworthy codes in the affective-intrapersonal category were "client experiences increased self-esteem" and "client self-soothes not using therapist." One interpersonal-affective code was noteworthy: "client feels in control of treatment." The minor codes within the subarea of therapeutic effects were "client feels empowered," "client experiences child state," and "client recognizes that therapist is fallible." Excerpts associated with the noteworthy codes follow:

Client experiences increased self-esteem (6 transcripts, 55%):

The biggest piece really is that I feel much better about myself than I ever did, I just feel much more okay than I ever did.

With Therapist #2...she really really helped me to reinforce that...I'm a good person.... It was other people that were in my life that caused these things to happen that made me the way I am. So in...reinforcing that with me, I know she was probably one of the...therapists that really helped me enhance my self-esteem that, you know, you...are a good person, you know.

Client self-soothes not using therapist (6 transcripts, 55%):

I would pick up the phone and call a fellow survivor just to share because I realized after some time in therapy that sharing the memory and the feelings cut it in half, sometimes even more.

I would deal with them [the memories] the best I could. I would go for a walk, I would call friends. Mostly the friends I would relate to are mostly other survivors and I didn't find it helpful to talk so much about it with people who weren't survivors 'cause I felt more...it was pity than support. So I would take a bath, I would just do a lot of nurturing. I would even practice yoga, relaxation and yoga, and sometimes just had to sit with the feelings...the discomfort.

Client feels in control of treatment (6 transcripts, 55%):

I'm totally in charge of where my therapy goes. I've had...months where it's been hard for me to try to get to the feelings...like I said, she's...pretty patient with the process. She knows it can't be forced.

She gave me complete...freedom to set my own direction. I think there may have even been times when I tried to get her to direct me more and she did not do that so I was really very much always in the driver's seat when it came to my therapy.... I'm a real hard worker, I work very hard on myself, not just in therapy, but outside of therapy also so I really think I ran the show to tell you the truth and I think my therapist would agree with that.

The subarea of therapist characteristics was represented by the categories of competency and availability. One competency code was noteworthy: "client perceives therapist as competent." Two availability codes were noteworthy: "client perceives therapist as emotionally available" and "client perceives therapist as emotionally unavailable." A minor code in the subarea of therapist characteristics was "therapist is available by phone." Illustrative excerpts of noteworthy codes follow:

Client perceives therapist as competent (6 transcripts, 55%):

I feel that she's extremely knowledgeable about how to deal with...survivors.

[My therapist has] ability, and he has incredible insight.

Client perceives therapist as emotionally available (8 transcripts, 73%):

I could do everything that I was doing outside of therapy because I knew that I wasn't alone, you know, that I had the support and that was just very powerful for me.

I think with Therapist #2, with her being older and more of a mother figure and her nurturing, kind ways...I felt the memories emerge.

Client perceives therapist as emotionally unavailable (6 transcripts, 55%):

When we talked about this, it was very...much more business-like, and...it just felt...not very therapeutic.

Sometimes she would feel a little anxious herself and before I would say oh, get to this is what I need to do for myself, she would suggest it and that would always rile me like...or make me think she can't tolerate this, that she has to hurry me up to make me do something to relieve it or so.... If she would suggest it because she was in a hurry, I would get that right away and that...was not helpful because I needed to get through that.

Table 1
Noteworthy Codes and Minor Themes

Subarea, category, and code	No. of transcripts	% of total
Noteworthy codes		
Therapeutic relationship		
Safety and trust	11	100
Client trusts therapist	11	100
Client feels safe	8	73
Valued and respected	9	82
Client-therapist bond	6	55
Client feels listened to	6	55
Therapeutic effects		
Affective-intrapersonal	7	64
Client experiences increased self-esteem	6	55
Client self-soothes not using therapist	6	55
Interpersonal-affective	9	82
Client feels in control of treatment	6	55
Therapist characteristics		
Competency	10	91
Client perceives therapist as competent	6	55
Availability	10	91
Client perceives therapist as emotionally available	8	73
Client perceives therapist as emotionally unavailable	6	55
Therapy techniques		
Active verbal	11	100
Therapist facilitates client awareness of strengths	8	73
Therapist facilitates client expression of feeling	8	73
Therapist helps client gain insight	6	55
Active verbal/active-nonverbal	9	82
Therapist gives client control	6	55
Active nonverbal	8	73
Therapist use of touch[a]	6	55
Minor themes		
Therapist modulates intensity and/or pace of treatment	5	45
Therapist is available by phone	5	45
Client feels empowered	4	35
Client experiences child state	4	35
Client recognizes that therapist is fallible	4	35
Therapist believes client	4	35

Note. Noteworthy codes occurred in 6 or more transcripts, and minor themes occurred in 4 or 5 transcripts.
[a] This code was qualified on the basis of participant feedback.

Within the subarea of therapy techniques were three categories: active verbal, active-verbal/active-nonverbal, and active nonverbal. In the active verbal category were the codes "therapist facilitates client awareness of strengths," "therapist facilitates client expres-

sion of feeling," and "therapist helps client gain insight." One active-verbal/active-nonverbal code was noteworthy ("therapist gives client control"), and one active nonverbal code was noteworthy ("therapist use of touch"). Minor codes in the subarea of therapy techniques were "therapist modulates intensity and/or pace of treatment" and "therapist believes client." Illustrative excerpts associated with noteworthy codes follow:

Therapist facilitates client awareness of strengths (8 transcripts, 73%):

I was aware, and I think that he helped foster this too, aware of my strengths and aware...that I wouldn't crumble without him and...that I was aware of that.

I feel like she's proud of the work I've done. She's proud of me. She knows that I'm working hard, and she's pleased that I have the courage to do this. I...can really feel that with her.

Therapist facilitates client expression of feeling (8 transcripts, 73%):

I'll be having an emotion that doesn't seem to fit present day life and...so...it might be happening for quite a few days, and then I'll finally get to her office and... she'll ask me to go ahead and...feel the feeling rather than trying to keep pushing it away.

He's allowed me to grieve if I needed to, to get in touch with all the feelings surrounding the memory. I cry, he's allowed me to cry.

Therapist helps client gain insight (6 transcripts, 55%):

It answered so many questions. It explained so many different negative feelings that I had about myself that I think it was...really helpful for me to have had the memories because it really did validate it.... [I]t helped me understand why I felt so bad about myself...why I had so much shame, why I saw myself the way that I did. It helped me understand my relationships a lot more, what I did in relationships.

I tended to minimize my experience for a long time, but I always had memories. I thought, "Well it happened. Well I'll get over it." And then somehow it really works. To talk about it. And there's this little...unconscious...worthlessness there I think that I always had.... I gained some confidence and that's probably the biggest thing. And I don't deserve that, I never deserved that. There's nothing that I did...it was lousy parenting...criminal behavior.

Therapist gives client control (6 transcripts, 55%):

Um, it was always what I wanted to do at the session.... I always felt that everything that she said was a suggestion and she often said that...this is a suggestion, I have an idea...would you like to try this?

She'll invite me to do whatever I feel I need to do to get rid of the mad, and if I can't think of anything, she'll give me a list of suggestions and ask me if any of those sound good.

Therapist use of touch (6 transcripts, 55%):

When they touched me that was helpful...just like a hand on the knee or...the first couple times they did it, they were clear to ask permission...and...if it was like a hand on the knee or going like this on my hand, that was very helpful.

What I really think was helpful with the first therapist

710 was when she would touch me, put her hand on my
shoulder or hug me or I really really craved physical
contact but was frequently way too scared or ashamed to
ask for it. So that was really significant and important.

715 Thirty-three codes were repeated but did not
achieve noteworthiness. Of these, 6 codes appeared in
4 or 5 transcripts. These codes, or minor themes, which
were briefly noted in the previous section, merit further
comment because they are consistent with the clinical
literature and inform the manner in which memory
720 retrieval occurs. As such, they are highly relevant to
the study. These codes may not have achieved noteworthiness because factors associated with memory
retrieval may vary among individuals. Two codes appeared in five transcripts. "Therapist is available by
725 phone" is not frequently addressed in the clinical literature but can be viewed as an extension of therapist
emotional availability. Second, "therapist modulates
intensity and/or pace of treatment" has been repeatedly
discussed as an important factor in the literature and
730 informs the ideal climate in which client expression of
feeling may occur.

Four codes appeared in four transcripts. "Therapist
believes client" represents a component of the therapist's validation of the client's experience and willing-
735 ness to explore traumatic material, and "client experiences child state" is consistent with the importance of
helping the client deal with dissociated memories or
with her vivid sense of herself as a child with a reser-
voir of previously forgotten memories. "Client recog-
740 nizes that the therapist is fallible" is likely to support
the client's efforts to be self-directed and to assume as
much responsibility and control of the psychotherapy
process as is feasible. The final repeated code, "client
feels empowered" is consistent with a variety of note-
745 worthy codes including those that dealt with self-
soothing, the experience of increased self-esteem,
awareness of strengths, and feeling in control of treatment.

"Therapist lead" appeared in only 3 of the 11 tran-
750 scripts. The issue of leading the client has often been
discussed in relation to dissociative clients, who may
be more highly suggestible than other clients. In order
to determine whether the process of memory retrieval
differed in a client with dissociative features, we un-
755 dertook a closer examination of the data from 1 participant who identified herself as having a dissociative
identity disorder. Whereas this participant's interview
contained 9 of the 15 noteworthy codes and all 6 repeated codes that appeared in 4 or 5 transcripts, it did
760 not contain any theme associated with the use of therapist suggestion or leading. To the contrary, it contained
the following codes: "client initiates discussion of sexual abuse" and "client shares issue of sexual abuse with
therapist." The data from this participant's interview
765 reflected the major results of the study—that the therapist who is perceived as helpful is one who modulates
the intensity and pace of treatment, empowers the cli-

ent, helps the client develop self-esteem, and facilitates
insight and self-soothing within a relationship in which
770 the therapist is perceived as safe, trustworthy, emotionally available, and competent.

Only 1 participant cited a significantly negative experience and reported having deteriorated during
treatment. This negative experience occurred with the
775 first of two therapists. Closer analysis of this experience can be used to compare the experience of this
woman with the experiences of other participants. The
participant was a single, 46-year-old, Caucasian administrator whose history included sexual abuse by an
780 older peer. Describing her first therapist, the participant
stated:

Well, probably if Therapist #1…if I had continued with
her…I feel I was getting very angry and resentful
of…how she was pushing me into this. It was like I had
785 no say in it…. Probably if I hadn't terminated geographi-
cally I probably would have terminated eventually because…I felt like it was making matters worse in my life.

The transcript of this interview included several
major (noteworthy) and minor (repeated) themes in her
790 description of her first negative experience. On the
positive side, only two codes were observed: "therapist
use of touch" and "client trusts therapist." On the
negative side, several codes were observed: "client
perceives therapist to be in control of treatment," "cli-
795 ent perceives therapist to be emotionally unavailable,"
and "therapist fails to modulate intensity and/or pace of
treatment." One other code that did not achieve noteworthiness was "client perceives therapist to be incompetent." In contrast, the same participant's commentary
800 about her positive experience with a different therapist
included eight noteworthy codes: "client perceives
therapist as emotionally available," "client trusts therapist," "client-therapist bond," "therapist gives client
control," "client feels in control of treatment," "thera-
805 pist use of touch," "therapist facilitates client's awareness of strengths," and "client experiences increased
self-esteem."

Participant Feedback

Seven of the 11 participants returned the questionnaire that inquired about the accuracy of the notewor-
810 thy codes. No individuals suggested additional major
codes. With one exception, participants provided confirmation for all codes, either by indicating simple
agreement or by stating agreement with qualification.
One participant suggested incorporating humor within
815 the category of self-soothing strategies. In response to
the code "patient self-soothing," she wrote,

I've been very grateful to my therapist for teaching me
these strategies. I was in the shit all the time 'till [*sic*] I
was encouraged not only by her but by those friends I
820 called to not forget to live my life! I'd add humor to the
list.

Similarly, in response to the code "control," another
participant wrote,

825 This was very important to me and it was helpful to me that [my therapist] asked me how I could feel in control in healthy ways as opposed to my trying to be in control in old, destructive ways.

"Therapist use of touch" was the only code that produced disagreement or qualified agreement in 50%
830 or more of participants who provided feedback. Four of the 7 participants expressed disagreement or qualified agreement about the use of touch. The qualifications indicated either ambivalence about or rejection of the idea of therapist touch. One respondent indicated that
835 touch would only be acceptable if the client gave the therapist permission. Portions of their comments follow:

(#1) As a sexual abuse survivor I found this difficult in the therapy process. Touch was not a part of the ther-
840 apy and did not feel safe to pursue, 'though I did have a separate massage therapist I worked with.
(#2) Now you are into uncharted territory for me. I crave touch, good touch, 24 hours a day. Recently I've allowed one friend to rub my back and my head. I see a
845 massage therapist [one time per month]. The thought of putting my head on [my therapist's] lap and letting her rub my head makes me cry. I desperately want it but I won't let it happen.
(#3) I agree [with the code, "therapist touch"]! With
850 permission!
(#4) [Therapist touch is appropriate] when [the client] asked and if [the] therapist feels comfortable with it. Touch is discussed.

Discussion

Olio (1989) stated, "Although the relationship is
855 important in all psychotherapy, in the treatment of adult survivors of sexual abuse it is probably the single most important factor" (p. 98). Six of the noteworthy codes that emerged in this study emphasize the importance of the therapeutic relationship, and the results are
860 consistent with the writings of many authors who indicate that it is the therapeutic relationship that, at least in part, supplies the necessary environment in which clients often access forgotten memories (e.g., Cornell & Olio, 1991, 1992; Courtois, 1988; Herman, 1992; Olio
865 & Cornell; 1993). The major relationship codes revealed by the present data involved safety, trust, the therapeutic bond, the experience of feeling listened to, and the emotional availability (or unavailability) of the therapist. The importance of the relationship is under-
870 scored by the finding that the only unhelpful code to achieve noteworthiness was "client perceives therapist as emotionally unavailable."

Six of the seven themes identified as important in the literature on relationship factors and psychotherapy
875 with sexual abuse survivors either achieved noteworthiness (safety, trust, client control, and therapist emotional availability) or were repeated in four or five transcripts ("therapist modulates the intensity and pace of treatment," "therapist believes client," "client experi-
880 ences child state"). The exception was "therapist lead,"

or discussion of abuse initiated by the therapist. This theme was mentioned as a factor in three transcripts; in these cases, "therapist lead" emerged as a participant-generated item of discussion. Because of the practical
885 and political importance of the issue of leading, this theme warrants further comment. One of the questions of the semistructured interview was "How did the issue of sexual abuse originally come up in your therapy?" The clients in the present study had, as a group, worked
890 with 16 therapists. Participants indicated that in 11 treatments, the client opened discussion of the sexual abuse and in 5 cases, the therapist initiated discussion of abuse.

Taken together, the present results suggest that the
895 non-specific aspects of the therapeutic relationship may be more important for clients who are accessing sexual abuse memories than is the therapist's use of specific techniques. Few specific therapeutic techniques or interventions were mentioned as important by partici-
900 pants, although interview questions designed to elicit information about techniques were included in the interview protocol. This finding is especially intriguing in light of recent interest in techniques of "memory recovery therapy" and the belief that a substantial
905 number of psychologists use risky and suggestive techniques that may lead clients to deteriorate psychologically and develop pseudomemories (Lindsay & Read, 1994; Ofshe & Watters, 1994; Ornstein, Ceci, & Loftus, 1996). The results of this study emphasize the
910 centrality of relational qualities and the ways in which these qualities facilitate memory work and the enhancement of functioning.

The importance of nonspecific relationship variables is also consistent with a great deal of research in
915 the general psychotherapy literature. When different approaches to psychotherapy are compared, few significant differences in client outcome emerge (Garfield, 1990, 1992; Smith, Glass, & Miller, 1980; Stiles, Shapiro, & Elliott, 1986). However, the therapeutic alli-
920 ance significantly predicts treatment outcome (Garfield, 1990; Orlinsky & Howard, 1986). Although a strong therapeutic alliance does not appear to be sufficient by itself to guarantee positive therapeutic outcome, the therapeutic alliance is a necessary condition
925 for promoting client change (Garfield, 1990; Highlen & Hill, 1984). Highlen and Hill (1984) summarized this position succinctly:

The sine qua non of therapy is the relationship between the therapist and the client. In order for the counselor to
930 become a potent source of influence in client change, a bond between the participants must be developed. If this solid base is not established, clients will not risk themselves to engage in the "pain of change." (pp. 360–361)

The findings imply that successful therapy for indi-
935 viduals who are accessing and dealing with memories of abuse resembles high-quality psychotherapy for other populations. Specific techniques may be "rela-

tively unimportant except as vehicles for enacting the therapeutic alliance" (Stiles et al., 1986, p.173).

940 Five codes reflect client capacities that emerged during treatment: engaging in self-soothing, gaining insight, experiencing increased self-esteem, becoming aware of strengths, and feeling in control. The importance of self-direction was also a significant component 945 of two noteworthy codes: "client feels in control" and "therapist gives client control." The theme of control has been noted rather extensively in the literature, specifically with regard to the importance of the client's experiencing as much authority and influence as possi- 950 ble during memory work (Briere, 1992; Courtois, 1992; Harvey, 1996; Meiselman, 1990). In addition, self-soothing can be viewed as a method for establishing self-control. The findings regarding control are especially consistent with feminist literature, which empha- 955 sizes that therapists should collaborate with their clients in the definition of problems as well as about choices regarding direction, goals, and the timing and pacing of psychotherapy (Brown, 1994; Laidlaw & Malmo, 1990; Worell & Remer, 1992). An egalitarian 960 climate is empowering and leads to the awareness of strengths and the capacity to reorganize and integrate traumatic memories in a meaningful framework.

Feminist authors in particular have addressed the importance of encouraging the client to become aware 965 of strengths (Brown, 1994; Morrow & Smith, 1995; Worell & Remer, 1992). Knowledge of personal capacities may help clients withstand the intensity of affect that often accompanies traumatic memory retrieval. Awareness of strengths may help bolster self- 970 esteem, which may, in turn, help clients rely on positive coping mechanisms during periods of emotional turbulence. The results suggest that effective therapists directly teach their clients methods to develop personal resources, such as tools for self-soothing.

975 The clinical literature suggests that the activities coded as "therapist facilitates client expression of feeling" and "therapist facilitates awareness of strengths" should be used in combination with each other. The therapist must be cognizant of the "thera- 980 peutic window" (Cole & Barney, 1987) or the "affective edge" (Cornell & Olio, 1991, 1992; Olio & Cornell, 1993), that is, the personal material that the client is prepared to work through without triggering a flood of unmanageable new material. This principle implies 985 that therapists should not promote expression of feelings at the expense of facilitating an awareness of strengths and coping skills.

Another noteworthy code, "client perceives therapist as competent," may be especially significant 990 within the context of traumatic memory retrieval. The client's confidence in the therapist may enable him or her to believe that the therapist can deal effectively with the intense affect and temporary disorganization that may be associated with traumatic memory re- 995 trieval.

A substantial number of noteworthy codes emphasize the enhancement of current functioning and are consistent with the conclusions of the APA's Working Group on Investigation of Memories of Childhood 1000 Abuse (Alpert et al. 1996), whose final report stated, "It is important to remember that the goal of therapy is not archeology; recollection of trauma is only helpful insofar as it is integrated into a therapy emphasizing improvement of functioning" (p. 5). This principle is 1005 also consistent with a recent survey of psychologists which revealed that 92% reported the most important goal of treatment with survivors of child sexual abuse to be " 'focusing on current behaviors, cognitions, thoughts, and/or feelings' or addressing both past and 1010 current clinical issues in therapy" (Polusny & Follette, 1996, p. 45).

A final noteworthy code, "therapist use of touch," merits further comment. As noted in the Results section, "therapist use of touch" was the only noteworthy 1015 code that was not consistently confirmed by participant feedback. Four participants expressed ambivalence toward or rejection of the idea of the therapist's touching them or stated that touch was acceptable only if the client gave the therapist permission for such touch. 1020 This feedback indicates that touch should be used with great caution and only after careful consideration of individual differences between clients and of the costs and benefits of touch.

Most of the noteworthy codes identified by this 1025 study are related to the outcome criteria proposed in Harvey's (1996) ecological-multidimensional model of recovery from trauma. The first criterion, authority over the remembering process, is especially consistent with the two noteworthy codes that highlight the im- 1030 portance of client control of the psychotherapy process. The client develops the capacity to influence and control traumatic or intrusive memories so that these experiences no longer disable him or her. Second, the integration of memory and affect, or the ability to connect 1035 emotion in a meaningful way with past and present experiences, is a logical outcome of "therapist facilitates client expression of feeling." The outcome criteria labeled as affect tolerance and symptom mastery emphasize the client's capacity to manage troubling emo- 1040 tions and are likely to be associated with "client self-soothes not using therapist." Fourth, the outcomes of self-esteem and self-cohesion are consistent with the noteworthy codes "awareness of strengths" and "increased self-esteem." Fifth, safe attachment, the capac- 1045 ity for whole relationships, is likely to be facilitated by a variety of experiences connected to the therapeutic relationship, including trust, safety, emotional availability, the client-therapist bond, and the experience of being listened to. Finally, the capacity to make mean- 1050 ing out of one's experience is likely to be enhanced by therapist assistance with insight. In summary, the results suggest that a positive therapeutic experience for sexually abused clients tends to occur when the therapist provides them with a corrective emotional experience in which new learning experiences are used to develop a sense of meaning and trust in the world.

The experience of the 1 participant who cited a significantly negative therapeutic experience points out outcomes that may occur when the therapeutic factors described above are not present. The participant perceived this therapist as emotionally unavailable, as taking control of the treatment, as incompetent, and as failing to modulate the intensity and/or pace of the therapy. The themes described in this transcript are consistent with the personal account of Hauser-Hines (1997), whose negative account of psychotherapy related to child sexual abuse described a controlling therapist who encouraged a level of emotional intensity that she found overwhelming. The participant in this study, in contrast to her early negative experience, viewed a second and helpful therapist as allowing her to establish control and set her own pace and as facilitating her awareness of strengths, all within a safe, supportive therapeutic relationship.

One of the strengths of this study is associated with sample selection. Given the controversy surrounding whether childhood sexual abuse memories can be repressed (e.g., Loftus, 1993), the self-selection method for recruiting participants was important in decreasing potential sources of bias. The fliers and advertisements used to recruit volunteers were equally capable of attracting individuals who believed their memories were legitimate as well as those who believed they suffered from "false memory syndrome" at the hands of a therapist who had used leading or suggestive techniques. To ensure that there was no inherent demand to report only positive therapy experiences, we did not solicit clients through their therapists. Given these factors, it is notable that no individual who volunteered for the study claimed false memories.

Several limitations associated with sample selection should also be noted. First, the participants' reports about the retrieval of forgotten memories were retrospective and taken at face value. There was no external confirmation that the participants' psychotherapy experiences were successful inasmuch as no objective data regarding therapists' perspectives were obtained. In terms of external validity limitations, women who responded to the flier and who were willing to be interviewed may have differed from those who did not volunteer. Furthermore, all participants were Caucasian women, which points to the limited diversity of this sample. Because 75% of the participants identified their perpetrators as family members, it is possible that therapeutic experiences differ when the perpetrator is not a family member.

The type of qualitative analysis used in this study can be construed as both a strength and a limitation. The method of qualitative data analysis used in this research is most consistent with a postpositivistic paradigm (Highlen & Finley, 1996). In accord with this paradigm, we attempted to achieve objectivity but recognized that researcher-participant interactions and researchers' subjective impressions influence data. Grounded theory (Strauss & Corbin, 1990, 1994) provided us with specific steps for creating and modifying theory within this postpositivistic framework. The coding procedures we used were designed to "force the researcher's own voice to be questioning, questioned, and provisional" (Strauss & Corbin, 1994, p. 280). Efforts to decrease bias included the use of triangulation (Yin, 1994), or the use of multiple sources of evidence. The multiple sources in this study included the use of two panels, one of judges and one of card sorters; the comparison of findings with a specific body of clinical literature; and feedback by participants. For this research, efforts to maintain objectivity seemed especially important given the controversial nature of retrieved memories of sexual abuse and the divergent and highly subjective opinions that many individuals hold.

Although the goal of this study was to reveal and clarify the client's experience, our use of these methods (relatively objective analysis) may have distanced us somewhat from respondents' views and may have limited the degree to which we were able to fully understand the psychotherapy experience from the client's perspective. The procedures we implemented and the criteria for establishing major and minor codes may have also resulted in the loss of some important data that may have revealed a more complex picture of the unique and varied experiences of clients. For these reasons, we recommend that future research on this topic incorporate alternative qualitative procedures that are consistent with interpretive-constructivist, critical, and poststructural paradigms (Highlen & Finley, 1996).

The most obvious direction for future research is the replication of this study with a larger and more heterogeneous sample that includes both men and women clients with differing racial-ethnic backgrounds, victims of familial and nonfamilial abuse, and hospitalized patients. Second, although the present study suggested that the nonspecific aspects of the therapeutic relationship are more important to memory work than are specific techniques, an important area for future study lies in defining how the activities identified operate. The question "How?" can be asked of many of the codes, even those as fundamental as "client feels safe" (e.g., "How does the therapist convey that he or she is a safe person, worthy of trust?"). Third, research should explore in depth what types of therapist behaviors are helpful (a) at the various stages of psychotherapy, (b) with diverse affective and cognitive states of clients, and (c) with clients with different backgrounds and presenting concerns (Beutler & Hill, 1992). Fourth, the present study's findings could be tested with alternative research methods, such as quantitative designs or single-case studies.

Future studies should continue to examine the client's experience of psychotherapy. The clinical litera-

1170 ture pertaining to the influence of the therapeutic relationship on the retrieval of traumatic memories has generally been written from the therapist's rather than the client's perspective. Research could also be conducted with therapist-client dyads in order to obtain
1175 both therapist and client perspectives.

References

Alpert, J. L., Brown, L. S., Ceci, S. J., Courtois, C. A., Loftus, E. F., & Ornstein, P. A. (Eds.). (1996). *Working group on investigation of memories of childhood abuse: Final report*. Washington, DC: American Psychological Association.

American Psychological Association. (1987). *Ethical principles in the conduct of research with human participants*. Washington, DC: Author.

Beutler, L. E., & Hill, C. E. (1992). Process and outcome research in the treatment of adult victims of childhood sexual abuse: Methodological issues. *Journal of Consulting and Clinical Psychology, 60*, 204–212.

Briere, J. (1989). *Therapy for adults molested as children: Beyond survival*. New York: Springer.

Briere, J. (1992). *Child abuse trauma: Theory and treatment of the lasting effects*. Newbury Park, CA: Sage.

Briere, J., & Conte, J. (1993). Self-reported amnesia for abuse in adults molested as children. *Journal of Traumatic Stress, 6*, 21–31.

Brown, L. S. (1994). *Subversive dialogues: Theory in feminist therapy*. New York: Basic Books.

Cameron, C. (1994). Women survivors confronting their abusers: Issues, decisions and outcomes. *Journal of Child Sexual Abuse, 3*, 7–35.

Cole, C. H., & Barney, E. E. (1987). Safeguards and the therapeutic window: A group treatment strategy for adult incest survivors. *American Journal of Orthopsychiatry, 57*, 601–609.

Cornell, W. F., & Olio, K. A. (1991). Integrating affect in treatment with adult survivors of physical and sexual abuse. *American Journal of Orthopsychiatry, 61*, 59–69.

Cornell, W. F., & Olio, K. A. (1992). Consequences of childhood bodily abuse: A clinical model for affective interventions. *Transactional Analysis Journal, 22*, 131–143.

Courtois, C. (1988). *Healing the incest wound: Adult survivors in therapy*. New York: Norton.

Courtois, C. A. (1992). The memory retrieval process in incest survivor therapy. *Journal of Child Sexual Abuse, 1*, 15–31.

Davies, J. M., & Frawley, M. G. (1994). *Treating the adult survivor of childhood sexual abuse: A psychoanalytic perspective*. New York: Basic Books.

Dominiak, G. M. (1992). Attachment dynamics in the opening phase of psychotherapy with sexually abused women. In S. Shapiro & G. M. Dominiak (Eds.), *Sexual trauma and psychopathology: Clinical intervention with adult survivors* (pp. 17–33). New York: Lexington Books.

Elliott, D. M., & Briere, J. (1995). Posttraumatic stress associated with delayed recall of sexual abuse: A general population study. *Journal of Traumatic Stress, 8*, 629–647.

Enns, C. Z., McNeilly, C. L., Corkery, J. M., & Gilbert, M. S. (1995). The debate about delayed memories of child sexual abuse: A feminist perspective. *The Counseling Psychologist, 23*, 181–279.

Feldman-Summers, S., & Pope, K. S. (1994). The experience of "forgetting" childhood abuse: A national survey of psychologists. *Journal of Consulting and Clinical Psychology, 62*, 636–639.

Garfield, S. L. (1990). Issues and methods in psychotherapy process research. *Journal of Consulting and Clinical Psychology, 58*, 273–280.

Garfield, S. L. (1992). Major issues in psychotherapy research. In D. K. Freedheim, H. J. Freudenberger, J. W. Kessler, S. B. Messer, D. R. Peterson, H. H. Strupp, & P. L. Wachtel (Eds.), *History of psychotherapy: A century of change* (pp. 335–359). Washington, DC: American Psychological Association.

Glaser, B. G., & Strauss, A. (1967). *The discovery of grounded theory: Strategies for qualitative research*. Chicago: Aldine.

Gurman, A. S. (1977). The patient's perception of the therapeutic relationship. In A. S. Gurman & A. M. Razin (Eds.), *Effective psychotherapy: A handbook of research* (pp. 503–543). New York: Pergamon Press.

Harvey, M. R. (1996). An ecological view of psychological trauma and trauma recovery. *Journal of Traumatic Stress, 9*, 3–23.

Hauser-Hines, S. (1997). A retrospective tale of psychotherapy: An incest dream. *Psychotherapy Bulletin, 32*(1), 33–37.

Herman, J. L. (1992). *Trauma and recovery*. New York: Basic Books.

Herman, J. L., & Schatzow, E. (1987). Recovery and verification of memories of childhood sexual trauma. *Psychoanalytic Psychology, 4*, 1–14.

Highlen, P. S., & Finley, H. C. (1996). Doing qualitative analysis. In F. T. L. Leong & J. T. Austin (Eds.), *The psychology research handbook* (pp. 177–192). Thousand Oaks, CA: Sage.

Highlen, P. S., & Hill, C. E. (1984). Factors affecting client change in individual counseling: Current status and theoretical speculations. In S. D. Brown & R. W. Lent (Eds.), *Handbook of counseling psychology* (pp. 334–396).

New York: Wiley.

Laidlaw, T. A., & Malmo, C. (Eds.). (1990). *Healing voices: Feminist approaches to therapy with women*. San Francisco: Jossey-Bass.

Lindsay, D. S., & Read, J. D. (1994). Psychotherapy and memories of childhood sexual abuse: A cognitive perspective. *Applied Cognitive Psychology, 8*, 281–338.

Loftus, E. F. (1993). The reality of repressed memories. *American Psychologist, 48*, 518–537.

Loftus, E. F., Polonsky, S., & Fullilove, M. T. (1994). Memories of childhood sexual abuse: Remembering and repression. *Psychology of Women Quarterly, 18*, 67–84.

McCracken, G. (1988). *The long interview*. (Sage University Paper Series on Qualitative Research Methods, Vol. 13). Newbury Park, CA: Sage.

Meiselman, K. C. (1990). *Resolving the trauma of incest: Reintegration therapy with survivors*. San Francisco: Jossey-Bass.

Miles, M. B., & Huberman, A. M. (1984). *Qualitative data analysis: A sourcebook of new methods*. Beverly Hills, CA: Sage.

Miles, M. B., & Huberman, A. M. (1994). *An expanded sourcebook: Qualitative data analysis* (2nd ed.). Newbury Park, CA: Sage.

Morrow, S. L., & Smith, M. L. (1995). Constructions of survival and coping by women who have survived childhood sexual abuse. *Journal of Counseling Psychology, 42*, 24–33.

Ofshe, R., & Watters, E. (1994). *Making monsters: False memories, psychotherapy, and sexual hysteria*. New York: Scribner.

Olio, K. A. (1989). Memory retrieval in the treatment of adult survivors of sexual abuse. *Transactional Analysis Journal, 19*, 93–106.

Olio, K. A., & Cornell, W. F. (1993). The therapeutic relationship as the foundation for treatment with adult survivors of sexual abuse. *Psychotherapy, 30*, 512–523.

Orlinsky, D. E., & Howard, K. I. (1986). Process and outcome in psychotherapy. In S. L. Garfield & A. E. Bergin (Eds.), *Handbook of psychotherapy and behavior change* (3rd ed., pp. 311–384). New York: Wiley.

Ornstein, P. A., Ceci, S. J., & Loftus, E. F. (1996). Reply to the Alpert, Brown, and Courtois document: The science of memory and the practice of psychotherapy. In J. L. Alpert et al. (Eds.), *Working group on investigation of memories of childhood abuse: Final report*. Washington, DC: American Psychological Association.

Polusny, M. A., & Follette, V. M. (1996). Remembering childhood sexual abuse: A national survey of psychologists' clinical practices, beliefs, and personal experiences. *Professional Psychology: Research and Practice, 27*, 41–52.

Poole, D. A., Lindsay, D. S., Memon, A., & Bull, R. (1995). Psychotherapy and the recovery of memories of childhood sexual abuse: U.S. and British practitioners' opinions, practices, and experiences. *Journal of Consulting and Clinical Psychology, 63*, 426–437.

Pruitt, J. A., & Kappius, R. E. (1992). Routine inquiry into sexual victimization: A survey of therapists' practices. *Professional Psychology: Research and Practice, 23*, 474–479.

Saakvitne, K. W. (1990, August). *Psychoanalytic psychotherapy with incest survivors: Transference and countertransference paradigms*. Paper presented at the Annual Convention of the American Psychological Association, Boston, MA.

Smith, L. L., Glass, G. V., & Miller, T. I. (1980). *The benefits of psychotherapy*. Baltimore: Johns Hopkins University Press.

Stiles, W. B. (1993). Quality control in qualitative research. *Clinical Psychology Review, 13*, 593–618.

Stiles, W. B., Shapiro, D. A., & Elliott, R. (1986). Are all psychotherapies equivalent? *American Psychologist, 41*, 165–180.

Strauss, A., & Corbin, J. (1990). *Basics of qualitative research: Grounded theory procedures and techniques*. London: Sage.

Strauss, A., & Corbin, J. (1994). Grounded theory methodology. In N. K. Denzin & Y. S. Lincoln (Eds.), *Handbook of qualitative research* (pp. 273–285). Thousand Oaks, CA: Sage.

Taylor, S.J., & Bogdan, R. (1984). *Introduction to qualitative research methods: The search for meanings*. New York: Wiley.

Williams, L. M. (1994). Recall of childhood trauma: A prospective study of women's memories of child sexual abuse. *Journal of Consulting and Clinical Psychology, 62*, 1167–1176.

Worell, J., & Remer, P. (1992). *Feminist perspectives in therapy: An empowerment model for women*. New York: Wiley.

Yapko, M. (1994). *Suggestions of abuse: True and false memories of childhood sexual trauma*. New York: Simon & Schuster.

Yin, R. K. (1994). *Case study research design and methods* (2nd ed.). London: Sage.

About the Authors: Alisa Phelps and Myrna L. Friedlander, Department of Counseling Psychology, University at Albany, State University of New York; Carolyn Zerbe Enns, Psychology Department, Cornell College.

Alisa Phelps is now at North Star Mental Health Services, Malone, New York.

Acknowledgments: This research was based on a doctoral dissertation by Alisa Phelps under the direction of Myrna L. Friedlander (Chair) and Carolyn Zerbe Enns. We are grateful to the other committee member, Dianne Newman, and to Emily Abbott, Geret Giles, Ray Gornell, Debra Klinger, and Bob Verno for their assistance with coding and sorting.

Address correspondence to: Carolyn Zerbe Enns, Psychology Department, Cornell College, 600 First Street West, Mount Vernon, Iowa 52314-1098. Electronic mail may be sent via Internet to enns@cornell-iowa.edu.

Exercise for Case 6

1. Introduction

A. Is the problem area for the research clearly described? Explain.

B. Have the researchers convinced you that the problem area is important? Explain.

C. To what extent does the literature presented in the introduction help you understand the problem? Is the literature used to put the problem in context? Explain.

D. Do the researchers indicate how this study is different from and/or similar to earlier ones reported in the literature?

E. Do the researchers reveal their personal perspectives on the problem area, including any possible biases? Explain.

2. Methods

A. Are the demographics of the participants (i.e., background characteristics such as age, race, and so on) described in sufficient detail? Explain.

B. Considering the problem area for the research, do you think that appropriate participants were selected? If you had been conducting the study, would you have selected the same type(s) of participants? Would you have used the same number of participants? Explain.

C. Which strategies listed in Table 1 on page 161 of this book were employed by the researchers? Are they described in sufficient detail? Explain.

D. In addition to those you named in response to question 2C, have the researchers used any additional strategies to help assure the validity of the study? If yes, what are they? Are they described in sufficient detail? Explain.

3. Analysis and Results

A. Are the steps taken in the analysis described in sufficient detail? Explain.

B. Are the results clearly organized? Explain.

C. Are the results discussed in terms of a theory or theories (either theories that emerged from this study or previously existing ones)? Explain.

D. Were the direct quotations of the participants' statements, if any, judiciously selected? Do they help you understand the results? Explain.

E. Are there other ways the results could have been organized and interpreted? Explain.

4. Conclusions/Implications

A. Are the researchers' concluding remarks appropriate? Do they flow logically from the material presented earlier?

B. Do the researchers describe any implications? If yes, are they appropriate? Are there other implications that are not discussed by the researchers? Explain.

5. Ethical Considerations

A. In your opinion, could this research have caused physical or psychological harm to the participants? If yes, did the researchers take adequate measures to ameliorate the potential for harm? Explain.

B. If you had conducted this research, would you have obtained written, informed consent from the participants before conducting the study? Explain. Does this research report indicate that the researchers obtained such consent?

6. Overall Evaluation

A. Throughout the article, are all specialized terms and jargon defined to your satisfaction? Explain.

B. Briefly describe your overall evaluation of the research report, noting any special strengths and weaknesses.

C. If you had been a reviewer for the journal in which this report was published, would you have recommended publication of the report? If yes, would you have recommended that it be published "as is" or modified before publication? Explain. If no, what is the primary reason why you would recommend not publishing it?

Case 7

A Really Good Art Teacher Would Be Like You, Mrs. C.: A Qualitative Study of a Teacher and Her Artistically Gifted Middle School Students

POLLY WOLFE
Ball State University

ABSTRACT. In this paper, I examine the experiences of a teacher and her artistically gifted middle school students over the course of a school year in an attempt to add to the definition of effective teaching for that population. Identified as artistically gifted through a formal, multimethod process, the students experienced a five-phase curriculum rhythm (a construct devised to describe the chronology of the class content). The phases—image flood, reflection, art work, critique, and exhibition—enabled the veteran teacher to "translate" meaning in both the student world and the adult art world. The translation process influenced students' self-identification as artists and their abilities to reflect and to be more articulate about their art. Possible ramifications of this study include further exploration of the themes of curriculum rhythm and translation as components of art teacher effectiveness with artistically gifted and other student populations.

From *Studies in Art Education*, 38, 232–245. Copyright © 1997 by the National Art Education Association. Reprinted with permission.

A really good art teacher would be like you, Mrs. C. She would do neat projects, like this mural. And we would learn all that stuff, like mixing colors. She would be funny, too. Oh yea, she'd let us drink cokes during class,
5   too. (Kelly, transcript; December 9, 1993)[1]

This quote by a seventh-grade participant in an artistically gifted program presents his simplified view of an area infrequently addressed in research: definitions of excellent or effective teaching relevant to the needs
10 of artistically gifted students. Within his statement, Kelly addresses both pedagogical actions (high-interest projects, technical instruction) and personal attributes (flexibility and a sense of humor), which are mentioned in the literature as central to art teacher effectiveness
15 (Clark & Zimmerman, 1995; Saunders, 1989).

In education literature, extensive effort has been

expended to describe or define excellence and/or effectiveness (Amidon & Flanders, 1967). Long lists of qualities are proffered as characteristics of effective
20 teachers (Langlois & Zales, 1991). In art education, studies disclose teacher traits such as artistic competence (Bradley, 1984; Hathaway, 1980; Saunders, 1989; Zimmerman, 1991, 1992), and the concomitant ability to share that capability with students as impor-
25 tant to art teacher effectiveness. Assuming a variety of roles, valuing art education, having organizational and evaluative skills, and being aware of student developmental and emotional needs exemplify the types of skills, knowledge, and behaviors that excellent art
30 teachers exhibit (Capet, 1986; May, 1993; Saunders, 1989; Stokrocki, 1991; Thomas, 1992).

With the exception of two studies (Zimmerman, 1991, 1992), Clark and Zimmerman's (1984) statement that the "question of ideal teacher characteristics for
35 students with superior abilities in the arts is virtually unexplored and unanswered at this time" (p. 94), still holds true. In learning more about effectiveness, there is a need to go beyond the "armchair lists" (Clark & Zimmerman, 1984) of teacher behaviors and charac-
40 teristics. For example, what does artistic competence imply (Bradley, 1984; Hathaway, 1980; Saunders, 1989; Zimmerman, 1991)? How does a teacher use that competence with students?

Zimmerman (1991, 1992) studied painting instruc-
45 tors working with middle and high school artistically gifted students in a summer enrichment program. She noted one instructor who used storytelling to impart art history or technique information, allowing the reader a sense of the students' and teacher's intensity and
50 learning atmosphere in the short-term program. However, no similar narratives of in-school artistically gifted programs and teachers exist. In this study, I explore what a group of artistically gifted students are doing, talking about, or thinking as their teacher plans
55 and executes lessons directed toward their differentiated needs. Discerning how the teacher's and students' actions and reactions evolve as a year progresses has the potential to expand comprehension of teacher effectiveness beyond the listing of teachers' skills and

---

[1] Material which came directly from the collected data, such as Kelly's quote, is cited by type of data and date of data collection. The three types of data used were field notes, video notes, and transcripts. As unpublished raw data, these are not listed in the reference section.

60   characteristics.

Research Framework

The theoretical framework of most qualitative research depends on the issues to be explored, the types
of guiding questions asked by the researcher, the roles
assumed by the researcher, and ways in which the
65   study is written (Bresler, 1994; Ettinger, 1987; Jacob,
1987; Patton, 1990). Instead of generating hypotheses,
as is common in quantitative research, broad-based
open-ended guiding questions are developed for qualitative research. In this study such questions pertain to
70   the teacher's role as instructional leader, the ways in
which the teacher and students interact to construct
meaning (or learn together), and the effects of the
wider context (school, peers, family, and community)
on learning. These questions reflect the broad-based
75   focus of qualitative research. My intent in this study is
to enhance the broad descriptive term *effectiveness*
through the in-depth study of a teacher and her artistically gifted students.

Blumer's (1967) social interaction theory, which
80   describes meaning-making as a social interactionary
process modified through self and social interpretation,
forms the theoretical basis of the study. Blumer posits
that one learns through social interaction combined
with internal dialogue and interpretation. In this study,
85   I concentrated on the interactions between the teacher
and students, between students and teacher and student,
as well as students' internal dialogue revealed in their
art work.

The Setting and Participants

Criteria for site selection included conditions such
90   as the presence of an ongoing artistically gifted program and a school district with administrative and
community history of support for gifted and talented
programming. The researcher selected the school district because it was one of the first in the state to act as
95   a model site for gifted programs, initiating artistically
gifted programs along with academic ones. The selected program began in 1987 as a pilot program for
the school district.

The Community

The selected school is a largely middle-class com-
100   munity of 43,764 inhabitants (Department of Commerce, 1990) across the river from a university town of
25,907. With a low (3.8%) unemployment rate, the city
has a varied economic base with 88% of the adults employed in manufacturing, service, government, and
105   retail (Indiana Department of Work Force Development, 1993). The school district has one large high
school (grades 9–12), two middle schools (grades 6–8),
and 11 elementary schools (grades K–5). There are also
9 religion-based schools. A modest art museum, a his-
110   torical museum, a performing and visual arts center, a
library, a community orchestra, and the variety of offerings typical to a large university community provide

opportunity for community arts involvement.

The School

Although school selection criteria were auxiliary to
115   the teacher selection, administrative support for the
artistically gifted program was central to the school site
selection. The district and middle school administration
supply the teacher with procedural aid in the gifted
identification process, scheduling assistance, and
120   funding for the teacher's inservice growth.

Sunnydale Middle School (a pseudonym, as are
those of the teacher and students) is a typically midwestern set of brick rectangles, squatting in an "L"
shape in an older section of the city. The middle school
125   reflects the community both economically and ethni-
cally. Of the students, 94% are Caucasian, 2% are African American, with the other 4% Hispanic, Asian, or
"other." One third of all students receive the free or
reduced-price lunch. Compared to students of similar
130   economic constituency, the Sunnydale students score
slightly better on the standardized tests than other middle schoolers across the state.

The Teacher

KC (or "Mrs. C." to her students) was selected because of her continuing educational pursuits, gifted and
135   talented training (Feldhusen & Hansen, 1994), her activity in local and state art organizations, and community recognition as an active artist and teacher (Clark &
Zimmerman, 1984, 1992; Zimmerman, 1991, 1992).
Receiving a fellowship to attend Clark and Zimmer-
140   man's Artistically Talented Program in 1992, KC continually seeks ways to keep abreast of educational and
artistic developments. She frequently mentors student-
and first-year teachers. On the executive board of the
state art education association, she is also active in sev-
145   eral arts groups in the city.

The Students

All 26 students who participated in the program
(called "Challenge Art") were part of the study. The
sixth, seventh, and eighth graders were identified
through a formal multimethod screening process based
150   on self, teacher, and parent nomination forms, along
with three drawing elements from the Clark's Drawing
Abilities Test (Clark, 1989). An identification committee consisting of the teacher, the gifted-talented
coordinator, and other art teachers rated the drawings
155   and nomination forms, with the highest scoring students being invited to join the Challenge program. In
1993–1994, all of the Challenge Art Students were
Caucasian, although a few African-American and
Asian students enrolled in prior Challenge Art classes.
160   Fifty percent of the 1993–1994 students were also enrolled in one or more academic Challenge courses.
First semester of the 1993–1994 year, the 21 students
were evenly divided among grades six, seven, and
eight. Five students dropped out second semester, and
165   5 new students were added, leaving a total of 9 seventh

and eighth graders and 3 sixth graders. First semester there were 12 girls and 9 boys, while second semester there were 11 girls and 10 boys.

Researcher Role

In anthropology, the participant observer is one who attempts to become part of the target culture (Ettinger, 1987; Maitland-Gholson & Ettinger, 1994; Patton, 1990). Assuming that role, I attempted to blend with the Challenge Art class in order to experience things as they did.

Initially, I participated as a learner, sitting with different student social groups, who seemed to designate certain tables or room areas as their own. I listened, learned, drew, and painted with them, and they watched me struggle with similar decisions and problem solving. I asked their advice, and they reciprocated. As the year progressed, I shifted more into an assistant teacher role, circulating among the students, asking questions, coaching, and talking with participants. I also used that time to informally interview students, take notes, take photographs, and record class interactions on audio and video tape.

Beginning in October, the class met weekly after school for 1 to 2½ hours. I attended 32 hours (95%) of the first semester meetings. Second semester I attended 29 hours (87%) of scheduled meetings. I met a few times with the summer school Challenge Art group, which contained many students who participated during the school year.

Data Sources and Collection

Primary data sources were field notes, taken during or shortly after class, audio or video tapes of observed classes, and interviews, along with slides and photos of student work. The video camera was placed to provide an overview of the entire classroom, while the audio recorder was placed on a table among 4 to 6 students, and moved to different tables each week. Since student social groups seemed to "claim" different areas of the room, or certain tables, moving the audio recorder allowed data collection from different social groups. Transcripts were made from both audio and video tapes, or notes taken while viewing video tapes. Multiple copies of transcripts were made, some of which were cut and placed in color-coded files to reflect analytic categories.

Slides, photos, and videos of art works became important data. These items were analyzed to reflect students' learning processes. Artifacts such as copies of student artwork, handouts, lesson plans, in-school bulletins, notes home, newspaper articles, and tapes of newscasts served as secondary data sources, augmenting the primary sources.

Data Analysis

Focusing on teacher-student, student-teacher, and student-student interactions, I began preliminary analysis within the first month of observation, using the constant comparison method of analysis which involves combining inductive behavior coding with simultaneous comparison of all observed events (Glaser & Strauss, 1967; Strauss, 1987). The codes, which began as interaction descriptors, began to reveal patterns within the accumulation of coded transcripts. Using the coding system, 7 graduate and undergraduate art education students rated representative interaction behaviors in five video clips. Their coding reflected an inter-rater reliability of .91 with the codes I had assigned the same clips.

Linkages were sought between patterns, usually emerging from theoretical memos written as analysis progressed (Strauss, 1987). These codes, patterns, and linkages were triangulated with interview and secondary data information, and particularly scanned for disconfirming data, causing assertions to be revised to include that data.

Challenge Art Description

The Teacher-Translator

The translation process is a construct the researcher developed to describe the complex phenomena of teacher and student behaviors, interaction patterns, and art work manifestations which reflect the intentional and unintentional classroom curricula in Challenge Art. Similar to Dillon's (1989) teacher as a cultural broker, the teacher-translator bridges the cultures/worlds of the artistically gifted middle school student and the artworld. The students' world includes school, peers, family, and community, while the artworld includes the local, regional, and international art world.

A translator is one who is fluent in more than one language. To translate efficiently, one must be able to clearly understand in one language, and almost simultaneously repeat the thought in another, retaining the same clarity, emphasis, and nuance. KC is a translator. Her "languages" are those of the artworld and the students' world. The artworld language is full of images, galleries, history, critical analyses, contact with other artists, aesthetic discussions, museums, books. The language of the students' world is full of references to the middle school culture of teachers, peers, who did what during lunch, who "likes" whom, who called whom last night, who got in trouble third period....

KC is a veteran teacher. KC is an artist. She melds the two in a life-web which attracts artistically gifted middle school students around her in a bubble of giggly enthusiasm. "I have to do art," she says, and the kids begin to feel the love she has for her field. "My kids..." she says, and they know the beginning of trust. One cannot talk to her without hearing about one or the other—her kids, art. The synergy resulting from her dual passions of art and teaching forms the basis for KC's effectiveness as a teacher-translator.

KC's personal time is filled with the vocabulary of the artworld. Travel involves visits to galleries and museums, as she and her spouse deliver and retrieve his paintings from Chicago, or take their works to exhibitions in other Midwestern cities. She reads a number of art magazines regularly, feeling that it is important to be "on the cutting edge of our profession...as artists" (Transcript; December 2, 1992).

As part of the school world, KC operates successfully in both adult and student circles. With her colleagues, she serves on school and district committees, helps reading teachers by assisting on a bookmaking unit, is part of a Friday breakfast "club," and uses the Art Club to assist in school decoration and scenery construction for music and drama productions.

As part of the student world, KC interacts with the Challenge Art students as they burst through the door on Thursday afternoons, asking one how he did on an English test, another about a musical audition. Frequently snapping pictures, she tells them that "this one's for the yearbook," or "I want to show other art teachers what you're really like" (Transcript; March 3, 1994). The class milieu is full of energy and laughter. Even her disciplinary statements are humor-laced. "Tank, the Chumpette, forgot to put up his chair again," she says in mock desperation. "Poor Mrs. C." is the response (Video notes; December 9, 1993). The cheerful by-play is the background for the more serious work of artistic teaching-learning conducted through the translation process. This translation is conducted through the medium of KC's curriculum rhythm.

Curriculum Rhythm

Curriculum rhythm is a construct developed by the researcher to reflect what was observed in this classroom over time. KC's teaching has a pattern to it. Reflecting the need for differentiated instruction, the pattern used with her "regular" students is different from the one used with her Challenge Art students. KC gives her regular students a chronological overview of art history, an introduction to critical and aesthetic learning experiences combined with varied media experiences. Highly structured, her regular art classes extend 9 or 12 weeks, depending on grade level.

In Challenge Art, the thematic subject matter differs each semester, yet the pattern of learning and experience remains consistent. The thematic curriculum accommodates in-depth study and extended immersion in student-selected art projects. In Challenge Art, KC provides problem finding and problem solving. For the regular classes, KC's curriculum rhythm is staccato; for her Challenge Art class, the rhythm resembles a more sustained melody reflecting the differentiated needs of her high-interest students.

The curriculum rhythm is the medium through which KC translates the artworld to the students. Art teachers easily recognize the concept of the rhythm of an art class. If it is a production lesson, the students enter the room, put their backpacks, food, and assorted clothing aside, retrieve what they are working on, and settle down to listen to the teacher, who introduces or demonstrates the day's lesson. The students work on their projects, clean up and leave—a cycle repeated throughout the day for the teacher, throughout the term for the students.

KC employs that familiar rhythm for some Challenge Art classes, but her class rhythms fall within a larger overall pattern consisting of five phases. KC's Challenge Art classes are semester based, as is the duration of her curriculum rhythm cycle. The rhythm cycle is repeated each semester, differing in its thematic content. As the translation vehicle, each of the five phases serves to further meld the student world and the artworld. The five phases are: image flood, reflection, art work, critique, and exhibition. I observed two complete cycles and part of a third during this study. Each semester evidenced all five phases of the rhythmic cycle. Through these rhythmic cycles the translation process occurs as described here.

Phase one: The image flood. KC begins each cycle with a flood of images for her students. Assembling many books, slides, and visuals on the selected topic, she floods her students with visual images. The first semester of the study, KC selected the theme of American Western art for her Challenge Art curriculum. She showed slides and snapshots of a prior trip through the Southwest, had dozens of books and magazines (such as *Arizona Highways*) available to the students, while discussing the physical characteristics of the Southwest. She then showed slides of noted Southwestern artists' work. Some were 19th-century; some were current. She discussed various techniques used, along with color choices. Remington, T.C. Cannon, Victor Higgins, and O'Keeffe illustrate the exemplar variety. Following the slides, the students went to a museum specializing in Western art. Not one to overlook an instructional opportunity, KC distributed many of the books and magazines on Western art to the students on the bus, reiterating technique, subject matter, and style. At the museum, a capable, denim-clad docent discussed artists, painting, and historical context of the works. Finally, the students were allowed to explore. The 18 kids who attended the field trip went nose-close to works of interest, or sprawled on the floor to sketch. A museum patron commented to me about their keen absorption. When informed that they were middle schoolers, she expressed surprise. Informed that they were artistically gifted, she no longer wondered at their intensity (Field notes; October 13, 1993).

Winter semester, which centered on both public art and Victorian architecture, in preparation for painting a mural on a bridge underpass, included a similar image flood phase. Field trips included investigating community public art, visits to the city historical museum and a lovingly restored Victorian home, as well as a bus tour around the historic neighborhood. Experiences were supplemented with slides and with opportunities for students to photograph selected homes or architectural details for future reference. Student sketch books reveal gas lamps, intricate wrought iron fences, and replications of fish scale shingles. Along with visual stimulation, the students heard "stories" about the city founders who populated the neighborhood, providing a visual and verbal picture of 1800s life.

KC explained to a group of fellow art teachers the necessity of the image flood:

> As adults we have built a large store of images. We have looked at a lot of art. My students have limited experience. So it is my job to fill them with a wide variety of images to build up their imagic store. (Field notes; October 29, 1994)

As the students are bombarded with these images, they are also making critical choices in selecting images of interest and recording them either photographically or in their sketch books.

Phase two: Reflection. The second phase of the teaching-learning rhythm begins during the first, as the students select which images to sketch or photograph. This is the reflection phase wherein the students reflect upon what they have seen, and begin generating ideas for further development.

One student, intrigued with a tree seen at the Western art museum, began to sketch it at the museum. Upon returning to the classroom, Ward transferred that sketch to a masonite board as the centerpiece of his Western painting. His sketch book revealed that the texture of the tree was of greatest interest, while the form of the tree was altered and refined as he continued the painting and drawing process. That same semester, another sixth grade boy was drawn to the smooth surface of an O'Keeffe pueblo painting at the museum. Pursuing his interest in O'Keeffe, he found a black-and-white photo of a skull drawing showing an intricate antler structure. Using that as a springboard, Biker also used real bovine skulls as further reference for his drawing (Video notes; November 4, 1993).

As part of the reflective process, this combining and altering visual references occurred during the second semester as well, with a notable addition, that of written reflection. KC asked the students questions such as "Why did you choose your house or object? What style is it?" (Video notes; February 24, 1994). Sketchbook journaling included information such as chronological data about chosen buildings, architectural style, as well as stories about the object or building. Much of the resource information came from materials KC had photocopied at the historical museum. As work continued on the actual bridge murals, KC asked them to record how they felt about their work and the collaborative nature of the project. She indicated that the students should "have a record of what you did, so you can show your children someday" (Video notes; February 24, 1994). While the students laughed at the vision of their own progeny, the permanence of the project was impressed upon them.

The journals/sketchbooks were not only used in recording interesting images, developing ideas, and writing about personal and historic documentation, but were also used as references in later presentations. As the work on the mural progressed, the students were asked on numerous occasions to discuss their work with interested community groups and community media. The sketchbook material became a resource for those comments

Phase three: Art work. As the students researched material for their art, using the abundant resources available, some generated ideas almost immediately. Others took more time, beginning with one idea, abandoning it and exploring another. KC helped them formulate ideas by referring them to the visual resources in the room (the slides, magazines, books, photos) and through technical instruction. Jack, a tall, bright, energetic seventh grader, talked about his Western art idea:

> I want it to represent all those old cowboy pictures. You know the ones where the cowboy rides off into the sunset. Only this is supposed to represent *all* the horses riding off into the sunset in *all* those movies. (Interview transcript; June 16, 1994)

Along with idea generation, two other components were central to the art-work phase, that of technical instruction and problem solving.

KC knew her students "wanted things to look real," so she gave them technique instruction which would aid them (Field notes; March 19, 1994). She used visual resources, demonstrated and repeatedly spoke of changing values to create the illusion of depth. "Those flat colors are a good start, Drake, now add some darker and some lighter right here" (Transcript; December 2, 1993). "See how this artist did that?" (Video notes; April 21, 1994). "Look at how these clouds are really flat on the bottom (referring to a photo), can you do that with yours?" (Transcript; December 9, 1993).

Formal and informal demonstrations were part of the mix. She spent two class periods in November discussing color theory and demonstrating scumbling, blending, and impressionistic paint strokes on her own painting. During the demonstration she discussed how painting was fun "because you can't make a mistake. You can let it dry and paint right over it" (Field notes; October 20 and 28, 1993).

In one-to-one situations, she would mix a bit of paint on the newspaper next to a painting, or add a little to a student's picture. The students seemed to regard this positively, as Elenie indicated: "Mrs. C. will start something on a little part of my painting, and then I get it" (Interview transcript; June 16, 1994). Most students did indeed "get it," demonstrating sophisticated layers of subtle shading in each semester's paintings.

When students encountered difficulty, they usually raised their hands or asked a friend. KC worked around the class clockwise, trying to touch base with each student as work sessions progressed. Students were confident in her help. Asked what they did when they had a problem, most responded "I ask Mrs. C." If KC was unavailable, most indicated that they would wait until she was (Interview transcripts; June 21 and 22, 1994). Jack, however, admitted that he would "walk around and get noisy" until he figured out what to do (Interview transcript; June 21, 1994). Besides demonstrating, KC frequently referred students to the visual resources. "Why don't you look in…" "See if you can find the book where the picture of…" was a repeated song in Challenge Art. The book/visual reference table usually had two or three students thumbing through visuals to find their own help.

Informal peer instruction was common. However, it seemed limited to problems like color mixing or texture. "I mixed red and that dark blue and a little brown for this" (Video notes; March 10, 1994). They also sought affirmation from each other: "Clara, what do you think of this?" "It's great, Mildred, but you need some more of that dark stuff there. It's all the same" (Transcript, December 1, 1993). They sought this affirmation in the same tone as they asked about social things like "Do you like my new sweater?" From their friends, they expected positive answers. From KC they expected help.

While giving them tools to help them achieve realism, KC also encouraged individual styles. "Wow, that's surrealistic, Jack" (Transcript; December 21, 1993). "Your clouds have that impressionistic feel, Clara" (Transcript; December 21, 1993). The art history and stylistic references were not accidental; rather, she attempted to reinforce earlier learning along with providing affirmation.

Phase four: The critique. Two sorts of critical activities were evident in the Challenge Art class: in-process assessment and whole class critique. Documented in several studies (Stokrocki, 1991), in-process assessment occurs as a teacher helps a student decide how well he or she is progressing. Adler (1982) refers to the practice of facilitating the fine tuning of student skills as "coaching."

In the Challenge Art class it was difficult to separate the one-on-one technical instruction from in-process assessment, as the instructional and assessment comments were so interwoven. Students sought affirmation and direction at the same time. Clara said: "What do you think, Mrs. C?" KC replied: "Oh, Clara. it's beautiful. The way you have layered those colors is wonderful. Let's put it up there so you can see it from a distance" (Transcript; December 9, 1993). Balancing the painting on the chalk tray, KC and Clara discussed the contrast. Clara could see that her dark colors needed a little light to afford more clarity. Since she seemed to love thickly layered colors, she would happily continue, following KC's gentle suggestions. The chalkboard sessions would also be used to demonstrate a student's successful use of a technique to the class. Elenie's skull and cactus was used as an exemplar of skillful shading. The now familiar "dark-medium-light" exhortation was heard as KC showed how Elenie's highlighting and shading made her cactus seem real enough to prickle (Video notes; December 16, 1993).

At the end of the Western art unit, the students entered the room in a chorus of "oohs and aahs," discovering their paintings carefully balanced on drawers and counters along the north wall. As students perched on tables and chairs, KC announced that they would be "looking for things that work well, and for things that can be improved" (Transcript; December 21, 1993). Pointing out similarities and differences in technique and subject matter, KC had students point out evidences of scumbling, blending, and shading. She contrasted stylistic and color treatments of similar subject matter in discussing the several skull pastels and paintings. The effects of color on mood were tied to those who used Cannon's riotous colors and those who demonstrated "soft, velvety colors" (Transcript; December 21, 1993). Although teacher talk dominated, students were encouraged to voice opinions, make connections, and find further examples of concepts under discussion.

Phase five: Exhibition. The exhibition phase of KC's teaching/learning rhythm brings the students into the adult artworld. KC firmly believes in ensuring that her students' work is seen publicly. She takes slides of all finished work, using some slides to show her other students as exemplars, others for presentations at state and national conferences. Inevitably, she shows the students these slides before a presentation, telling them she is "showing them off to other art teachers" (Transcript; October 9, 1993; March 3, 1994). One major difference between this phase and the others is that it occurs beyond the semester framework. Thus, the work from the fall semester may be exhibited in the spring, depending on exhibition schedules. However, with the number of continuing students, and KC's consistency, each student knows his or her work will be exhibited.

KC organizes a county-wide K–8 art show, inviting friends and family to the opening. Two of the last three such exhibitions have shared space with adult artists. KC feels that this is important, as the arts community can recognize the quality of student work, while the students have the opportunity to interact with adult artists and their patrons (Interview transcript; December 2, 1992). A fall exhibition at a university gallery allowed students to explain how they had devised their sculptures to assembled friends, family, and art educators. Even the quietest students responded with alacrity to professors' questions, with answers like "I just stuffed the gloves with cotton and painted on them" (Video notes; October 30, 1993).

The second semester public art project gave students numerous opportunities to make public statements about their art. The first arose when they spoke to the local historic neighborhood association con-

620 cerning their proposals for bridge murals. Using their sketch book information, students gave presentations on their drawings of buildings and events in the district, including historical information about the drawings' subjects. Mildred: "I did the circus wagon because they used to have a circus which would play in Murdock Park," followed by a bit she had written

625 about circus day in the late 1800s. Two girls who had worked together on a drawing did a well-rehearsed presentation which included historical fact, architectural preference, and comments on their collaborative process. A blurb on the evening television news about

630 the project was a precursor to other newscasts and newspaper features as the murals progressed. After the first newscast, KC made it a point to steer the reporters to the students, as she noted "they are the ones doing all the work" (Field notes; May 1, 1994).

635 The exhibitions, presentations, and news coverage had the effect of solidifying students' cognition about both art process and subject matter. The students' historical facts about local residences and events were well researched and accurately delivered. Describing

640 their research and art process to an audience served to increase their identification as "real" artists among themselves, their peers, their families, and the community (Interview transcripts; June 16 and 21, 1994).

Discussion and Implications for Further Research
Discussion

In this study, I attempted to describe how an effec-

645 tive art teacher and her artistically gifted students learn together over the course of a school year. Such description demonstrates how teacher and learning rhythms can impact a middle school class for artistically gifted students. The rhythm created by KC gave

650 the students a familiarity with several art processes, both as observers and creators, as they absorbed, reflected upon, created, and interpreted art images. Through exhibition and their own explanations to various publics, the artistically gifted middle school stu-

655 dents became part of the art world as they helped others interpret and understand their work. Finally, the circular, rhythmic translation process cemented students' self-identification as "real" artists with peers, family, and community.

660 Clark and Zimmerman (1984, 1988) and Zimmerman (1991, 1992) discussed the importance to artistically gifted students of peer interaction and substantive teaching. KC and her students extend the understanding of what substantive teaching may be.

665 The nature of qualitative research is a collaboration between researcher and researched, as interpretations are clarified, or transcriptions revisited. The research process itself has helped KC reflect upon her own practice. Discussing and watching the growth of her

670 students, through her own and another's eyes, has made her more aware of the choices she makes as she plans, prepares for, and teaches these students. She

recognizes the rhythmic nature of her curriculum.

675 "That's what I do, all right" (Field notes; October 29, 1994). She comprehends the translation concept, linking it with Renzulli's (1977) real products for real audiences (Field notes; October 29, 1994). Reflecting and collaborating allowed KC to perceive the effects of the publicity surrounding the bridge murals from her

680 students' point of view. As a result, she plans to continue community-based projects for her Challenge students. Included in her future plans are a sculpture for the school and murals for a local community center.

Implications for Research

KC and teacher effectiveness definitions. This study

685 began in a quest to understand more about teacher effectiveness in conjunction with artistically gifted students. Reflecting the nature of qualitative study, the results of this research are idiosyncratic. Yet KC does demonstrate some characteristics noted in effective art

690 teachers such as valuing art education, organizational skills, and awareness of students' developmental and social needs (Capet, 1986; May, 1993; Saunders, 1989; Stokrocki, 1991; Thomas, 1992). She also meets some of Clark and Zimmerman's (1988, 1992, 1995) rec-

695 ommendations for teaching artistically gifted students: substantive teaching, providing access to professional level visual resources, and solid technical instruction. Evidenced in the discussion of each of the five phases is the way in which KC combines these qualities as she

700 translates student-artworld languages making her teaching and the learning of her students effective.

Translation. The translation concept may be potentially significant for those responsible for developing meaningful artistically gifted/talented programming.

705 Teachers and administrators may be able to discern the importance of bringing the outside world to the gifted/talented classroom and vice versa. Particularly at the tumultuous middle-school age, self-identification is an important issue. Clark and Zimmerman (1988) dis-

710 cussed the effects of positive peer interaction in artistically gifted classes. KC's students reflected that positive peer, family, school, and teacher influence. It may be meaningful to continue to monitor the students' self-identification as artists to discern any long-lasting ef-

715 fects.

If teachers and administrators can develop programs that allow students to see themselves as real contributors, artistically gifted students may have a better understanding of the positive ramifications of

720 their special abilities.

Curriculum rhythm. The concept of curricular rhythm has potential as a tool for understanding more about teacher effectiveness. Although the idea developed as a way of describing the chronology of content

725 in one class, it is a concept with resonance. Research may determine other styles of rhythms which exist in effective art teaching. Patterns of common traits may be found in particularly effective curricular rhythms, or

730 effective rhythms may be found to be idiosyncratic to class or teacher. Rhythm types may link with specific teaching styles or unique populations in effective classrooms. Cross-case analysis, the method by which many qualitative studies are analyzed, may provide more illumination into the possibilities of the rhythm concept 735 and its relationship to teaching effectiveness.

Eisner (1993) called for "fine grained study, description, interpretation, and evaluation of what actually goes on in art classrooms" (p.54). This paper is an attempt to heed that call. KC is a highly effective 740 teacher, working with her school's "best artists." She demonstrates many qualities cited in research as part of being effective. However, through her unique translation process, involving a carefully developed curriculum rhythm conducted with her gifted students' needs 745 at the forefront, KC has forged her own brand of effectiveness from which we each may take pieces to use in our own practical or theoretical applications.

References

Adler, M. (1982). *The paideia proposal.* New York: Collier Books, MacMillan.

Amidon, E., & Flanders, N. (1967). *The role of the teacher in the classroom.* Minneapolis, MN: Paul Amidon and Associates.

Blumer, H. (1967/1986). *Symbolic interactionism: Perspective and method.* Englewood Cliffs, NJ: Prentice Hall.

Bradley, L. (1984). Legislative impact on art teacher certification standards. *Action in Teacher Education 6*(4), 43–46.

Bresler, L. (1994). Zooming in on the qualitative paradigm in art education: Educational criticism, ethnography, and action research. *Visual Arts Research, 20*(1), 1–21.

Capet, M. (1986). An exploratory study of teaching visual arts grades one through eight: A phenomenological account of teacher cues, assumptions, intuition, and dialog during a studio experience and their implications for future research. (Doctoral dissertation, University of California, Los Angeles, 1986). *Dissertation Abstracts International.* (University Microfilms no. ADD85-00582).

Clark, G. (1989). Screening and identifying students talented in the visual arts: Clark's Drawing Abilities Test. *Gifted Child Quarterly, 33*(3), 98–105.

Clark, G., & Zimmerman, E. (1984). *Educating artistically talented students.* Syracuse, NY: Syracuse University Press.

Clark, G., & Zimmerman, E. (1988). Views of self, family background, and school: Interviews with artistically talented students. *Gifted Child Quarterly, 32*(4), 340–346.

Clark, G., & Zimmerman, E. (1992). *Issues and practices related to identification of gifted and talented students in the visual arts.* Storrs, CT: The National Research Center on the Gifted and Talented.

Clark, G., & Zimmerman, E. (1995). Programming opportunities for students gifted and talented in the visual arts. *Translations: From theory to practice, 5*(1), 1–6.

Department of Commerce. (1990). *1990 Census of population and housing: Population and housing characteristics for census tracts and block numbering areas 1990 CPH-3-199, Lafayette-West Lafayette, IN MSA.* Washington, DC: U.S. Government Printing Office.

Dillon, D. (1989). Showing them that I want them to learn and that I care about who they are: A microethnography of the social organization of a secondary low track English reading classroom. *American Educational Research Journal, 26*(2), 227–259.

Eisner, E. (1993). The emergence of new paradigms for educational research. *Art Education, 46*(6), 50–55.

Ettinger, L. (1987). Styles of on-site descriptive research: A taxonomy for art educators. *Studies in Art Education, 28*(2), 79–95.

Feldhusen, J., & Hansen, J. (1994). A comparison of trained and untrained teachers of gifted students. *Gifted Child Quarterly, 38*(3), 115–123.

Glaser, B., & Strauss, A. (1967). *The discovery of grounded theory: Strategies for qualitative research.* Chicago: Aldine.

Hathaway, J. (Ed.). (1980). *Art education: Middle/junior high school* (3rd printing). Reston, VA: National Art Education Association, 59–63.

Indiana Work Force Development (1993). *Highlights: Tippecanoe County, 1993 edition.* Lafayette, IN: Indiana Work Force Development.

Jacob, E. (1987). Qualitative research traditions: A review. *Review of Educational Research, 57*(1), 1–50.

Langlois, D., & Zales, C. (1991). Anatomy of a top teacher. *American School Board Journal, 178,* 44–46.

Maitland-Gholson, J., & Ettinger, L. (1994). Interpretative decision making in research. *Studies in Art Education, 36*(1), 18–27.

May, W. (1993). Good teachers making the best of it: Case studies of elementary art and music teaching. *Elementary Subjects' Center Series No. 100.* East Lansing, MI: Office of Educational Research and Improvement, Washington, DC, Center for Learning and Teaching of Elementary Subjects. (ERIC Documentation Reproduction Service No. ED 360 230.)

Patton, M. (1990). *Qualitative evaluation and research methods* (2nd edition). Newbury Park, CA: Sage Publications.

Renzulli, J. (1977). *The Enrichment triad model: A guide for developing defensible programming for the gifted and talented.* Mansfield Center, CT: Creative Learning Press.

Saunders, H. (1989). How to select an effective art teacher. *NASSP Bulletin,* May 1989, *4,* 54–69.

Stokrocki, M. (1991). A decade of qualitative research in art education: Methodology expansions and pedagogical explorations. *Visual Arts Research, 17*(1), 42–51.

Strauss, A. (1987). *Qualitative analysis for social scientists.* New York: Cambridge University Press.

Thomas, R. (1992). Art Education: Program evaluation report. Orlando, FL: Orange County Public Schools. (ERIC Document Reproduction Service No. ED 357 057.)

Zimmerman, E. (1991). Rembrandt to Rembrandt: A case study of a memorable painting teacher of artistically talented 13–16 year old students. *Roeper Review, 13*(2), 76–80.

Zimmerman, E. (1992). A comparative study of two painting teachers of talented adolescents. *Studies in Art Education, 33*(3), 174–185

Exercise for Case 7

1. Introduction

A. Is the problem area for the research clearly described? Explain.

B. Has the researcher convinced you that the problem area is important? Explain.

C. To what extent does the literature presented in the introduction help you understand the problem? Is the literature used to put the problem in context? Explain.

D. Does the researcher indicate how this study is different from and/or similar to earlier ones reported in the literature?

E. Does the researcher reveal her personal perspectives on the problem area, including any possible biases? Explain.

2. Methods

A. Are the demographics of the participants (i.e., background characteristics such as age, race, and so on) described in sufficient detail? Explain.

B. Considering the problem area for the research, do you think that appropriate participants were selected? If you had been conducting the study, would you have selected the same type(s) of participants? Would you have used the same number of participants? Explain.

C. Which strategies listed in Table 1 on page 161 of this book were employed by the researcher? Are they described in sufficient detail? Explain.

D. In addition to those you named in response to question 2C, has the researcher used any additional strategies to help assure the validity of the study? If yes, what are they? Are they described in sufficient detail? Explain.

3. Analysis and Results

A. Are the steps taken in the analysis described in sufficient detail? Explain.

B. Are the results clearly organized? Explain.

C. Are the results discussed in terms of a theory or theories (either theories that emerged from this study or previously existing ones)? Explain.

D. Were the direct quotations of the participants' statements, if any, judiciously selected? Do they help you understand the results? Explain.

E. Are there other ways the results could have been organized and interpreted? Explain.

4. Conclusions/Implications

A. Are the researcher's concluding remarks appropriate? Do they flow logically from the material presented earlier?

B. Does the researcher describe any implications? If yes, are they appropriate? Are there other implications that are not discussed by the researcher? Explain.

5. Ethical Considerations

A. In your opinion, could this research have caused physical or psychological harm to the participants? If yes, did the researcher take adequate measures to ameliorate the potential for harm? Explain.

B. If you had conducted this research, would you have obtained written, informed consent from the participants before conducting the study? Explain. Does this research report indicate that the researcher obtained such consent?

6. Overall Evaluation

A. Throughout the article, are all specialized terms and jargon defined to your satisfaction? Explain.

B. Briefly describe your overall evaluation of the research report, noting any special strengths and weaknesses.

C. If you had been a reviewer for the journal in which this report was published, would you have recommended publication of the report? If yes, would you have recommended that it be published "as is" or modified before publication? Explain. If no, what is the primary reason why you would recommend not publishing it?

In the Service of Citizenship: A Study of Student Involvement in Community Service

ROBERT A. RHOADS
Michigan State University

From *The Journal of Higher Education*, 69, 277–297. Copyright © 1998 by Ohio State University Press. Reprinted with permission.

Introduction

I learn more through my volunteer work than I ever do in any of my classes at school. Talking to people from diverse backgrounds provides so much insight that people just can't imagine. I study all these different theories in
5 political science and sociology, but until you get a chance to see how the social world influences people's everyday lives, it just doesn't have that much meaning.

I have been involved in volunteer work ever since I was in high school, and I'll probably continue to do stuff like
10 Habitat [for Humanity] until I'm old and gray. I get a lot out of working to serve others, and it's a good feeling to know that I have helped someone even if it's in some small way. It helps me to cherish people more and understand what life is all about.

15 The preceding comments are from college students who discussed their involvement in community service and the meaning they derive from such activities. Both of these students give voice to a form of learning that may be termed "citizenship education" in that a con-
20 cern for the social good lies at the heart of the educational experience (Delve, Mintz, & Stewart, 1990). These students are reflective of others described throughout this article who through participation in community service explore their own identities and
25 what it means to contribute to something larger than their individual lives.

In recent years, the role of higher education as a source of citizenship preparation has come to the forefront. In this regard, higher education reflects a rising
30 tide of concern for national service and the common good, as programs such as AmeriCorps, Learn and Serve America, Habitat for Humanity, and Big Brothers and Big Sisters have evoked our most prominent leaders as well as citizens across the country to commit
35 themselves to the service of others. The influence this national movement has had on the academy is most apparent in the growth of organizations such as Campus Compact and Campus Outreach Opportunity League (COOL) whose memberships and influence

40 increased dramatically in the early 1990s (Markus, Howard, & King, 1993). Professional organizations associated with the academic enterprise also have added fuel to the growing concern over social responsibility and citizenship. For example, in 1997 the call
45 for proposals from the American Association for Higher Education Conference on Faculty Roles and Rewards specifically identified an interest in how community service and service learning contribute to a more engaged faculty. The 1996 Annual Meeting of the
50 American Educational Research Association was organized around the theme of "Research for Education in a Democratic Society," and at the 1995 American College Personnel Association Annual Convention, one of the keynote speakers, Dr. Robert Coles, ad-
55 dressed the issue of moral education when he called for greater commitment to service learning and community service.

Although it is hard to argue with calls to foster social responsibility among our students, our future lead-
60 ers, there also is a tremendous need for clarification. With this said, the following key questions offer a guide for addressing some of the confusion revolving around community service: (1) Are community service and service learning interchangeable concepts or are
65 there important differences? (2) What is the role of community service in engaging students as democratic citizens in a culturally diverse society? (3) Are there variations in the structure of service activities which produce different experiences for students? The first
70 question is examined as I explore the relevant literature on community service and service learning. The second and third questions are addressed primarily through discussions of the theoretical perspective, findings, and implications. Thus, the latter two questions form the
75 heart of the theoretical and empirical analysis offered throughout this article. In weaving theoretical and empirical work together to address these questions, I follow the tradition of critical theory and support the argument that all research is theoretically rooted: Some-
80 times the perspective of the author is spelled out (as in this case), while at other times it must be interpreted based on the assumptions undergirding the work (Tierney & Rhoads, 1993). This is by no means a rejection of empiricism in favor of theory, but instead should be

85 understood as an effort to bridge the gap separating the two.

Community Service and Service Learning

Over recent years there has been an incredible growth in attention paid to community service and service learning (Jacoby & Associates, 1996; Kendall, 90 1990; Kraft, 1996; Kraft & Swadener, 1994; Rhoads, 1997; Waterman, 1997; Zlotkowski, 1995). The increasing interest in service reflects to a large degree a concern that institutions of higher education be more responsive to society and that higher learning in gen-95 eral ought to have greater relevance to public life (Boyer, 1987, 1994; Study Group, 1984; Wingspread Group, 1993). A convincing argument could be made that for American colleges and universities a commitment to service "is a movement whose time has come" 100 (Rhoads & Howard, 1998, p. 1).

The issue to be addressed in this brief review of the literature concerns distinguishing community service from service learning. The primary difference between these two concepts is the direct connection service 105 learning has to the academic mission. Typically, service learning includes student participation in community service but with additional learning objectives often associated with a student's program of study. For example, a student majoring in social work may par-110 ticipate in service activities at a local homeless shelter in conjunction with a course of study on urban poverty. Specific activities designed to assist the student in processing his or her experience are included as part of the service learning project. The student, for example, 115 may be expected to write a reflective paper describing the experience and/or there may be small-group interactions among students involved in similar kinds of experiences. The learning objective might be to help students interpret social and economic policies through 120 a more advanced understanding of the lived experiences of homeless citizens. Seen in this light, service learning seeks to connect community service experiences with tangible learning outcomes. Assessing such outcomes becomes a central concern of research and 125 evaluation (Boss, 1994; Giles & Eyler, 1994).

Although service learning often is specifically tied to classroom-related community service in which concrete learning objectives exist, some writers suggest that student involvement in community service may be 130 tied to out-of-class learning objectives and thus constitute a form of service learning as well (Jacoby & Associates, 1996; Rhoads, 1997). From this perspective, student affairs professionals who involve students in community service activities may engage in the 135 practice of service learning when there are clearly articulated strategies designed to bridge experiential and developmental learning. The confusion between "class-related" versus "out-of-class-related" service learning led Rhoads and Howard (1998) to adopt the term "aca-140 demic service learning" to distinguish the formal cur-

riculum (largely faculty initiated) from the informal curriculum (largely student affairs initiated). Howard (1998), for example, defined academic service learning as "a pedagogical model that intentionally integrates 145 academic learning and relevant community service" (p. 22). For Howard there are four components of academic service learning. First, it is a pedagogical model and is therefore to be understood as a teaching methodology. Second, academic service learning is inten-150 tional; that is, there are specific goals and objectives tying the service experience to course work. Third, there is integration between experiential and academic learning. And finally, the service experience must be relevant to the course of study. As Howard explains, 155 "Serving in a soup kitchen is relevant for a course on social issues, but probably not for a course on civil engineering" (p. 22).

From an educational standpoint, it makes sense to link community service activities with intentional 160 learning objectives whenever possible. Obviously, when student participation in community service can be connected to specific learning activities involving reflection, group interaction, writing, and so on, the experience is likely to have a greater impact on student 165 learning and move into the realm of service learning (Cooper, 1998; Eyler, Giles, & Schmiede, 1996).

In addition to varying degrees of connection community service may have to academic learning objectives, there are also differing opinions on which goals 170 of higher education service ought to address. Whereas Howard stresses the role of service as a pedagogical model used to assist in course-related learning, others see service (community service and service learning) as a key strategy for fostering citizenship (Harkavy & 175 Benson, 1998; Mendel-Reyes, 1998; Rhoads, 1998). This vision of community service and service learning is captured most pointedly in the philosophical work of John Dewey, in which education is fundamentally linked to the social good and what it means to exist in 180 relation to others.

Theoretical Perspective: Dewey, Mead, and Gilligan

This article is grounded in the philosophical work of John Dewey and his contention that education has a vital role to play in a democratic society. In his classic work *Democracy and Education,* Dewey argued that a 185 democratic society demands a type of relational living in which one's decisions and actions must be made with regard to their effect on others. "A democracy is more than a form of government; it is primarily a mode of associated living, of conjoint communicated experi-190 ence. The extension in space of the number of individuals who participate in an interest so that each has to refer his own action to that of others, and to consider the action of others to give point and direction to his own" (1916, p. 93). Dewey's vision of democracy 195 challenges all citizens to take part in a form of decision making that balances the interests of oneself with those of others. Democracy seen in this light demands that individuals understand the lives and experiences of other members of a society. How else can we weigh the effect of our actions if others remain distant and unknown?

Implied throughout Dewey's conception of democracy is an ethic-of-care philosophy akin to the work of feminist scholars such as Gilligan (1982) and Young (1990), in which caring for others forms a core component of identity (often discussed as the "relational self"). This is conveyed in Dewey's view of liberty: "Liberty is that secure release and fulfillment of personal potentialities which take place only in rich and manifold association with others" (1927, p. 150). Recent political theorists such as Battistoni (1985) also have recognized the importance of developing relational understandings of social life. For example, Battistoni supported Tocqueville's (1945) claim that American democracy is dependent upon "the reciprocal influence of men upon one another" (p. 117). For Battistoni, reciprocal influence is fostered through participatory forms of education, which he claimed are more likely to foster citizens who see themselves as active participants in the political process. Similarly, in discussing the relationship between citizenship and education, Barber argued that citizens must recognize their dependence upon one another and that "our identity is forged through a dialectical relationship with others" (1992, p. 4). Barber calls attention to the idea that citizenship is fundamentally tied to identity. Mead and Gilligan provide additional insight into the connection between citizenship and identity through their respective concepts of the "social self" and the "relational self."

Mead's (1934) idea of the social self derives in part from James (1890) and Cooley (1902), who both suggested that an individual's self-conception derives from the responses of others mirrored back to the individual. Mead argued that the self forms out of the interaction between the "I" and the "me." The "I" is the individual acting out some sort of behavior; the individual doing something such as talking, listening, interacting with others, expressing an idea. The "me" relates to the sense one has about the "I" who is acting out a behavior or set of behaviors. The sense we develop about the "I" derives from the interpretations we suspect that others have of us. We cannot develop an initial sense about ourselves without the help of others, who provide feedback and interact with the behaving "I." Through the imagined thoughts of others, we envision ourselves as a "me" as we become the object of our own thoughts. According to Mead, an individual cannot develop a sense of self without the interactive context of a social group or a community. Therefore, the other, either the particularized or generalized other, is essential to the development of the self.

Feminist theorists such as Gilligan also have developed a conception of the self strongly rooted in other-

ness. Gilligan (1979, 1982) was one of the first theorists to point out that women often make moral decisions based on a sense of connection with others. She argued that women's moral decision making reflected a fundamental identity difference based on gender. Whereas men tend to seek autonomy and make moral decisions founded on abstract principles such as justice, women, in general, seek connectedness and weigh moral decisions based on maintaining or building relationships.

As a result of early child-parent interactions and ongoing gender socialization (which arguably begins at birth), relationships become central to the social world of women (Chodorow, 1974, 1978). For men, the relational quality of social life is often displaced by a strong sense of individualism. The other is fundamentally a part of women's experience and kept at somewhat of a distance for men. The development of the self for females may be characterized by connectedness. Male development may be characterized by individuation. These general patterns (which obviously vary in degree from one individual to the next) have significant implications for how males and females relate to others and how they understand themselves in the context of the social world.

Based in part on early feminist work, various scholars have argued that regardless of gender differences, society is likely to benefit when its members develop a commitment to caring (Larrabee, 1993; Noddings, 1984, 1992, 1995; Oliner & Oliner, 1995). This is poignantly noted by Sampson (1989), who argued,

> The feminist perspective should no longer be understood as developing a psychology of women but, I believe, is better seen as developing a psychology of humanity tomorrow. The real issue, therefore, does not involve gender differences per se, as much as it speaks to an emerging theory of the person that is appropriate to the newly emerging shape of a globally linked world system. (p. 920)

Of course, Sampson's point about the "globally linked world" reminds us of an earlier issue raised in this article concerning how cultural diversity might influence citizenship education (recall key question Number 2: What is the role of community service in engaging students as democratic citizens in a culturally diverse society?). Arguably, as a society grows increasingly diverse, communications are likely to become more challenging. Cultural differences, though they may be understood as a source of community for learning and sharing among citizens (Tierney, 1993), nonetheless pose a significant challenge to social interaction and an individual's ability to connect with the other, who, in the case of a heterogeneous society, is likely to be a diverse other.

Woven together, Dewey, Mead, and Gilligan, among others, provide insight into how citizenship education might encompass learning about the self, the other, and the larger society in which one exists. The

"caring self" is the term I use to capture the synthesis of their work. The caring self is intended to convey the
315 idea of a socially oriented sense of self founded on an ethic of care and a commitment to the social good. Furthermore, it is reasonable to assume that community service, with its focus on caring for others, would offer excellent settings to explore the development of the
320 caring self. But is this the case, and if so, in what kinds of service contexts are the qualities associated with the caring self likely to be forged?

This brings me to the crux of my argument and what I intend to shed light on through a study of stu-
325 dent involvement in community service. Arguably, unless individuals have a deep sense of caring for others, it is less likely that they will engage in interactions with diverse others in a meaningful way. Caring may be seen as the solution to the challenge presented by a
330 postmodern society characterized by difference. In essence, I contend that fostering a deep commitment to caring is the postmodern developmental dilemma all of education faces, including higher education. If we are to promote democratic citizenship in these challenging
335 times, then we must foster in our citizens a commitment to caring. Higher education has a major part to play in this process, and involving students in community service may be one vehicle for meeting this challenge. The question that needs to be asked then, is,
340 How and in what kinds of community service settings is caring to be fostered? Before addressing this question through a discussion of the findings, I first clarify the methodology used in conducting the study.

Methodology

The primary goal of this article is to advance under-
345 standing of community service as a strategy for citizenship education. Through a qualitative study of college students involved in community service, I shed light on various facets of the service context that may be most beneficial to challenging students as caring citizens.
350 The focus is not on student learning per se; instead, I target the kind of meaning students construct about their service encounters as a means to identify important aspects of community service associated with caring. I need to be clear here. This article does not at-
355 tempt to assess developmental change by examining student involvement in community service. Although such a strategy is important and falls in line with the tradition of student outcomes research (Astin, 1979, 1993; Feldman & Newcomb, 1970; Pascarella & Ter-
360 enzini, 1991), this article takes more of a phenomenological direction in which the essence of community service is the primary concern. Hence, the kind of experiences students describe are important in this study, not as learning outcomes, but as indications of the na-
365 ture of the service context.

The data for this article were derived from research and participation in community service projects conducted in conjunction with three universities: Pennsyl-
370 vania State University, the University of South Carolina, and Michigan State University. Community service projects ranged from week-long intensive experiences requiring travel to distant out-of-state communities to ongoing student service projects in the local communities or states in which these universities are
375 situated. I participated as a volunteer in many of the service projects described throughout this article. My role ranged from a staff supervisor in a few cases to that of a graduate student volunteer with limited responsibility in other instances. In every case, my pri-
380 mary role was as a volunteer and not as a researcher; the data I collected was more of an outgrowth of the community service experience and was not the central objective. The comments here are not meant to shortchange the research strategy employed, but instead are
385 intended to clarify for the reader the context of my interactions and involvement with the student volunteers. In fact, my role as a volunteer may actually add strength to the naturalistic strategies used in collecting data as I was able to engage in ongoing and meaningful
390 dialogue with the research participants (Denzin, 1989).

Based on the methodological strategies associated with naturalistic inquiry, data were collected using a variety of techniques, including formal and informal interviews, surveys, participant observation, and
395 document analysis (Lincoln & Guba, 1985). The principal documents used as a source of data were journals students were asked to keep as part of their community service experience. The use of multiple data collection techniques provides a degree of triangulation and offers
400 the researcher an opportunity to confirm or reject tentative interpretations (Denzin, 1989).

The early phase of the study was conducted in conjunction with Pennsylvania State University and the data obtained was part of a formal evaluation of com-
405 munity service activities by students. This phase of the project involved surveys of students' experiences and was considered program evaluation and as such did not require human subject approval at Penn State. The second phase, which primarily involved interviews and
410 observations, necessitated gaining human subject approval. Students were informed of the study and given the opportunity to participate or decline. It was during this phase of the study that student journals were used, but only with student approval.
415 During the six-year period (1991–1996) in which data were collected, 108 students participated in interviews, 66 students completed open-ended surveys, and more than 200 students were observed at various project sites in which participant observation was central.
420 Approximately 90% of the students involved in the community service projects were undergraduates, and about 10% were graduate students. The vast majority (approximately 80%) of the undergraduates were traditional-age students in the range of 18 to 24 years old.
425 Females represented approximately 60% of the sample, and in terms of race, the majority were Caucasian

(roughly 85%), with African Americans constituting the largest minority group—about 8 to 10% of the overall group.

Interview transcripts (from both formal and informal interviews), open-ended surveys, field notes from participant observation, student journals, and documents collected in conjunction with various service projects form the entire data base for the study. Once collected, the data were read repeatedly in an effort to identify important and relevant themes. The process followed the kind of analytical strategy stressed in the work of cultural anthropologists and interpretivists (Geertz, 1973; Rosaldo, 1989). Specifically, themes were identified based on their contextual significance and relevance to the overall goal of the project: *to better understand the context of community service and how such activities might challenge students' understandings of citizenship and the social good.* In a procedure described by Lincoln and Guba (1985) as "member checks," themes and interpretations were shared with several students as part of a process to obtain feedback and incorporate student reactions into the final manuscripts.

Based on the data analysis, several themes were identified. Three of those themes—students' explorations of the self, understandings of others, and views of the social good—form the basis for this article. Other issues, such as "student motivation" for getting involved in community service and "attitudes toward community service," are examples of additional themes that emerged from the data analysis but are peripheral to this article and thus are not discussed in any substantive way.

Findings

In keeping with the theoretical concern of democratic citizenship and fostering more caring selves, the findings are organized around three general concerns suggested by students in discussing their participation in community service: self-exploration, understanding others, and the social good. These themes are highly interactive and, in general, students' exploration in all of these areas contributes to understanding what I describe as the caring self.

Self-Exploration

Participation in community service is an educational activity that lends itself to identity clarification. For example, a student who was part of an intensive week-long community service project in South Carolina talked about identity issues and her participation in the project: "I'm kind of in a search for my own identity, and this trip is part of that search. I just don't know quite who I am yet. I'm struggling to figure it all out. These kinds of experiences help. I'm most genuine in these kinds of settings." Another student added, "Getting involved in community service helps me to get back in touch with who I really am. It reminds me that I have more to live for than merely myself." A

third student offered the following comments:

I've always done service work. During my freshman year at USC [University of South Carolina] I worked on the City Year project and the Serv-a-thon. I believe service is an important part of leadership. It's important to give back to the community. The last four weeks I've been totally into myself, like running for vice president of the student body. I signed up for this project because I wanted to get outside myself for awhile.

This student saw the service project as an opportunity to connect with others and in her words "get outside" of herself. For her, the service project offered a chance to become more other-focused and to contribute to her community.

A second student described her involvement in community service as part of a journey to better understand herself: "My work as a volunteer has really helped me to see that I have so much more to understand about myself in order to grow. I'm still on the journey and have a long way to go." And a third student discussed what he learned about himself: "I got involved in volunteerism because I wanted to learn more about myself. I've learned how to love a wide range of people despite differences between us. I've learned not to be judgmental." A fourth offered insight into the kind of soul searching students often go through as a result of service work:

Sometimes I feel like I'm only fooling myself and that I'm really only into service so that I can help myself. I list this stuff on my resume and I feel guilty because I know it will help me get a teaching job. Is that why I do this? I know it makes me feel better about what I do in my spare time, but who am I really serving?

This student recognized, like others, the positive returns of service, not only in terms of experience helpful for landing employment, but for the feelings reflected back to the self.

Self-exploration through community service often involved a kind of self-interrogation that helped students to think more seriously about their lives. Listen to the following student as she recalled her volunteer work with troubled youth:

I got involved in a lot of self-esteem work, primarily with teenagers. It helped me to think more seriously about my understanding of myself and how others think of me. I began to wonder about what kind of person I was and was going to be. I began to ask questions of myself: "Am I too judgmental? Am I open to others? Am I sensitive to how other people see the world?"

Once again, the role of community service in challenging one's sense of self is clear. Equally clear is how one's sense of self is tied to the social context and the views others hold of us.

Understanding Others

A significant learning experience associated with community service was the opportunity to better understand the lives students worked to serve. Students were able to put faces and names with the alarming statistics and endless policy debates about homelessness as well as rural and urban poverty. As one student explained,

> Expressing what it has meant to me to actually have the chance to engage in conversations with people who used to be total strangers is next to impossible. It has been eye opening. My understanding of homeless people was based on what I'd see on the news, in magazines, or on TV shows. They were not real people and I could easily turn my back on them and the problem in general.

Similar comments were offered by Penn State and Michigan State students involved in community service projects working with homeless citizens in DC, Louisville, and New York City:

> Every homeless person has a name, a story.

> They just want to be recognized and treated as human beings. There are names behind the statistics.

> Working with the people of the streets has transformed "those people" into real faces, real lives, and real friends. I can no longer confront the issue without seeing the faces of my new friends. This has an incredible effect on my impetus to help.

> All the statistics about homeless people and the stories of people freezing to death in the winter never really sunk in until I made friends with Harry and Reggie. There are faces now.

Students who worked in rural areas with low-income families also derived benefit from personal interactions with those they worked to serve. One student commented on the general outcomes associated with having personal interactions in service settings: "The whole experience helps you to see that others are real people and have real problems and yet can come together to help one another.... When you work with the people on their houses or in their back yard it adds to the experience. You get a chance to know the people. You have a face or a personality to go with the work." A second student stated, "The fact that we were able to interact a great deal with the people in the community added so much to the overall experience. I've done volunteer work in the past where I never really got the chance to meet with the people who I was actually trying to help." A third student, who participated in a week-long service project in a low-income rural area, added, "This week has taught me so much about other people and the problems they face in life. You can read about growing up poor, but getting to share a conversation with someone who has overcome so much during their lifetime is quite a different matter.... It's made me much less judgmental of others and their place in life."

A common point made by students was the fact that community service work with people of diverse cultural backgrounds forced students to confront generalizations they had of the other. For example, students talked about various stereotypes they held about poor people and how such stereotypes were erased as a result of their service work. Several students noted how surprised they were to find so many intelligent and educated people without jobs or places to live. One student maintained that the only accurate stereotype relates to the amount of bad luck that most homeless people have experienced. A second added, "I learned that all people are innately afraid and that no one deserves to be without a voice and a safe place and that stereotypes can be more damaging than can be fathomed." A third student talked about how his preconceptions about homeless people had been shattered through his interactions with them. As he explained, "This experience gave my beliefs and convictions about the homeless a personal basis that I'll never forget."

Many of the preconceptions students had about the poor were rooted in their limited experience with cultural diversity. Although socioeconomic factors were the primary source of difference between students and community members, race was another factor. Interactions with a variety of low-income individuals and families often challenged students' conceptions of the diverse other. Because the vast majority of the student volunteers were Caucasians and many of the community members served by the students were African Americans, a number of racial issues emerged from time to time. A Penn State sophomore talked about the difference she felt between herself and the large number of homeless African Americans she encountered during her volunteer work in DC: "I definitely felt a major barrier between Blacks and Whites in this country. There were times working in the soup kitchens where I felt very uncomfortable." A college junior studying mathematics commented on a similar feeling: "It was an experience for me simply to be placed in the awkward environment of walking around in predominantly African American, poor neighborhoods. I want to remember that feeling of insecurity. It reminds me of the vast differences between races in our society."

Often, issues of race and class blended together and challenged students' prejudices in a multifaceted way. Listen to the following two students discuss their experiences:

> There is something that I'm not proud of and I always considered myself open-minded and not prejudiced, but when I worked at Sharon's house [Sharon is an African American woman who needed repairs done to her home] it reminded me that some of my previous thinking about the poor had been based on stereotypes. I mean I've always kind of thought in the back of my mind that people become poor or destitute because they are not motivated or not as intelligent. But Sharon has a master's degree and is very articulate. I see now that there may be many causes or barriers that people face that can limit them. It was an eye opener and I see now that I was carrying this misconception about them being to blame for their plight.

> Meeting homeless people and talking with them taught me that some of my stereotypes about the poor, about

Blacks, have been rooted in my own life of White, middle-class privilege. I have never had to work that hard to get a college education, for example, yet I've bought into the idea that others who have less than me are somehow lazy because they are poor. Heck, they may have worked twice as hard as I have. I've never really had my views of the poor challenged until this experience working with homeless people.

The generalizations and stereotypes to which students referred were seen by several as the by-product of the media. As one student, a senior in geography, pointed out, "I learned that my perceptions of poverty, crime, and homelessness are influenced and perhaps shaped by misconstrued images that I see on television." Another student also talked about how television had played a major role in how she had come to envision African Americans. She pointed out that in her rural Pennsylvania community, "there wasn't a single African American family. I never even met an African American until I attended college."

The Social Good

As one might expect, given the context of caring for others, issues related to the social good often surfaced. Community service is ripe for such discussions and offers a context conducive to serious thought about the larger social body. One student offered an example of the kind of serious thought that may evolve from community service work:

> There are a lot of people in this country who need help to make ends meet. You can choose to help them or you can turn your back on them. I want to help people, and I want those who choose not to help to know that there are consequences for walking away. There are children who will go hungry and people who will be living in the streets. I cannot live with that on my conscience.

For this student, the social good suggests a world in which no one starves or goes homeless. Giving up some of his own time and energy to help others "make it" is in line with his vision of social responsibility.

Other students offered similar remarks about the social good. For example, one student commented, "Intellectual exploration has been rewarding but also suffocating at times and so I find the desire to commit myself to experiential work. I found one way could be by working in a homeless shelter and understanding social issues from a political standpoint as well as from the perspective of those living and breathing poverty."

For another student, the common good included the role of education in assisting the poor. He saw service as important, but there were deeper issues underlying poverty. He explained,

> Service activities are important, but we also have to help teach people how to fish. You just can't give people food or build houses for them without also helping them develop the skills to take care of their own lives and their own families.... Part of my goal is to help others to develop their own abilities so that they can lead productive lives.

This student alludes to the idea that simply providing "bandages," though important and necessary, may not heal deeper wounds. In this case, the student highlights how sometimes the problems rest with the poor and their limited skills.

Other students also concerned with the deeper roots of economic inequities chose to focus on social structure instead of individuals as part of their effort to make sense of the social good. For example, one student saw community service as a stepping stone to larger work for social change: "I need to be in community with people who are interested in radical social change. Together we can work and witness all kinds of changes, and perhaps come closer to finding some answers." Another student alluded to the structural aspects of poverty as she discussed her learning experiences:

> Community service is something that I think everybody should get involved doing. You see a different side of our country when you see some of the struggles the poor face. You begin to understand the barriers to their economic situation and why it is so hard to get out of poverty. I talked to this one woman, and she explained to me how expensive day care is for her children and that in order for her to take a job she needs to make at least eight to ten dollars an hour. And no one will pay her that.

For the preceding student, community service experience helped her identify a structural problem that limits low-income workers—the lack of affordable day care.

Not everyone who participated in this study saw service as necessarily a positive force for improving society. Listen to the following student take issue with some of the general comments he heard about the positive aspects of service:

> To be honest, and it's hard to say this around all these "do gooders," I'm not sure all this volunteer stuff really does a whole lot of good. I know, I'm one of those volunteers too. But I keep asking myself a bunch of questions: "Am I doing this to help the homeless or am I doing this to help myself? Who really benefits?" Maybe I'm being too skeptical, but I think most of the students here are like me but won't admit it. It makes them feel good to help feed someone, and that way they can go back to living their happy little lives without feeling too guilty.

Despite the biting cynicism of the preceding student's comments, he makes an important point that turns our attention back to the theoretical thrust of this article: The idea that one often develops positive feelings about oneself as a result of involvement in service reminds us that our sense of self indeed is tied to others. When warm feelings are shared with a student engaged in service, then logically, that student may see him or herself in a more favorable manner. The interactional context is one reason why community service is so critical to forging more caring selves. Through acts designed to serve others, students learn to feel better about themselves. At the same time, their relationship to others and to the larger social body is strengthened. Hopefully, reaching out becomes a way of life and the diversity that offers the potential to divide one from another becomes instead a source of sharing. This is the essence of the caring self.

Implications for Structuring Community Service

As noted earlier, this study was phenomenological in nature. The study did not seek to determine whether students become more caring citizens as a result of their service. Instead, by approaching the subject phenomenologically, I was able to identify aspects of the community service context that might contribute to students' considerations of the self, others, and the social good. The underlying assumption of course is that such considerations are likely to contribute positively to one's ongoing development as a caring citizen. Thus, in thinking about the implications of the findings I was able to identify three structural components of community service that appear to be critical to advancing citizenship as defined in this article. These key components are *mutuality, rejection,* and *personalization.*

There are two aspects of mutuality I stress: One aspect relates to a recognition that both parties—the so called "doers" and the "done to," in Radest's (1993) terms—benefit from the service encounter. Students involved in service receive incredible rewards for their work in the form of personal satisfaction. And, if their work is effective, community members also receive rewards in the form of a service provided. Thus, one might say that the experience is mutual.

The gifts that students receive through their community service offerings are not without complications. Students frequently expressed a degree of guilt for feeling good about themselves as a result of their service to others. A line from the great American poet, Delmore Schwartz, comes to mind here: "Nothing is given which is not taken." Taking or "receiving" the gifts offered by community members is something students engaged in service must learn to do. In fact, effective leadership training for students ought to prepare them to be recipients of the rewards of service. "In giving, one must learn to receive," noted one student who worked with homeless citizens in Washington, DC.

The second aspect of mutuality relates to the structure of the relationship between service providers and community members who may receive a specific service. Too often we are guilty of determining the needs of those to be served with little to no involvement on their part. For community service to be most effective for the development of caring citizens, then, the planning of such activities ought to include those to be served in an equal and empowering manner. After all, Dewey's conception of democracy entails each person taking others into consideration when making decisions affecting the public realm.

A second key to making community service most

effective for citizenship development is the inclusion of reflection as part of the service work. By the term "reflection" I refer to activities designed to help students process their service experiences in a manner involving serious thought. Small-group discussions and writing assignments are common tools used to foster student reflection. As is noted earlier in this article, community service that incorporates reflection moves closer to what is typically considered service learning in that the reflective activity helps to link service to an educational outcome.

Several of the service projects observed through this study did not involve structured reflection and the students' experiences suffered. One example occurred in New York City, where a young woman became so intimidated by her interactions with a homeless man who screamed profanities at her that she vowed to never again work with the homeless. The project she worked on was led entirely by students and there was no opportunity for guided reflection. In interviewing this student, I was left to ponder how her reaction might have been different had she been able to interact with an experienced facilitator. Would she have been able to work through her feelings and perhaps take something positive from the traumatic encounter?

Other examples from this study reveal the power of reflection. Recently, I accompanied a group of 23 students from Michigan State University to Merida in the Yucatan where we worked at a Salvation Army shelter for children, a low-income health facility, and a women's resource center. As part of helping MSU students process their experiences, staff volunteers facilitated reflection groups each evening after students returned from their work sites. At the end of the week, we evaluated the project and consistently students described the reflection activities as one of the highlights of their cross-cultural experience (despite the "educational" overtones such activities carried!).

Perhaps the most significant aspect of community service that I found to contribute to caring is what may be called the personalization of service. For community service to be challenging to a student's sense of self, it seems most beneficial for service to involve opportunities for meaningful interaction with those individuals to be served. Time and time again students discussed how significant it was for them to have the opportunity to interact with individuals and families on a personal basis.

Conclusion

The challenge of education to foster caring citizens has taken on enormous proportion in contemporary society as the struggle between individualism and social responsibility has taken on new meaning (Bellah, Sullivan, Swidler, & Tipton, 1985; Coles, 1993; Palmer, 1993; Parks Daloz, Keen, Keen, & Daloz Parks, 1996; Wuthnow, 1991, 1995). Community service is one option educators can select to enhance

880 the development of citizens concerned with the social good. Caring is central to the effectiveness of community service, and thus students are challenged to give serious thought to what it means to care as they strug-gle to evaluate their commitment to the lives of others.
885 Because the relationship between individuals and their obligation to one another is a cornerstone of democracy, community service may be seen to contribute to citizenship in a democratic society.

The students in this study highlight how cultural
890 diversity poses additional challenges to one's development as a caring citizen. They described how community service often is an interaction between diverse others. This is the essence of Radest's (1993) argument when he maintained that community service may be
895 seen as an "encounter with strangers" in which the challenge of service is that we each learn from the other and we each give as well as receive. From this perspective, community service represents a dialogical encounter with diverse others and serves as a bridge to
900 build communal ties. Thus, community service offers one vehicle for preparing students to communicate in a culturally diverse world.

Finally, because service encourages students to see themselves as intimately connected to the other, a
905 learning context is created in which the caring self is more likely to emerge. Fostering a sense of self grounded in an ethic of care is one of the central challenges of education and becomes increasingly important as our society grows more diverse. By fostering an
910 ethic of care, higher education encourages the sense of otherness needed for democracy to survive and, indeed, thrive in a complex and fragmented social world.

References

Astin, A. W. (1979). *Four critical years: Effects of college on beliefs, attitudes and knowledge*. San Francisco: Jossey-Bass.

Astin, A. W. (1993). *What matters in college?: Four critical years revisited*. San Francisco: Jossey Bass.

Barber, B. (1992). *An aristocracy of everyone: The politics of education and the future of America*. New York: Oxford University Press.

Battistoni, R. (1985). *Public schooling and the education of democratic citizens*. Jackson, MS: University Press of Mississippi.

Bellah, R. N., Sullivan, W. M., Swidler, A., & Tipton, S. M. (1985). *Habits of the heart: Individualism and commitment in American life*. New York: Harper & Row.

Boss, J. A. (1994). The effect of community service work on the moral development of college ethics students. *Journal of Moral Education, 23*(2), 183–198.

Boyer, E. L. (1987). *College: The undergraduate experience in America*. New York: Harper & Row.

Boyer, E. L. (1994, March 9). Creating the new American college. *Chronicle of Higher Education*, p. A 48.

Chodorow, N. (1974). Family structure and feminine personality. In M. Rosaldo & L. Lamphere (Eds.), *Women, culture and society* (pp. 43–66). Stanford, CA: Stanford University Press.

Chodorow, N. (1978). *The reproduction of mothering: Psychoanalysis and the sociology of gender*. Berkeley: University of California Press.

Coles, R. (1993). *The call of service: A witness to idealism*. Boston: Houghton Mifflin.

Cooley, C. H. (1902). *Human nature and the social order*. New York: Charles Scribner's Sons.

Cooper, D. (1998). Reading, writing, and reflection. In R. A. Rhoads & J. P. F. Howard (Eds.), *Academic service learning: A pedagogy of action and re-flection*. New Directions for Teaching and Learning, no. 73 (pp. 47–56). San Francisco: Jossey-Bass.

Delve, C. I., Mintz, S. D., & Stewart, G. M. (1990). *Community service as values education*. New Directions for Student Services, no. 50. San Fran-cisco: Jossey-Bass.

Denzin, N. (1989). *The research act* (3rd ed.). New York: Prentice-Hall.

Dewey, J. (1916). *Democracy and education*. New York: Macmillan.

Dewey, J. (1927). *The public and its problems*. New York: Henry Holt and Company.

Eyler, J., Giles, D. E., & Schmiede, A. (1996). *A practitioner's guide to reflec-tion in service-learning: Student voices and reflections*. Washington, DC: Corporation for National Service.

Feldman, K. A., & Newcomb, T. M. (1970). *The impact of college on students*. San Francisco: Jossey-Bass.

Geertz, C. (1973). *The interpretation of cultures*. New York: Basic Books.

Giles, D. E., Jr., & Eyler, J. (1994). The impact of a college community service laboratory on students' personal, social, and cognitive outcomes. *Journal of Adolescence, 17*, 327–339.

Gilligan, C. (1979). Woman's place in man's life cycle. *Harvard Educational Review, 9*(4), 431–446.

Gilligan, C. (1982). *In a different voice: Psychological theory and women's development*. Cambridge, MA: Harvard University Press.

Harkavy, I., & Benson, L. (1998). De-Platonizing and democratizing education as the bases of service learning. In R. A. Rhoads & J. P. F. Howard (Eds.), *Academic service learning: A pedagogy of action and reflection*. New Di-rections for Teaching and Learning, no. 73 (pp. 11–20). San Francisco: Jossey-Bass.

Howard, J. P. F. (1998). Academic service learning: A counternormative pedagogy. In R. A. Rhoads & J. P. F. Howard (Eds.), *Academic service learning: A pedagogy of action and reflection*. New Directions for Teaching and Learning, no. 73 (pp. 21–29). San Francisco: Jossey-Bass.

Jacoby, B., & Associates. (Eds.). (1996). *Service-learning in higher education: Concepts and practices*. San Francisco: Jossey-Bass.

James, W. (1890). *Principles of psychology* (Vol. 1). New York: Holt.

Kendall, J. C. (Ed.). (1990). *Combining service and learning: A resource book for community and public service* (Vol. 1). Raleigh, NC: National Society for Experiential Education.

Kraft, R. J. (1996). Service learning. *Education and Urban Society, 28*(2), 131–159.

Kraft, R. J., & Swadener M. (Eds.). (1994). *Building community: Service learning in the academic disciplines*. Denver: Colorado Campus Compact.

Larrabee, M. J. (Ed.). (1993). *An ethic of care: Feminist and interdisciplinary perspectives*. New York: Routledge.

Lincoln, Y. S., & Guba, E. G. (1985). *Naturalistic inquiry*. Beverly Hills: Sage.

Markus, G. B., Howard, J. P. F., & King, D. C. (1993). Integrating community service and classroom instruction enhances learning: Results from an ex-periment. *Educational Evaluation and Policy Analysis, 15*(4), 410–419.

Mead, G. H. (1934). *Mind, self, & society* (Charles W. Morris, Ed.). Chicago: University of Chicago Press.

Mendel-Reyes, M. (1998). A pedagogy for citizenship: Service learning and democratic education. In R. A. Rhoads & J. P. F. Howard (Eds.), *Academic service learning: A pedagogy of action and reflection*. New Directions for Teaching and Learning, no. 73 (pp. 31–38). San Francisco: Jossey-Bass.

Noddings, N. (1984). *Caring: A feminine approach to ethics and moral educa-tion*. Berkeley: University of California Press.

Noddings, N. (1992). *The challenge to care in schools: An alternative ap-proach to education*. New York: Teachers College Press.

Noddings, N. (1995). Teaching themes of care. *Phi Delta Kappan, 76*(9), 675–679.

Oliner, P. M., & Oliner, S. P. (1995). *Toward a caring society: Ideas into action*. Westport, CT: Praeger.

Palmer, P. (1993). *To know as we are known: Education as a spiritual journey*. San Francisco: Harper.

Parks Daloz, S., Keen, C. H., Keen, J. P., & Daloz Parks, L. A. (1996). *Com-mon fire: Lives of commitment in a complex world*. Boston: Beacon Press.

Pascarella, E. T., & Terenzini, P. T. (1991). *How college affects students: Findings and insights from twenty years of research*. San Francisco: Jossey-Bass.

Radest, H. (1993). *Community service: Encounter with strangers*. Westport, CT: Praeger.

Rhoads, R. A. (1997). *Community service and higher learning: Explorations of the caring self*. Albany: SUNY Press.

Rhoads, R. A. (1998). Critical multiculturalism and service learning. In R. A. Rhoads & J. P. F. Howard (Eds.), *Academic service learning: A pedagogy of action and reflection*. New Directions for Teaching and Learning, no. 73 (pp. 39–46). San Francisco: Jossey-Bass.

Rhoads, R. A., & Howard, J. P. F. (1998). *Academic service learning: A peda-gogy of action and reflection*. New Directions for Teaching and Learning, no. 73. San Francisco: Jossey-Bass.

Rosaldo, R. (1989). *Culture & truth: The remaking of social analysis*. Boston: Beacon.

Sampson, E. E. (1989). The challenge of social change for psychology: Glob-alization and psychology's theory of the person. *American Psychologist, 44*(6), 914–921.

Study Group on the Conditions of Excellence in American Higher Education. (1984). *Involvement in learning*. Washington, DC: National Institute of Edu-cation.

Tierney, W. G. (1993). *Building communities of difference: Higher education in the 21st century*. Westport, CT: Bergin & Garvey.

Tierney, W. G., & Rhoads, R. A. (1993). Postmodernism and critical theory in higher education: Implications for research and practice. In J. C. Smart (Ed.), *Higher education: Handbook of theory and research* (pp. 308–343). New York: Agathon.

Tocqueville, A., de (1945). *Democracy in America*. New York: Alfred A. Knopf.

Waterman, A. S. (Ed.). (1997). *Service learning: Applications from the research*. Mahwah, NJ: Lawrence Erlbaum Associates.

Wingspread Group on Higher Education. (1993). *An American imperative: Higher expectations for higher education*. Racine, WI: Johnson Foundation.

Wuthnow, R. (1991). *Acts of compassion: Caring for others and helping ourselves*. Princeton, NJ: Princeton University Press.

Wuthnow, R. (1995). *Learning to care: Elementary kindness in an age of indifference*. New York: Oxford University Press.

Young, I. M. (1990). The ideal of community and the politics of difference. In Linda J. Nicholson (Ed.), *Feminism/postmodernism* (pp. 300–323). New York: Routledge.

Zlotkowski, E. (1995). Does service learning have a future? *Michigan Journal of Community Service Learning*, 2(1), 123–133.

About the Author: Robert A. Rhoads is assistant professor in the Department of Educational Administration, Michigan State University.

Exercise for Case 8

1. Introduction

A. Is the problem area for the research clearly described? Explain.

B. Has the researcher convinced you that the problem area is important? Explain.

C. To what extent does the literature presented in the introduction help you understand the problem? Is the literature used to put the problem in context? Explain.

D. Does the researcher indicate how this study is different from and/or similar to earlier ones reported in the literature?

E. Does the researcher reveal his personal perspectives on the problem area, including any possible biases? Explain.

2. Methods

A. Are the demographics of the participants (i.e., background characteristics such as age, race, and so on) described in sufficient detail? Explain.

B. Considering the problem area for the research, do you think that appropriate participants were selected? If you had been conducting the study, would you have selected the same type(s) of participants? Would you have used the same number of participants? Explain.

C. Which strategies listed in Table 1 on page 161 of this book were employed by the researcher? Are they described in sufficient detail? Explain.

D. In addition to those you named in response to question 2C, has the researcher used any additional strategies to help assure the validity of the study? If yes, what are they? Are they described in sufficient detail? Explain.

3. Analysis and Results

A. Are the steps taken in the analysis described in sufficient detail? Explain.

B. Are the results clearly organized? Explain.

C. Are the results discussed in terms of a theory or theories (either theories that emerged from this study or previously existing ones)? Explain.

D. Were the direct quotations of the participants' statements, if any, judiciously selected? Do they help you understand the results? Explain.

E. Are there other ways the results could have been organized and interpreted? Explain.

4. Conclusions/Implications

A. Are the researcher's concluding remarks appropriate? Do they flow logically from the material presented earlier?

B. Does the researcher describe any implications? If yes, are they appropriate? Are there other implications that are not discussed by the researcher? Explain.

5. Ethical Considerations

A. In your opinion, could this research have caused physical or psychological harm to the participants? If yes, did the researcher take adequate measures to ameliorate the potential for harm? Explain.

B. If you had conducted this research, would you have obtained written, informed consent from the participants before conducting the study? Explain. Does this research report indicate that the researcher obtained such consent?

6. Overall Evaluation

A. Throughout the article, are all specialized terms and jargon defined to your satisfaction? Explain.

B. Briefly describe your overall evaluation of the research report, noting any special strengths and weaknesses.

C. If you had been a reviewer for the journal in which this report was published, would you have recommended publication of the report? If yes, would you have recommended that it be published "as is" or modified before publication? Ex-plain. If no, what is the primary reason why you would recommend not publishing it?

Urban Educators' Perceptions of Successful Teaching

STEVEN ILMER
Wayne State University

JO-ANN SNYDER
Wayne State University

SARAH ERBAUGH
Wayne State University

KAREN KURZ
Berry College

The publication of *A Nation at Risk* (National
Commission on Excellence in Education, 1983) stimulated several reports in the mid-1980s on the need for
reform in urban education (American Council on Education, 1983; Darling-Hammond, 1985; National Alliance of Black School Educators, 1984; National Coalition of Advocates for Students, 1985). Many initial
urban school reforms focused on the need for fundamental changes in the delivery of educational services.
Reformers argued for rapid expansion of specific programs and services in early childhood, health and social services in the schools, school-community partnerships, and alternative delivery systems (Oakes, 1987;
Yinger & Hendricks, 1990). Recently, considerable
emphasis has been on structural-based school reform
efforts including school choice, approaches to systemic
change, use of common core curricula, flexible scheduling, and the use of alternative methods for assessing
student performance (Carroll, Potthoff, & Huber, 1996;
Newmann & Wehlage, 1995).

Teachers' voices are absent from much contemporary school reform literature (Ascher, 1993; Koerner,
1992). When asked to cite factors most important for
successful urban teaching, how do experienced urban
teachers reply? How may urban teachers' voices affect
teacher preparation programs? How do experienced
urban teachers' voices compare with those of other
teachers? In this study, we examined these questions
and issues in the larger context of urban school reform.
Hargreaves (1996) persuasively argues that teachers'
voices are an important area of inquiry. He also cau-
tions investigators to avoid potential overgeneralization
and romanticism in teachers' voices when such voices
are presented in a decontextualized manner.

Corcoran, Walker, and White (1988) conducted
over 400 interviews with urban teachers, administrators, and staff concerning the conditions of teaching in
urban schools. They identified and categorized specific
conditions of urban teaching according to organizational, physical, and relational attributes.

Pasch et al. (1993) interviewed 90 teachers working
in Detroit, Cleveland, and Milwaukee to examine critically the voices of urban teachers and identify factors
the teachers perceived critical to successful urban
teaching. They interviewed participants to identify specific environmental, curricular, funding/resource, and
organizational factors they thought would directly affect urban teachers' success. They categorized teachers' responses and analyzed them by thematic codes
and found that teachers' direct understanding and fundamental knowledge of the urban community and culture inextricably linked with their perceptions of success in the classroom. Furthermore, they provided insight into the belief that factors internal and external to
the classroom and school building directly affect successful urban teaching. They categorized individual
themes as contextual, personological, or pedagogical.
Themes such as Home/Community and Class-
room/School Conditions represented contextual em-
phases. The category of Learner Needs and Characteristics is a theme representing a personological emphasis, whereas Subject Matter and Teaching Skills represented a pedagogical emphasis. Pasch et al. (1993) reported that themes in the contextual category were
most frequent, followed by themes in the personological and pedagogical categories.

We undertook this study as part of a national school
reform initiative supported by the AT&T Education
Foundation's *Teachers for Tomorrow* initiative, the
major goal of which was to improve the preparation of
urban teachers through school-university partnerships.
In Detroit, one of the first steps toward improving the
preparation of urban teachers was to describe factors
contributing to successful teaching in urban schools.
We addressed two questions:

- What factors do urban teachers identify as fundamental for successful teaching?
- How do these factors compare with those univer-

80 sity student teachers and university teacher educators identify as fundamental to successful urban teaching?

Pasch et al. (1993) focused solely on the voices of experienced teachers. We extended their findings by examining the voices of additional experienced urban 85 teachers and comparing those teachers' voices with the voices of other groups of educators.

Method

Seventy-three participants in the Detroit AT & T project—45 teachers, 18 student teachers, and 10 teacher education faculty—participated in this study. 90 Sixty-two (85%) of the subjects were female; 39 (53%) were African American; 31 (43%) were Caucasian; and 3 (4%) were Asian American. The university faculty were selected because of their experience and expertise in preparing urban teachers, as well as for their prior 95 experience as K–12 teachers in urban schools.

We conducted individual, audiotaped, face-to-face interviews of approximately 30 minutes with 73 educators at three Detroit elementary schools. We used Pasch et al.'s (1993) survey form to elicit responses to 100 eight statements. We designed the statements to elicit open-ended responses regarding urban educators' perceptions of successful teaching. Statements focused on critical knowledge, skills, attitudes, environmental factors, student characteristics, and professional prepa- 105 ration experiences affecting successful urban teaching.

We transcribed the audiotapes of each interview and conducted a thematic content analysis of each using a modified version of Spradley's domain analysis procedure (Spradley, 1979). Each member read each 110 transcription for familiarity and initial interpretation, then the research team discussed their initial interpretations, reached consensus on the names and definitions of the thematic codes, applied the definitions, and coded the transcriptions. We recorded all codes on the 115 master copy of the transcriptions and used a computer software program to tally all coded responses.

We intended the data interpretation and analysis to produce a gestalt of interviewees' perceptions and beliefs concerning factors directly contributing to suc- 120 cessful urban teaching (Miles & Huberman, 1994). The eight items in the interview had considerable content overlap. We intended the data analysis plan to identify key themes related to successful urban teaching. We counted the frequency of each theme across open- 125 ended responses for all eight items. Finally, we compared the themes with the highest frequencies across the eight items as a whole for each of the three groups.

Results

The first research question focused on perceptions of experienced urban teachers relative to identifying 130 factors responsible for teaching success. Illustrative teacher statements are identified.

Urban Teachers' Perceptions

We coded 45 themes from teachers' responses across the eight interview items. Among these 45 themes, the seven highest ranked (i.e., most frequent) 135 themes accounted for 41.2% of the responses. Knowledge of Community and Culture, the most frequent theme, accounted for 9.6% of the teachers' total responses. Several teachers thought that a working knowledge of the community and culture of the school 140 is necessary to be successful. "We're able to share the different cultures so that all children can respect one another. We try to incorporate it in the program so they can get a broader aspect of the world."

Teachers emphasized the need to understand and 145 respect individuals from different cultures and acknowledge that achievement potential is not dependent upon economic status. "I think of urban schools as being a variety of people, having a real social and economic mix, and I think that's great because you always 150 have kids from different economic backgrounds who are achievers. It reinforces that any kid can be great."

Teachers' responses underscored the importance of recognizing that children come to school with many attitudes and opinions about their neighborhoods. Chil- 155 dren face potential health problems in the community (e.g., drug abuse, violence). An important role of the teacher involves helping children cope with home and community problems. A teacher pointed out that there are cultural differences in teacher-student interactions 160 that teachers must understand. For example, children from some cultures may respond negatively to an authoritarian teacher. Experienced teachers adjust their style of instruction based upon the cultural makeup of the class. "We have had American Indian children in 165 our building, and their approach to authority was different. And if we don't understand that, we almost might think, well, you know, they're not listening to me. They're not paying attention and you get angry at that child for that instead of finding out."

170 The second most frequent theme, Teachers' Needs and Attitudes, accounted for 7.5% of the experienced teachers' responses. Teachers described important teacher characteristics. "You need to bring compassion. You need to bring diligence and you need to bring in- 175 tegrity."

Teachers stated that it was important to be a motivator who challenges children to learn. Positive motivation is an intrinsic characteristic of a teacher not dependent on school facilities, resources, or other extrin- 180 sic factors.

We can't use lack of materials as excuses for poor results, because if we get up in the front of the room, and if we present and we're prepared, and we motivate and we challenge them, we're going to get the job done.

185 Teachers have to have the attitude that all children can learn. You have to teach them in a way so they will learn.

Experienced teachers also thought that, to be effective, teachers must be open-minded and patient with children and parents. They must be aware of their personal biases and prejudices. In addition to being concerned about their own attitudes, teachers are in the unique position of imparting positive and constructive attitudes to their students. "You're always fighting biases that are placed on you by others. You always have to defeat that prejudice that is placed against you."

Children's Needs, the third most frequent theme, accounted for 7.1% of the teachers' responses. Teachers mentioned the special needs of individual children living in urban communities who bring a wide variety of problems from home to school. Successful teachers can anticipate children's needs by trying to understand their home background. "You have to know that these kids come from a setting you can't control. You just can't block yourself from it."

Instructional Style and Teaching Methods, the fourth most frequent theme, accounted for 5.9% of the teachers' overall responses. Several stated that teaching style and methods are important tools in the classroom. They often identified the topics of classroom management, discipline, and creativity. The skillful teacher uses creativity to develop instructional materials that address children's interests, needs, and abilities. Successful urban teachers modify their teaching styles to meet the special needs of children. They adapt to differences in children's learning styles. "This school has provided the children here with as many manipulatives as possible. They have to have hands-on; they have to see by doing."

The fifth most frequent theme, Community Resources, accounted for 4.0% of the teachers' responses. The urban community offers teachers a broad array of resources—libraries, museums, zoos, businesses, university facilities, and specialized recreational centers. Many successful teachers bring their own resources to the classroom. Parents also may provide the teacher with support and materials. The teacher must incorporate the available resources in the curriculum. "A good urban teacher learns how to use the resources of the community. We pretty much have everything that we could need. I don't mean everything that we want, but everything that we need."

The sixth most frequent theme, School Climate, accounted for 3.6% of the teachers' responses. Teachers thought that respect for others and a relaxed, congenial atmosphere were more important than the physical facility. Some teachers pointed out that it is the teacher's responsibility to improve a faulty facility or classroom in order to enhance instruction. Some teachers painted the classroom walls and created colorful and informative bulletin boards. "It's very important that the schools should be clean, safe and secure. It should be a very happy environment for urban children. The school has no control over the outside environment, but I'm certain we can control the inside."

The seventh most frequent theme, Subject Matter and Content Knowledge, accounted for 3.5% of the teachers' responses. The importance of subject matter was often a given; successful experienced teachers are very knowledgeable about subject matter. Furthermore, their high level of confidence about content enables them to focus more attention on culture and community aspects, children's needs, and classroom dynamics. "I think you should know your subject matter, of course. You can't guess your way through. You also have to know how to impart that knowledge. To be knowledgeable and not able to impart it is still as bad as not having the knowledge."

In summary, seven themes accounted for 41.2% of the experienced teachers' total responses to the first research question.

Comparisons of Perceptions Among Groups of Urban Educators

The second research question focused on the similarities and differences among the perceptions of experienced urban teachers and two additional groups, student teachers and experienced urban teacher educators. We compared frequency data for the three groups using a chi square analysis ($p < .05$).

Table 1 contains data for the five most frequent themes for the experienced teachers, student teachers, and university teacher educators. We compared results for the three groups to identify potential differences in perceptions of successful urban teaching.

Each group identified Knowledge of Community and Culture and Teacher Needs and Attitudes as critical themes for successful teaching. Differences among the groups were nonsignificant for these two analyses.

Differences among the groups for the next three themes in Table 1 were statistically significant ($p < .05$). The experienced teachers and the student teachers thought that Children's Needs were more important than did the university teacher educators. The experienced teachers and the teacher educators identified Instruction and Teaching as an important theme. Student teachers seldom mentioned this theme. The experienced teachers and the student teachers identified Community Resources as an important theme, while the teacher educators thought that it was less important.

Discussion

The first research question that this investigation focused upon concerned the identification of factors experienced urban teachers cite as fundamental for successful teaching in urban schools. In this study, the experienced teacher indicated that contextual, personal, and pedagogical factors have a direct impact and influence upon successful teaching in urban schools. Among the five highest ranked themes, the experienced teachers viewed the contextual themes of knowledge of community and culture and community resources as having a direct impact upon teaching success. These urban teachers recognized the importance of attempting to acquire some level of understanding of cultural dif-

Table 1
Frequency and Percent of Responses for Selected Major Themes Differentiated by Group

Selected Themes	Groups			
	Experienced Teachers (*n* = 45)	Student Teachers (*n* = 18)	University Teacher Educators (*n* = 10)	Chi Squared Value
Knowledge of Community and Culture	84(9.6)	35(11.1)	17(16.5)	< 1
Teacher Needs and Attitudes	66(7.5)	13(4.0)	9(8.7)	3.3
Children's Needs	62(7.0)	28(8.9)	5(4.8)	6.0*
Instruction and Teaching	52(5.9)	1(0.0)	8(7.8)	18.6*
Community Resources	35(4.0)	32(10.0)	5(4.8)	15.8*

*$p < .05$

300 ferences among students. They viewed awareness of local community issues as further affecting their teaching success. Acquiring some understanding of local housing circumstances, employment trends, and general economic conditions are examples of such is-
305 sues.

Early teacher preparation experiences should incorporate opportunities for preservice teachers to recognize the importance of learning about the communities in which they will work and the cultures of the students
310 they will teach. Preservice teachers should learn how to identify and access resources such as museums and libraries available in urban communities. Preservice teachers need ample opportunities to reflect upon these experiences as they progress through their professional
315 preparation programs.

The perceived importance of contextual factors upon successful urban teaching does not minimize the relative importance or influence of personological and pedagogical factors. Rather, it may be useful to view
320 the three factors as complementary and interactive. In this study, the influence of themes such as teacher needs and attitudes and children's needs upon successful teaching was evident in the frequency rankings of the experienced teachers. Pasch et al. (1993) report
325 similar findings.

The second research question in this study focused on comparing factors experienced teachers identify as fundamental to successful urban teaching with those factors a group of student teachers and a group of ur-
330 ban teacher educators identify. Within each of the three groups, there is a similar rank order for each of the major themes (see Table 1). However, significant differences are evident when we compared frequency rankings from individual themes across groups. For
335 example, in terms of percentage of responses as a function of impact upon successful urban teaching, the experienced teachers and the student teachers identified the theme of understanding children's needs more frequently than did the teacher educators. One possible
340 explanation for this finding is that teacher educators were more removed from daily contact with children in K–12 classrooms. Both experienced teachers and teacher educators thought that instructional methods and techniques were relatively more important than did
345 the student teachers. An explanation of this finding is

that responsibility of managing instruction for a whole class may initially overwhelm new teachers. Even when these teachers appropriately apply basic skills and techniques, they typically lack the broad array of
350 instructional planning and implementation strategies developed through reflection and experience. Preservice teachers must acquire the foundational skills upon which they will be able to build, with further experience, the teaching repertoires necessary to address
355 students' differential learning styles and needs.

This study supports the view that closer working partnerships between experienced urban teachers and urban teacher educators can enhance current improvement efforts for preparing preservice teachers. Teach-
360 ers must be empowered to share their knowledge and experience in the urban setting with teacher educators and preservice students. When placing preservice teachers in field work and practicum assignments, teacher preparation programs may wish to assign pre-
365 service teachers to the same school for a number of semesters or terms. Such extended experiences may enable preservice teachers to acquire a greater understanding of community and cultural factors that affect children in schools (Garibaldi, 1992; Jordan, 1995).
370 To help create an urban teaching corps capable of addressing the inherent challenges of working in urban settings, teacher preparation programs must infuse the lessons learned by experienced urban teachers. School reform literature must expand to incorporate teachers'
375 voices in authenticated contexts (Hargreaves, 1996). The knowledge and insights of urban educators may effectively contribute to the current dialogue and future direction of needed reforms in urban schools.

References

American Council on Education. (1983). *Demographic imperatives: Implications for educational policy.* Washington, DC: American Council on Education.

Ascher, C. (1993). *Changing schools for urban students: The School Development Program, Accelerated Schools, and Success for All* (Trends and Issues, No. 18). New York: ERIC Clearinghouse on Urban Education, Teachers College, Columbia University.

Carroll, J. A., Potthoff, D., & Huber, T. (1996). Learnings from three years of portfolio use in teacher education. *Journal of Teacher Education, 47,* 253–262.

Corcoran, T. B., Walker, L. J., & White, J. L. (1988). *Working in urban schools.* Washington, DC: Institute for Educational Leadership.

Darling-Hammond, L. (1985). *Equality and excellence: The educational status of Black Americans.* New York: College Entrance Examination Board.

Garibaldi, A. (1992). Preparing teachers for culturally diverse classrooms. In M. Dilworth (Ed.), *Diversity in teacher education: New expectations* (pp.

23–39). San Francisco: Jossey-Bass.

Hargreaves, A. (1996). Revisiting voice. *Educational Researcher, 26*(1), 12–17.

Jordan, M. L. R. (1995). Reflections on the challenges, possibilities, and perplexities of preparing preservice teachers for culturally diverse classrooms. *Journal of Teacher Education, 46,* 369–374.

Koerner, M. E. (1992). The cooperating teacher: An ambivalent participant in student teaching. *Journal of Teacher Education, 43,* 46–56.

Miles, M. B., & Huberman, A. M. (1994). *Qualitative data analysis: An expanded sourcebook.* Thousand Oaks, CA: Sage.

National Alliance of Black School Educators. (1984). *Saving the African-American child.* Washington, DC: National Alliance of Black Educators.

National Coalition of Advocates for Students. (1985). *Barriers to excellence: Our children at risk.* Boston: National Coalition of Advocates for Students.

National Commission on Excellence in Education. (1983). *A nation at risk: The imperative for educational reform.* Washington, DC: U. S. Government Printing Office.

Newmann, F. M., & Wehlage, G. G. (1995). *Successful school restructuring: A report to the public and educators by the Center on Organization and Restructuring of Schools.* Madison: Center on Organization and Restructuring of Schools, University of Wisconsin.

Oakes, J. (1987). *Improving inner-city schools: Current directions in urban district reform.* New York: RAND.

Pasch, S., Pasch, M., Johnson, R., Ilmer, S., Snyder, J., Stapleton, E., Hamilton, A., & Mooradian, P. (1993). *Reflections of urban education: A tale of three cities.* In M. J. O'Hair & S. J. Odell (Eds.), *Diversity and teaching: Teacher education yearbook I* (pp. 9–30). New York: Harcourt, Brace, Jovanovich.

Spradley, J. P. (1979). *The ethnographic interview.* New York: Holt, Rinehart & Winston.

Yinger, R. J., & Hendricks, M. S. (1990). An overview of reform in Holmes Group Institutions. *Journal of Teacher Education, 41,* 21–26.

Note: This research is based on work supported in part by a grant from the AT&T Education Foundation's *Teachers for Tomorrow* initiative. Any opinions, findings, or recommendations expressed in this article are those of the authors and do not necessarily reflect those of the AT&T Education Foundation.

About the Authors: Steven Ilmer is professor and associate dean at Wayne State University, Michigan. His specializations include urban education and sensorimotor learning and development. Jo-Ann Snyder is assistant professor at Wayne State University, Michigan. Her specializations include preparing effective urban teachers. Sarah Erbaugh is associate professor and assistant dean at Wayne State University, Michigan. Her specializations include urban teacher preparation and developmental issues in motor performance of children and youth. Karen Kurz is assistant professor at Berry College, Mt. Berry, Georgia. Her specializations include urban teacher preparation and motor development in young children.

Exercise for Case 9

Part A: Comparison of Quantitative and Qualitative

Directions: Compare the quantitative and qualitative parts of this research report and answer the following questions.

1. Was it appropriate to use both quantitative and qualitative methods for this research problem? Explain.

2. Did one method contribute more than the other in helping to advance knowledge in this area? Explain.

3. Which method did you personally find more interesting? Explain.

Part B: Evaluation of the Qualitative Aspects of this Research

Directions: Evaluate the qualitative aspects of this research by answering the following questions.

1. Introduction

A. Is the problem area for the research clearly described? Explain.

B. Have the researchers convinced you that the problem area is important? Explain.

C. To what extent does the literature presented in the introduction help you understand the problem? Is the literature used to put the problem in context? Explain.

D. Do the researchers indicate how this study is different from and/or similar to earlier ones reported in the literature?

E. Do the researchers reveal their personal perspectives on the problem area, including any possible biases? Explain.

2. Methods

A. Are the demographics of the participants (i.e., background characteristics such as age, race, and so on) described in sufficient detail? Explain.

B. Considering the problem area for the research, do you think that appropriate participants were selected? If you had been conducting the study, would you have selected the same type(s) of participants? Would you have used the same number of participants? Explain.

C. Which strategies listed in Table 1 on page 161 of this book were employed by the researchers? Are they described in sufficient detail? Explain.

D. In addition to those you named in response to question 2C, have the researchers used any additional strategies to help assure the validity of the study? If yes, what are they? Are they described in sufficient detail? Explain.

3. Analysis and Results

A. Are the steps taken in the analysis described in sufficient detail? Explain.

B. Are the results clearly organized? Explain.

C. Are the results discussed in terms of a theory or theories (either theories that emerged from this study or previously existing ones)? Explain.

D. Were the direct quotations of the participants' statements, if any, judiciously selected? Do they help you understand the results? Explain.

E. Are there other ways the results could have been organized and interpreted? Explain.

4. Conclusions/Implications

A. Are the researchers' concluding remarks appropriate? Do they flow logically from the material presented earlier?

B. Do the researchers describe any implications? If yes, are they appropriate? Are there other implications that are not discussed by the researchers? Explain.

5. Ethical Considerations

A. In your opinion, could this research have caused physical or psychological harm to the participants? If yes, did the researchers take adequate measures to ameliorate the potential for harm? Explain.

B. If you had conducted this research, would you have obtained written, informed consent from the participants before conducting the study? Explain. Does this research report indicate that the researchers obtained such consent?

6. Overall Evaluation

A. Throughout the article, are all specialized terms and jargon defined to your satisfaction? Explain.

B. Briefly describe your overall evaluation of the research report, noting any special strengths and weaknesses.

C. If you had been a reviewer for the journal in which this report was published, would you have recommended publication of the report? If yes, would you have recommended that it be published "as is" or modified before publication? Explain. If no, what is the primary reason why you would recommend not publishing it?

Case 10

Couples Watching Television:
Gender, Power, and the Remote Control

ALEXIS J. WALKER
Oregon State University

ABSTRACT. I sought to confirm that partners in close relationships "do gender" (West & Zimmerman, 1987) and exercise power (Komter, 1989) even in their ordinary everyday behavior and specifically in their selection of television programming via a remote control device (RCD). Individuals in 36 couples (86% heterosexual, 14% gay or lesbian) were interviewed. Men in heterosexual couples use and control the RCD more than women, and their partners find RCD use more frustrating than they do. Heterosexual women also are less able than men to get their partners to watch a desired show. The results confirm that couples create and strengthen stereotypical notions of gender through the exercise of power, even in the mundane, joint, leisure activity of watching television.

From *Journal of Marriage and the Family, 58,* 813–823. Copyright © 1996 by the National Council on Family Relations, 3989 Central Ave. NE, Suite 550, Minneapolis, MN 55421. Reprinted by permission. All rights reserved.

Five years ago, my parents bought a second television set because my mother refused to watch television with my father any longer. "I can't stand the way he flips through the channels," she said. Note that my fa-5 ther actually has the use of the new television, and my mother has been relegated to the den with the older model. Nevertheless, mother now has her own set, and conflicts about the remote control device have been reduced considerably.

10 Several years ago, journalist Ellen Goodman (1993, p. 181) published an essay in which she described the RCD as "the most reactionary implement currently used to undermine equality in modern marriage." Because family scholars rarely study such mundane, eve-15 ryday life experience, there is little research available to confirm Goodman's sentiments or to assess the prevalence of solutions to television-watching disagreements such as that employed by my parents. RCD use, however, presents a challenging arena in which to 20 examine gender and relationship issues in the experience of daily living.

Over the past 20 years, feminist scholars have shown that ordinary, routine, run-of-the-mill activities that take place inside homes every day bear an uncanny 25 resemblance to the social structure. For example, the distribution of household labor and of child care is gendered in the same way that paid work is gendered: The more boring and less desirable tasks are disproportionately performed by women, and status has a 30 way of reducing men's, but not women's, participation in these tasks. (See Thompson & Walker, 1989, for a review.) Examining television-watching behavior is a way to extend the feminist analysis to couples' leisure.

Despite the fact that television watching is the 35 dominant recreational activity in the United States today (Robinson, 1990), there is little research on this topic in the family studies literature. Indeed, there is little family research on leisure at all (but see Crawford, Geoffrey, & Crouter, 1986; Hill, 1988; Holman & 40 Jacquart, 1988), although scholars often mention that employed wives and mothers have very little of it (e.g., Coverman & Sheley, 1986; Hochschild, 1989; Mederer, 1993). Recently, Firestone and Shelton (1994), using data from the 1981 Study of Time Use, con-45 firmed that married women have less overall leisure time than married men. They also demonstrated gender-divergent patterns in the connection between paid work and both domestic (in-home) and out-of-home leisure time. Women who are employed have less 50 out-of-home leisure time than men do, but men who are employed have less domestic leisure time than employed women. Specifically, they found that employment hours do not affect the amount of leisure time that married women have at home. To explain this surpris-55 ing finding, Firestone and Shelton speculated that leisure at home appears to be the same for employed and nonemployed wives because leisure is compatible with household chores and with child care. In other words, women combine family work with leisure activities. 60 For example, they iron while watching television.

Although there is little research on leisure in family studies, there is considerable literature on gender and leisure in the field of leisure studies. For example, Henderson (1990), predating Firestone and Shelton 65 (1994), described women's leisure as fragmented because much of it takes place at home where it is mingled with domestic labor. In comparison with men, women say that leisure is less of a priority and that they do not deserve it. Some activities that are defined as 70 leisure pursuits, such as family picnics, are actually occasions for women's work, making leisure a possible source of internal conflict for women (Shank, 1986; Shaw, 1985). In fact, Henderson (1994) called for a deconstruction of leisure because the term embodies contradictions for women, contradictions that may be evident particularly in family leisure (Shaw, 1991).

To develop a way to measure couples' television-watching behavior, I sought guidance from the empirical research on television watching, which also is considerable. Here, studies describe various types of RCD use, sometimes referred to as (a) grazing (sometimes called surfing)—progressing through three or more channels with no more than 5 seconds on any one channel for the purpose of seeing what is available; (b) zapping—switching channels to avoid something, usually a commercial; and (c) zipping—fast-forwarding during a prerecorded program, mostly to avoid commercials (Cornwell et al., 1993; Walker & Bellamy, 1991).

Observational, survey, in-depth interview, and ethnographic data from communications researchers using a wide variety of sampling strategies revealed that when heterosexual families with children watch television together, fathers dominate in program selection and in the use of the RCD. Sons are active as well, using the RCD more than either their mothers or their sisters. That gender differences are smaller among younger persons, however, suggests a potential for women and men to be more similar in their remote control behavior in the future, when the RCD-using youth of today are adults (Copeland & Schweitzer, 1993; Cornwell et al., 1993; Eastman & Newton, 1995; Heeter & Greenberg, 1985; Krendl, Troiano, Dawson, & Clark, 1993; Lindlof, Shatzer, & Wilkinson, 1988; Morley, 1988; Perse & Ferguson, 1993). Note that the dominance in RCD use by men and boys in a family context is not evident when individuals are observed alone. In an experimental study, women were no less likely to use the RCD than were men (Bryant & Rockwell, 1993). The authors concluded that a social context is necessary to produce such gendered behavior.

Morley (1988) described fathers as using the RCD for unnegotiated channel switching—that is, changing channels when they want to—without explaining their behavior to or consulting other television watchers. Unemployed fathers, by the way, are less likely than employed fathers to use the RCD in this way, suggesting a possible connection between RCD use and the use of legitimate power—that is, power derived from and supported by societal norms and values (e.g., Farrington & Chertok, 1993).

Why so much channel switching? Men say they change channels to avoid commercials, to see if something better is on, to see what they are missing, to watch news reports, because they like variety, to avoid looking up the printed listings, to annoy others, and, my favorite reason, to watch more than one show at the same time (Perse & Ferguson, 1993). By contrast, women say they change channels to watch a specific program. A frightening finding is that the children of heavy RCD users are also heavy users, suggesting that parents pass on this behavior and that we can anticipate more grazing in the future (Heeter & Greenberg, 1985).

Copeland and Schweitzer (1993) concluded: "Men have usually been viewed as the persons who control program selection, and domination of the remote control seems to make visually explicit what may have previously been implicit" (p. 165). This notion of power, clearly stated in the language of the communications researchers, is missing from the family research on leisure. In their studies, however, the communications researchers have focused almost exclusively on parents watching television with their children. Rarely have they studied couples watching television. Furthermore, students of communication rarely have combined data about television watching and RCD use with questions of primary interest to those of us who study close relationships among adults. For example, are there any ways in which watching television with your partner is frustrating? Would you change the way that you watch television with your partner if you could? How do you influence your partner to watch something that *you* want to watch?

These questions address issues of power in relationships described by Aafke Komter (1989). She demonstrated that power is evident not only in the direct, observable resolution of conflict between partners, but also in covert or nonobservable events that reflect structural inequality. Direct expression of power reflects manifest power; covert expression reflects latent power. Examples of latent power are the ability to prevent issues from being raised, the anticipation of the desires of the more powerful partner, and resignation to an undesirable situation due to the fear of a negative reaction from the more powerful partner or worry that change might harm the relationship in some way (see also Huston, 1983; McDonald, 1980). In addition to other domains (e.g., family labor and sexual interaction), Komter included leisure in her study, but she focused only on hobbies and interaction with friends.

I chose to wed the focus of communications researchers on television-watching behavior with Komter's (1989) approach to studying power. I expected that heterosexual couples would "do gender" (West & Zimmerman, 1987) even in such a mundane activity as joint television watching. I anticipated that the creation and affirmation of gender would be evident in the (manifest and latent) power men have over their women partners in the domain of leisure activity. Furthermore, I sought to confirm the importance of gender in partner interaction by examining joint television watching behavior in lesbian and gay couples as well (see Kollock, Blumstein, & Schwartz, 1985).

Method

Participants

The sample for this study was characterized by its diversity. Participants were recruited primarily by students enrolled in an upper-division undergraduate course on gender and family relationships. In recruiting respondent pairs, students worked in groups of four to maximize diversity. Couples were chosen so that each group of four students would select a diverse set of pairs. All respondents were in a romantic (i.e., heterosexual married, heterosexual cohabiting, or cohabiting gay or lesbian) relationship in which both individuals were at least 18 years old. All couples had been living together for at least 1 year and had a television set with an RCD. Within each group, however, participants included (a) couples varying in relationship length, from shorter (1 year) to longer (15 years or more); (b) a lesbian or gay couple; (c) at least one married couple; (d) at least one heterosexual, cohabiting, or unmarried couple; (e) couples with and without children; (f) at least one couple in which at least one partner was Asian American, African American, Latino, or of mixed race; and (g) couples in which both partners were employed and couples in which only one partner was employed. Fourteen percent ($n = 5$ pairs) of the 36 couples (72 individuals) were gay or lesbian. Here, and for much of this report, I focus attention on the 31 heterosexual pairs.

Women and men in these heterosexual couples did not differ significantly on sociodemographic characteristics. (Table 1 shows these characteristics for all couples.) The typical respondent was 34 years old ($SD = 12.69$) and had completed 2 years of academic work beyond high school. Most (77%, $n = 48$) were White, although nearly one quarter were either African American, Hispanic, or of mixed race. Nearly three quarters (74%, $n = 48$) were married; one quarter was cohabiting. On average, their relationships had been in existence for 10 years. Most (77%, $n = 48$) respondents were employed, and just over 30% ($n = 19$) were students; only 16% ($n = 10$) of the sample, however, was nonemployed, nonretired students. Heterosexual respondents represented three income groups. Just over one third earned less than $20,000 annually, one third reported an annual household income between $20,000 and $39,999, and just under one third earned $40,000 or more. One third had children living at home.

Measures

A semistructured interview was administered to each member of the couple. In addition to sociodemographic questions, respondents were asked about the number and location of television sets and videocassette recorders in the home, the frequency with which they and their partners watched television, and other activities they engage in while watching television. They were asked about use of the RCD, in general, while watching with their partner and during the program most recently watched with the partner. They were also asked if their most recent experience was typical of their joint television watching. These questions were quantitative in nature and are similar to the types of questions asked of participants by communications researchers. Additional single-item, quantitative questions were derived from the family studies literature; that is, questions about relationship happiness, happiness with the way things are regarding watching television with the partner, and how much partners enjoy the time they spend together.

Other questions focused on issues of power à la Komter (1989). These questions were open-ended and concerned changed expectations about watching television with the partner over the history of the relationship, how the couple decides on a program to watch together, how partners get each other to watch programs that they want to watch, and their frustrations with watching television with their partner. Respondents were asked if they would like to change anything about the way they watch television together, if they thought they would be successful at making these changes, whether it would be worth it for them to make the changes, and how their partner would react to the changes. In addition, any changes they had already made in their joint television-watching behavior were described.

Procedures

A coin toss was used to determine which partner to interview first. Partners were interviewed separately, usually in their own homes, by trained student interviewers. Interviews were audiotaped and transcribed. SAS was used to analyze the quantitative data, and transcriptions were read and reread for analysis of the open-ended data.

Results

On average, the heterosexual couples had 1.81 television sets ($SD = 0.99$), but some had only 1, and a few had as many as 5. They had 1.30 videocassette recorders ($SD = 0.53$), with a range from 1 to 3. They also had 1.30 RCDs ($SD = 0.68$), with a range from 1 to 3. The typical home had basic cable television (with no extra channels) or a satellite dish.

These individuals watched television quite often—on average almost daily for nearly 3 hours per day ($M = 2.77$, $SD = 1.48$). During the week prior to the interview, they had, on average, watched television together on 4.87 days ($SD = 2.09$). Nearly all, 94% ($n = 29$) of the women and 87% ($n = 27$) of the men, reported that, regarding watching television with their partners, they were happy with the way things are. Yet two thirds of the women and three fifths of the men reported that there were things about their joint television watching that were frustrating to them. The interview transcripts were revealing about these frustrations. Women complained about their partners' grazing behavior, both during a show and when they first turned on the televi-

Table 1
Characteristics of Respondents in the Sample

	Heterosexual Partners (n = 62)		Lesbian or Gay Partners (n = 10)	
Characteristic	*M* or %	*SD* or *n*	*M* or %	*SD* or *n*
Age	34.1	12.69	36.4	7.52
Education level[a]	3.1	1.70	4.1	1.52
Race (% White)	77.4	48	100.0	10
Relationship status (%)				
Cohabiting	25.8	16	100.0	10
First marriage	58.1	36		
Previous marriage	16.1	10	10.0	1
Years in relationship	10.2	11.22	8.1	3.51
Children at home (%)	32.3	20	0.0	0
Employed (%)	77.4	48	90.0	9
Employment hours[b]	2.8	1.41	3.1	0.38
Income[c]	2.2	1.26	2.4	1.13

Note: Within heterosexual couples, there were no significant differences by gender for any of these variables.
[a]Education measured from 0 (*less than high school*) to 6 (*graduate degree*).
[b]Employment hours measured from 0 (*0 to 10 hours per week*) to 4 (*more than 40 hours per week*).
[c]Income measured from 1 (*less than $20,000*) to 5 (*more than $80,000*).

sion set. One woman in a 3-year cohabiting relationship said:

> I would say that the only thing that's frustrating for me is when we first turn on the TV and he just flips through the channels. It drives me crazy because you can't tell what's on, because he just goes through and goes through and goes through.

Another woman, in the 17th year of a first marriage, reported, "[I get frustrated] only if I get hooked into one show and then he flips it to another one. As soon as I get hooked into something else, he flips it to something else." Such reports from women were common. A married man spontaneously agreed: "We don't watch TV a lot together; I would rather do other activities with my wife. Channel switching wasn't a problem until...the remote control." Indeed, many men indicated that their women partners were bothered by this behavior.

In contrast, men reported being frustrated with the quality of the programming or the circumstances of watching, rather than with RCD activity. For example, one husband said, "I wish we had a VCR... I wish we had one of those TVs where you could watch two things on the screen at once." Another said, "It's sort of frustrating when I want to watch something she doesn't, and she goes into the other room and gets sort of pouty about it." A third reported, "No, [nothing is frustrating], but she does talk a little."

I looked specifically at the RCD; for example, where is the RCD usually located? Men were more likely than women to say that they usually hold the RCD or have it near them, $\chi^2(1, n = 62) = 7.38, p < .01$, and they were less likely than women to say that their partner usually holds it or has it near them, $\chi^2(1, n = 62) = 14.47, p < .001$. In half the couples ($n = 16$), according to both women and men, men have the RCD. In over 80% ($n = 25$) of the couples, according to both

the women and the men, the women do not have control of it solely. According to 16% ($n = 5$) of the women and 10% ($n = 3$) of the men, women control the remote. In roughly one third of the couples, the RCD is in a neutral location, or both take turns holding it. The pattern was the same when respondents were asked about the RCD's location during the most recent television show that they watched together. The RCD was more likely to be located near men than near women or near both members of the couple, $\chi^2(2, n = 59) = 13.12, p < .001$. The transcriptions support this general pattern of RCD location, as well. A husband reported, "I usually use the remote because I know how to use it, and it usually sits right in front of me while I am on the couch." A young married woman said, "I had the baby [the RCD] this time. This was a rare occasion." Roger (all names are pseudonyms), a married man, reported:

> I frequently have the remote at my side. I won't change the channel until we are ready to look for something else. If there is someone who wants to change the channel at a commercial, it will be Sally [his wife]. I will hand the remote to her, and she will change it to another favorite show, and then back. And that is very typical.

Sally agreed. The last time they watched television together, the RCD was in "Roger's pocket! Either in his shirt pocket or bathrobe pocket." A young, married man reported:

> I don't hold [the RCD], but I pretty much have control of it, and if I don't care what's on, then I let her have it. Sometimes we fight over it. Not like fight, but, I mean, it's like, "You always have the remote control."

Women were significantly more likely than men to say that RCD use was frustrating to them, $\chi^2(1, n = 62) = 8.42, p < .01$. Only 10% ($n = 3$) of the men, but 42% ($n = 13$) of the women evidenced such frustration. Furthermore, women ($M = 0.61, SD = 0.79$) reported that significantly more RCD behaviors were frustrating to them than men reported ($M = 0.15$, $SD = 0.37$) $t(48)$ = −2.70, $p < .01$. Yet 30% ($n = 9$) of the women in the sample and 16% ($n = 5$) of the frustrated men reported that they would like to change how the RCD is used during their joint television watching. This difference was not significant.

What was frustrating about RCD use? Respondents reported being frustrated by the amount of grazing, the speed of grazing, heavy use of the RCD, and the partner taking too long to go back to a channel after switching from it during a commercial. A few respondents actually indicated concern about their own frequent RCD use. Women and men, however, reported similar percentages of other television-watching behaviors that were frustrating (e.g., too much time watching television; bothersome behaviors of the partner, such as making fun of a program); 58% ($n = 18$) of the women and 48% ($n = 15$) of the men were frustrated by these other behaviors.

Thus far, I have shown that men control the RCD more than women and that women are more frustrated by RCD behaviors than men are. I also asked about the other activities engaged in while watching television. Two types of activities were mentioned: family work (e.g., child care, cooking, laundry) and pleasurable activities, such as doing nothing (i.e., relaxing), eating, drinking, playing computer games, and so on. When activities within each type were summed, the findings were revealing. When asked about their most recent joint television-watching episode, men ($M = 1.00$, $SD = 0.52$) responded that they were significantly more likely than women ($M = 0.74$, $SD = 0.44$) to engage in pleasurable behaviors while watching television, $t(62)$ = 2.11, $p < .04$. Women ($M = 0.36$, $SD = 0.71$) were not more likely than men ($M = 0.13$, $SD = 0.34$) to do family work while they watched television, although the data suggested a trend in this regard, $t(62) = −1.60$, $p < .12$. The small proportion of households with children (32%, $n = 10$) may have contributed to this finding. At least 80% of both women and men described this most recent experience as typical of their joint television watching and of their RCD use. Interestingly, women ($M = 2.84$, $SD = 0.74$) tended more than men ($M = 3.16$, $SD = 0.69$) to describe the particular show they watched as their partner's preference rather than their own, $t(60) = 1.78$, $p < .08$.

Recall that 30% of the women said they would change the use of the RCD during their joint television watching if they could. Only half as many men would make such a change. The open-ended data support these results. For example, a young married woman described her technique of standing in front of the television to interrupt the signal from the RCD. Another young married woman said that her partner used the RCD to watch more than one program at a time. "I should get him one of those TVs with all the little windows so he can watch them all," she said sarcastically. A middle-aged married woman said that she would like

to change their television watching so that she would have "control of the remote for half of our viewing time." Of those who would like to make any changes in their television watching, one in five women expected that they would *not* be successful.

Men typically admitted their heavier RCD use. For example, a middle-aged married man said that he switched channels to avoid commercials. "I'm the guilty party," he said. "My [family members] would leave it there and watch the commercial. I just change it because I'd rather not be insulted by commercials."

One of the most provocative questions asked of respondents was "How do you get your partner to watch a show that you want to watch?" The results were enlightening. A cohabiting woman said, "I tell him that would be a good one to watch, and he says, 'No,' and keeps changing [channels]. I whine, and then usually I don't get [my way]." A middle-aged married woman said:

Let me think here, when does that occur? [Laughing.] If I really want to watch, I'll say, "I want to watch this one."... I'll say, "Come in here and watch this" if he's not in the room, but pretty much we watch the same things a lot, whether or not that's because I let him. He, a lot of the time, turns it on, and I'll come in and join him. But, if it's something I really want to watch, I'll say, "Don't flip the channel; I want to see this."

In contrast, a young married man said that he gets his partner to watch a show he wants to watch in this way:

I just sneak the remote away from her if she has it, or, if I'm there first, then... I mean, if there's sports on, that's usually what we watch unless there's something else on. I mean, usually if there's...some kind of sports game on, we usually watch that, but unless there's...another show on that, you know, she can talk me into, deter my interest, or something...

When asked how his partner gets him to watch something that she wants to watch, he reported:

Oh, I guess, if there's not anything that I'm...real big on watching then I'll let her choose, or if she, you know, she's interested in something... A bunch of times, we watch TV, and it's like, well, we'll go back, and, well, that's kind of interesting, we go back and forth.

His wife agreed:

I usually don't have to beg him. I don't know. [Laughing.] I tie him down, and say, "You're watching this." I don't know. He usually just comes over, and if it's not what he wants, then he'll take the remote and try to find sports.

In other words, this couple watches sports when it is available. If there is no sports program on television and if the husband does not have something else he really wants to watch, then the wife may choose a show, but her husband will be looking for a sports program while her show is on, or at least he will go back and forth between her show and others.

A woman who has been married for 18 years was

deliberate in her efforts to watch a particular show:

> I usually start a couple of days ahead of time when I see them advertised, and it is something that I am going to want to watch. I tell him to "get prepared!" I have to be relatively adamant about it. When the time comes up, I have to remind him ahead of time that I told him earlier that I want to watch the program.

When her husband wants to watch a program, however, she said, "He just watches what he wants. He doesn't ask." Finally, a married man reported, "I just say I want to watch something, and if she wants to watch something really bad, I will let her watch what she wants to watch." Ultimately, the authority is his.

The data are much the same when people report on changes they would like to see in the way they watch television together. One man who has been cohabiting with his partner for one year said, "I should probably let her 'drive' sometimes, but [it] would bug me too much not to be able to do it." A woman who has been married for 37 years painted a brighter picture. When asked, "How do you feel about watching TV with your husband? Are you happy with the way things are?" she responded:

> Yes, right now. But see, without the VCR we'd be in trouble because I just tape anything I want to see. Without that, there'd be more conflict... Buying a second TV has changed the way we watch TV. It's made it easier—less stress, less conflict.

A young married man also was more positive. When asked, "Have you changed the way you watch television together?" he replied, "We take turns watching our programs, and I let her hold the remote during her programs."

Earlier, I mentioned that 14% ($n = 5$) of the couples in this study were gay or lesbian. In these couples, too, one partner usually is more likely than the other to use the RCD. In a gay male couple, one nearly always used the RCD, and the other almost never used it. When the RCD user was asked why they have this typical pattern, he responded: "Why? I don't know. I just like using the remote. I think I'm better at it than he is." In answer to a question regarding whether he used the RCD at all, his partner indicated: "He doesn't let me." In a second gay male couple, one partner again was far more likely to use the remote than the other partner, but both reported using controlling strategies to get their partner to watch a show they wanted to watch. Greg said, "I just tell him I want to watch it, and we do." Rob said, "I just turn it on, and that is what we watch." When asked, "How does your partner get you to watch a program he wants to watch?" Greg replied: "I usually don't watch programs I don't want to watch. If he asked me to watch it with him for a purpose, I would."

In contrast, one partner in a lesbian pair reported, "If we are both here, we try to make sure it's something that we both like." In fact, this couple limited their television viewing to avoid potential problems resulting from their different styles of RCD use. They also made it a practice to talk to each other during the commercials, in part, so that the one partner who tended to do so, would not graze. A second lesbian pair reported similar behavior. When asked, "Think back to the beginning of your relationship with [your partner]. Have your expectations about watching television with her changed over time?" she responded:

> In the beginning,...TV watching was something we could do when we didn't know each other very well yet. You know, it was kind of like a sort of a neutral or a little bit less personal activity that we could sit and watch TV together as a shared activity. And it's still a shared activity... We don't use it to tune each other out, and if someone wants to talk, we just click the mute button or turn it off.

Becky's partner, Mary, used the RCD much more often than Becky did. According to Becky, however, when Mary grazes, "she's perfectly willing, if I say, 'This looks really good,' she'll stop. She doesn't dominate that way." In fact, when Mary grazes, "she'll just say, 'Is this bothering you?'" Mary agreed that she was the one who usually held the RCD, but that they shared, too. "If Becky has a show she really likes, then I give her the remote so I'm sure I don't play with the TV while she's watching her show." Mary does not "let" her partner hold the RCD; she asks her to hold it to keep her own behavior in check. Indeed, Mary's frustration with their joint television watching comes from her own behavior: "Well, I feel self-conscious about how much I change the channels because I know that she doesn't like to change as often or as fast as I do." Although based on a very modest sample, these findings are intriguing and illustrate how couples successfully develop and maintain egalitarian or peer relationships.

Discussion

These data confirm that for women in heterosexual pairs leisure is a source of conflict—conflict between their own enjoyment and the enjoyment of their partners (Shank, 1986; Shaw, 1985, 1991). The data expose the contradictions between the goal and the reality of leisure for women. Support also comes from the findings that men, more than women, combine other pleasurable pursuits with television watching. Others (Coverman & Sheley, 1986; Firestone & Shelton, 1994; Hochschild, 1989; Mederer, 1993) have shown that women more than men dovetail family labor with their leisure activity.

The data also support previous work suggesting that when heterosexual couples watch television together, men dominate in program selection and in the use of the RCD (Copeland & Schweitzer, 1993; Cornwell et al., 1993; Eastman & Newton, 1995; Heeter & Greenberg, 1985; Krendl et al., 1993; Lindlof et al., 1988; Morley, 1988; Perse & Ferguson, 1993). Indeed, unnegotiated channel switching by male partners was a fre-

595 quent occurrence in this sample. Men use the RCD to avoid commercials, to watch more than one show at a time, and to check what else is on (Perse & Ferguson, 1993). And they do so even when their partners are frustrated by these behaviors.

600 The data reveal that men have power over women in heterosexual relationships (Komter, 1989). Men are more likely than women to watch what they want on television and to do so without considering their partner's wishes. Men control the RCD, which gives them

605 the means to watch what they want, when they want, in the way that they want. Men also persist in RCD use that is frustrating to their women partners. These are examples of manifest power. Men make overt attempts to get their way and are successful at doing so. Men's

610 power is evident, as well, in the lesser power of their women partners. For example, women struggle to get their male partners to watch a program they want to watch and are less able than men to do so. Furthermore, women watch a preferred show on a different

615 television set or videotape it so that they can watch it later. These options do not prevent a husband or male partner from watching a show that he wants to watch when he wants to watch it.

Men's latent power over women is evident as well.

620 Even though women rarely control the RCD, fewer than half report that RCD use is frustrating to them, and only 30% say they would like to change their partner's RCD behavior. According to Komter (1989), resignation to the way things are is evidence of latent

625 power. Another illustration of the effect of latent power is anticipation of a negative reaction. Only four women feel they would be successful if they attempted to change the way their partners use the RCD. In the heterosexual sample, women seem less able than men to

630 raise issues of concern to them, they anticipate the struggles they will encounter when and if their own preferences are made known, and they predict a negative reaction to their wishes from their male partners.

Confirmation of men's latent power over their

635 women partners also was demonstrated by a series of auxiliary analyses. I was unable to explain the dependent variables of respondent's relationship happiness or respondent's enjoyment of the time the couple spends together with independent variables such as frustration

640 with remote control use, dominance of the remote control, or desire to change frustrating remote control use. As Komter (1989) suggested, both lesser power and resignation on the part of women contribute to the appearance of balance in these pairs.

645 Joint television watching in heterosexual couples is hardly an egalitarian experience. As is true for my mother, some women use a second television or a videocassette recorder to level the playing field (i.e., so that they are able to watch the shows they want to

650 watch). A second television set, however, reduces joint leisure time among those couples who can afford it, and a VCR means that a woman may have to wait to

watch her show. Even these solutions to conflict around joint television watching demonstrate that cou-

655 ples watching television are not simply passive couch potatoes. They are doing gender, that is, acting in ways consistent with social structures and helping to create and maintain them at the same time.

Everyday couple interaction is hardly mundane and

660 run-of-the-mill. It is a systematic recreation and reinforcement of social patterns. Couples' leisure behavior is gendered in the same way that household labor is gendered: Social status enhances men's leisure activity relative to women's. Thus, leisure activity has gen-

665 dered meanings (Ferree, 1990). Through it, women and men are creating and affirming themselves and each other as separate and unequal (Ferree, 1990; Thompson, 1993). In other words, leisure activity is both an occasion for relaxation and an occasion for doing gen-

670 der (Fenstermaker, West, & Zimmerman, 1991; Shaw, 1991).

As Osmond and Thorne (1993) point out, "Gender relations are basically power relations" (p. 593). Because the power of men in families is legitimate—that

675 is, backed by structural and cultural supports—it constrains the less powerful to act to maintain the social order and the stability of their relationship (Farrington & Chertok, 1993). Few women make demands of their heterosexual partners so that their patterns of television

680 watching change. Instead, they say they are "happy" with their joint television watching. This same pattern is evident when we examine family labor. Most women describe the objectively uneven distribution of household work as fair (Thompson, 1991).

685 Hochschild (1989) argued that women give up leisure as an indirect strategy to bolster a myth of equality. Rather than resenting her male partner's leisure time, a woman uses the time when he is pursuing his own leisure or interests to engage in what she describes

690 as her interests: housework and child care. Overall, she defines their level of involvement at home as equal, a view that can be sustained only if she ignores her own lack of leisure time, as well as the amount of leisure time her partner has. Hochschild also suggested that a

695 woman sees her male partner's leisure time as more valuable than her own because she feels that more of his identity and time than hers are committed to paid work. She concludes, therefore, that he deserves extra relaxation. In Hochschild's view, and in Komter's

700 (1989), women cannot afford to feel resentment in their close relationships.

In a review of the literature, Szinovacz (1987) wrote that there were few studies of how people in families exercise power. She argued that such studies

705 are needed, as are studies on strategies of resisting power. The data reported here suggest that the exercise of power around couples' television watching behavior can be overt and relentless. Men's strategies to control the content and style of viewing are ways in which they

710 do gender. Women's resistance strategies (e.g., getting

a second television set, using the VCR) are also ways of doing gender. They do little to upset the intracouple power dynamics. Indeed, most women whose male partners are excessive grazers do not describe resistance strategies at all. Instead, they maintain the status quo (Komter, 1989).

Of interest is that in lesbian and gay couples one person was more likely to be the heavier RCD user, as well. Yet these couples had some unique patterns. The behavior of the lesbian couples, in particular, is suggestive for those of us wishing to establish and maintain egalitarian partnerships. One lesbian woman demonstrated a solution to the conflict between partners when one is distressed by the other's RCD behavior. Asked, "Is there anything else you'd like to tell us?" she responded:

> Well, I think that the most important thing for me is to remember to be sensitive to the fact that she doesn't have the same tastes as me, and I try to think about that. And, if she mentions that she likes something, then I ask her before I change the channel if she's done watching it, or if she's not interested, if I could change the channel.

In this act, she elevates the importance of her partner's wishes to the level of her own. She demonstrates the consideration that her partner desires and deserves (Hochschild, 1989; Thompson, 1991). When asked if it would be important for them to make changes in the way they watch television together, her partner expressed insight into her own behavior. Mary, the RCD user, likes to "veg out" and watch TV, but Becky likes to:

> pretend I'm not going to watch, I'm going to get a magazine or the newspaper,...or I'll bring some desk paper work over to do... I think, well, I'll just sit there in the living room while Mary watches TV. I'll work on our bills or something... Then, what happens is I'll look around and think that looks kind of interesting. Although usually by the time I've looked around, she's changed the channel... I think what happens is that she's more up front about saying, "Hey, I'm going to veg out here and watch some TV," and I pretend I'm going to do more worthwhile things, and I end up just watching TV anyway.

Perhaps these two women, with their honesty to themselves, their sensitivity to each other, and their concern about the ways in which their own behavior is or could be a problem in their relationship, are doing gender, too. They are concerned with the relationship, rather than with getting their own way. This is how women are said to make connection and to demonstrate care, to give what Hochschild (1989) described as a gift of gratitude. Using these strategies, they maximize joint enjoyment of leisure and minimize power imbalances. Rather then reproducing structural hierarchies, they create a bond of equality and provide a different course for the resolution of inherent conflict within couples.

The results from this study are hardly definitive. They are based on a small, volunteer sample, albeit one sufficiently diverse to include different types of close, romantic relationships. Additionally, the very small number of lesbian and gay couples suggests a need to exercise caution when generalizing from these findings. Further study with larger, representative samples will be required to extend these findings beyond the couples interviewed here.

Nevertheless, the patterns I identified are similar to those found in other studies of television watching in families and of the intersection of gender and power in close relationships. Mundane activities are important for understanding the intersection of gender and power in close relationships. Indeed, as Lull (1988) noted:

> Television is not only a technological medium that transmits bits of information from impersonal institutions to anonymous audiences, [but] it is a social medium, too—a means by which audience members communicate and construct strategies to achieve a wide range of personal and social objectives. (p. 258)

Others (Morley, 1988; Spigel, 1992) have pointed out that the way men engage with television programming and women watch more distractedly are illustrations of cultural power. Daytime television programming in the 1950s, for example, was designed to be repetitive and fragmented to facilitate joint housework and television watching for women (Spigel, 1992), thus helping to create and reinforce the view that leisure at home is problematic for women. The availability of the RCD does not change the fact that women's leisure is fragmented.

Recently, I toured an area of Portland, Oregon, billed as "The Street of Dreams," where there are a half dozen homes costing nearly a million dollars apiece. Each year, such homes are opened temporarily to members of a curious public who will never be able to afford them. Inside one was a theater room with three television sets mounted side-by-side along the back wall. A moment after we arrived, a middle-aged heterosexual couple entered the room. The woman smiled and said to the man, "Look, Dan, you could get rid of the remote!" If three television sets in one room is a solution to the problem of being able to watch only one show at a time, gendered struggles inherent in such mundane, everyday activity as watching television are destined to continue. They will do so until women and men are equal in both their microlevel interactions and in the broader social structure.

References

Bryant. J., & Rockwell, S. C. (1993). Remote control devices in television program selection: Experimental evidence. In J. R. Walker & R. V. Bellamy, Jr. (Eds.). *The remote control in the new age of television* (pp. 73-85). Westport, CT: Praeger.

Copeland, G. A., & Schweitzer, K. (1993). Domination of the remote control during family viewing. In J. R. Walker & R. V. Bellamy, Jr. (Eds.), *The remote control in the new age of television* (pp. 155-168). Westport, CT: Praeger.

Cornwell, N. C., Everett, S., Everett, S. E., Moriarty, S., Russomanno, J. A., Tracey, M., & Trager, R. (1993). Measuring RCD use: Method matters. In J. R. Walker & R. V. Bellamy, Jr. (Eds.), *The remote control in the new age of television* (pp. 43-55). Westport, CT: Praeger.

Coverman, S., & Sheley, J. F. (1986). Change in men's housework and child-care time, 1965-1975. *Journal of Marriage and the Family, 48,* 413-422.

Crawford, D. W., Geoffrey, G., & Crouter, A. C. (1986). The stability of leisure preferences. *Journal of Leisure Research, 18,* 96-115.

Eastman, S. T., & Newton, G. D. (1995). Delineating grazing: Observations of remote control use. *Journal of Communication, 45,* 77-95.

Farrington, K., & Chertok, E. (1993). Social conflict theories of the family. In P. G. Boss, W. J. Doherty, R. LaRossa, W. R. Schumm, & S. K. Steinmetz (Eds.), *Sourcebook of family theories and methods: A contextual approach* (pp. 357-381). New York: Plenum.

Fenstermaker, S., West, C., & Zimmerman, D. H. (1991). Gender inequality: New conceptual terrain. In R. L. Blumberg (Ed.), *Gender, family, and economy: The triple overlap* (pp. 289-307). Newbury Park, CA: Sage.

Ferree, M. M. (1990). Beyond separate spheres: Feminism and family research. *Journal of Marriage and the Family, 52,* 866-884.

Firestone, J., & Shelton, B. A. (1994). A comparison of women's and men's leisure time: Subtle effects of the double day. *Leisure Sciences, 16,* 45-60.

Goodman, E. (1993). Click. In *Value judgments* (pp. 180-182). New York: Farrar Strauss, & Giroux.

Heeter, C., & Greenberg, B. S. (1985). Profiling the zappers. *Journal of Advertising Research, 25,* 15-19.

Henderson, K. A. (1990). The meaning of leisure for women: An integrative review of the research. *Journal of Leisure Research, 22,* 228-243.

Henderson, K. A. (1994). Perspectives on analyzing gender, women, and leisure. *Journal of Leisure Research, 26,* 119-137.

Hill, M. S. (1988). Marital stability and spouses' shared time. *Journal of Family Issues, 9,* 427-451.

Hochschild, A. (with Machung, A.) (1989). *The second shift: Working parents and the revolution at home.* New York: Viking.

Holman, T. B., & Jacquart, M. (1988). Leisure-activity patterns and marital satisfaction: A further test. *Journal of Marriage and the Family, 50,* 69-77.

Huston, T. L. (1983). Power. In H. H. Kelley, E. Berscheid, A. Christensen, J. H. Harvey, T. L. Huston, G. Levinger, E. McClintock, L. A. Peplau, & D. R. Patterson (Eds.), *Close relationships* (pp. 169–219). New York: W. H. Freeman.

Kollock, P., Blumstein, P., & Schwartz, P. (1985). Sex and power in interaction: Conversational privilege and duties. *American Sociological Review, 50,* 34-46.

Komter, A. (1989). Hidden power in marriage. *Gender and Society, 3,* 187-216.

Krendl, K. A., Troiano, C., Dawson, R., & Clark, G. (1993). "OK, where's the remote?" Children, families, and remote control devices. In J. R. Walker & R. V. Bellamy, Jr. (Eds.), *The remote control in the new age of television* (pp. 137-153). Westport, CT: Praeger.

Lindlof, T. R., Shatzer, M. J., & Wilkinson, D. (1988). Accommodation of video and television in the American family. In J. Lull (Ed.), *World families watch television* (pp. 158-192). Newbury Park, CA: Sage.

Lull, J. (1988). Constructing rituals of extension through family television viewing. In J. Lull (Ed.), *World families watch television* (pp. 237-259). Newbury Park, CA: Sage.

McDonald, G. W. (1980). Family power: The assessment of a decade of theory and research, 1970-1979. *Journal of Marriage and the Family, 42,* 841-854.

Mederer, H. (1993). Division of labor in two-earner homes: Task accomplishment versus household management as critical variables in perceptions about family work. *Journal of Marriage and the Family, 55,* 133–145.

Morley, D. (1988). Domestic relations: The framework of family viewing in Great Britain. In J. Lull (Ed.), *World families watch television* (pp. 22-48). Newbury Park, CA: Sage.

Osmond, M. W., & Thorne, B. (1993). Feminist theories: The social construction of gender in families and society. In P. G. Boss, W. J. Doherty, R. LaRossa, W. R. Schumm, & S. K. Steinmetz (Eds.), *Sourcebook of family theories and methods: A contextual approach* (pp. 591-623). New York: Plenum.

Perse, E. M., & Ferguson, D. A. (1993). Gender differences in remote control use. In J. R. Walker & R. V. Bellamy, Jr. (Eds.), *The remote control in the new age of television* (pp. 169-186). Westport, CT: Praeger.

Robinson, J. P. (1990, September). I love my TV. *American Demographics, 12,* 24-27.

Shank, J. W. (1986). An exploration of leisure in the lives of dual-career women. *Journal of Leisure Research, 18,* 300-319.

Shaw, S. M. (1985). Gender and leisure: Inequality in the distribution of leisure time. *Journal of Leisure Research, 17,* 266-282.

Shaw, S. M. (1991). Gender, leisure, and constraint: Towards a framework for the analysis of women's leisure. *Journal of Leisure Research, 26,* 8-22.

Spigel, L. (1992). *Make room for TV: television and the family idea in postwar America.* Chicago: University of Chicago.

Szinovacz, M. E. (1987). Family power. In M. B. Sussman & S. K. Steinmetz (Eds.), *Handbook of marriage and the family* (pp. 651-693). New York: Plenum.

Thompson, L. (1991). Family work: Women's sense of fairness. *Journal of Family Issues, 12,* 181-196.

Thompson, L. (1993). Conceptualizing gender in marriage: The case of marital care. *Journal of Marriage and the Family, 55,* 557-569.

Thompson, L., & Walker, A. J. (1989). Gender in families: Women and men in marriage, work, and parenthood. *Journal of Marriage and the Family, 51,* 845–871.

Walker, J. R., & Bellamy, R. V., Jr. (1991). Gratifications of grazing: An exploratory study of remote control use. *Journalism Quarterly, 68,* 422-431.

West, C., & Zimmerman, D. H., (1987). Doing gender. *Gender and Society, 1,* 125-151.

Note: This is an expanded version of the presidential address presented at the 1995 annual meeting of the National Council on Family Relations, Portland, Oregon. I thank the following individuals for their help: Kinsey Green, for providing funds to support a graduate research assistant for this project; Alan Acock, for releasing me from a course during academic year 1994-1995; Janet Lee and Rebecca Warner, for their assistance with measurement; Linda Eddy and the students enrolled in HDFS 442 in the spring of 1994, for their role in data collection; Lori Schreiner, for coding the quantitative data; and Sally Bowman, Alan Acock, Fuzhong Li, John Bratten, and, especially, Takashi Yamamoto, for their help with data analysis. I am grateful also to Katherine Allen, Mark Fine, and two anonymous reviewers for their careful and thoughtful reading of an earlier draft of this article.

Exercise for Case 10

Part A: Comparison of Quantitative and Qualitative

Directions: Compare the quantitative and qualitative parts of this research report and answer the following questions.

1. Was it appropriate to use both quantitative and qualitative methods for this research problem? Explain.

2. Did one method contribute more than the other in helping to advance knowledge in this area? Explain.

3. Which method did you personally find more interesting? Explain.

Part B: Evaluation of the Qualitative Aspects of this Research

Directions: Evaluate the qualitative aspects of this research by answering the following questions.

1. Introduction

A. Is the problem area for the research clearly described? Explain.

B. Has the researcher convinced you that the problem area is important? Explain.

C. To what extent does the literature presented in the introduction help you understand the problem? Is the literature used to put the problem in context? Explain.

D. Does the researcher indicate how this study is different from and/or similar to earlier ones reported in the literature?

E. Does the researcher reveal her personal perspectives on the problem area, including any possible biases? Explain.

2. Methods

A. Are the demographics of the participants (i.e., background characteristics such as age, race, and so on) described in sufficient detail? Explain.

B. Considering the problem area for the research, do you think that appropriate participants were selected? If you had been conducting the study, would you have selected the same type(s) of participants? Would you have used the same number of participants? Explain.

C. Which strategies listed in Table 1 on page 161 of this book were employed by the researcher? Are they described in sufficient detail? Explain.

D. In addition to those you named in response to question 2C, has the researcher used any additional strategies to help assure the validity of the study? If yes, what are they? Are they described in sufficient detail? Explain.

3. Analysis and Results

A. Are the steps taken in the analysis described in sufficient detail? Explain.

B. Are the results clearly organized? Explain.

C. Are the results discussed in terms of a theory or theories (either theories that emerged from this study or previously existing ones)? Explain.

D. Were the direct quotations of the participants' statements, if any, judiciously selected? Do they help you understand the results? Explain.

E. Are there other ways the results could have been organized and interpreted? Explain.

4. Conclusions/Implications

A. Are the researcher's concluding remarks appropriate? Do they flow logically from the material presented earlier?

B. Does the researcher describe any implications? If yes, are they appropriate? Are there other implications that are not discussed by the researcher? Explain.

5. Ethical Considerations

A. In your opinion, could this research have caused physical or psychological harm to the participants? If yes, did the researcher take adequate measures to ameliorate the potential for harm? Explain.

B. If you had conducted this research, would you have obtained written, informed consent from the participants before conducting the study? Explain. Does this research report indicate that the researcher obtained such consent?

6. Overall Evaluation

A. Throughout the article, are all specialized terms and jargon defined to your satisfaction? Explain.

B. Briefly describe your overall evaluation of the research report, noting any special strengths and weaknesses.

C. If you had been a reviewer for the journal in which this report was published, would you have recommended publication of the report? If yes, would you have recommended that it be published "as is" or modified before publication? Explain. If no, what is the primary reason why you would recommend not publishing it?

Case 11

The Process of Mentoring Pregnant Adolescents: An Exploratory Study

LYNN BLINN-PIKE
University of Missouri

DIANE KUSCHEL
University of Missouri

ANNETTE McDANIEL
University of Missouri

SUZANNE MINGUS
University of Missouri

MEGAN POOLE MUTTI
Caring Communities, Columbia, Missouri

ABSTRACT. The goal of this exploratory study was to describe, empirically, the process that occurs in relationships between volunteer adult mentors and pregnant adolescent mentees. A second goal was to generate testable hypotheses based on the findings concerning the mentor role. Case records from 20 mentors were analyzed and the results revealed that the mentors spent time in quasi-parenting roles helping the mentees access services and resources, discussing interpersonal issues and infant development, and being involved in intimate details of the mentees' lives. Criteria are discussed for conceptualizing some mentors as fulfilling quasi-parenting roles. It is hypothesized that there is a relationship between the neediness of pregnant adolescents and the extent of the quasi-parental roles that mentors assume.

From *Family Relations*, *47*, 119–127. Copyright © 1998 by the National Council on Family Relations. Reprinted with permission.

Although lacking a clearly identified theoretical and empirical foundation, programs designed to establish and support formal mentoring programs for at-risk youth have grown in popularity since the 1980s
5 (Freedman, 1993). In 1989, the William T. Grant Foundation Commission on Work, Family, and Children recommended that multiple mentoring programs for youth be developed, evaluated, and refined. By 1990, organizations such as Chrysler, Proctor & Gam-
10 ble, IBM, the United Way of America, the National Urban League, and the National Education Association were involved in supporting mentoring programs. Several states, including Rhode Island, New York, and California, established public offices and governmental
15 task forces on mentoring high-risk youth (Freedman, 1993).

Recent popularization has not afforded adequate time for theory-building, conceptualization, or evaluations of mentoring programs (Freedman, 1993; Rhodes,
20 1994). As a result, empirical data are needed about the mentoring process itself (Goodman, 1989). One goal of the present study was to describe, empirically, the process that occurs during relationships between volunteer adult mentors and adolescent mentees. The second goal
25 was to generate hypotheses about the mentoring role. In this case, the mentees were all pregnant adolescents, a subgroup of high-risk youth that has received little attention in the mentoring literature. The hypotheses will be discussed in the discussion section of the arti-
30 cle.

Adolescents' Relationships With Nonparental Adults

Current research on adolescent outcomes reveals that having a positive relationship with at least one caring adult, not necessarily the parent, is one of the most important elements in protecting youth from mul-
35 tiple risks (Carnegie Council on Adolescent Development, 1989; Scales & Gibbons, 1996; Werner & Smith, 1982; Wynn, Costello, Halpern, & Richman, 1994). However, Scales and Gibbons (1996) stated that there is a surprisingly limited empirical research base re-
40 garding adolescent relationships with nonparental adults. Rhodes (1994) described the number of studies on extrafamilial adults in the lives of adolescents as "sparse but growing" (p. 187). According to Rhodes (1994), the few studies that exist on this topic can be
45 characterized as outcome-based, cross-sectional, and small scale.

Scales and Gibbons (1996) stated that there is a major gap in understanding how the functional roles of parents and nonparents compare. The few studies that
50 have made such a comparison have shown mixed results. One study by Munsch and Blyth (1993) found correspondence between the functions of parents and nonparents in their relationships with adolescents. On the other hand, Hendry, Roberts, Glendinning, and
55 Coleman (1992) found that nonfamilial adults and parents differed in their role with adolescents.

Mentoring. Researchers and practitioners attempting to understand the roles of nonparental adults in adolescents' lives have begun to examine adult-youth
60 mentoring processes. Anderson and Shannon (1988) defined mentoring as a nurturing process in which a more skilled or experienced person serves as a role model to teach, sponsor, encourage, counsel, and be-

102

friend a less skilled or less experienced person for the purpose of promoting the latter's professional and/or personal development. The present interest in mentoring is evident in a recently developed typology of youth mentoring styles: classic, individual-team, friend-to-friend, peer group, and long-term (Philip & Hendry, 1996).

The value of the mentoring experience can be explained by social support theory. Thompson (1995) defined social support as social relationships that provide (or can potentially provide) material and interpersonal resources that are of value to the recipient, such as access to information and services, sharing of tasks and responsibilities, and skill acquisition. Several authors have identified the functions of the mentoring process as providing: instrumental (tangible) support, expressive (emotional) support, and instruction (information) (National Black Child Development Institute, 1990; Phillips-Jones, 1983; Saito & Blyth, 1992).

Mentoring relationships can be divided into those that evolved naturally (informal mentoring) and those that were created by an outside party or organization (formal mentoring). Rhodes, Ebert, and Fisher (1992) described informal mentors as an overlooked resource in the social networks of adolescent mothers. In their study of natural mentors among African-American adolescent mothers, Rhodes and colleagues found that there was strong preference for extended family members as natural mentors (aunts, older female relatives, grandmothers, and boyfriend's female relatives) over nonrelated helpers such as teachers, clergy, counselors and neighbors. In a similar study of Latina adolescent mothers by Rhodes, Contreras, and Mangelsdorf (1994), only 15% of the subjects nominated teachers or counselors as natural mentors.

While natural helpers have always played a role in adolescent development, formal mentoring relationships are a relatively recent phenomena. Freedman (1993) summarized the positive functions of formal mentoring as supplying information and opportunities, providing nurturance and support, and preparing youth for adulthood. He also cautioned that issues surrounding formal mentoring programs include: limited time on the part of volunteer mentors, social class differences between mentors and mentees, and a lack of programmatic infrastructure to support mentoring and follow-up.

In a rare large-scale evaluation of a formal mentoring program, Tierney, Grossman, and Resch (1995) studied the effects of the Big Brothers/Big Sisters program on over 900 youths from 10 to 16 years of age. The results showed that mentored, as opposed to nonmentored, children were less likely to initiate the use of alcohol or drugs, less likely to report having hit someone, and more likely to report better attitudes toward school. No significant differences were reported for self-concept or participation in social and cultural activities.

Zippay (1995) conducted an exploratory study of formal mentoring by pairing 20 adolescent mothers with professionally employed mentors in order to increase the mothers' education and job skills. The results showed that mentors linked the adolescents with information and resources not readily available in their personal networks. In one of the few experimental evaluations of formal mentoring programs, Silfven (1990) randomly assigned 110 adolescent mothers to a mentored or nonmentored control group. The results showed a significant negative relationship between perceived social support on the part of the mentored group and depression scores.

While efforts to evaluate the impact of mentoring programs, such as those described above, are to be applauded, a review of the literature revealed that future research on this topic needs to be more process-oriented and theory-driven, as well as target specific subpopulations of youth. The present study was an attempt to meet these three needs. It was a micro-examination of the actual mentoring process as described by volunteer mentors of pregnant adolescents. The examination of the mentoring process led to the generation of testable hypotheses that can be further explored in an attempt to begin to develop a theoretical base related to formal mentoring.

Research Questions

One goal of the current research was to explore what mentors provide that promotes the positive development of pregnant adolescents. A second goal was to generate tentative hypotheses about the roles of mentors in the lives of pregnant adolescents. Based on a specific mentoring program for pregnant adolescents, two process-oriented research questions emerged. First, when pregnant adolescents and adult volunteers are involved in mentoring relationships for six months: (a) how much time do they spend together, (b) where do they spend their time, (c) what issues within the adolescents' lives do they deal with, and (d) what services and information are provided by the mentors? And second, based on the above description, how can the mentor role be conceptualized in order to begin to generate theory?

Research Methods

Sample

The sample for this study consisted of 20 mentors involved in the Missouri Volunteer Resource Mothers Project (MVRM), a mentoring program for pregnant adolescents. The MVRM project was adapted from a home visiting program developed by the National Commission to Prevent Infant Mortality (International Medical Services for Health, 1990). The goals of the MVRM project were to: (a) improve the health of the adolescent mother and her baby, (b) decrease parenting stress, and (c) decrease child abuse potential. In the MVRM project, volunteer mentors were matched with pregnant adolescents and served as sources of support, and information and referral at least until the babies' first birthdays. Adolescent participants were recruited through referrals from community agencies, schools, and health care providers and mentors were recruited through local media and word-of-mouth.

All of the mentors were female and lived in or within 20 miles of a Midwestern city of 69,000 people. Two mentors were Black and 18 were White, with a mean age of 30.5 ($SD = 9.21$) years. Seven mentors had high school degrees, 10 had bachelors degrees, 2 had masters decrees, and 1 had a law degree. Mentors had an average of 1.35 ($SD = .77$) children and were homemakers, teachers, home day care providers, nurses, and an administrative judge. Only one mentor was unmarried. Five of the mentors had been adolescent mothers themselves.

In the MVRM project, 15 of the mentored adolescents were White, four were Black and one was Hispanic with a mean age of 17.5 years ($SD = 1.42$). Mentees were pregnant for an average of 4.8 months ($SD = 2.22$) when they enrolled in MVRM and all delivered their babies during the six-month period being studied. One member of the group was married. Eleven mentees were enrolled in high school, 6 had dropped out, and 3 had already graduated. Nineteen were primiparous and one already had a child. All mentees were receiving at least one type of public assistance: Aid to Families With Dependent Children (15), food stamps (16), and Medicaid (16).

Data Collection

In order to conduct a micro-examination of the mentoring process, each mentor kept separate written records of each contact with her mentee using the Resource Mothers Contact Form (see appendix). This form was developed based on a review of the literature concerning the support needs of pregnant and parenting adolescents and a review of forms used in other mentoring programs. The contact form consisted of a series of quantitative descriptive questions and checklists, as well as a space for qualitative comments. The descriptive questions asked the mentor to identify the location of the contact, how much time was spent with the mentee, what issues were identified in the adolescent's life, and what information and services the mentor provided during that particular contact. The categories of issues, services and information corresponded to the functions of supportive relationships described by Lazarus and Folkman (1984): emotional, instrumental, and informational. The qualitative part asked the mentor to describe, in more detail, actions taken, issues identified, and services provided. The mentors' comments ranged from a paragraph to approximately a page in length.

Data Analysis

The data for this analysis were taken from the contact forms completed by 20 mentors, beginning with their first meeting with their mentees and spanning approximately a six-month period of continuous mentoring. The contact forms were analyzed using two-step, sequential triangulation. Morse (1991) stated that sequential triangulation is used if the results of one method are essential for planning the second method. In this case, the goal was not to find correspondence between the two methods but, rather, to examine the quantitative results to select themes for the qualitative content analysis. The first step in the sequence involved computing frequencies on the numerical data and checklists. The second step involved selecting the items with the greatest frequency and importance that emerged from the quantitative results and using them as the major themes for the content analysis of the qualitative comments. The content analysis was done independently by the authors and then the answers were compared for reliability. Differences were discussed and reconciled. The data were analyzed via a computer program called Ethnograph (version 4.0) (Seidel, Friese, & Leonard, 1995).

Quantitative Results

When recruited into the MVRM project, each mentor was asked to spend approximately three hours per week with her mentee. Over the approximately six months (26 weeks) of data used in this analysis, the 20 mentors spent a total of 1,561 hours or an average of 78 hours per mentor ($SD = 34.29$, range of 38 to 159 hours). They had a total of 288 contacts or an average of 14 contacts per pair ($SD = 10.15$, range of 5 to 27 contacts). They spent their time with their mentees in the following locations: in the community (60% of their time together or 937 hours), in either of their homes (21% or 328 hours), in MVRM-organized activities (12% or 187 hours), and in telephone conversations (7% or 109 hours). All of the mentors reported spending time in the first three locations. Two of the mentees did not have telephones, and therefore no telephone contact was reported.

Issues Identified

On the contact form, mentors were asked to check any of 14 issues that they identified in the adolescents' lives. Issues associated with abuse/neglect, furniture, insurance, substance abuse, and utilities were each checked fewer than 17 times over the six months and were dropped from the analyses. However, the topics that were checked a total of 593 times were: infant/children care (28% or 168 times), interpersonal issues (17% or 100 times), transportation (16% or 92 times), financial matters (9% or 50 times), emotional needs (8% or 49 times), health care (7% or 43 times), housing (6% or 38 times), clothing (5% or 28 times), and food/nutrition (4% or 25 times).

Services Provided

The mentors were asked to check any of six possible services that they provided to their mentees during the contact being recorded. The following services were checked as being provided a total of 813 times: emotional support (29% or 240 times), modeling life skills (23% or 187), transportation (20% or 163), problem solving (18% or 147), securing resources (7% or 64), and referral to other agencies or services (1% or 12).

Information Provided

The mentors were asked to check any of 11 possible types of information that they provided during the contact being recorded. Information identified as being provided 489 times included child growth and development (35% or 170 times), infant nutrition (11% or 56), safety (10% or 49), personal nutrition (8% or 41), breast feeding (8% or 39), labor and delivery (7% or 36), postnatal care (5% or 25), prenatal care (5% or 24), family planning (5% or 23), school (4% or 22), and substance abuse (< 1% or 4).

Qualitative Results

The second step in the sequential triangulation was to provide further elaboration on two of the descriptive categories: time spent in the community and issues identified in the adolescents' lives. The first was selected as a theme because the descriptive results showed a significant amount of community involvement (60% of their time together). The second was selected as a theme because of the critical importance of further delineating the issues experienced by pregnant adolescents. There was obvious overlap among the issues identified and the information and services provided to address those issues, thus, duplication was avoided by selecting only the issues category.

Time In the Community

In their qualitative narratives the mentors provided additional data about their community activities with their mentees. In the community, the mentors served as role models for the mentees, and provided emotional, tangible, and informational support. Mentors mentioned community activities 298 times across ten categories: recreation (30% or 91 times), shopping (17% or 52), health care (16% or 46), basic needs (12% or 39), social service agencies (7% or 20), classes/meetings (7% or 20), special occasions (4% or 13), church (3% or 10), time with the adolescent's family (2% or 5), and school (< 1% or 2). Table 1 provides more detail about the mentors' time in the community. The "miscellaneous" subcategory in Table 1 represents the number of individual items that were mentioned only once.

The distribution of activities revealed that all of the mentors reported being involved in at least four categories: recreation, shopping, meeting basic needs, and health care. The most frequent recreational event in which the mentors and mentees engaged was eating out (70% or 64 out of 91 recreational events mentioned). Shopping was primarily at the local mall (69% or 36 out of 52 descriptions of shopping). Health care issues were dealt with in the hospital during delivery of the baby (68% or 31/46) and at doctors' offices (26% or 12/46). Meeting basic needs included buying groceries (25% or 10/39), and learning to drive (15% or 6/39). The social service agencies they visited most often together were the Department of Family Services (45% or 9/20) and the Department of Health (35% or 7/20). Classes or meetings attended together included childbirth classes/hospital tours (45% or 9/20), and child care/child development classes (25% or 5/20). Baby showers were the special occasions that were celebrated together most often (69% or 9/13). The ten religious activities attended were all at the mentors' places of worship. The five visits with the adolescents' families were with their mothers/fathers (4 times) and sister (1 time). Two school-related visits were at a high school and at the GED office.

Identified Issues

Each mentor mentioned all five of the issues shown in Table 2. The mentors wrote about mentees' issues a total of 463 times. The categories listed on the contact form, with some adaptations, were used as the basis for the outline shown in Table 2. For example, interpersonal and emotional issues were combined into one category called "adolescent's mental health." The general heading of "securing and managing resources" was created and provided more detail about some of the issues related to obtaining tangible items.

The frequencies of the categories were: (a) transportation (28% or 131 times), (b) infant care (23% or 107 times), (c) adolescent's mental health (18% or 79 times), (d) securing and managing resources (16% or 74 times), and (e) adolescent's physical health (15% or 72 times). The items listed under the subcategories of "interpersonal issues" and "public assistance" totaled to more than the sum for those subcategories because multiple items were mentioned under the same subcategory. For example, a statement about interpersonal issues may have included feelings about both partner and parents, and therefore, was counted twice.

The following selected quotations further illustrate the five issues-related categories and subcategories. They also illustrate how the mentors met the mentees' emotional, tangible and information needs. The subcategories are identified in brackets after each quotation.

Transportation. The mentors were asked to provide the transportation (tangible support) the mentees needed to be able to access services either because mentees: did not know how to drive and had no support system (such as parents or relatives) to provide them with transportation, or they knew how to drive but did not have access to a car. Mentors mentioned transportation as an issue for the adolescents 131 times. The subcategories included driving them places 123 times, teaching them to drive six times, and providing information about buying a car twice. The following quotations reflect these results.

395 I took ____ to Family Services to pick up food stamps, to the grocery store and then to her mom's house for a visit. [mentor-provided transportation]

I took ____ to the mall and then to study for the driver's test. [learning to drive]

____ needs to get a car, asked me to help her look for one. [information]

Table 1

Content Analysis of Mentors' Qualitative Comments: Time In the Community

Category	# of Times Mentioned
Recreation	91
Eating out	64
Movies	12
Walking	7
Bowling	2
Swimming	2
Miscellaneous	4
Shopping	52
Local mall	36
Discount stores	15
Garage sales	1
Health care	46
Delivery of baby	31
Doctors' offices	12
Hospital	2
Department of Health	1
Basic needs	39
Groceries	10
Learning to drive	6
Post office	3
Car repair	3
Public library	3
Pharmacy	2
Miscellaneous	12
Social Service Agencies	20
Department of Family Services	9
AFDC	6
Medicaid	1
Food Stamps	1
Welfare To Work Program	1
Department of Health	7
Birthright	2
Miscellaneous	2
Classes/meetings	20
Childbirth classes/hospital tours	9
Child care/child development	5
Home visitation program	3
Miscellaneous	3
Special occasions	13
Baby showers	9
Miscellaneous	3
Religious Services	10
Adolescent's Family	5
Adolescent's mother/father	4
Adolescent's sister	1
Schools	2
High school	1
GED office	1

400 *Infant Care.* While emotional support was involved, providing information was most frequently mentioned under the "infant care" category. Mentors mentioned issues concerning infant care 107 times with 405 the following subcategories: health and illness (54 times), child development (25), parenting (21), and child/day care (7). The following quotations from the mentors' narratives are illustrative of the infant care category.

410 We discussed her feeling of inadequacy as a mother and her concerns and issues with breast feeding. I encouraged her to keep trying, that she's doing the right thing. [health—breast feeding]

She asked me if it was too early [too young] to give him cereal—I told her it was! [health—infant feeding]

415 ____ and I attended a group meeting and sat in on a speaker about newborn development—learned about baby's senses, how to feed, hold and diaper, and about illnesses in newborns. [child development]

____ told me she is afraid the baby sleeps too much, goes 420 to the bathroom too little, and that she's not doing the right thing. [child development]

We talked about the importance of holding her baby (she doesn't) and interacting with him (she doesn't like to). [parenting]

425 We talked about ____ quitting her job and her baby staying in day care. [child/day care]

Adolescent's Mental Health. Most of the mentees had mental health issues of various degrees of seriousness and received emotional support from the mentors. 430 Three received professional mental health counseling. The adolescent's mental health was the third most frequent issues-related category in the narratives (mentioned 79 times), with two subcategories—interpersonal issues (64) and general mental health (15). The 435 interpersonal issues involved the adolescent's partner or partner's family (36) and her own parents (23). The following quotations from the mentors' narratives are illustrative of the adolescent's mental health category.

____ and her boyfriend have been having issues. They 440 talked about the importance of having the father around for the baby, even if they decided not to stay together.

____ had some issues with her own father as a child and blames many things on him, so it is hard for her to let the baby's father be around unless he is going to be very 445 supportive and loving. [interpersonal issues—partner]

____ would like to be reunited with the baby's father (who has physically abused her). Her mother will not allow this to happen. We talked about how this causes her to feel depressed. [interpersonal issues—parents]

450 ____ admitted that she sometimes feels jealous of the baby because of all the attention she gets. We had a long talk about postpartum depression. [interpersonal issues—baby]

____ is lonely and needs a friend. She spent the day at my house. [general]

455 I visited ____ at her house. She is depressed and doesn't leave the house (or want to). We talked about getting up

and dressed in the a.m.—that both she and baby need stimulation. [general]

460   *Securing and Managing Resources.* All mentors assisted their mentees in securing tangible resources. Of the five subcategories under "securing and managing resources" (mentioned 74 times), the two most frequent were securing infant care items (35) and securing pub-465 lic assistance (20). The following quotations from the mentors' narratives are illustrative of the adolescents' needs to learn to secure and manage resources.

I offered the Voluntary Action Center as an idea for getting (free) baby clothes and items and I promised to go 470   through friends' baby clothes and bring her some. [infant care items]

I took ____ to apply for food stamps, Medicaid for the baby and to look into the Futures Welfare to Work program. [public assistance]

Table 2
Content Analysis of Mentors' Qualitative Comments: Adolescent's Issues

Category	# of Times Mentioned
Transportation	131/463
Provided by mentor	123
Learning to drive	6
Information	2
Infant Care	107/463
Health and illness	54
Illness	20
Breast feeding	17
Infant feeding	9
Safety	8
Child development	25
Parenting	21
Child/day care	7
Adolescent's Mental Health	79/463
Interpersonal issues	64
Partner/partner's family	36
Parent(s)	23
Friends	8
Other relatives	6
Baby	3
General mental health	15
Securing and Managing Resources	74/463
Infant care items	35
Public assistance	20
WIC	9
Food stamps	6
AFDC	3
Medicaid	2
Social Security	2
Futures Welfare To Work Program	1
Money management	9
Child support/paternity	6
Space/living arrangements	5
Adolescent's Physical Health	72/463
Labor and delivery/postnatal care	35
Prenatal care	30
Nonpregnancy-related	7

475   *Adolescent's Physical Health.* Addressing mentees' physical health issues required mentors to provide both emotional and informational support. Labor and delivery/postnatal care (35 times) and prenatal care (30) were the most frequent subcategories under the heading 480   of "adolescent's physical health" (72). Nonpregnancy-related health issues were mentioned seven times. The following quotations from the mentors' narratives are illustrative of the adolescents' physical health category.

____ will be induced Saturday. We discussed her expec-485   tations, concerns…who will be there…she's unsure of her mom's role. [labor and delivery]

____ had an ultrasound this past week and found out the baby's head is down. She also had some spotting. So while this was a fun outing, serious issues were discussed 490   and emotional support given. [prenatal]

____ is still not able to find a bed for herself or the baby and she is having back problems from sleeping on the floor. [non-pregnancy related]

Mentor Roles

The mentors' narratives were content analyzed and 495   similar mentor roles emerged as having been identified previously by other authors: providing expressive (emotional), instrumental (tangible), and instructional (informational) support (e.g., Saito & Blyth, 1992). As Tables 1 and 2 indicate, the mentors spent considerable 500   time providing all three types of support. The high frequency with which mentors assumed all three of the roles resulted in the identification of a fourth, overarching, role labeled "quasi-parenting." Quasi-parenting was defined as (a) providing the mentee with 505   the types of emotional, instrumental and instructional support that are generally assumed to be the purview of the family, (b) being informed by the mentee about personal and intimate details of her life, and (c) being involved in both the significant and mundane aspects 510   of the mentee's life. As a quasi-parent, a mentor might be the individual who instructs the adolescent about breast feeding (instructional), is confided in about previous sexual abuse (emotional), and assists the adolescent with weekly laundry and/or grocery shopping 515   (tangible).

The following vignettes illustrate in more detail the quasi-parental roles performed by three different mentors. These vignettes show how mentors in their respective situations met the criteria for being labeled as 520   quasi-parents.

Vignette #1. Dee, a 17-year-old African American, entered the program at three months pregnant. She lived with a roommate, was unemployed, and was enrolled in high school. She was receiving AFDC, food 525   stamps, Medicaid, Social Security, and WIC. This was Dee's first pregnancy. She and her mentor spent 45 hours together and had 18 contacts over the six-month period being analyzed. A critical issue frequently addressed by Dee and her mentor was Dee's lack of adequate housing. She was forced to leave her apartment two days before her baby was due. As a result, her mentor helped her seek emergency housing, as well as financial and legal advice.

> I am having a hard time finding Dee, when I did finally reach her she was very upset. She and her roommate have not been getting along. We spent all day together talking about these issues, family issues, her future educational and career desires, and social services available to her. I took her to look at two different subsidized housing complexes, picked up an application at one, and to the grocery store on the way home. [contact #4]

> Dee has to move out of her apartment—baby is due in two days and she is not in a very stable housing arrangement. Owes rent money and is concerned about bad credit (or worse) that will be the result of not being able to pay for the broken lease. [contact #10]

> …went to her dad's house to pick up food stamps, went to the post office to do a change of address, went to DFS (Department of Family Services), and the Social Security office. [contact #11]

> Went to see Dee in the hospital. They kept her and the baby for almost a week because they thought they might have herpes, also baby has elevated fever. [contact #12]

> Spent some time with Dee. Took her to get a certified letter to send to the landlord that wants to sue her. Took her to get pictures of her and her baby. [contact #15]

Vignette #1 shows that the mentor met the criteria of a "quasi-parent" by being involved in both the mundane (e.g., grocery shopping), as well as the more significant aspects of Dee's life (finding emergency housing). The mentor provided three types of support: transportation to find emergency housing (tangible), emotional support during a period of homelessness (emotional), and information about career and educational options (instructional).

Vignette #2. Anita was an 18-year-old Caucasian when she entered the program at three months pregnant. She lived with her father, was unemployed, and was enrolled in high school. She was receiving food stamps. This was Anita's first pregnancy. She and her mentor spent 52.75 hours together and had 19 contacts over the six-month period being analyzed. Two recurring issues for Anita and her mentor were legal issues surrounding the baby's father and Anita's pregnancy-related health issues. Her mentor provided transportation to a variety of community services, assisted her with job seeking, served as a sounding board for her concerns about her serious emotional and medical issues, and provided emotional support during labor and delivery.

> Anita and I met at her home and then did a mall walk and talk thing. She is talking about a wide range of issues. I think things are going well for us. The main issue right now is child support/financial issues. Anita is talking to Division of Family Services, her family and the child's father before consulting legal advice. [contact #1]

> Anita and I spent part of the day together shopping and having lunch. She helped me pick out a baby gift for a friend. We looked at maternity clothes and then I bought her a pregnancy book—she seemed real interested in it and we talked about some of the concerns and questions regarding her pregnancy. She is also looking for a job and has an interview at a day care center Monday that I suggested. She's anxious for the next [MVRM] group activity. [contact #3]

> Anita had an ultrasound this past week and found out the baby's head is down. She has also had some spotting. So while this was a fun outing, serious issues were discussed and emotional support given. Also discussed estranged boyfriend possibly wanting visitation. Anita is worried he might make things difficult for her. [contact #6]

> Anita went into the hospital for observation—is in labor but moving slowly. [contact #17]

> Visited Anita and new baby. Breast feeding didn't work, went to formula. Had made the switch before I could talk to her. We set up an appointment to sign up for AFDC. [contact #18]

Vignette #2 shows that the mentor was involved in both everyday activities with her mentee, such as shopping, as well as more serious issues such as preparation for labor and delivery, visitation by the baby's father, and finding suitable employment. The support provided included transportation to social services (tangible), counseling related to a variety of personal and medical issues (emotional), and information about pregnancy (informational).

Vignette #3. Laurel was an 18-year-old Caucasian who was eight months pregnant when she entered the program. She lived with her father, was employed, and had graduated from high school. She was receiving AFDC, food stamps, and WIC. This was Laurel's first pregnancy. She and her mentor spent 91 hours together and had 27 contacts over the six-month period being analyzed. Laurel's most pressing and long term issue involved her divorced parents and their respective roles in her and her baby's lives. This issue came to a head and made the delivery time extremely complicated for both Laurel and her mentor. Her mentor provided transportation to community services, served as a sounding board for serious issues, helped with the emotional preparation for labor and delivery, and provided emotional support during labor and delivery, as well as during the postpartum period.

> We spent the day getting to know each other and playing with my daughter. We talked about her abusive relationship with the baby's father and her family structure. We also discussed meal planning and she wrote down recipes. She had dinner with my husband, daughter and me. [contact #3]

> I took Laurel to the GED office, Social Security office and then back to my house to visit…she is lonely and needs a friend…she was extremely upset. She needed a friend and confidant. [contacts 7–9]

> Laurel thought she might be in labor so we spent the day walking, talking and timing contractions. [contact #10]

> Laurel will be induced Saturday. We discussed her ex-

pectations, concerns...who will be there, whether or not I'll attend the actual delivery—she's unsure of her mom's role. [contact #14]

650 Laurel had her baby today, Doug Michael. I was with her through most of her labor and postpartum. Today was a stressful day. Her parents were a big stressor to Laurel which did not help her labor. They each had a significant other with them. Poor Laurel. Finally the nurse made us 655 all leave except her mom. After delivery Laurel hemorrhaged so she didn't get her baby for a few hours. I was the designated photographer. [contact 15]

Visited Laurel and Doug in the hospital. Took Laurel to lunch. Discussed how her parents were fighting over her 660 and how she feels guilty. Discussed her feeling of inadequacy as a mother and her concerns and issues with breast feeding. Encouraged her to keep trying, that she's doing the right thing. [contact #16]

Laurel and Doug finally going home. My husband and I, 665 along with Laurel's dad, helped her leave and gave her support. She's excited but scared of the responsibility. [contact #18]

Today Laurel is exhausted and stressed. Doug had her up all night, she's insecure about breast feeding and her par-670 ents continue to fight over her. Today she's going to her mom's in {city} for a few days. She's afraid the baby sleeps too much, goes to the bathroom too little, and that she's not doing the right thing. She's also apprehensive about the future—getting a job, child care, losing her 675 Medicaid, food stamps...Also afraid the baby's father will come after her and try to get the baby. [contact #19]

Laurel asked me to take her to her WIC appointment but I couldn't so I took her to lunch instead and a friend took her to WIC. I think it was good for her to get out and re-680 lax. This evening she asked me if she could go to a Bible study with my husband and I so I said okay. This was at her request. We attempted to discuss a budget but she doesn't want to. [contact #23]

Vignette #3 shows that in assuming a quasi-685 parenting role with Laurel, her mentor became involved in both routine activities (e.g., meal planning) and serious activities (e.g., labor and delivery). Tangible support included transportation for needed social services, as well as transportation home from the hos-690 pital, emotional support included assistance in dealing with concerns over labor and delivery, and instructional support included information about infant care and development.

Discussion

This discussion will center on two important as-695 pects of the study: methodology (replication) and findings (process description and hypothesis testing). Both of these have direct application for future mentoring programs. The use of mentor-produced contact records demonstrated a practical way of gain-700 ing insiders' perspectives of the mentoring process and these led to the generation of testable hypotheses.

Methodology

Three caveats are in order. First, as is the case with

most qualitative research, this study had limited exter-705 nal validity because of the small sample. Second, the locations in which mentors and mentees chose to spend time together and the services that were available were community-specific. And third, this was an exploratory study with a group of pregnant adolescents. Further research comparing pregnant versus non-pregnant 710 adolescents is needed to verify the findings and conclusions. On the other hand, the internal validity of the study was strong given the two methodologies that were employed. As was to be expected, there was close correspondence between the issues identified on the 715 checklists and what the mentors chose to write about in the narratives. For example, transportation, infant care, and interpersonal issues were the top three categories in both the quantitative and qualitative analyses, although their relative rankings varied slightly.

720 Currently, there are numerous manuals designed to assist family life educators in establishing youth mentoring programs (e.g., Abell Foundation, 1989; Kanfer, Englund, Lennhoff, & Rhodes, 1995; National Black Child Development Institute, 1990; Saito & 725 Blyth, 1992; Tierney, Grossman, & Resch, 1995). Typically, chapters in these manuals contain specific information on recruiting, training, and retaining mentors and mentees. Generally, however, this advice is neither empirically grounded nor specific for sub-730 populations of at-risk youth, such as pregnant and parenting adolescents.

While providing instruction on how to establish a project similar to MVRM is beyond the scope of this article, the following are practical recommendations for 735 family life educators to assist in facilitating the mentor role. Programs providing formal mentoring for pregnant adolescents need to pay close attention to supporting the mentor in the quasi-parenting role, through effective orientation, training, and "mentoring of the 740 mentor." First, provide systematic and ongoing mentor training in the areas shown in Table 2: infant care, counseling and helping skills, securing and managing resources, and managing medical issues related to pregnancy. Mentors need to be well prepared to answer 745 questions and provide information about these and related topics. Second, make potential mentors aware of the nature of the quasi-parental relationship in which they may be involved by having them read the vignettes included in this article and/or roleplay their 750 responses to various situations that may arise. Third, ask mentors to complete an adapted and expanded descriptive portion of the contact form to gather more details about the venue in which the contact occurred.

Fourth, ask mentors to complete a portion of the 755 contact form that has been adapted according to the outline in Table 2 to more accurately reflect the actual issues that pregnant adolescents confront. The contact form could be revised to include more specific information about infant care, adolescent mental health, and 760 securing and managing resources, topics mentioned

most often in the qualitative portion of the analysis. It could serve as both a needs assessment and form of process evaluation. It would give family life educators greater detail about the issues being faced by the ado-
765 lescents they are serving. With this detail, family life educators can work with mentors to individualize and tailor the nature of the activities and information provided to the particular needs of the adolescents. And fifth, provide mentors the opportunity to meet together,
770 provide support for each other, share joys and concerns about their mentoring experience, and build their helping skills.

Findings

The quasi-parenting relationship as defined here needs to be compared with both the classic career-
775 based and more recent social service-based definitions of mentoring. In terms of career-based mentoring, Endsley and colleagues (Endsley & Giles, 1988; Giles & Endsley, 1988; Watkins, Giles, & Endsley, 1987) have made a useful distinction between mentors and spon-
780 sors. According to Endsley and Giles, classic mentoring relationships in academe are high on four dimensions: reciprocity in communication, affective bond, influence, and power. A sponsor, on the other hand, plays more of an administrative role in the men-
785 tee's life and the relationship is low on the first three dimensions (communication, affective bond, and influence) and high on power. The role of the quasi-parent described here is more similar to that of the classic mentor than the sponsor, with the exception of the
790 power dimension.

The relationships between the mentors and pregnant adolescents were high on reciprocal communication (frequency of communication, enjoyment, frankness and mutual understanding), affective bond (shared
795 respect, love, trust, and support) and influence (breadth and depth of impact). However, the quasi-parenting relationship was moderate on power because the relationship was voluntary and the mentor did not have the legal power over the mentee that is afforded a parent or
800 guardian. Likewise, the quasi-parenting relationship was moderate on power because the mentor did not have influence due to money, career status or social status. In fact, these factors were intentionally minimized by matching the mentor and mentee based on
805 race and similar socioeconomic status. The mentors were trained to relate to the mentee on her level. The mentor's power came from being able to assist the mentee in meeting some of her emotional, tangible, and educational needs. The loss of the relationship would
810 deprive the mentee of social support and friendship but not career advancement, employment, social standing, or income.

In terms of social service-based mentoring, not all successful mentoring programs are planned to inten-
815 tionally fit the three criteria for quasi-parenting listed earlier. Some mentoring relationships, such as school-

based tutors or site-specific recreational leaders, may be more closely aligned with the description of a sponsor rather than a mentor. Likewise, not all successful
820 mentoring programs are designed to afford the mentor the type of reciprocal intimacy and range of types of involvement necessary to be classified as quasi-parenting.

There are at least four explanations why the quasi-
825 parenting role was evident in the MVRM data. The first explanation for the emergence of the quasi-parenting role is that the mentors were given the freedom to spend time with their mentees as they felt necessary. The fact that the mentors were not confined to
830 one location (such as the adolescent's home or school), confined to one role (such as tutor), or restricted in the time available to interact with their mentees (such as after school), afforded them the opportunity to provide critical support when and where it was needed. The
835 second explanation is that quasi-parenting may have emerged because of the unique medical and emotional needs of pregnant adolescents. Third, mentors' personal experiences with pregnancy, and in five cases personal experiences with adolescent pregnancy, may
840 have sensitized them to the unique needs of these adolescents and motivated them to become quasi-parents. Lastly, the methodology itself may have contributed to the identification of the quasi-parenting role. The mentor-produced contact forms provided an insider's
845 perspective that is unique to mentoring research.

From the results obtained here, two hypotheses were generated. First, it is hypothesized that there is a direct relationship between the "neediness" of the pregnant adolescent and the degree of quasi-parenting
850 required of the volunteer mentor. Neediness can be deemed as the absence of critical tangible, emotional, and/or instrumental resources necessary to function and grow. As the medical and emotional needs of the pregnant adolescent increase and are not met by her family,
855 partner, or other non-related adults, the closer the successful mentor moves to assuming the role of a parent.

Second, it is hypothesized that as mentors are afforded freedom to determine where and when to spend time with their mentees, the greater likelihood of them
860 assuming quasi-parental roles. Mentoring programs vary greatly in the freedom afforded mentors. They range from site-specific and content-specific models, such as school-based tutoring and community center-based recreational programs (e.g., Boys and Girls
865 Clubs of America), to relatively unstructured models such as Big Brothers/Big Sisters and MVRM. Accordingly, less structured models may afford mentors the time and freedom necessary to assume greater quasi-parenting roles with their mentees.
870 In order to test these hypotheses in the future, both "neediness" and "quasi-parenting" will need to be further defined and operationalized. There are many unanswered questions that need exploration. For example, is assumption of the quasi-parental role most closely cor-

875 related with the medical or emotional needs of the adolescent, the presence of a less restrictive meeting venue, and/or the unmet needs of the mentor? What cultural values impact the definition of a quasi-parent? Is quasi-parenting needed more during adolescent
880 pregnancy or parenting? How does the quasi-parenting role change as adolescents move from being pregnant to being mothers? How does the quasi-parenting relationship contribute to building resiliency in youth?

Conclusion

Scales and Gibbons (1996) asked a key question:
885 What do nonfamilial adults provide that is helpful to adolescents? The emergence of the quasi-parenting role provided a preliminary answer for the subpopulation of pregnant adolescents. The willingness of a volunteer, previously unknown to the adolescent, to be involved
890 in a mix of both significant and mundane activities shows commitment and caring. Likewise, reciprocity is important. The adolescent must be willing to allow the mentor into both the everyday and private areas of her life.
895 Mentors of pregnant adolescents face the challenge of assuming more intimate quasi-parental roles than they may have anticipated. This may be due, at least in part, to the fact that pregnant adolescents have unique and immediate medical and emotional needs: one ado-
900 lescent called her mentor when she found herself homeless and expecting a baby in two days; another contacted her mentor after she attempted suicide over rejection by both her family and boyfriend; and several adolescents had no one, other than their mentors, to be
905 present during labor and delivery. One young mother in the MVRM program showed how meaningful this voluntary relationship was to her when she said, "I know she cares about me because she is not being paid to be with me." In most cases, when the mentors assumed
910 quasi-parental roles, it was due to the absence of supportive parents or other nonparental adults and the mentors were the contact of last resort. It may be that adolescents who lack support from both family and nonfamilial adults are most in need of mentors who can
915 assume quasi-parenting roles.

References

Abell Foundation. (1989). *Mentoring manual: A guide to program development and implementation.* Baltimore, MD: Author.

Anderson, E. M., & Shannon, A. L. (1988). Toward a conceptualization of mentoring. *Journal of Teacher Education, 39,* 16–20.

Carnegie Council on Adolescent Development. (1989). *Turning points: Preparing American youth for the 21st century.* Washington, DC: Author.

Endsley, R. C., & Giles, H. W. (1988). Assessing career development relationships in academe. *Career Planning and Development Journal, 4,* 22–28.

Freedman, M. (1993). *The kindness of strangers.* San Francisco, CA: Jossey Bass.

Giles, H. W., & Endsley, R. C. (1988). Early career development among child and family development professionals: The role of professor and peer relationships. *Family Relations, 37,* 470–476.

Goodman, S. (1989). *Patterns in mentoring relationships: An exploratory study in a selected educational setting.* Unpublished master's thesis, University of Tennessee, Knoxville, Tennessee.

Hendry, L. B., Roberts, W., Glendinning, A., & Coleman, J. C. (1992). Adolescents' perceptions of significant others in their lives. *Journal of Adolescence, 15,* 255–270.

International Medical Services for Health. (1990). *Resource mothers handbook.* Sterling, VA: Author.

Kanfer, F. H., Englund. S., Lennhoff, C., & Rhodes, J. (1995). *A mentor manual for adults who work with pregnant and parenting teens.* Washington, DC: Child Welfare League of America.

Lazarus, R. S., & Folkman, S. (1984). *Stress, appraisal, and coping.* New York: Springer.

Morse, J. (1991). Approaches to qualitative-quantitative methodological triangulation. *Nursing Research, 40,* 120.

Munsch, J., & Blyth, D. A. (1993). An analysis of the functional nature of adolescents' supportive relationships. *Journal of Adolescent Research, 13,* 132–153.

National Black Child Development Institute. (1990). *Each one reach one: The spirit of excellence: Tutor's manual.* Washington, DC: Author.

Philip, K., & Hendry, L. B. (1996). Young people and mentoring—Towards a typology? *Journal of Adolescence, 19,* 189–201.

Phillips-Jones, L. (1983). Establishing a formalized mentoring program. *Training and Development Journal, 15,* 38–41.

Rhodes, J. (1994). Older and wiser: Mentoring relationships in childhood and adolescence. *Journal of Primary Prevention, 14,* 187–196.

Rhodes, J., Contreras, J. M., & Mangelsdorf, S. C. (1994). Natural mentor relationships among Latina adolescent mothers: Psychological adjustment, moderating processes, and the role of early parental acceptance. *American Journal of Community Psychology, 22,* 211–227.

Rhodes, J., Ebert, L., & Fisher, K. (1992). Natural mentors: An overlooked resource in the social networks of young, African-American mothers. *American Journal of Community Psychology, 20,* 445–461.

Saito, R. N., & Blyth, D. A. (1992). *Understanding mentoring relationships.* Minneapolis, MN: Search Institute.

Scales, P., & Gibbons, J. (1996). Extended family members and unrelated adults in the lives of young adolescents. *Journal of Early Adolescence, 16,* 365–389.

Seidel, J., Friese, S., & Leonard, D. C. (1995). *The ethnograph v4.0: A users guide.* Amherst, MA: Qualis Research Associates.

Silfven, S. T. (1990). Postpartum depression in unwed teenage mothers. *Dissertation Abstracts International, 52,* 1738B.

Thompson, R. A. (1995). *Preventing child maltreatment through social support.* Thousand Oaks, CA: Sage.

Tierney, J. P., Grossman, J. B., & Resch, N. L. (1995). *Making a difference: An impact study of Big Brothers/Big Sisters.* Philadelphia, PA: Public/Private Ventures.

Watkins, H. D., Giles, W. F., & Endsley, R. C. (1987). The career development relationships (CDR) model: An expanded view of dyadic relationships in career development. *International Journal of Mentoring, 1,* 3–8.

Werner, E. E., & Smith. R. S. (1982). *Vulnerable but invincible: A longitudinal study of resilient children and youth.* New York: McGraw-Hill.

Wynn, J., Costello, J., Halpern, R., & Richman, H. (1994). *Children, families and communities: A new approach for social services.* Chicago: University of Chicago Chapin Hall Center for Children.

Zippay, A. (1995). Expanding employment skills and social networks among teen mothers: Case study of a mentor program. *Child and Adolescent Social Work Journal, 12,* 51–69.

Appendix

Resource Mothers Contact Form

Resource Mother's Name _____
Date(s) of Contact _____ ID# _____
Time spent together (number of hours) _____
Location of contact:

__ Community   __ MVRM activity
__ Homes   __ Telephone call
__ Other: _____

Issues you and/or the teen mother identified:

__ Abuse/neglect   __ Housing
__ Clothing   __ Infant/child care
__ Emotional   __ Insurance
__ Financial   __ Interpersonal
__ Food/nutrition   __ Substance abuse
__ Furniture   __ Transportation
__ Health care   __ Utilities
__ Other: _____

Services that you offered:

__ Emotional support
__ Modeling life skills
__ Issues solving
__ Referral

___ Securing resources
___ Transportation
___ Other: _____

Information you provided to her:

___ Breast feeding	___ Postnatal care
___ Child growth and development	___ Prenatal care
___ Family planning	___ Safety
___ Infant nutrition	___ School
___ Labor and delivery	___ Substance abuse
___ Personal nutrition	
___ Other: _____	

Comments: (Please describe your contact in greater detail, indicate specific actions taken, describe issues identified and services provided.)

Note: Support for this project was provided by the Missouri Children's Trust Fund, Missouri Department of Health and University of Missouri Extension Service. Sincere appreciation is expressed to the project participants, both mentors and mentees.

About the Authors: Lynn Blinn-Pike is an Associate Professor in the Department of Human Development and Family Studies and Director of the Center on Adolescent Sexuality, Pregnancy and Parenting at the University of Missouri, Columbia. Her interests include adolescent sexuality, research methods, and program evaluation. Diane Kuschel is a doctoral student in Sociology at the University of Missouri, Columbia. Her interests are in the areas of feminism, sociology of the body, historical sociology, and social control/deviance. Annette McDaniel is a masters student in Human Development and Family Studies at the University of Missouri, Columbia. Her interests include program evaluation and adult development. Suzanne Mingus is an Instructor in Human Development and Family Studies and previous Project Coordinator of the Missouri Volunteer Resource Mothers Project. Her interests include adolescent pregnancy and parenting, psychosocial needs of hospitalized children and adolescents, therapeutic play, and child health and well-being issues. Megan Poole Mutti is a site coordinator for Caring Communities in Columbia, Missouri. Her research interests include divorce and family mediation, adolescent risk-taking behaviors, and family life education.

Address correspondence to: Lynn Blinn-Pike, Human Development and Family Studies, 162B Stanley Hall, University of Missouri, Columbia, Missouri.

Exercise for Case 11

Part A: Comparison of Quantitative and Qualitative

Directions: Compare the quantitative and qualitative parts of this research report and answer the following questions.

1. Was it appropriate to use both quantitative and qualitative methods for this research problem? Explain.

2. Did one method contribute more than the other in helping to advance knowledge in this area? Explain.

3. Which method did you personally find more interesting? Explain.

Part B: Evaluation of the Qualitative Aspects of this Research

Directions: Evaluate the qualitative aspects of this research by answering the following questions.

1. Introduction

A. Is the problem area for the research clearly described? Explain.

B. Have the researchers convinced you that the problem area is important? Explain.

C. To what extent does the literature presented in the introduction help you understand the problem? Is the literature used to put the problem in context? Explain.

D. Do the researchers indicate how this study is different from and/or similar to earlier ones reported in the literature?

E. Do the researchers reveal their personal perspectives on the problem area, including any possible biases? Explain.

2. Methods

A. Are the demographics of the participants (i.e., background characteristics such as age, race, and so on) described in sufficient detail? Explain.

B. Considering the problem area for the research, do you think that appropriate participants were selected? If you had been conducting the study, would you have selected the same type(s) of participants? Would you have used the same number of participants? Explain.

C. Which strategies listed in Table 1 on page 161 of this book were employed by the researchers? Are they described in sufficient detail? Explain.

D. In addition to those you named in response to question 2C, have the researchers used any additional strategies to help assure the validity of the study? If yes, what are they? Are they described in sufficient detail? Explain.

3. Analysis and Results

A. Are the steps taken in the analysis described in sufficient detail? Explain.

B. Are the results clearly organized? Explain.

C. Are the results discussed in terms of a theory or theories (either theories that emerged from this study or previously existing ones)? Explain.

D. Were the direct quotations of the participants' statements, if any, judiciously selected? Do they help you understand the results? Explain.

E. Are there other ways the results could have been organized and interpreted? Explain.

4. Conclusions/Implications

A. Are the researchers' concluding remarks appropriate? Do they flow logically from the material presented earlier?

B. Do the researchers describe any implications? If yes, are they appropriate? Are there other implications that are not discussed by the researchers? Explain.

5. Ethical Considerations

A. In your opinion, could this research have caused physical or psychological harm to the participants? If yes, did the researchers take adequate measures to ameliorate the potential for harm?

Explain.

B. If you had conducted this research, would you have obtained written, informed consent from the participants before conducting the study? Explain. Does this research report indicate that the researchers obtained such consent?

6. Overall Evaluation

A. Throughout the article, are all specialized terms and jargon defined to your satisfaction? Explain.

B. Briefly describe your overall evaluation of the research report, noting any special strengths and weaknesses.

C. If you had been a reviewer for the journal in which this report was published, would you have recommended publication of the report? If yes, would you have recommended that it be published "as is" or modified before publication? Explain. If no, what is the primary reason why you would recommend not publishing it?

Case 12

A Comparison of Alternatively and Traditionally Prepared Teachers

JOHN W. MILLER
Florida State University

MICHAEL C. MCKENNA
Georgia Southern University

BEVERLY A. McKENNA
Georgia Southern University

From *Journal of Teacher Education, 49,* 165–176. Copyright ©
1998 by the American Association of Colleges of Teacher Education and Corwin Press, Inc., A Sage Publications Company.
Reprinted with permission of Corwin Press, Inc.

By 1993, 40 states had instituted alternative certification (AC) programs for degree holders wishing to teach (Sindelar & Marks, 1993). Although these alternative certification programs have occasioned contro-
5 versy over their value, researchers have conducted very few substantive investigations on their effectiveness. The few extant studies have somewhat contradictory results.

One problem with investigations and even discus-
10 sion of AC and traditional certification (TC) is the variety of the former. Cornett (1990) provides useful descriptions of the broadly differing ends of the spectrum of AC programs:

[Some AC programs] simply give teachers without the
15 proper credentials (requirements such as education hours completed) an interim status and allow them to be employed while they work to earn the college credits that are equivalent to standard requirements for teacher education programs. On the other hand, several states have
20 developed **alternative certification programs**—ones that permit Arts and Sciences graduates to go through intensified but shorter programs (not requiring the typical accumulation of education hours), or meet requirements by demonstrating competencies, or by gaining the neces-
25 sary expertise through field-based experiences while holding a teaching position (p. 57, emphasis in original).

In this article, we compare TC program graduates with individuals completing a carefully constructed AC program. The AC program required condensed
30 coursework to meet provisional certification standards, an induction mentoring program, and ongoing casework to meet minimal state certification guidelines. It did not meet the full requirements for a degree program in middle-level education.

35 Darling-Hammond (1992), reviewing the literature on alternative teacher certification programs, reports:

Studies of teachers admitted through quick-entry alternate routes frequently note that the candidates have difficulty with curriculum development, pedagogical content
40 knowledge, attending to students' differing learning

styles and levels, classroom management and student motivation (Feiman-Nemser & Parker, 1990; Grossman, 1989; Lenk, 1989; Mitchell, 1987). Novice teachers without full training show more ignorance about student
45 needs and differences and about teaching basics than trained beginners (Rottenberg & Berliner, 1990) (Darling-Hammond, 1992, p. 131).

Some researchers question the content preparation of AC teachers, a supposed strength of AC programs.
50 McDiarmid and Wilson (1991) compared the mathematical knowledge of teachers from two different AC programs with that of TC teachers and noted that teachers with AC preparation lacked depth of content knowledge. They did not improve appreciably through
55 teaching the content:

Our analyses should raise questions about assumptions that underlie policy initiatives such as alternate routes: Specifically, should a major in mathematics—or in any discipline—be accepted as a proxy for the kinds of un-
60 derstandings of the subject essential to helping diverse learners understand critical ideas and concepts (McDiarmid & Wilson, 1991, p. 102)?

Several studies support the equivalence and occasional advantages of AC programs when compared
65 with TC programs. Adelman (1986) found that AC programs attract individuals with greater classroom effectiveness than that possessed by TC teachers. In an evaluation of Texas programs, Wale and Irons (1990) found that administrators held favorable opinions of
70 AC teachers. Hawk and Schmidt (1989) found no difference between AC and TC teachers, either in observed classroom performance or National Teacher Examination scores. Other researchers (Barnes, Salmon, & Wale, 1989; Dewalt & Ball, 1987;
75 Etheridge, Butler, Etheridge, & James, 1988; Guyton, Fox, & Sisk, 1991; Hutton, 1987; Mishima, 1987; Soares, 1989, 1990) report similar findings. Comparisons based on achievement test performance suggest that AC programs do not necessarily lead to lower stu-
80 dent outcomes (Barnes, et al., 1989; Denton & Peters, 1988; Gomez & Grobe, 1990; Stafford & Barrow, 1994).

Yet, legitimate reasons exist to continue examining the value of alternative programs, especially those em-
85 ploying innovative methodologies. First, a substantial database suggests that AC teachers are not inherently

inferior to their TC colleagues. Second, alternative certification programs have been in place as long as there have been certification programs of any kind. All states award probationary certificates in areas of shortage of people from TC programs. Third, widespread desire exists to create diversity in the teaching force by recruiting people with a variety of life experiences. AC populations are demonstrably more diverse than TC populations (McKibbin & Ray, 1994; Sindelar & Marks, 1993). Fourth, the periodic need to meet specific teacher shortages is likely to continue. Fifth, conflicting results of comparative studies suggest that AC programs cannot be easily lumped together for generalization. McKibbin (1995), for example, has listed nine different alternative routes to teaching in California. Alternative certification is here to stay; researchers should investigate not whether such programs work, but which ones work best.

The present research evidence comparing AC with TC teachers is inconclusive and somewhat contradictory. Numerous reasons for such inconsistent results exist: methodological differences across studies, lack of accepted dependent variables, problems with operationally defining the term *alternative certification,* and other measurement problems. Hawley (1990) cites key problems with such studies:

- Alternative certification teachers from a given district are not compared with TC teachers from that district, but with teachers statewide or nationally or some other jurisdiction that is very different from the district being studied.
- Demonstrating that, on average, AC teachers have higher test scores, or grade point averages, or knowledge of subject matter when such criteria are used to screen out AC applicants, attests not to the superiority of AC programs in attracting candidates, but to the simple fact that different requirements for entry result in different entrants.
- Measures of teaching performance are often administered by principals. Principals usually must commit to support of the AC program before AC teachers are assigned to their schools. And they must devote resources to mentoring and other support.
- Most studies of AC do not try to systematically assess teacher performance. When such assessments do take place, they typically rely on measures that are required by the district or the state.
- Some of the more interesting studies comparing TC teachers with those who enter teaching through alternate routes involve very small numbers of teachers and the reader has no way of knowing whether the teachers studied are representative.
- Some studies fail to distinguish between types of (AC) programs when the data are analyzed (pp. 7-8).

In the remainder of this article, we report our studies investigating the efficacy of an AC program for middle-grade teachers designed by faculty at a southeastern university and funded by the BellSouth Foundation. We designed these studies to overcome the methodological limitations Hawley (1990) cited to answer questions about programmatic strengths on which to capitalize and weaknesses to reduce or eliminate in AC programs.

The Alternative Program

In May 1989, the university initiated an AC training model for 70 middle-grade teachers. The program included individualized and intensive programs of study that comply with Georgia Certification Standards (provisional). Coursework was undertaken in the 1989 summer quarter to qualify the 70 participants for provisional certification and fall 1989 employment in Georgia public schools. Sixty-seven participants successfully completed the coursework and were in classrooms in Fall 1989. Depending on initial assessments, students took between 15 and 25 quarter hours (the equivalent of 9-15 semester hours) prior to the beginning of their teaching assignments in the fall.

During their initial year as teachers, participants were heavily involved with additional coursework and mentoring from university and public school faculty to support their initial instruction. The experiences were designed recognizing that placing teachers in classrooms without university supervision or carefully controlled mentor interaction can lead to ineffective practices (Grossman, 1989; Hawley & Rosenholtz, 1984; McKibbin & Ray, 1994) and in the belief that on-the-job feedback from supervisors and mentors is a distinguishing feature of effective AC programs.

Interns had their own classrooms; they received a substantial amount of supervision. A university supervisor observed each teacher eight times during the year and held post-observation conferences. The supervisor met with mentors individually to monitor the success of the teacher-mentor relationship. During their first year, teachers took a biweekly class taught by the university supervisor that focused on examining common problems, exploring solutions collaboratively, and providing support. Teachers took regular course offerings depending on their assessed needs for certification.

In subsequent years, university support ceased except for additional coursework required of some participants to earn regular certification. Mentor relationships continued on an informal basis.

Study 1

We conducted the initial study to examine differences in teaching practices between those educated in TC and AC programs. We examined behavioral differences of teachers in relationship to training differences.

Subjects

Sixty-seven of the 70 summer participants were placed in classrooms in fall 1989. Three years later, we traced 41 of the 67 AC students to teaching positions accessible to the campus. They became the AC sample. We matched them with TC counterparts, teachers who began in the same year and thus had 3 years of teaching experience. They taught the same subjects, at the same grade level, at the same school; all had graduated from varying TC programs from instate and out-of-state public and private institutions.

Instrument and Data Collection

We used a 15-item, 4-node rating scale to evaluate observed lessons for specific dimensions of instruction known to be causally related to learning (e.g., Hunter & Russell, 1977; Rosenshine, 1986). The instrument has two subscales, Effective Lesson Components (9 items) and Effective Pupil-Teacher Interaction Components (6 items). The Effective Lesson Components include Focus, Objective and Purpose, Goal Direction, Exposition, Modeling, Practice, Monitoring, Feedback and Adjustment, and Closure. The Effective Pupil-Teacher Interaction Components include Questioning Strategies, High Pupil Participation, Creative and Enthusiastic Presentation, Appropriate Reinforcement, Appropriate Constructive Criticism, and Appropriate Negative Consequences.

We labeled rating-scale nodes as follows:

1 = *No attempt to exhibit the behavior*
2 = *Limited effectiveness in exhibiting the behavior*
3 = *Moderate effectiveness in exhibiting the behavior*
4 = *High effectiveness in exhibiting the behavior*

We allowed an NA rating (no appropriate opportunity to exhibit the behavior) for some categories (e.g., Focus, Practice) because circumstances might have prevented the teacher from applying the categories during a given observation. For other categories (e.g., Monitoring, High Pupil Participation), we assumed that evaluation was possible during any observation, and we did not permit the NA.

Prior to the study, we precisely defined each category of teacher behavior and developed instructional materials (including printed manuals and videotaped lessons) to train observers in script taping and converting completed script tapes into viable ratings. The instrument and the training program had been carefully and systematically validated prior to the present study (Miller & McKenna, 1988; Miller, McKenna, & Davison, 1990; Miller, McKenna, & Harris, 1989). We trained two certified teachers as observers because of their extensive classroom experience and because the instrument had been validated on the basis of practitioner observers. Each observer observed and evaluated all 82 of the subjects. The observations were blind; observers did not know that 41 subjects were alternatively certified and 41 were traditionally certified. They were informed that they would be observing teachers to establish an evaluation data base for the instrument. The observations were unscheduled; if an intact lesson was not being taught, the observer would stay until an intact lesson was begun or return on another occasion. They then arranged observations of each pair of teachers. Two observers were present for all lessons ob-

served so that ratings for each category could be juried in case of disagreement after the completion of their script tapes. In nearly all cases, jurying was unnecessary because the two ratings coincided. Observers visited both teachers in each pair on the same day. They observed at a time the teachers had suggested; teachers were encouraged to select a time when they were introducing new material. Both observers had their observational skills validated prior to any data collection.

Results

We conducted preliminary analysis steps to identify outliers and assess assumptions for the multivariate analysis of variance (MANOVA) procedure. First, inspection of histograms of each dependent variable for each group did not suggest the presence of outlier observations. Second, we assessed the assumption of multivariate normality by examining the histograms mentioned above. Inspection of the plots suggested the assumption of multivariate normality was tenable. Finally, we considered the scores of each teacher to be independent. Thus, we identified no unusual data values, and MANOVA assumptions appeared to be met.

We computed means and standard deviations for all 15 categories of teacher behavior for both groups. Occasional ratings of NA caused the number of subjects to vary for some categories. We also computed means and standard deviations for the two subscales. We eliminated teachers from the computation of the mean for that subscale who received a rating of NA for any item in one of the two subscales. Descriptive statistics for all categories and for the two subscales appear in Table 1. The difference in sample means between the two groups appears small for all the individual categories, with the largest difference being approximately 0.2.

We used three separate MANOVAs to determine if the small sample differences between groups obtained in the study reflect real differences in the populations or are due to sampling variability. In the first MANOVA, we used the two subscales as the dependent variables. A nonsignificant Wilks's lambda resulted, Wilks's lambda = .98, $F(2,31) = 0.4$, $p = .69$. No group differences on the two subscales were present. In the second MANOVA, the nine Effective Lesson Component categories were used as the dependent variables. Again, we detected no significant differences, Wilks's lambda = .76, $F(9,24) = 0.8$, $p = .59$. Finally, we used the six Effective Pupil-Teacher Interaction measures as dependent variables. Once again, we observed no significant differences, Wilks's lambda = .93, $F(6, 66) = 0.9$, $p = .53$. The analyses suggest that the differences obtained in the study between traditional and alternative groups were due to sampling variability and do not reflect true differences in the populations.

We performed follow-up analyses to identify whether the study had adequate precision to support a

Table 1
Contrasts Between the Traditional and Alternative Groups

	Group						Point estimate of contrast	SE	99% confidence interval
	TC			AC					
Variable	n	M	SD	n	M	SD			
Focus	32	2.9	1.0	41	2.8	0.9	0.15	0.27	(−0.57, 0.87)
Objective and purpose	16	2.6	1.0	18	2.7	0.9	−0.14	0.26	(−0.81, 0.54)
Goal direction	41	3.4	0.6	41	3.3	0.6	0.12	0.14	(−0.25, 0.49)
Exposition	41	3.1	0.4	41	3.1	0.6	0.03	0.12	(−0.29, 0.35)
Modeling	41	3.1	0.6	41	3.0	0.7	0.09	0.16	(−0.34, 0.52)
Practice	34	3.2	0.5	41	3.3	0.5	−0.10	0.13	(−0.45, 0.25)
Monitoring	41	3.2	0.7	41	3.2	0.7	0.01	0.15	(−0.37, 0.39)
Feedback and adjustment	41	3.3	0.6	41	3.1	0.7	0.19	0.15	(−0.20, 0.58)
Closure	34	2.1	1.0	40	2.2	0.9	−0.01	0.25	(−0.66, 0.64)
Effective lessons subscale		27.9	4.4		26.8	4.2	1.16	1.47	(−2.87, 5.19)
Questioning strategies	27	3.2	0.5	38	3.1	0.6	0.06	0.13	(−0.28, 0.40)
High pupil participation	41	3.4	0.7	41	3.5	0.6	−0.05	0.15	(−0.45, 0.35)
Creative and enthusiastic presentation	41	3.1	0.7	41	3.0	0.7	0.12	0.16	(−0.31, 0.55)
Appropriate reinforcement	40	3.1	0.5	35	2.9	0.5	0.16	0.12	(−0.16, 0.48)
Appropriate constructive criticism	41	3.1	0.5	36	2.9	0.6	0.22	0.14	(−0.15, 0.58)
Appropriate negative consequences	33	2.8	0.6	41	2.8	0.6	0.09	0.14	(−0.28, 0.46)
Effective pupil-teacher interaction subscale		18.7	2.6		18.2	2.6	0.49	0.60	(−1.10, 2.08)

310 finding of no practical importance in the population. To identify whether the study had adequate precision, we computed 99% confidence intervals for each of the contrasts. We selected the more stringent 99% confidence level to protect against the inflation of fam-
315 ily-wise error rate. We then compared intervals against a threshold value of 1 for the individual categories and values of 9 and 6 for the two subscales, respectively, with the belief that a 1-unit change on the 4-node rating scale reflects an important difference. Confidence in-
320 tervals that lie completely below the value of practical importance allow us to conclude that we have high confidence that the true population difference is of no practical importance. The results, shown in Table 1, suggest that this study had sufficient precision of esti-
325 mation, as the range of each of the confidence intervals lies entirely below the threshold values of importance. There appear to be no reliably important differences between the alternative and traditional teaching groups for the behavior examined in this study. We accept the
330 null hypothesis that groups do not differ on these sets of teaching behaviors.

Discussion

That the two groups did not significantly differ on any of the dimensions surveyed suggests alternative explanations. The most apparent is that certification
335 programs did not differentially affect teachers' performance. Two conditions affected this result: Data were gathered 3 years after preservice preparation for TC teachers had ended, and intervening professional experiences may have had an equalizing effect. Ongo-
340 ing mentorship was designed to accomplish this result. A second factor is that the AC teachers, like their tra-ditional colleagues, faced annual evaluations based on a rating scale that, while different from the instrument used in the study, drew on the same effectiveness lit-
345 erature.

An unlikely alternative explanation is that the two observers exhibited a response set in which ratings clustered around the moderate node (rating = 3) even when observed evidence suggested otherwise. Exami-
350 nation of Table 1 reveals sizeable standard deviations (for a scale spanning only three units), indicating considerable variance in the ratings. In Closure, the mean for both groups differed markedly from the means for most other categories. Finally, the training program to
355 prepare the observers had been validated through studies establishing its effectiveness in developing the ability to produce ratings consistent with observed evidence (Miller & McKenna, 1988).

The most reasonable conclusion is the most obvi-
360 ous: Alternative certification did not lead to inferior practice among teachers evaluated 3 years into their careers. The program through which these teachers passed did not end with graduation but included a two-part mentoring component supporting them
365 through their initial year. Preparatory coursework followed by supervised application of what is learned exemplifies the direct instruction model on the basis of which these teachers were evaluated.

Study 2

We conducted a second study to examine the ef-
370 fects of AC versus TC teachers on the achievement outputs of their students. The treatments previously discussed in relation to Study 1 remain the same in Study 2. The sample, instrument, data collecting, and

statistical analysis all differ.

Sample

375   From the 41 AC teachers and 41 TC teachers from the observational analysis, we selected only those in self-contained fifth- and sixth-grade classrooms. We did so to have students taught all of their basic subject matter competencies in a given year by a single
380   teacher. Teachers in subject-matter-defined middle-grade classrooms, such as middle-grade science, could not be fairly evaluated because of the indirect alignment between their teaching, the teaching of others, and the focus of the achievement test score. In the
385   self-contained classrooms, where both pre- and post-achievement test scores were available, we could determine entry level differences to control for prior differences of achievement based on interaction with other teachers or any other related factors. We could
390   attribute posttest gains to the instruction of a single teacher rather than that of several teachers for each individual student.

Eighteen classrooms of students participated in the achievement test score analysis done in Study 2. For
395   each of these 18 classrooms, we utilized all students present for the entire year and having pretest and posttest scores. This resulted in a sample of 188 students taught by AC teachers and 157 students taught by TC teachers.

400   There were no apparent systematic biases in the way students were placed into these classrooms. They were not ability grouped; therefore, there was no systematic reason to suspect that there would be pretest differences. Nevertheless, we collected pretest scores
405   for all subjects and analyzed differences between the AC and the TC distributions of students' scores. There were no entry level differences approaching significance on either the total reading or total math variables, or on any of the other subtest scores.

Instrument and Data Collection

410   Students took the Iowa Test of Basic Skills (ITBS) as a posttest at the conclusion of the academic year. The total reading and total math subtest normal curve equivalent scores (NCEs) were the primary bases of analysis. To provide general indicators of some differ-
415   ent types of thinking skills, we analyzed three other math subtests: concepts, problem solving, and computation NCE scores.

The achievement tests were administered under normal standardized procedures by the classroom
420   teachers and were retrieved from the district's database. Students with posttest scores in AC and TC teachers' classrooms were then traced backwards to pretest scores.

Results

NCE means and standard deviations for total math
425   and total reading subtests, and the three additional math subtests are in Table 2. After determining that there

were no preexisting differences based on pretest measures, we concluded no covariate was necessary. The data met the same major assumptions for MANOVA as
430   the data analyzed for Study 1. We used the posttest MANOVA procedure to control for family-wise error rate and test the hypothesis that group population means did not differ for any of the dependent measures and combinations. A conceptual relationship existed
435   between the nature of the dependent variables; a statistical test of the quality of variance assumption was conducted and met. The normality of the distributions was examined with histograms and appeared to be met. Comparison between the AC and TC students' test
440   score means was then conducted by a multivariate analysis of variance (MANOVA). A nonsignificant Wilks's lambda resulted, $F(1,158) = .99$, $p = .83$. No significant difference was observed in the effect of the independent variable (method of training) on the col-
445   lective dependent measures. Further examination of the five posttest means indicated that there were virtually no differences on any of the dependent measures.

Table 2
Means and Standard Deviations of NCEs for Total Math, Total Reading, and Math Subtests

Test	Group			
	TC		AC	
	M	SD	M	SD
Total math	47.6	18.4	46.9	19.1
Total reading	44.5	16.2	45.9	16.1
Math concepts	46.1	17.2	46.0	16.9
Math problem solving	44.5	15.8	46.3	17.6
Math computation	41.3	15.1	45.2	15.2

N: TC = 157, AC = 188

Follow-up analyses indicated that Study 2 had adequate precision to support a finding of no practical im-
450   portance in the population.

Discussion

The results of the student output measures closely parallel those of the observational study. There was no difference in average student achievement test score levels, based upon whether students had been taught by
455   AC or TC teachers. Although this was not an experiment in that there was no random assignment of classrooms, little indication exists that any entry-level biases would have affected these test scores. The school district did not use any grouping or clustering assign-
460   ment processes that would create differences and used a random procedure within grade levels and within buildings to assign students to classrooms. Insofar as the ITBS reflects student learning in reading and mathematics, there were no relative advantages or dis-
465   advantages in terms of student mean output whether AC or TC teachers taught them.

Although the value of these achievement test scores may be questioned, no indications existed of trends of differences in student output based on these measures
470   used in a district-wide procedure. There appeared to be

no effect of type of teacher training on student achievement.

Study 3

The third study was qualitative. We conducted it to gain insight into AC and TC teachers' perceptions of their teaching abilities.

Subjects

The 82 teachers in the 41 pairs of matched subjects in Study 1 were the total sample for Study 3. The same selection and matching procedures in Study 1 apply in Study 1.

Instrument and Data Collection

We developed a direct interview protocol to collect qualitative data. The protocol contained three major areas of questions and some recommended supportive probes in each of these three areas.

The interviews were face-to-face meetings between trained interviewers and all subjects in their classrooms. To avoid formalization of response and to create a more discussion-oriented atmosphere, interviewers did not tape-record the interviews. They conducted the interviews as informal discussions between teachers concerning perceptions of their experiences. We used practicing teachers to gather data because of their classroom experience and because interviewees might be forthcoming reflecting with a peer. The three major areas discussed included teachers' perceptions of their preparation level when they began teaching 3 years previously, their perception of their current level of competency, and their perception of problems encountered across their 3-year careers. Interviewers kept complete notes; these notes were later transcribed. Interviewers did not know that some subjects were AC teachers and some were TC. Questions in the interview protocol were composed to not reveal to the interviewer the type of preparation the interviewee had undergone.

Results and Discussion

All 82 subjects responded to discussion probes in each of the three areas. Content analysis of the resulting commentary reveals interesting trends. Although there were differences in the qualitative aspects of the AC and TC teachers' responses, differences within those categories were greater than differences across the categories. The following are generalizations about teachers' feelings of adequacy of preparation at the beginning of their teaching experience.

Neither AC nor TC teachers felt particularly well prepared. TC teachers sometimes tried to explain this more as the natural tendency to feel inadequate at the beginning of a career, whereas AC teachers felt that something was missing. Typical comments from TC teachers, when asked, *How prepared did you feel as a teacher when you started your job?* included

- I did not feel very prepared. Of course, no one ever

feels truly prepared.
- Not too prepared, but not because of the program I was in—it's just the nature of teaching.
- I'm sure that like all first-year teachers I had some problems and felt uneasy.
- Like anyone, there was the uncertainty of a new job.
- I had all the theories for teaching, but lacked any real classroom experience in my undergraduate program.

Some AC teachers also felt inadequate. They believed they had gaps that could be traced to their preparation.

- I did not know how to control behavior.
- I did not know how to write a lesson plan.
- Very unprepared. I'm not sure whether student teaching would have helped, but I think so.
- Very shaky. I don't think I would have made it without my mentor.
- Some hands-on experience would have been helpful. I had no earthly idea of how to do a lesson.

More TC teachers felt adequately prepared than not. The percentage expressing confidence was higher for TC than AC teachers. They made comments like

- I was very confident. I felt pleased with how my undergraduate program prepared me.
- Fairly prepared. I had been involved some with the schools beforehand.
- Pretty prepared, but then I guess no one goes in completely prepared.

Responses to the first question indicated that both groups were somewhat unsure of themselves. Some TC teachers had a higher confidence level, whereas others felt similarly to AC teachers. TC teachers explained some of their inadequacies as the natural by-product of beginning a new job.

Question 2 concerning the current feeling of competence to practice elicited little or no differences between the groups. The TC teachers said things like

- I feel very prepared. On-the-job experience does wonders.
- I owe a great deal to my mentor. I feel very confident now.
- Experience is the best teacher. There is no substitute for actual classroom experience.
- Now I am very prepared. I feel the comfort that comes from experience.

AC teachers, who might have been expected to place even more value in the more practical experience, did not differ from their TC counterparts who also placed a great deal of faith in on-the-job practice. AC teachers made comments like

- I am very prepared now. I have learned how to have good rapport with my students.
- Now I feel I am on equal footing with the teachers who went through the traditional route.
- I have taught several years at the same school, so now I feel confident.
- I am very grateful for the opportunity that this pro-

580 gram created for me and for all the help that was pro-
     vided in the induction program.
     • I enjoy teaching more now, I am more relaxed and
       prepared. The veteran mentor really helped.

     Both TC and AC teachers, after having had experi-
585 ence, felt competent. At the end of the 3-year experi-
     mental period, TC and AC teachers were not distin-
     guishable based upon their comments concerning their
     competence.

     The types of problems TC and AC teachers en-
     countered seem not to differ. Discipline and classroom
590 management were by far the most common problems
     both cited. Both groups cited the ability to deal with
     special need students, to work with emerging technolo-
     gies, and to deal with parents less often, but equally
     frequently. A number of the AC teachers commented
595 favorably on the induction program and the help of
     their mentors in overcoming some of their initial diffi-
     culties.

Summary and Implications

     We conducted three studies to address basic issues
     of research design Hawley (1990) identified as charac-
600 teristic of comparative investigations of AC and TC
     teachers. We addressed his observation that AC teach-
     ers are too often compared with TC teachers from other
     districts by using same-school pairs of TC and AC
     teachers. We further matched each pair by subject
605 matter taught and years of experience. Hawley's obser-
     vation that different screening criteria for AC and TC
     trainees may skew samples even before training begins
     was not a problem in these studies because the AC co-
     hort was not subject to special admission requirements,
610 such as higher test performance. We met his concern
     that classroom observation data often come from prin-
     cipals through using trained observers who were out-
     siders to the school and who visited classrooms without
     knowledge of the certification history of those ob-
615 served. We used a well-validated instrument with
     which none of the teachers was familiar.

     Hawley also noted that the small sample sizes in
     some studies raise questions about the representative-
     ness of the teachers included as subjects. We consis-
620 tently used a relatively large cohort of AC teachers.
     Finally, Hawley noted some studies fail to distinguish
     types of AC programs in data analysis, a difficulty oc-
     curring when results of several investigations are ag-
     gregated. Our results are limited to a single AC pro-
625 gram with well-defined characteristics. This clarity of
     identity gives the results their strength.

     The preceding does not mean no design limitations
     were present. Examining the trainees of a single pro-
     gram and after an interval of only 3 years constrains
630 the generalizability of findings and leaves unaddressed
     such matters as first-year efficacy. Nevertheless, two
     circumstances make it possible to arrive at important
     conclusions about alternative certification on the basis
     of these results. The first is that we systematically ac-

635 counted for notable past difficulties with research. The
     second is the logical progression in planning the sec-
     ond and third studies to extend and clarify the results.

     The combined results of Study 1, dealing with ob-
     servable differences in classroom teaching behaviors;
640 Study 2, dealing with achievement test score perform-
     ance of students; and Study 3, dealing with qualitative
     differences in the perceptions of teachers, support the
     conclusion that, after 3 years of experience and
     mentoring, no major differences exist between AC and
645 TC teachers. Yet, these studies provide no solace for
     those who believe that anyone with a bachelor's degree
     can be placed in a classroom and expect to be equally
     as successful as those having completed traditional
     education programs.

650 We can clearly say that after 3 years, there appear
     to be no observable teaching behavior differences, stu-
     dent output differences, or attitudinal differences con-
     cerning perceptions of competence of people prepared
     under the two conditions. Other indicators might have
655 revealed differences between the two groups of teach-
     ers compared in these studies. Student behaviors, for
     example, might have been examined with respect to
     library use, cooperative group work, engaged time, and
     many other potential impact measures. Teacher be-
660 haviors might have been more broadly indexed to in-
     clude professional memberships, integration into the
     school culture, emergent philosophical orientations,
     and any number of other conceivable outcomes. Al-
     though interesting, such possibilities seem less central
665 to the principal issues involving issues addressed by
     the outcomes examined in the present systematic series
     of investigations. Carefully constructed induction pro-
     grams may be a good means of including a broader,
     more diverse teaching population than limiting all ave-
670 nues of entrance to the profession through TC prepara-
     tion. The three studies reported here support carefully
     constructed AC programs with extensive mentoring
     components, post-graduation training, regular inservice
     classes, and ongoing university supervision.

675 A most constructive result of data interpretation
     would be to examine the relevance of the induction
     program presented to AC teachers as a model for all
     beginning professionals. Extensive mentoring with
     peer professionals, continued university support, and
680 specifically constructed inservice classes during the
     first 3 years of preparation may be a model that would
     enhance the teaching abilities of all. Rather than con-
     struing these results as supporting a means of dimin-
     ishing potential differences, it may be more appropriate
685 to envision a comprehensive induction model that pro-
     vides a baseline of support for those entering service
     through AC routes and enrichment or even remediation
     for those entering via TC programs.

References

Adelman, N. E. (1986). *An exploratory study of teacher alternative certification and retraining programs* (U.S. Department of Education, Data Analysis
Support Center, Contract No. 300-85-0103). Washington, DC: Policy Stud-

ies Associates.

Barnes, S., Salmon, J., & Wale, W. (1989, March). *Alternative teacher certification in Texas.* Paper presented at the meeting of the American Educational Research Association, San Francisco. (ERIC Document Reproduction Service No. 307 316)

Cornett, L. M. (1990). Alternative certification: State policies in the SREB states. *Peabody Journal of Education, 67*(3), 55-83.

Darling-Hammond, L. (1992). Teaching and knowledge: Policy issues posed by alternate certification for teachers. In W. D. Hawley (Ed.), *The alternative certification of teachers* (Teacher Education Monograph No. 14, pp. 123-154). Washington, DC: ERIC Clearinghouse on Teacher Education.

Denton, J. J., & Peters, W. H. (1988, September). *Program assessment report: Curriculum evaluation of a non-traditional program for certifying teachers.* College Station: Texas A & M University. (ERIC Document Reproduction Service No. 300 361)

Dewalt, M., & Ball, D. W. (1987). Some effects of training on the competence of beginning teachers. *Journal of Educational Research, 80,* 343-347.

Etheridge, C. P., Butler, E. D., Etheridge, G. W., & James, T. (1988, February). *The effects of type of teacher preparation program on internships in secondary schools.* Paper presented at the meeting of the American Association of Colleges for Teacher Education, New Orleans. (ERIC Document Reproduction Service No. 293 807)

Feiman-Nemser, S., & Parker, M. B. (1990). *Making subject matter part of the conversation or helping beginning teachers learn to teach.* East Lansing, MI: National Center for Research on Teacher Education.

Gomez, D. L., & Grobe, R. P. (1990, April). *Three years of alternative certification in Dallas: Where are we?* Paper presented at the meeting of the American Educational Research Association, Boston.

Grossman, P. L. (1989). A study in contrast: Sources of pedagogical content knowledge for secondary English teachers. *Journal of Teacher Education, 40*(5), 24-31.

Guyton, E., Fox, M. C., & Sisk, K. A. (1991). Comparison of teaching attitudes, teacher efficacy, and teacher performance of first year teachers prepared by alternative and traditional teacher education programs. *Action in Teacher Education, 13(2),* 1-9.

Hawk, P. P., & Schmidt, M. W. (1989). Teacher preparation: A comparison of traditional and alternative programs. *Journal of Teacher Education, 40*(5), 53-58.

Hawley, W. D. (1990). The theory and practice of alternative certification: Implications for the improvement of teaching. *Peabody Journal of Education, 67*(3), 3-34.

Hawley, W. D., & Rosenholtz, S. (1984). Good schools: What research says about improving student achievement. *Peabody Journal of Education, 61*(4), 1-178.

Hunter, M., & Russell, D. (1977). How can I plan more effective lessons? *Instructor, 87*(2), 74-75, 88.

Hutton, J. B. (1987). *Alternative teacher certification: Its policy implications for classroom and personnel practice.* Austin: University of Texas. (ERIC Document Reproduction Service No. 286 264)

Lenk, H. A. (1989). *A case study: The induction of two alternate route social studies teachers.* Unpublished doctoral dissertation, Teachers College, Columbia University.

McDiarmid, G. W., & Wilson, S. M. (1991). An exploration of the subject matter knowledge of alternate route teachers: Can we assume they know their subject? *Journal of Teacher Education, 42*(2), 93-103.

McKibbin, M. D. (1995, April). *A longitudinal study of the effectiveness of district intern alternative certification programs in California.* Paper presented at the meeting of the American Educational Research Association, San Francisco.

McKibbin, M., & Ray, L. (1994). A guide for alternative certification program improvement. *The Educational Forum, 58,* 201-208.

Miller, J. W., & McKenna, M. C. (1988, April). *Effects of a training program on the ability to observe and analyze instruction.* Paper presented at the meeting of the American Educational Research Association, New Orleans.

Miller, J. W., McKenna, M. C., & Davison, R. G. (1990, April). *The relationship of observational notes to the quality of post-observation teacher conferences.* Paper presented at the meeting of the American Educational Research Association, Boston.

Miller, J. W., McKenna, M. C., & Harris, B. (1989, March). *The utility of differing scripting strategies in evaluating teaching performance.* Paper presented at the meeting of the American Educational Research Association, San Francisco.

Mishima, P. (1987). *The California teacher trainee program: A review.* Sacramento, CA: California State Office of the Legislative Analyst. (ERIC Document Reproduction Service No. 293 801)

Mitchell, N. (1987). *Interim evaluation report of the alternative certification program* (REAB7027-2). Dallas, TX: DISD Department of Planning, Evaluation and Testing.

Rosenshine, B. V. (1986). Synthesis of research on explicit teaching. *Educational Leadership, 43*(7), 60-69.

Rottenberg, C. J., & Berliner, D. C. (1990, April). *Expert and novice teachers' conceptions of common classroom activities.* Paper presented at the meeting of the American Educational Research Association, Boston.

Sindelar, P. T., & Marks, L. J. (1993). Alternative route training: Implications for elementary education and special education. *Teacher Education and Special Education, 16,* 146-154.

Soares, L. M. (1989, February). *Correlates of self-attribution and competency of liberal arts graduates in teacher training programs.* Paper presented at the annual meeting of the Eastern Educational Research Association, Savannah, GA. (ERIC Document Reproduction Service No. 304 408)

Soares, L. M. (1990, April). *Comparisons of student teachers and alternative route candidates.* Paper presented at the meeting of the American Educational Research Association, Boston.

Stafford, D., & Barrow, G. (1994). Houston's alternative certification program. *The Educational Forum, 58,* 193-200.

Wale, W. M., & Irons, E. J. (1990, April). *An evaluative study of Texas alternative certification programs.* Paper presented at the meeting of the American Educational Research Association, Boston.

About the Authors: John W. Miller is dean of the College of Education at Florida State University, Tallahassee. His specializations include administration of teacher education programs. Michael C. McKenna is professor at Georgia Southern University, Statesboro. His specializations include teacher education and literacy education. Beverly A. McKenna is instructor at Georgia Southern University, Statesboro. Her specializations include internships in elementary and middle-level education.

Exercise for Case 12

Part A: Comparison of Quantitative and Qualitative

Directions: Compare the quantitative and qualitative parts of this research report and answer the following questions.

1. Was it appropriate to use both quantitative and qualitative methods for this research problem? Explain.

2. Did one method contribute more than the other in helping to advance knowledge in this area? Explain.

3. Which method did you personally find more interesting? Explain.

Part B: Evaluation of the Qualitative Aspects of this Research

Directions: Evaluate the qualitative aspects of this research by answering the following questions.

1. Introduction

A. Is the problem area for the research clearly described? Explain.

B. Have the researchers convinced you that the problem area is important? Explain.

C. To what extent does the literature presented in the introduction help you understand the problem? Is the literature used to put the problem in context? Explain.

D. Do the researchers indicate how this study is different from and/or similar to earlier ones reported in the literature?

E. Do the researchers reveal their personal perspectives on the problem area, including any possible biases? Explain.

2. Methods

A. Are the demographics of the participants (i.e., background characteristics such as age, race, and so on) described in sufficient detail? Explain.

B. Considering the problem area for the research, do you think that appropriate participants were selected? If you had been conducting the study, would you have selected the same type(s) of participants? Would you have used the same number of participants? Explain.

C. Which strategies listed in Table 1 on page 161 of this book were employed by the researchers? Are they described in sufficient detail? Explain.

D. In addition to those you named in response to question 2C, have the researchers used any additional strategies to help assure the validity of the study? If yes, what are they? Are they described in sufficient detail? Explain.

3. Analysis and Results

A. Are the steps taken in the analysis described in sufficient detail? Explain.

B. Are the results clearly organized? Explain.

C. Are the results discussed in terms of a theory or theories (either theories that emerged from this study or previously existing ones)? Explain.

D. Were the direct quotations of the participants' statements, if any, judiciously selected? Do they help you understand the results? Explain.

E. Are there other ways the results could have been organized and interpreted? Explain.

4. Conclusions/Implications

A. Are the researchers' concluding remarks appropriate? Do they flow logically from the material presented earlier?

B. Do the researchers describe any implications? If yes, are they appropriate? Are there other implications that are not discussed by the researchers? Explain.

5. Ethical Considerations

A. In your opinion, could this research have caused physical or psychological harm to the participants? If yes, did the researchers take adequate measures to ameliorate the potential for harm? Explain.

B. If you had conducted this research, would you have obtained written, informed consent from the participants before conducting the study? Explain. Does this research report indicate that the researchers obtained such consent?

6. Overall Evaluation

A. Throughout the article, are all specialized terms and jargon defined to your satisfaction? Explain.

B. Briefly describe your overall evaluation of the research report, noting any special strengths and weaknesses.

C. If you had been a reviewer for the journal in which this report was published, would you have recommended publication of the report? If yes, would you have recommended that it be published "as is" or modified before publication? Explain. If no, what is the primary reason why you would recommend not publishing it?

Sexual Attraction Toward Clients, Use of Supervision, and Prior Training: A Qualitative Study of Predoctoral Psychology Interns

NICHOLAS LADANY
Lehigh University

KAREN M. O'BRIEN
University of Maryland College Park

CLARA E. HILL
University of Maryland College Park

DEBORAH S. MELINCOFF
Lehigh University

SARAH KNOX
University of Maryland College Park

DAVID A. PETERSEN
University of Maryland College Park

ABSTRACT. Interviews were conducted with 13 predoctoral psychology interns about an experience of sexual attraction toward a client, use of supervision to address the sexual attraction, and prior training regarding sexual attraction. Results indicated that sexual attraction to clients consisted of physical and interpersonal aspects. Therapists believed they were more invested and attentive than usual to clients to whom they were sexually attracted, and they indicated that sexual attraction created distance, distraction, and loss of objectivity. In terms of supervision, only half of the participants disclosed their sexual attraction to supervisors, and supervisors seldom initiated the discussion. Furthermore, trainees found it helpful when supervisors normalized the sexual attraction and provided the opportunity to explore feelings in supervision. Finally, trainees believed their training programs did not adequately address therapist sexual attraction.

From *Journal of Counseling Psychology, 44*, 413–424. Copyright © 1997 by the American Psychological Association, Inc. Reprinted with permission.

Historically, sexual attraction toward clients has been considered an aspect of countertransference (i.e., a reaction to the client's transference; Freud, 1915/ 1983) or to stem from a problem with the therapist
5 (Kaplan, 1977). Recently, therapists' sexual feelings toward clients have been recognized as a common, although complicated, dynamic involving both realistic and unrealistic reactions that most therapists experience at some point in their professional lives (Gabbard,
10 1994, 1995; Pope, Keith-Spiegel, & Tabachnick, 1986). In fact, research has indicated that more than 84% of therapists become sexually attracted to a client at some point during their practice of psychotherapy (Pope et al., 1986; Rodolfa et al., 1994). The purpose
15 of our study was to examine the process of therapists' sexual attraction toward clients, the manner in which therapists are able to use supervision to assist them in managing and resolving their feelings of sexual attrac-

tion, and the training they receive regarding such feel-
20 ings.

To date, participants in studies on therapist sexual attraction have been psychologists in private practice (Pope et al., 1986) and in university counseling centers (Rodolfa et al., 1994) and social workers (Bernsen,
25 Tabachnick, & Pope, 1994). A summary of the results of these survey investigations (combined sample sizes exceeding 385) indicated that most therapists have been sexually attracted to at least one client, with male therapists consistently reporting greater sexual attrac-
30 tion than female therapists. Although therapists rarely considered sexual involvement, they occasionally had sexual fantasies about the client. Also, therapists were sexually attracted to physical and psychological characteristics of their clients, and they often experienced
35 discomfort, guilt, or anxiety as a result of having the sexual attraction. Many therapists also perceived the sexual attraction to be, more often than not, beneficial to the therapy process (with nearly half also noting negative effects). Furthermore, many therapists be-
40 lieved the client was not aware of the therapist's sexual attraction, but most believed that the sexual attraction was reciprocal. In terms of supervision and training, more than half of the therapists sought supervision or consultation at least once, which they believed would
45 involve a positive supervisory or collegial relationship; during their training programs or internships, about half of the therapists had received no, or at best poor, education about issues of sexual attraction.

The consistency of findings across these studies is
50 impressive. These studies indicate reliable trends and thus strengthen our understanding of sexual attraction to clients. However, the generalization of the results to specific client-counselor interactions is limited because of the manner in which the information was elicited.
55 Using a survey methodology, the authors of the aforementioned studies assessed the sexual attraction process for all clients to whom a therapist had been sexually attracted instead of for a specific client-counselor

interaction. Furthermore, the surveys contained predominantly structured, closed-ended questions that failed to capture the inner experiences of trainees. Thus, a more in-depth qualitative analysis of specific instances of therapists' experiences of sexual attraction seemed warranted, and this was the first purpose of our investigation. By examining specific instances in which trainees felt sexually attracted to clients, we hoped to learn more about what may have caused them to feel this sexual attraction and how they managed these feelings.

One aspect of the therapist sexual attraction process that has received limited attention is therapists' use of supervision when sexually attracted to clients. Pope, Sonne, and Holroyd (1993) have suggested that by disclosing in supervision feelings of sexual attraction to clients, therapists can be assisted in working through their sexual feelings in a healthy, rather than a destructive, manner. Rodolfa et al. (1994) found that 60% of their sample of postdoctoral psychologists sought supervision or consultation to examine their feelings of sexual attraction. Those who did not seek supervision reported that the sexual attraction was not interfering with therapy or that they feared a negative reaction from a supervisor. Similarly, Stake and Oliver (1991) found that about 50% of their sample of psychologists discussed with a supervisor their sexual attraction toward a client, and 19% discussed these issues with a therapist.

Whereas most of the research to date has assessed the attitudes and behaviors of practicing psychotherapists, none has specifically examined psychology trainees, who are in a prime position to benefit from supervisory interventions. Unique to trainees is their involuntary involvement in individual psychotherapy supervision (Bernard & Goodyear, 1992; Blocher, 1983), which ostensibly provides them with the opportunity to discuss, work through, and prevent potentially damaging consequences of their sexual attraction toward clients (Ellis & Douce, 1994; Pope et al., 1993). However, in a related study on trainees' nondisclosure, Ladany, Hill, Corbett, and Nutt (1996) found that trainees did not disclose many things to their supervisors, including their sexual attraction toward their clients. Moreover, a primary reason for the nondisclosure to their supervisors was that these predoctoral trainees felt their sexual attraction to clients was unimportant (Ladany et al., 1996). Hence, it is unclear whether trainees, even though they are in a position to benefit from supervision, actually use supervision to help them with sexual feelings toward clients. Thus, our second purpose was to examine the extent to which supervision was used when therapists-in-training were sexually attracted to a client.

Training programs in which therapists learn about sexual attraction to clients have been noted as another relevant research area (Rodolfa et al., 1994; Vasquez, 1988; Yarris & Allgeier, 1988). No training—or poor training—in sexual attraction issues has been reported by more than half of surveyed psychologists (Pope et al., 1986; Pope & Tabachnick, 1993; Rodolfa et al., 1994), marriage and family therapists (Nickell, Hecker, Ray, & Bercik, 1995), and social workers (Bernsen et al., 1994). Although training was generally described as inadequate, the specifics of therapists' dissatisfaction are unclear. Hence, our third purpose was to determine the helpful and unhelpful aspects of training in graduate programs and internships regarding sexual attraction issues.

In sum, the first purpose of our study was to describe the experience of therapists' sexual attraction toward clients, particularly the thoughts and feelings associated with the sexual attraction, how the sexual attraction developed, client and therapist factors associated with the sexual attraction, the impact of sexual attraction on therapy, dreams and fantasies associated with the sexual attraction, and how the sexual attraction was managed and resolved. Our second purpose was to explore how therapists used supervision to address their sexual attraction—specifically, whether therapists disclosed their sexual attraction in supervision, supervisors' reactions to disclosures or supervisory factors associated with nondisclosures, and the manner in which the supervisory relationship influenced their disclosures or nondisclosures. We studied therapists who were in their predoctoral internships because we assumed that they would have a greater understanding than novices would of the therapy process and, unlike postdoctoral therapists, would be in a unique position to use supervision. Our third purpose was to examine the extent to which therapists were trained during their graduate programs and internships to manage and examine their sexual attraction toward clients. Finally, we used a consensual qualitative research (Hill, Thompson, & Williams, in press) approach because we wanted to obtain an in-depth understanding of therapists' experiences of sexual attraction to clients.

Method

Participants

Thirteen psychology interns (10 White, 2 Latina, and 1 Middle Eastern; 8 women, 5 men; 11 heterosexuals, 1 gay man, 1 lesbian) who ranged in age from 27 to 39 years ($M = 31.23$, $SD = 4.15$) participated in this study. Participants were from doctoral programs in either counseling ($n = 9$) or clinical ($n = 4$) psychology. On average, interns had 45.23 months ($Mdn = 48.00$, $SD = 15.42$) of counseling experience since entering their doctoral programs. Twelve of the 13 interns had been in therapy themselves ($M = 27.50$ months, $Mdn = 9.00$, $SD = 35.62$). Participants noted that in general, they were sometimes ($n = 6$) or rarely ($n = 7$) sexually attracted to clients. None of the participants reported any sexual activity with the clients to whom they were sexually attracted.

The therapists reported being sexually attracted to

eight male clients (seven clients were White and one was Latino; seven were heterosexual and one was bisexual) and five female clients (four clients were White and one was Latina; all were heterosexual). Eleven cases involved heterosexual attraction and two cases involved gay male or lesbian attraction. The clients' presenting problems had to do with issues of relationship-trust (nine cases), drugs and alcohol (four cases), individuation-self-esteem (four cases), family of origin (two cases), anger management (one case), depression (one case), sex addiction (one case), and lack of direction (one case). At the time of the sexual attraction, participants were supervised by 3 White male and 10 White female supervisors (9 PhD psychologists, 1 PsyD psychologist, 1 EdD psychologist, 1 psychiatrist, and 1 licensed clinical social worker).

Researchers

The primary researchers for this study were three White doctoral-level counseling psychologists (Nicholas Ladany, Karen O'Brien, and Clara E. Hill); three White graduate students (Deborah S. Melincoff, Sarah Knox, and David A. Petersen) in doctoral programs in counseling psychology served as the interviewers. All six served as judges for the coding tasks.

Prior to collecting data, we noted our biases and expectations regarding the potential findings of the study. We discussed these biases and expectations to increase awareness and to minimize their impact on the data analysis. Four of us believed that most trainees would admit that they had been sexually attracted to a client, and that shame, guilt, and embarrassment would accompany the sexual attraction. One of us expected that the sexual attraction would not be extremely intense. Three believed that the guilt and shame might inhibit disclosure of the sexual attraction to the participant's supervisor. Four of us agreed that the trainee would be more likely to disclose to a supervisor if the supervisor was supportive, open, and caring and if there was a strong working alliance between them. One of us suspected that most of the trainees would disclose the sexual attraction to their supervisors, whereas another expected that the supervisor would need to broach the topic if it was to be discussed at all. Two of us believed that the participants would have received less than adequate training in this area. In sum, we were quite interested in the topic and reported some range of expectations about it. None of us reported particularly traumatic experiences having to do with sexual attraction to clients, and all of us indicated an openness to discovering what was to be found in the data.

Measure

After reviewing the literature on sexual attraction in therapy (e.g., Pope, 1990; Pope et al., 1986), we composed a semistructured interview. In the final version of the interview, questions were open-ended, as suggested by McCracken (1988), to ensure that partici-

pants would have the freedom to answer in an unstructured fashion. The interview questions were divided into 10 areas: (a) discussion of the client to whom the intern was sexually attracted (description of the sexual attraction, client's awareness of the sexual attraction, the client's attractive qualities, whether the client reciprocated the sexual attraction, demographic questions about the client), (b) the course of the sexual attraction (what led to the intern's awareness of the sexual attraction, thoughts and feelings about the sexual attraction, dreams and fantasies related to the sexual attraction), (c) the influence of the sexual attraction on the counseling relationship (influence on outcome of therapy, personal factors that may have been related to the sexual attraction, management and resolution of the sexual attraction), (d) the discussion of the sexual attraction in supervision (whether the intern disclosed sexual attraction to supervisor, what was helpful or not helpful, the relationship with the supervisor, the ways in which the sexual attraction affected the supervisory relationship), (e) the extent to which the interns' training programs dealt with the issue of sexual attraction, (f) how they were trained to deal with sexual attraction issues, (g) the ways in which internships dealt with sexual attraction issues, (h) thoughts about how training programs and internships should deal with the issue of sexual attraction, (i) biographical information about the participants, and (j) biographical questions about supervisors. Interviewers were encouraged to probe the participants' answers to clarify any issues. We conducted pilot interviews with three advanced graduate students in psychology, and we used their suggestions to revise the interview.

Procedure

We used a qualitative methodology to answer the research questions of this investigation. Specifically, we followed the procedures suggested by Hill et al. (in press) for consensual qualitative research, which are detailed below.

Recruiting. We gave a total of 77 packets to colleagues at 18 college counseling centers nationally, who agreed to distribute these packets to their intern trainees or fellow interns who might consider participating in the study. The contacts were not aware of whether or not the interns chose to participate. Once the potential participants opened the materials, they were asked in a cover letter if they would participate in a study regarding sexual attraction to clients. Specifically, we mentioned that as part of the study, we were going to have them reflect on their experiences doing therapy over the past 2 years and describe the client to whom they were most sexually attracted. We also noted in the cover letter that we believed sexual attraction toward clients to be a normal part of the therapy process. We informed potential participants that they would need to be available for two phone interviews over the span of 2 weeks. We then asked them to complete a questionnaire containing demographic questions, an item asking if they had been sexually attracted to a client, and, if they wished to participate, a first name, phone number, and time when they could be reached. A list of the interview questions was enclosed so that participants could review the questions prior to the interview. We informed potential participants that they would be given Pope et al.'s (1993) book in appreciation for their participation. Questionnaires were returned in self-addressed, stamped envelopes.

Of the 77 interns sampled, 22 responded. Seven people declined to participate, 1 person participated but reported he had not experienced sexual attraction to a client, and 1 person could not be reached by phone. The 8 nonparticipants did not differ from the 13 participants in terms of gender, race, or age, but the nonparticipants reported that they had never been sexually attracted to a client.

Interviews. We randomly assigned participants to interviewers. The assigned interviewer called the participant to arrange a time for the interview. Only the first name of the participant was used to set up and conduct the interviews. We informed participants that the interview would be taped and that their responses would be kept anonymous. At the end of the first 30–45 min interview, the interviewer and participant set up a time for a 10–15 min follow-up interview. During the time between the two interviews, another researcher on the team listened to the initial interview and gave suggestions for further probing during the follow-up interview. Also, the follow-up interview gave interviewers a chance to think of areas to probe further and provided participants with an opportunity to reflect on the initial interview and provide additional information. After the follow-up interview, interviewers asked participants to send their names and addresses on a postcard to one of the graduate students on the research team so that the participants could receive the book that served as the research incentive. Thus, there was no way to link the name of the intern to a specific interview. Following the interviews, we assigned each participant a code number, which was subsequently used to ensure anonymity.

Data preparation. Research assistants transcribed the audiotapes verbatim (except for minimal phrases such as "um hmm"), omitting any identifying information about the participant. A different research assistant than the original transcriber checked these transcripts against the audiotape for accuracy. The original interviewer then again checked the transcripts against the audiotape for accuracy.

Coding into domains. After developing an initial "start list" of domains (topic areas) based on the interview questions, the six of us independently reviewed three transcribed interviews to categorize all material in a transcript that related to the same idea into domains and then argued to consensus about the best assignment. For example, we coded in the emergence-of-

sexual-attraction domain information related to the point in therapy when the sexual attraction was noticed by the therapist. We modified the domains to fit the data during the coding process, resulting in the following final list of 19 domains: (a) emergence of sexual attraction, (b) therapist experience of sexual attraction, (c) client factors associated with therapist sexual attraction, (d) client awareness of therapist sexual attraction, (e) client reciprocation of sexual attraction, (f) influence of sexual attraction on therapy process, (g) influence on termination, (h) influence on outcome, (i) dreams and fantasies about client, (j) sexual activity with client, (k) management of sexual attraction, (l) resolution of sexual attraction, (m) therapist factors concurrent with sexual attraction, (n) disclosed to supervisor, (o) not disclosed to supervisor, (p) how training program dealt with sexual attraction issues, (q) how internship dealt with sexual attraction issues, (r) suggestions for training programs and internships, and (s) other thoughts and reactions. Rotating teams of two judges completed the domain coding for the remaining transcripts (i.e., judges independently assigned domains and then the two judges discussed each categorization and came to consensus).

Abstracting core ideas within domains. Rotating teams of three judges independently read the raw data within each domain and formulated core ideas (i.e., summary statements). The purpose of creating core ideas was to capture the content of all the interview data in the domain in a succinct manner. For example, when questioned about what a participant was trained to do if feelings of sexual attraction occurred, the participant responded, "Uh…consult. Talk to a supervisor or if you're not being supervised, then talk to a peer." The abstracted core idea was "intern was trained to consult with supervisors or peers." Next, the team of three judges discussed their core ideas until they reached consensus about the wording of each core idea. We developed a consensus version for each case that consisted of these core ideas and the corresponding interview data for each domain.

Auditing of core ideas. After the consensus version was completed, two other persons from the larger team audited the consensus version to check if the raw data were appropriately coded into the domains, as well as to check the accuracy and wording of the core ideas. The auditors gave their written feedback individually to the primary team, who discussed the feedback and agreed on any changes made to the consensus version.

Cross-analysis. The purpose of the cross-analysis was to identify patterns of responses across participants within specific domains. We divided into rotating teams of three to examine the data within each domain. These teams developed categories by looking for similarities in the core ideas for each domain across the 13 cases. For example, we divided the data in the resolution-of-sexual-attraction domain into two categories: "completely resolved" (5 cases) and "not completely resolved" (8 cases).

400   Once the categories had been created, the team re-
examined the abstracted core ideas and the raw data
within each domain for each participant to determine
whether information relevant to each of the categories
had been coded adequately. If additional information
405 was found, the team determined by consensus whether
or not to add the information to the core ideas and the
appropriate category in the cross-analysis.

Auditing of cross-analyses. The three people who
were not involved in developing the categories for a
410 domain in the cross-analysis served as auditors for that
domain. These auditors reviewed the cross-analysis to
make sure that the data had been captured adequately.
The initial team discussed and agreed on any necessary
changes.

415   *Review by entire team.* The entire team discussed
the results to ensure that there was consensus.

Results

Tables 1 and 2 show the number of cases fitting
into each of the categories and subcategories within the
domains. Using criteria suggested by Hill et al. (in
420 press), we described a category as *general* if it applied
to all 13 cases, *typical* if it applied to 7–12 cases, and
variant (occasional, in a few cases) if it applied to 3–6
cases. We dropped categories that applied to only 1–2
cases. (The actual differences between general and
425 typical categories, or between typical and variant categories, were minimal in some instances and hence
should be treated cautiously.)

Emergence of Sexual Attraction

The sexual attraction typically emerged after therapy began (e.g., developed over the first third of ther-
430 apy as the relationship grew closer), whereas it occurred at first sight (e.g., at intake or first session) occasionally.

Therapist Experience of Sexual Attraction

The feelings associated with the sexual attraction
were typically negative (e.g., the therapist felt scared,
435 guilty, and hyperaware when realizing the attraction to
the client), but in a few cases the feelings were positive
(e.g., the therapist enjoyed being in a therapeutic relationship in which he or she felt well-matched intellec-
tually with the client). Therapists typically noted that
440 they experienced a physical response during sessions
with the client (e.g., the therapist experienced a visceral
physical response to client).

*Client Factors Associated With Therapist Sexual
Attraction*

Therapists typically reported that their clients were
physically attractive (e.g., the therapist noted that client
445 was his or her "type"). Therapists also typically noted
interpersonal factors associated with their attraction to
the client, which could be divided into four subcategories, the first of which was typical and the last three,
variant: (a) client was a good therapy client (e.g., client

450 was brilliant, articulate, sophisticated, and richer in
attributes than other clients), (b) client seemed needy or
vulnerable (e.g., therapist saw client as vulnerable because client's fiancée recently broke off their engagement), (c) client was sexually provocative or flirtatious
455 (e.g., client was coy and childlike), and (d) client had
an attractive personality (e.g., pensiveness, philosophy
of life, intellectualism). As additional variants, therapists noted a similarity between themselves and their
clients (e.g., client was similar to therapist in age and
460 minority status, and therapist identified with client's
struggles about ways to relate more genuinely with
people), therapists mentioned that the client was similar to the therapist's previous or current romantic partner (e.g., the client resembled therapist's wife), and
465 therapists indicated that clients were not the usual type
to whom they were attracted.

Client Awareness of Sexual Attraction

Therapists typically reported that they had no indication that the client was aware of their sexual attraction. For example, one therapist believed that the cli-
470 ent's lack of awareness was partially due to the client's
not assuming that a same-sex therapist would be sexually attracted to him.

Client Reciprocation of Sexual Attraction

Instead of a typical pattern in this category, there
were three variants: (a) there was no indication that
475 client was sexually attracted to therapist, (b) therapist
was uncertain if client was sexually attracted to her or
him (e.g., therapist was uncertain about level to which
client reciprocated the attraction, although he hoped
she was attracted to him), and (c) therapist thought that
480 client was sexually attracted to her or him (e.g., client
wanted a relationship with therapist outside of therapy).

Influence of Sexual Attraction on Therapy Process

Therapists typically believed that they were more
invested, caring, and attentive than usual because of the
485 sexual attraction (e.g., the therapist was more psychi-
cally invested than in other short-term cases). They
also typically believed that the sexual attraction created
tension or distance (e.g., therapist was cautious and
distanced herself from client to compensate for sexual
490 attraction). Occasionally, therapists reported that the
sexual attraction (a) contributed to the therapist's being
too giving and losing boundaries with the client (e.g.,
therapist recognized her tendency to be protective of
client), (b) was intrusive and distracting (e.g., therapist
495 was distracted in session by client's physical attributes,
which caused therapist to be less attentive to what client was saying), or (c) created less objectivity (e.g.,
therapist was concerned about attributing insight to the
client that client did not have).

*Influence of Sexual Attraction on Termination and
Outcome*

500   Twelve of the 13 cases had been terminated at the

127

Case 13 Sexual Attraction Toward Clients, Use of Supervision, and Prior Training: A Qualitative Study of Predoctoral Psychology Interns

Table 1
Number of Cases for Categories From the Cross-Analysis of the 13 Cases About Sexual Attraction and Related Factors

Domain and category	No. of cases	Domain and category	No. of cases
Emergence of sexual attraction		*Dreams and fantasies about client (continued)*	
Sexual attraction emerged after therapy began	8	Dreams alerted therapist to, or intensified, sexual attraction	3
Sexual attraction at first sight	5	Fantasies	
Therapist experience of sexual attraction		None reported	8
Negative feelings	10	Reported fantasies of possible sexual nature	5
Physical response evoked in therapist	7	*Management of sexual attraction*	
Positive feelings	5	Thought/reflected/worked through sexual attraction feelings	
Client factors associated with therapist sexual attraction		on own	7
Client was physically attractive	10	Discussed with supervisor	6
Client was interpersonally attractive	12	More attentive or cautious with case than usual	4
Client was a good therapy client	8	Discussed with someone other than supervisor	4
Client seemed needy or vulnerable	5	Denied, refocused, or repressed feelings or thoughts	4
Client was sexually provocative or flirtatious	4	*Resolution of sexual attraction*	
Client had attractive personality	4	Not completely resolved	8
Client was similar to therapist	6	Completely resolved	5
Client was similar to therapist's previous or current romantic		*Therapist factors concurrent with sexual attraction*	
partner	4	Relationship status	
Client was not usual type therapist finds attractive	3	In problematic romantic relationship	5
Client awareness of therapist sexual attraction		In relatively good romantic relationship	5
No indication client aware of therapist's sexual attraction	12	Not currently in romantic relationship	3
Client reciprocation of sexual attraction		Concurrent stressors	5
No indication client sexually attracted to therapist	6	*How training program dealt with sexual attraction issues*	
Therapist uncertain if client sexually attracted to therapist	4	Sexual attraction not addressed adequately	9
Client sexually attracted to therapist	3	Instructed to talk to their supervisors, consult, or seek own	
Influence of sexual attraction on therapy process		therapy	8
More investment, caring, attention	10	Addressed in ethics class	7
Created tension or distance	7	Environment not open to, or safe for, discussing sexual	
Too giving/lost boundaries	6	attraction	5
Intrusive/distracting	4	Understood they should not act on feelings	4
Less objectivity	4	*How internship dealt with sexual attraction issues*	
Influence on termination[a]		Sexual attraction addressed didactically	7
Difficulty with termination	8	Sexual attraction addressed (or could have been) in	
Perceived no effect on termination	4	supervision	7
Influence on outcome[a]		Sexual attraction not addressed	3
No effect or uncertain effect	8	*Suggestions for training programs and internships*	
Dreams and fantasies about client		Include didactic instruction in curriculum	9
Dreams		Normalize sexual attraction	8
None reported	8	Address sexual attraction individually in supervision	5
Reported dreams of possible sexual nature	5	Discuss appropriate behaviors	4
		Create a safe environment	3

Note. Categories that included fewer than 3 cases are not shown.
[a] Only 12 cases had terminated.

time of the study. Of these 12 cases, therapists typically had difficulty with termination (e.g., the therapist felt more rejected than typical when client terminated uni-laterally), although as a variant, therapists reported no effect on termination. As for outcome, therapists typically believed that there was no effect or they were uncertain of the effects of the sexual attraction on outcome.

Dreams and Fantasies About Client

Typically, therapists reported that they had no dreams about the client. However, a few occasionally reported having dreams of a sexual nature, some of which alerted the therapist to the sexual attraction or intensified the sexual attraction. One therapist reported becoming aware of the sexual attraction after the first session when she had a sexual dream about the client. She dreamed of a fire that had not quite reached her house. She was trying to evacuate her family and dog. She opened the door and her client, who was dressed as a firefighter, had come to rescue them. In the dream, she felt relieved and attracted, and she thought of her client as a hero. The therapist interpreted the dream as sexual because the fire connoted sexuality and passion to her. She felt disturbed by the dream because it felt incestuous (she had previously been aware of having a maternal countertransference toward the client), and it suggested a reversal of roles in that the client rescued the therapist and took care of her needs.

Therapists typically reported no fantasies, although a few therapists reported having fantasies of a sexual nature (e.g., a therapist had fantasies of sexual seduction that took place in the therapist's office). Overall, therapists typically reported having either dreams or fantasies but not both.

Management of Sexual Attraction

Therapists reported that they managed their feelings
535 and thoughts of sexual attraction in five ways. First,
therapists typically thought about, reflected on, or
worked through the sexual attraction feelings and
thoughts on their own (e.g., one participant tried to be
honest with herself and aware of her attraction to the
540 client). Second, therapists occasionally discussed the
sexual attraction with their supervisors. Third, therapists occasionally became more attentive or cautious
with the case (e.g., one therapist was more planful than
usual). Fourth, therapists occasionally discussed the
545 sexual attraction with others such as their therapists.
Finally, therapists occasionally denied, refocused, or
repressed the feelings or thoughts of sexual attraction
(e.g., one therapist "shoved" the sexual attraction out of
his mind and kept busy).

Resolution of Sexual Attraction

550 Therapists typically reported that the sexual attraction was not completely resolved or worked through
(e.g., one therapist felt sexual attraction was mostly
resolved; one therapist felt that he would still be attracted to the client if he worked with her now). In a
555 few cases, however, the therapists reported that the
sexual attraction was completely resolved.

Therapist Factors Concurrent With Sexual Attraction

Two therapist factors were occasionally reported at
the time of the therapist's sexual attraction to the client.
First, in terms of relationships, a few therapists were in
560 problematic romantic relationships (e.g., at the time of
the work with the client, the therapist was being
"strung along" in a relationship, and this made her take
the client's side when working with similar relationship
issues), a few were in relatively good romantic rela-
565 tionships (e.g., the therapist was involved in a 4-year,
committed, monogamous, fulfilling, fun relationship at
the time), and a few were not currently involved in
romantic relationships. Second, a few therapists reported being under a lot of stress at the time of the sex-
570 ual attraction (e.g., graduate school was very difficult
for the therapist).

Supervision

Table 2 shows the number of cases for the supervision domain. Seven of the participants disclosed their
sexual attraction to their supervisors, and six did not
575 disclose their sexual attraction to their supervisors.
Results are described separately for these two groups.
For each of the two subgroups, we considered the category to be general if it applied to all of the cases, typical if it referred to at least half of the cases, and variant
580 if it referred to at least two but less than half of the
cases.

Disclosed to supervisor. For those who disclosed,
the disclosure was typically initiated by the trainee. In
terms of the supervisor's response, all trainees reported
585 that the supervisor was helpful by normalizing, vali-

dating, and supporting. Trainees also typically reported
that supervisors enabled them to explore and cope with
the sexual attraction. In one case, the trainee stated that
the supervisor helped monitor the sexual attraction and
590 provided objective feedback about it. In another example, the trainee mentioned that the supervisor asked in a
nonintrusive fashion about personal issues that might
have fostered the sexual attraction. However, trainees
occasionally reported that some of the supervisors'
595 responses were not helpful because the sexual attraction was not discussed enough or the supervisor probed
too much (e.g., the therapist did not find it helpful
when the supervisor tried to process physical attraction
that the therapist did not feel was there).

Table 2

*Number of Cases for the Supervision Domain and Catego-
ries From the Cross-Analysis of the 13 Cases of Sexual
Attraction*

Domain and category	No. of cases
Disclosed to supervisor	
Who initiated discussion of sexual attraction	
Trainee	5
Supervisor	2
Supervisor response	
Helpful	7
Sexual attraction normalized, validated, and supported	7
Enabled trainee to explore and cope with sexual attraction	6
Not helpful/not enough discussion/probed too much	3
Relationship with supervisor	
Positive aspects	7
Negative aspects	3
Disclosure of sexual attraction strengthened supervisory relationship	6
Not disclosed to supervisor	
Reasons for nondisclosure	
Negative feelings about supervisor/would not be supportive	4
Sexual attraction not significant enough/not relevant	3
Relationship with supervisor	
Positive aspects	4
Negative aspects	4
Nondisclosure of sexual attraction weakened supervisory relationship	4
Beneficial discussion with others (peers, family members, therapist)	5

Note. For the supervision domain, the total number of cases possible was 7 for the disclosure group and 6 for the nondisclosure
group. Categories that included fewer than 2 cases are not shown.

600 In terms of the supervisory relationship, positive
aspects emerged for all cases in the disclosure group
(e.g., excellent relationship, relationship was honest,
supportive, and good). A few therapists also reported
negative aspects (e.g., supervisor discussed tangential
605 topics, supervisory relationship was initially difficult).
Finally, therapists typically reported that discussing the

sexual attraction strengthened the supervisory relationship. One therapist mentioned that the discussion of the sexual attraction confirmed a good relationship, and another believed that the sexual attraction issue brought the therapist closer to the supervisor.

Not disclosed to supervisor. Typically, those therapists who did not disclose to their supervisors their feelings of sexual attraction reported negative feelings about the supervisor or concern that the supervisor would not be supportive. One therapist believed that the supervisor was not competent enough, and another mentioned that the supervisor was insensitive and disrespectful toward her. Another reason for not disclosing to supervisors was that the sexual attraction was not considered significant enough or relevant to supervision (e.g., the therapist thought attraction was more appropriate to talk about with her therapist and her friends in a peer supervision group).

In terms of the supervisory relationship, therapists typically mentioned positive and negative aspects. Examples of positive aspects included statements that the supervisor was supportive or complimentary. Negative aspects included statements that the supervisor was distant and competitive or sexually harassed the therapist. The sexual attraction issue typically had a negative effect on the supervisory relationship. One trainee reported that not discussing the sexual attraction added distance to an already distant supervisory experience. Relatedly, therapists who did not disclose their sexual attraction to their supervisors typically found it beneficial to discuss the sexual attraction with others, including peers, family members, and their therapists.

How Training Program Dealt With Sexual Attraction Issues

Table 1 shows that therapists typically reported that sexual attraction was not addressed adequately in their training programs. For example, one therapist stated that sexual attraction was only mentioned by some faculty in practice, and another stated that there was minimal exposure in the training program to the topic of sexual attraction. Therapists also typically reported that they were instructed to talk to their supervisors, seek consultation, refer the client elsewhere, or obtain therapy when they felt sexually attracted to their clients. In addition, therapists typically stated that sexual attraction issues were addressed in ethics classes. A few therapists, however, reported that the training programs were not open or safe environments in which to discuss sexual attraction (e.g., one therapist stated that students were hesitant to discuss sexual attraction because it could be dangerous professionally to do so).

How Internship Dealt With Sexual Attraction Issues

Table 1 also shows that sexual attraction was typically addressed didactically in internships (e.g., interns were given a book on the topic, or sexual attraction was discussed in the context of a seminar). Therapists typically reported that they knew they could talk to their supervisors, suggesting that sexual attraction was addressed informally. In a few cases, sexual attraction toward clients was not addressed in any manner.

Suggestions for Training Programs and Internships

Therapists typically suggested that training programs and internships include didactic instruction in the curriculum (e.g., discuss case examples and use videotape training to educate students). Also, participants typically felt a need for sexual attraction to be normalized by training programs and internships. Other suggestions by a few therapists included addressing sexual attraction individually in supervision, discussing appropriate behaviors (e.g., emphasizing not to act on the feelings in therapy), and creating a safe environment (e.g., discussing sexual attraction in a safe setting where students can explore their feelings and talk openly; see Table 1).

Narrative Example of a Therapist's Experience of Sexual Attraction

The intern, "Martin," was a White man in his early 30s who used both cognitive-behavioral and humanistic theory in his work. The client was a 21-year-old White woman who sought therapy for depression and substance abuse. The supervisor was a White man in his 30s who was psychodynamically oriented. Martin met with his client once a week for about 6 months before ending treatment with her about 1 week before being interviewed for the study.

At the time of therapy, Martin was dating, but he was not in a serious, long-term relationship. He noticed that he was sexually attracted to his client in about the second session, when he experienced an emotional and physical response to her presence. The client was not only physically attractive to Martin but also impressed him as articulate, sophisticated, and generally richer in interpersonal attributes than other clients. Martin had never been sexually attracted to a client before and was very distressed by the situation; he experienced a range of negative feelings. For example, he felt embarrassed that he was sexually attracted to someone who had numerous complex problems. He felt guilty that he was devoting more attention to this client than to others, and he felt "tortured" inside because he enjoyed being attracted to her and did not try to change his feelings. In fact, as the sessions progressed, Martin found himself looking forward to seeing the client each week. Thus, the sexual attraction created an emotional dilemma that he struggled to manage.

Although his training program and internship neglected the discussion of sexual attraction to clients, Martin understood that the proper procedure in such cases was to address the issue in supervision. Unfortunately, he felt he could not discuss his predicament with his current supervisor for several reasons. For instance, he felt that discussing sexual issues with this supervisor was off limits because of related issues Martin was aware of in the supervisor's life. Also, be-

715 cause this was a high-risk case that Martin wanted to keep, he feared that if he disclosed in supervision that he was sexually attracted to the client, his supervisor would ask him to give up the case. Despite these con-
720 cerns, Martin said that he would have talked about the sexual attraction if the supervisor had broached the topic, but the supervisor never did. Martin suspected that the supervisor might have sensed the presence of the sexual attraction but did not bring it up out of re-spect for Martin's privacy.

725 Martin speculated that the main benefit of discuss-ing the situation in supervision would have been to reduce his turmoil rather than to change how he was working with the client. Indeed, he believed that be-cause the sexual attraction forced him to stay focused
730 on the client's issues, the client received better care than Martin's other clients. Despite not addressing the situation in supervision, his experience was normalized to some degree when he discussed his sexual attraction to the client with a fellow intern who had a similar ex-
735 perience. Martin's additional strategy for managing the sexual attraction was to read Pope et al.'s (1993) book on sexual feelings in therapy and to be mindful of not harming the client. Thus, although his feelings for the client never changed, he believed the sexual attraction
740 did not have a detrimental effect on the client.

Nevertheless, Martin noticed a blurring of his pro-fessional boundaries in this situation, as evidenced by his eager anticipation of sessions with this client. He also realized that his sexual attraction to her created
745 distance between them as he struggled to compensate for his feelings. For example, although it was not his usual style to avoid physical contact with clients, he became cautious about avoiding casual touch with this client.

750 According to Martin, the termination did not go well in this case. The client had to leave therapy on short notice because she had to move away from the area unexpectedly, and this, in addition to Martin's strong feelings for her, made it difficult for him to pre-
755 pare for termination as he normally would. In fact, when he ended treatment with this client, he regretted not having addressed issues that he typically would have covered when terminating with other clients. Al-though Martin was not sure if the client was attracted
760 to him, he believed that neither of them was ready to end the relationship. Martin's feelings for the client ended when she left, but he was uncertain if the issue of being sexually attracted to her was resolved.

Discussion

The results of this study indicate that interns report
765 feeling sexual attraction toward their clients, and there appears to be consistent patterns in their experiences of sexual attraction. The development of sexual attraction toward clients typically occurred in the beginning stages of therapy, which coincides with the therapeutic
770 phase in which the working alliance is rapidly maturing

(Bordin, 1979; Gelso & Carter, 1985). Perhaps the emotional intensity of a developing relationship, com-bined with physically and interpersonally attractive client qualities, facilitated the development of sexual
775 attraction to clients. Given this scenario, it is not sur-prising that most therapists will at some point in their practice become sexually attracted toward a client. Relatedly, the beginning phase of therapy has also been found to be when sexual contact with clients often oc-
780 curs (Bouhoutsos, Holroyd, Lerman, Forer, & Green-berg, 1983).

Although some therapists found the sexual attrac-tion exciting, most noted negative feelings of guilt and fear, which was consistent with previous research ex-
785 amining the sexual attraction process (e.g., Pope et al., 1986; Rodolfa et al., 1994). Although the physical and some of the interpersonal aspects of a therapist's at-traction to a client appear to be common to relation-ships in general, some of the interpersonal aspects were
790 clearly specific to therapy (e.g., client was a good ther-apy client and client seemed needy or vulnerable). Furthermore, the interpersonal aspects, such as the cli-ent's neediness and flirtatiousness, may be diagnostic of key therapeutic issues for therapists and clients (e.g.,
795 a therapist or a client may tend to sexualize relation-ships; Brodsky, 1985). Ultimately, additional research that investigates how these interpersonal aspects are related to therapeutic process and outcome is neces-sary.

800 Almost all of the therapists perceived no indication that the client was aware of the therapist's sexual at-traction. This finding presumes that the therapist was able to hide the sexual attraction or that the client was not insightful enough to recognize the sexual attraction.
805 Given that these ideas stem from the therapist's per-ception, it would be fruitful to explore clients' reac-tions and perceptions to determine whether clients are in agreement with therapists (Hill, Thompson, Cogar, & Denman, 1993). Furthermore, none of the therapists
810 disclosed their sexual feelings to their clients, which may be appropriate given that the treatment efficacy of such disclosures is uncertain (Goodyear & Shumate, 1996; Pope et al., 1993).

Most of the therapists believed that their clients
815 were not sexually attracted to them, indicating that the sexual attraction was predominately in one direction. However, it might be expected that the sexual attrac-tion was reciprocal because of the mutuality of the therapeutic experience. It is important for future re-
820 searchers to assess the client's perspective to determine the extent to which the therapist's perception is indeed accurate. Trainees' typical beliefs and their reactions to having someone attracted to them or the manner in which their sexual attraction to others is usually mani-
825 fested may prove fruitful to explore as potential inter-ventions in supervision. In this way, supervisors could determine the extent to which the sexual attraction is indeed unidirectional.

131

830 According to the therapists, their sexual attraction appeared to have an effect on the therapy process. Consistent with the survey findings (Bernsen et al., 1994; Pope et al., 1986; Rodolfa et al., 1994), most therapists perceived that the sexual attraction led to both beneficial and negative therapeutic effects. Therapists re-
835 ported becoming more invested and caring about the clients to whom they were sexually attracted while recognizing that the sexual attraction contributed to their overinvestment (i.e., their becoming too giving and their losing touch with their emotional boundaries).
840 Ultimately, without clients' reports or objective observations, it is unclear whether a therapist's overinvestment is actually beneficial or harmful to therapy.

More than half of the therapists reported either dreams or fantasies of a sexual nature about their clients. These dreams or
845 fantasies sometimes alerted therapists to the sexual attraction and related problems. These results suggest that therapists should pay attention to their dreams and fantasies for clues about their feelings toward clients. In addition, supervisors should be alert to therapists'
850 dreams and fantasies about clients and their relevance to discussion in supervision.

More than half of the therapists believed that their sexual attraction was not resolved and that some residual feelings of sexual attraction remained at the end of
855 treatment. Research is needed to investigate how to help trainees resolve their feelings appropriately and effectively. Moreover, what constitutes resolution of sexual attraction needs to be clarified. Specifically, resolution need not imply that therapists no longer have
860 thoughts or feelings about their sexual attraction to clients. Perhaps resolution consists of greater understanding and insight into the feelings of sexual attraction rather than of a complete absence of thoughts and feelings of this nature (Bridges, 1994).
865 The results regarding therapist factors provided a mixed picture of the status of therapists' relationships and of concurrent stressors and therefore must be interpreted with caution. It seemed that there was an equal mix of therapists in good and in problematic romantic
870 relationships. Furthermore, only some of the therapists reported concurrent stressors. It is unclear if the relationship statuses and stressors described here are characteristic of most predoctoral interns or are unique to therapists who are sexually attracted to their clients.
875 Thus, although linking relationship status or concurrent stressors to sexual attraction is intuitively appealing, the results do not support this notion.

Supervision

About half of the participants disclosed to a supervisor their feelings of sexual attraction. Thus, trainees
880 in this study who had direct access to supervisors did not use supervision as a resource for dealing with issues of sexual attraction any more frequently than did postdegree therapists (Rodolfa et al., 1994). The findings indicated that the trainees were the ones who typi-

885 cally initiated the discussion about the sexual attraction. In fact, out of the 13 cases of sexual attraction, only two supervisors initiated the discussion of issues of sexual attraction. In one of the nondisclosure cases, the trainee told her supervisor that the client was the
890 most sensual person she had ever met, yet the supervisor did not investigate this further. Perhaps supervisors did not initiate discussion of sexual attraction because of their own discomfort with the topic or because the trainees avoided mentioning their sexual attraction. As
895 has been found in previous research, trainees seemed adept at not disclosing what they did not want their supervisors to know, especially when they had a negative supervisory relationship (Ladany et al., 1996). When the supervisor initiated a discussion of the sexual
900 attraction, the trainees felt relieved and welcomed the opportunity to process the issue. These results suggest that it might be helpful for supervisors to attend more closely to sexual attraction issues and to initiate exploration of these issues in a gentle and supportive man-
905 ner.

Overall, trainees found it particularly helpful when supervisors normalized and validated their experiences and enabled them to explore feelings. Thus, for some trainees, supervision became a primary place in which
910 to work on their issues of sexual attraction. The effectiveness of the supervisory intervention seemed to stem from a blend of supervisory approaches involving both didactic (e.g., normalization) and counseling (e.g., exploration) styles. These approaches highlight the im-
915 portance of supervisory styles involving flexibility, understanding, and comprehensiveness to meet the needs of trainees.

The supervisory relationship seemed to be a key factor in the decision for trainees to disclose their sex-
920 ual attraction issues to supervisors. Specifically, trainees were more likely to make disclosures about sexual attraction when the supervisory relationship was mostly positive and supportive than when it had relatively equal amounts of positive and negative aspects.
925 Several trainees who did not disclose their sexual attraction toward a client thought that their supervisor would not be helpful or supportive. As in therapy, the supervisory working alliance may be a very important factor in determining trainee—and ultimately client—
930 outcome (Bordin, 1983; Efstation, Patton, & Kardash, 1990; Ladany & Friedlander, 1995; Patton & Kivlighan, 1997). Not surprisingly, disclosure to a supervisor strengthened an already positive relationship, whereas nondisclosure weakened an already weak re-
935 lationship.

The results also demonstrate that whether or not they disclosed to a supervisor, trainees were very likely to reveal and discuss sexual attraction issues with peers and therapists. They found these discussions beneficial
940 for the same reasons as did those who discussed the sexual attraction issue with their supervisors (i.e., normalization and support). Thus, when they believed

their supervisors would not be helpful, some trainees were able to approach others to satisfy their need for supervision on these issues. As in Ladany et al.'s (1996) study, it appears that peer supervisors provide a great deal of supervision.

On the basis of the results of this study, we have several suggestions for supervision. Given that previous research suggests that disclosure of sexual attraction in supervision facilitates positive outcome in therapy, we suggest that supervisors (a) be alert to the possibility among trainees of their sexual attraction to clients (Ellis & Douce, 1994), (b) foster a supervisory relationship that is mutually warm, understanding, and trusting, (c) initiate discussions regarding sexual attraction in the context of a positive and open supervisory relationship, (d) be flexible in their approach to supervision, and (e) process sexual attraction issues extensively when trainees ask (or hint) for assistance. Furthermore, assessing and assisting trainees with their sexual feelings toward clients seem to be relevant focal points in the training of clinical supervisors.

Training

Overall, the majority of the participants believed that sexual attraction to clients was not addressed adequately in their training programs and was addressed somewhat during their internships. Perhaps psychotherapy educators may not believe that beginning trainees are ready to handle advanced skills such as examining sexual feelings in therapy and working through countertransference issues. However, this developmental stance may be without merit (e.g., Ellis & Ladany, 1997; Holloway, 1987); further study is warranted to determine the extent to which beginning and advanced trainees can manage and understand issues of therapist sexual attraction to clients. In terms of internships, it appears that in some cases an attempt was made to provide didactic information, but the information may have been inadequate. Thus, it seems important that professors and internship supervisors approach therapist sexual attraction in a more comprehensive fashion than currently exists (Ellis & Douce, 1994; Rodolfa, Kitzrow, Vohra, & Wilson, 1990; Vasquez, 1988). The interns suggested that beyond normalizing sexual attraction, training programs and internships should address sexual attraction issues in practice to provide students with knowledge about how to manage sexual attraction to clients. The trainees also felt it would be beneficial if the instruction on sexual attraction was not solely didactic but also included experiential components as well as examples of how senior therapists or faculty dealt with sexual attraction in their work with clients. Furthermore, according to trainees, this discussion should be conducted in a safe and open environment so that the topic of sexuality can be broached and students' sexual feelings can be explored.

Limitations

One limitation of this study is the generalizability from a small sample. At best, only tentative hypotheses can be generalized to psychology interns. In addition, postdoctoral therapists (who may be able to choose their supervisors) or beginning practicum therapists (who may also be contending with other developmental issues; Stoltenberg & Delworth, 1987) may not experience similar processes with regard to sexual attraction to clients. A second limitation pertains to participant self-selection and response rate. Although the return rate for this study was consistent with other qualitative studies (e.g., Rhodes, Hill, Thompson, & Elliott, 1994), we do not know whether those therapists who did not participate would have reported different reactions. For example, it is unknown if those who did not participate were more or less likely to have been sexually attracted to, or involved with, a client than those who participated. Third, although we attempted to address the influence of researcher bias on the data analysis, it is possible that some of the findings are unique to the manner in which we as a group interpreted the data. Furthermore, some uniqueness can be attributed to the manner in which the interview questions were originally formulated, as well as addressed, in the interview. Thus, replications and extensions with other subsamples of participants and with other researchers to code the data as well as to formulate and direct the interview questions are warranted.

Directions for Future Research

We suggest that investigators attend more closely to the manner in which therapists' sexual attraction to clients influences the process and outcome of therapy. Also, it is important to determine the extent to which client factors, therapist factors, and client-therapist interactions contribute to the development of therapists' sexual attraction. In addition, the manner in which sexual attraction in therapy has been assessed should be expanded. A full understanding of the sexual attraction process and how it might influence therapy process and outcome involves identifying clients' reactions and attraction to the therapist (i.e., not only therapists' perceptions) as well as making behavioral observations of the therapeutic interactions.

Another potential area of investigation is to determine the manner in which parallel process issues are occurring in the therapy and supervisory relationships (Alpher, 1991; Ekstein & Wallerstein, 1972; Friedlander, Siegel, & Brenock, 1989; Pope, Schover, & Levenson, 1980). Specifically, it seems salient to examine the extent to which sexual issues are manifested in both the therapy relationship and the supervisory relationship. A further area of study is the extent to which the supervisory relationship influences the likelihood of therapist disclosure in supervision. In particular, examining the relation between the supervisory working alliance and trainee self-disclosure of sexual attraction to a client might prove worthwhile. Furthermore, delineating the salient features of sexual attrac-

1055 tion that lead to sexual contact (Bates & Brodsky, 1989) is important. Moreover, it is necessary to determine the extent to which supervisors are able to identify and provide adequate interventions for trainees who are sexually attracted to their clients (e.g., what do supervisors look for and how do they decide to broach 1060 the topic?). Finally, investigating the most effective methods of training therapists and supervisors to manage and resolve therapists' feelings of sexual attraction toward their clients is relevant to psychotherapy training programs.

References

Alpher, V. S. (1991). Interdependence and parallel processes: A case study of structural analysis of social behavior in supervision and short-term dynamic psychotherapy. *Psychotherapy, 28,* 218–231.

Bates, C., & Brodsky, A. (1989). *Sex in the therapy hour: A professional case of incest.* New York: Guilford Press.

Bernard, J. M., & Goodyear, R. (1992). *Fundamentals of clinical supervision.* Carmelle, IN: Allyn & Bacon.

Bernsen, A., Tabachnick, B. G., & Pope, K. S. (1994). National survey of social workers' sexual attraction to their clients: Results, implications, and comparison to psychologists. *Ethics & Behavior, 4,* 369–388.

Blocher, D. H. (1983). Toward a cognitive developmental approach to counseling supervision. *The Counseling Psychologist, 11,* 27–34.

Bordin, E. S. (1979). The generalizability of the psychoanalytic concept of the working alliance. *Psychotherapy: Theory, Research, and Practice, 16,* 252–260.

Bordin, E. S. (1983). A working alliance based model of supervision. *The Counseling Psychologist, 11,* 35–42.

Bouhoutsos, J. C., Holroyd, J., Lerman, H., Forer, B., & Greenberg, M. (1983). Sexual intimacy between psychologists and patients. *Professional Psychology: Research and Practice, 14,* 185–196.

Bridges, N. A. (1994). Meaning and management of attraction: Neglected areas of psychotherapy training and practice. *Psychotherapy, 31,* 424–433.

Brodsky, A. M. (1985). Sex between therapists and patients: Ethical gray areas. *Psychotherapy in Private Practice, 3,* 57–62.

Efstation, J. F., Patton, M. J., & Kardash, C. M. (1990). Measuring the working alliance in counselor supervision. *Journal of Counseling Psychology, 37,* 322–329.

Ekstein, R., & Wallerstein, R. S. (1972). *The teaching and learning of psychotherapy* (2nd ed.). New York: Basic Books.

Ellis, M. V., & Douce, L. A. (1994). Group supervision of novice clinical supervisors: Eight recurring issues. *Journal of Counseling and Development, 72,* 520–525.

Ellis, M. V., & Ladany, N. (1997). Inferences concerning supervisees and clients in clinical supervision: An integrative review. In C. E. Watkins, Jr. (Ed.), *Handbook of psychotherapy supervision* (pp. 447–507). New York: Wiley.

Freud, S. (1983). Further recommendations in the technique of psychoanalysis: Observations on transference-love. In P. Reiff (Ed.), *Freud: Therapy and technique* (pp. 167–180). New York: Collier Books. (Original work published 1915).

Friedlander, M. L., Siegel, S. M., & Brenock, K. (1989). Parallel process in counseling and supervision: A case study. *Journal of Counseling Psychology, 36,* 149–157.

Gabbard, G. O. (1994). Sexual excitement and countertransference love in the analyst. *Journal of the American Psychoanalytic Association, 42,* 1083–1106.

Gabbard, G. O. (1995). The early history of boundary violations in psychoanalysis. *Journal of the American Psychoanalytic Association, 43,* 1115–1136.

Gelso, C. J., & Carter, J. A. (1985). The relationship in counseling & psychotherapy: Components, consequences, and theoretical antecedents. *The Counseling Psychologist, 13,* 155–243.

Goodyear, R. K., & Shumate, J. L. (1996). Perceived effects of therapist self-disclosure of attraction to clients. *Professional Psychology: Research and Practice, 27,* 613–616.

Hill, C. E., Thompson, B. J., Cogar, M. C., & Denman, D. W. (1993). Beneath the surface of long-term therapy: Therapist and client report of their own and each other's covert processes. *Journal of Counseling Psychology, 40,* 278–287.

Hill, C. E., Thompson, B. J., & Williams, E. N. (in press). A guide to conducting consensual qualitative research. *The Counseling Psychologist.*

Holloway, E. L. (1987). Developmental models of supervision: Is it supervision? *Professional Psychology: Research and Practice, 18,* 209–216.

Kaplan, H. S. (1977). Training of sex therapists. In W. H. Masters, V. E. Johnson, & R. D. Kolodny (Eds.), *Ethical issues in sex therapy and research* (pp. 182–189). Boston: Little, Brown.

Ladany, N., & Friedlander, M. L. (1995). The relationship between the supervisory working alliance and supervisee role conflict and role ambiguity. *Counselor Education and Supervision, 34,* 220–231.

Ladany, N., Hill, C. E., Corbett, M. M., & Nutt, E. A. (1996). Nature, extent, and importance of what psychotherapy trainees do not disclose to their supervisors. *Journal of Counseling Psychology, 43,* 10–24.

McCracken, G. D. (1988). *The long interview.* Newbury Park, CA: Sage.

Nickell, N. J., Hecker, L. L., Ray, R. E., & Bercik, J. (1995). Marriage and family therapists' sexual attraction to clients: An exploratory study. *American Journal of Family Therapy, 23,* 315–327.

Patton, M. J., & Kivlighan, D. M., Jr. (1997). Relevance of the supervisory alliance to the counseling alliance and to treatment adherence in counselor training. *Journal of Counseling Psychology, 44,* 108–115.

Pope, K. S. (1990). Therapist-patient sexual involvement: A review of the research. *Clinical Psychology Review, 10,* 477–490.

Pope, K. S., Keith-Spiegel, P., & Tabachnick, B. (1986). Sexual attraction to clients: The human therapist and the (sometimes) inhuman training system. *American Psychologist, 41,* 147–158.

Pope, K. S., Schover, L. R., & Levenson, H. (1980). Sexual behavior between clinical supervisors and trainees: Implications for professional standards. *Professional Psychology, 10,* 157–162.

Pope, K. S., Sonne, J. L., & Holroyd, J. (1993). *Sexual feelings in psychotherapy: Explorations for therapists and therapists-in-training.* Washington, DC: American Psychological Association.

Pope, K. S., & Tabachnick, B. G. (1993). Therapist anger, hate, fear, and sexual feelings: National survey of therapist responses, client characteristics, critical events, formal complaints, and training. *Professional Psychology: Research and Practice, 24,* 142–152.

Rhodes, R. H., Hill, C. E., Thompson, B. J., & Elliott, R. (1994). Client retrospective recall of resolved and unresolved misunderstanding events. *Journal of Counseling Psychology, 41,* 473–483.

Rodolfa, E., Hall, T., Holms, V., Davena, A., Komatz, D., Antunez, M., & Hall, A. (1994). The management of sexual feelings in therapy. *Professional Psychology: Research and Practice, 25,* 168–172.

Rodolfa, E. R., Kitzrow, M., Vohra, S., & Wilson, B. (1990). Training interns to respond to sexual dilemmas. *Professional Psychology: Research and Practice, 21,* 313–315.

Stake, J., & Oliver, J. (1991). Sexual contact and touching between therapists and clients: A survey of psychologists' attitudes and behavior. *Professional Psychology: Research and Practice, 22,* 297–307.

Stoltenberg, C. D., & Delworth, U. (1987). *Supervising counselors and therapists: A developmental perspective.* San Francisco: Jossey-Bass.

Vasquez, M. J. T. (1988). Counselor-client sexual contact: Implications for ethics training. *Journal of Counseling and Development, 67,* 238–241.

Yarris, E., & Allgeier, E. R. (1988). Sexual socialization for therapists: Applications for the counseling/psychotherapy of women. *Women & Therapy, 7,* 57–75.

Editor's Note: Charles D. Claiborn served as the action editor for this article.—CEH

About the Authors: Nicholas Ladany and Deborah S. Melincoff, Department of Education and Human Services, Lehigh University; Karen M. O'Brien, Clara E. Hill, and Sarah Knox, Department of Psychology, University of Maryland College Park; David A. Petersen, Department of Counseling and Personnel Services, University of Maryland College Park.

Acknowledgements: Earlier versions of this article were presented at the annual meeting of the Society for Psychotherapy Research, Amelia Island, Florida, June 1996, and at the 104th Annual Convention of the American Psychological Association, Toronto, Ontario, Canada, August 1996. We are grateful to Robert A. Brown, Leslie K. Orysh, and Kenneth S. Pope for their comments on an earlier version of this article. We also thank Linda Tipton for her assistance with the data coding and Michelle Bosio, Shawn Eigenbrode, Michele Forstot, Jennifer Hudson, Gopa Kahn, Elisaida Mendez, Susan Reynolds, Sharon Weiss Cohen, and Jamell White for their assistance with transcribing the interviews.

Address correspondence to: Nicholas Ladany, Counseling Psychology Program, Department of Education and Human Services, Lehigh University, 111 Research Drive, Bethlehem, Pennsylvania 18015. Electronic mail may be sent via Internet to nil3@1ehigh.edu.

Exercise for Case 13

Note: Article 14 is a *quantitative study* on the same general topic as this one. If you are assigned Article 14, you will find questions asking you to compare the two articles in the exercise for that article.

1. Introduction

A. Is the problem area for the research clearly described? Explain.

B. Have the researchers convinced you that the problem area is important? Explain.

C. To what extent does the literature presented in the introduction help you understand the problem? Is the literature used to put the problem in context? Explain.

D. Do the researchers indicate how this study is different from and/or similar to earlier ones reported in the literature?

E. Do the researchers reveal their personal perspectives on the problem area, including any possible biases? Explain.

2. Methods

A. Are the demographics of the participants (i.e., background characteristics such as age, race, and so on) described in sufficient detail? Explain.

B. Considering the problem area for the research, do you think that appropriate participants were selected? If you had been conducting the study, would you have selected the same type(s) of participants? Would you have used the same number of participants? Explain.

C. Which strategies listed in Table 1 on page 161 of this book were employed by the researchers? Are they described in sufficient detail? Explain.

D. In addition to those you named in response to question 2C, have the researchers used any additional strategies to help assure the validity of the study? If yes, what are they? Are they described in sufficient detail? Explain.

3. Analysis and Results

A. Are the steps taken in the analysis described in sufficient detail? Explain.

B. Are the results clearly organized? Explain.

C. Are the results discussed in terms of a theory or theories (either theories that emerged from this study or previously existing ones)? Explain.

D. Were the direct quotations of the participants' statements, if any, judiciously selected? Do they help you understand the results? Explain.

E. Are there other ways the results could have been organized and interpreted? Explain.

4. Conclusions/Implications

A. Are the researchers' concluding remarks appropriate? Do they flow logically from the material presented earlier?

B. Do the researchers describe any implications? If yes, are they appropriate? Are there other implications that are not discussed by the researchers? Explain.

5. Ethical Considerations

A. In your opinion, could this research have caused physical or psychological harm to the participants? If yes, did the researchers take adequate measures to ameliorate the potential for harm? Explain.

B. If you had conducted this research, would you have obtained written, informed consent from the participants before conducting the study? Explain. Does this research report indicate that the researchers obtained such consent?

6. Overall Evaluation

A. Throughout the article, are all specialized terms and jargon defined to your satisfaction? Explain.

B. Briefly describe your overall evaluation of the research report, noting any special strengths and weaknesses.

C. If you had been a reviewer for the journal in which this report was published, would you have recommended publication of the report? If yes, would you have recommended that it be published "as is" or modified before publication? Explain. If no, what is the primary reason why you would recommend not publishing it?

Case 14

The Management of Sexual Feelings in Therapy

EMIL RODOLFA
University of California, Davis

TOM HALL
Private Practice

VALERIE HOLMS
University of Manitoba

ANITA DAVENA
Ohio State University

DAVID KOMATZ
St. Norbert College

MALU ANTUNEZ
University of California, Davis

ANNA HALL
Private Practice

Editor's note: This is a *quantitative* research article on the same general topic as Article 13, which is *qualitative*. The questions at the end of this article ask you to compare and contrast the two articles.

ABSTRACT. This research project examined the incidence, experience, salient features, and management of sexual attraction between psychologists and clients and assessed 908 American Psychological Association member psychologists who work in university counseling centers (43% return rate). Only 12% reported never having been attracted to any client, and 96% never had acted out sexually against a client. Almost half reported that their feelings of attraction benefited the therapy process and 43% reported negative consequences. Sixty percent sought consultation or supervision to discuss this attraction. The results of this study support the need for increased awareness and education in this area.

From *Professional Psychology: Research and Practice, 25,* 168–172. Copyright © 1994 by the American Psychological Association, Inc. Reprinted with permission.

It is well documented that therapist-client sexual intimacy results in damaging, painful client experiences (Bates & Brodsky, 1989; Bouhoutsos, Holroyd, Lerman, Forer, & Greenberg, 1983; Chesler, 1973; Feldman-Summers & Jones, 1984; Freeman & Roy, 1976; Gartrell, Herman, Olarte, Feldstein, & Localio, 1987; Hotelling, 1988; Kluft, 1989; Pope, 1988; Pope & Bouhoutsos, 1986; Rutter, 1989; Sonne, Meyer, Borys & Marshall, 1985). Stake and Oliver (1991) noted that sexual contact between therapist and client has had almost universally negative consequences for the client. The acting out of feelings of sexual attraction toward clients is a profound problem for our profession.

The American Psychological Association's Ethics Committee (1991) reported that exploitation of clients, including sexual acting out, is the most frequently investigated complaint. Additionally, the APA Trust reported that 53 cents out of each malpractice dollar goes to sexual misconduct claims (Vasquez, 1991).

Previous researchers (Borys & Pope, 1989; Holroyd & Brodsky, 1977; Pope, Keith-Speigel, & Tabachnick, 1986; Pope, Tabachnick, & Keith-Speigel, 1987; Stake & Oliver, 1991) have reported that between 3% and 12% of psychologists become sexually involved with their clients. Consistently, investigators have found that male psychologists report higher incidence rates of sexual content with clients than do female psychologists, although these differences have narrowed in more recent surveys. Brodsky (1989) reported a decreasing trend in the incidence of sexual contact between psychologist and patient between 1977 and 1987.

How do psychologists manage these feelings of sexual attraction? Pope et al. (1986) and Stake and Oliver (1991) found that approximately 50% of psychologists sought supervision or consultation. Stake and Oliver also found that 19% discussed their feelings with their own therapists.

Pope and his colleagues (1986) emphasized that limited consultation and supervision-seeking is based on the countertransference hypothesis. Limited education about this topic also influences the decision to consult. Pope et al. (1986) and Glaser and Thorpe (1986) reported that the vast majority of psychologists have received minimal training on this topic. Edelwich and Brodsky (1982, 1991) summarized that most professionals felt inadequately prepared to respond to the sexual dilemmas they encounter in their therapeutic work. As a result, there has been a call for increased education on this topic (Bates & Brodsky, 1989; Edelwich & Brodsky, 1982, 1991; Gabbard, 1989; Glaser & Thorpe, 1986; Pope et al., 1986; Pope & Vasquez, 1991; Rodolfa, Kitzrow, Vohra, & Wilson, 1990; Rodolfa & Reilley, 1991; Rutter, 1989; Schoener & Gonsiorek, 1988; Simon, 1989; Stake & Oliver, 1991).

The present study was undertaken to investigate (a) the incidence of sexual attraction and sexual acting out by psychologists; (b) the salient features that contribute to these feelings; (c) how psychologists manage these feelings; (d) how these feelings influence the therapeutic relationship; and (e) previous training experiences.

Method

Procedure

In 1990, we contacted the APA's Office of Research and requested a randomly drawn list of names of psychologists who identified their primary workplace as a university counseling center. A two-page questionnaire, cover letter, and return envelope were mailed to these 908 APA member psychologists (454 men and 454 women). Subjects were informed that the purpose of the investigation was to expand previous knowledge in this area and that their responses would be kept completely anonymous.

Questionnaire

A 30-item questionnaire[1] (22 structured and 8 open-ended items) was developed, on the basis of the survey used in the Pope et al. (1986) study, to investigate the following areas: demographic characteristics, incidence and management of sexual attraction, clients' awareness of and reciprocation of the attraction, the impact of the attraction on the therapy process, and training.

Analysis

The analysis of parametric data is based on a 2 x 2 analysis of variance (ANOVA) to evaluate the response categories as a function of age (44 years and under and 45 years and over) and sex. Chi square analysis was used to analyze nonparametric data. Analyses were considered significant at $p < .01$ to compensate for the increased probability of Type I error with multiple tests.

Results

Demographic Characteristics

Questionnaires were returned by 386 (199 male and 187 female) subjects (43% response rate). The median age of the respondents was 44 years, and there was no significant difference in the average age between male ($M = 46$ years) and female ($M = 42$ years) respondents. For the purpose of data analysis, the 202 respondents 44 years of age and younger were designated "younger therapists," and the 184 respondents 45 years and older were designated "older therapists."

Fifty-six percent of the respondents were counseling psychologists, 39% were clinical psychologists, and 5% were from other specialty areas (e.g., counselor education). Respondents averaged 15.33 ($SD = 9.05$) years of professional experience. Male therapists had significantly more experience than did female therapists, $F(1, 348) = 92.3, p < .003$.

Incidence and Salient Characteristics of Sexual Attraction to Clients

Incidence. Only 47 (12%) of 386 respondents reported never having been attracted to any client. Among the 339 who were attracted, 109 (104 women

---

[1] To receive a copy of the questionnaire used in this research project, contact Emil Rodolfa, Counseling Center, University of California, Davis, California 95616.

and 5 men) reported attraction only to male clients, l66 (163 men and 3 women) only to female clients, and 64 (45 women and 19 men) to both male and female clients. The 187 male psychologists were significantly more often attracted to clients than were the 152 female psychologists ($F(1, 348) = 100.92, p < .001$). Younger therapists were significantly more often attracted to clients than were older therapists, $F(1, 385) = 168, p < .001$.

Salient features. Respondents were asked to list the client characteristics that elicited feelings of sexual attraction. Sixty-three percent of respondents in this study reported physical attractiveness as the primary characteristic that elicited feeling sexually attracted to a client. Other client characteristics reported to elicit feelings of attraction included positive mental-cognitive traits (31%), the positive character of the client (15%), the sexual nature of the client's presentation (10%), the kind nature of the client (10%), and a vulnerable presentation by the client (9.5%).

Another salient characteristic is whether the respondents had fantasies about their clients. Most psychologists reported that they never had sexual fantasies about former clients (78.8%), $\chi^2 (1, N = 386) = 512.0, p < .001$, nor did they have sexual fantasies about current clients (75%), $\chi^2 (1, N = 386) = 533.5, p < .001$, while engaging in sexual activity with their current partner. Male psychologists reported having more sexual fantasies about clients than did female psychologists (past clients, 33% vs. 16%; current clients, 30% vs. 17%, $\chi^2 (3, 386) = 18.39, p < .001$). There were no differences based on age.

Management of Sexual Feelings Toward Clients

Emotional responses. About half (55%) of all respondents indicated that their feelings of attraction caused them discomfort, guilt, or anxiety. No differences between male and female or younger and older psychologists were noted.

Behavioral responses. The vast majority of respondents (91.9%) reported that they had never seriously considered actual sexual involvement with a client, $\chi^2 (1, N = 386) = 923.27, p < .001$. Of the 31 psychologists who had considered sexual involvement, 27 had considered it only once or twice. Male psychologists had considered sexual involvement with clients more often than had female psychologists, $\chi^2 (1, N = 381) = 7.25, p < .007$. Older psychologists were significantly more inclined to seriously consider sexual involvement than were younger psychologists, $\chi^2 (1, N = 386) = 8.89, p < 01$.

The respondents reported the following reasons for refraining from sexual involvement with clients: 55% felt it was exploitative or countertherapeutic, and 50% felt it was unethical. Additionally, they noted it was against their personal values (19%), was unprofessional practice (15%), damaging to them personally or professionally (14%), or illegal (5%). Eleven percent refrained because they were in a committed relationship.

The majority of respondents (96%) have never become sexually involved (defined as touching in a sexually arousing manner or having genital contact) with their clients, $\chi^2 (1, N = 383) = 325.34, p < .001$. Sexual intimacies with clients occurred rarely (once or twice) for the remaining 4% of the respondents. Male psychologists engaged in sexual intimacies with clients more often than did female psychologists (5.55% vs. 2.16%); however, this difference did not reach statistical significance, $\chi^2 (1, N = 383) = 2.96, p < .085$. Factors that contributed to therapists' sexual behavior with clients included the break-up or absence of a primary relationship, poor self-concept, and environmental stress (job problems). One psychologist reported that the sexual interaction resulted from being a naive therapist.

Consultation seeking. Approximately 60% of the respondents reported that they had sought supervision or consultation to discuss their feelings of attraction, 27% said that they had not sought supervision or consultation, and 13% failed to answer. Male psychologists were more likely to seek supervision than were female psychologists (66.3% vs. 54%), $\chi^2 (1, N = 386) = 30.39, p < .001$. No age differences were found.

Psychologists sought consultation or supervision because they were concerned for client welfare, felt that they had lost their objectivity, or desired to gain understanding of their attraction. A generally positive supervisory or collegial relationship influenced consultation seeking. Most psychologists who sought consultation did not fear acting out the sexual attraction.

Respondents did not consult because they felt the attraction did not interfere with the course of therapy. A small number of psychologists reported that they were fearful of a negative supervisor reaction or that anxiety or shame inhibited their desire to speak with their supervisor.

Effects on the Therapeutic Process

Forty-eight percent of respondents indicated that their sexual attraction had been beneficial to the psychotherapy process in at least some instances. These therapists noted that the beneficial aspects included enhanced empathy for the clients, increased awareness of transference and countertransference reactions, and increased awareness of clients' nonverbal behaviors. No differences between male and female or younger and older psychologists were found.

Forty-three percent of the respondents in this study believed that their sexual attraction had negatively influenced the process of therapy on at least one occasion. The harmful effects included therapists feeling distracted from client issues, difficulty confronting clients, early referral or termination, or feeling overly involved with the client. No differences were found between younger and older or male and female psychologists.

Our respondents believed that a client's awareness of a therapist's attraction has a strong negative influence on the therapeutic process, $F(3, 317) = 16.35, p < .001$. Most psychologists (85%), however, believed that the clients were not aware of the psychologists' attraction, $\chi^2 (1, N = 334) = 49, p < .001$. Male psychologists were much more likely to suspect that the client knew of their attraction than were female psychologists, $F(1, 332) = 18.24, p < .001$.

Sixty-four percent believed that the attraction was mutual. Their judgment of mutual attraction was based on the verbal expressions of the client (e.g., client asking personal questions, seeking extra contact, giving gifts), as well as nonverbal actions (e.g., client dress, eye contact, behavior, and client touching the therapist). Fourteen percent reported that the attraction had never been reciprocated, and 20% indicated that they did not know or were unsure, $\chi^2 (2, N = 336) = 46.10, p < .001$. More female than male psychologists felt that the attraction had gone unreciprocated (28% vs. 11%, $\chi^2 (1, N = 265) = 7.41, p < .006$). There were no age group differences.

Graduate Training

Forty percent of the respondents had not received education about sexual attraction during graduate school, and 51% had not received training during their internship. When training did occur, it primarily occurred during supervision, rather than during a structured seminar or class. It was surprising that no significant differences between older and younger psychologists were noted. Additionally, no significant differences between male and female psychologists were discovered.

Discussion

This study has attempted to discover the salient features of sexual attraction between client and psychologist, and steps taken to manage these feelings.

The Incidence of Sexual Attraction

This study found 88% of psychologists (94% men and 81.3% women) were sexually attracted to at least one client. Client physical attractiveness was the most frequently reported salient client characteristic. The percentage of men reporting attraction is similar to the responses reported in past surveys (eg., Pope et al., 1986), whereas the percentage of women who reported feeling attracted has increased. There are some possible explanations for this change. Possibly, this increase results from a client population in university counseling centers that is more attractive to women psychologists. Perhaps female psychologists have become more accepting of these feelings. In 1976, Abramowitz, Abramowitz, Roback, Corney, and McKee noted that female therapists tend to avoid treating attractive male clients. As female psychologists become more accepting of these feelings, perhaps this pattern of behavior reported by Abramowitz et al. will decrease.

Psychologists' Management of Sexual Attraction Toward Clients

Approximately half the respondents who felt attracted to clients reported greater empathy and awareness of transferential and countertransferential aspects of the psychotherapeutic process. They also reported that the negative effects included becoming over- or underinvolved with clients. No significant differences between men's and women's views of the effects of sexual attraction to the therapy process were found.

The majority of psychologists experienced distress when feeling sexually attracted to a client. This distress may result from a lack of acceptance of these feelings or may be due to the lack of appropriate behavioral responses. Pope et al. (1986) described the negative effects of the transference-countertransference explanation and the inhibitory reactions that can result. Psychologists who do not accept their feelings will be inadequately prepared to effectively use them appropriately in therapy.

Approximately one quarter of our respondents did not seek consultation when sexually attracted to a client. Although it may be that the feelings were fleeting or did not interfere with therapy, it also may be that psychologists deny the importance of these feelings or the effects they have on their therapy experiences.

Four percent of the psychologists reported sexual interactions with clients. This finding is part of a recent trend (Borys & Pope, 1989; Pope et al., 1986; Pope et al., 1987; Stake & Oliver, 1991) of lower sexual acting out incidence rates than those originally reported in the research conducted in the late 1970s (Holroyd & Brodsky, 1977; Pope, Levenson, & Shover, 1979). Our results add that the differences between male and female psychologists who report sexually acting out has become statistically insignificant.

There are many possible explanations for this outcome. As discussed by Brodsky (1989), psychologists, particularly male psychologists, may be learning to more effectively keep their libidinal desires in check and not act on their feelings of attraction. Additionally, psychologists may more fully understand the negative, painful, exploitative consequences for clients who have been sexually involved with their therapist. Reports of malpractice suits, as well as the criminalization of psychotherapist-client sex document the harmful consequences therapists experience, which may further inhibit psychologists from acting out their feelings of attraction. Perhaps the findings of the often-quoted early investigations overestimated the actual incidence of sexual acting out against clients, and the more recent investigations are painting a more accurate picture of the actual incidence. Another less hopeful explanation may be that psychologists are less willing to report, even anonymously, their sexual interactions with clients.

Age Differences

Respondents were arbitrarily divided into groups of younger and older psychologists, with the cutoff being 44 years old. The only differences found between these groups were that younger psychologists more frequently reported attraction to clients than did older psychologists, and older psychologists were significantly more inclined to consider sexual involvement with clients than were younger psychologists. Although no significant differences were noted in the training received by younger and older psychologists, perhaps the arbitrary nature of the grouping clouded the true differences between older and younger psychologists. It would be useful to investigate what factors contribute to the contemplation of sexual acting out. Specifically, has the increased recent attention our profession has paid made a difference to psychologists? Have the clarifications of the ethical principles, the legal rulings, and the recent publications influenced the responses of psychologists when experiencing sexual feelings toward clients?

Training Implications

Sixty percent of the respondents had received some education about sexual attraction during their graduate programs, and even fewer of the respondents (50%) had received training during their internships. These numbers are comparable to those from past surveys.

Stake and Oliver (1991) hypothesized that training on this topic is increasing. We believe it would be useful to investigate the current incidence of training on this topic at the doctoral and internship levels. Exploring the effects of training on therapists' emotional and behavioral responses will provide important information.

We believe that it is important to enhance training opportunities on this topic. To do so, doctoral- and intern-program faculty must assess their program atmosphere (Vasquez, 1988) and determine how gender dynamics influence student-teacher interactions. Robinson and Reid (1985), Pope et al., (1979), and Hall (1987) reported that between 25% and 75% of female graduate students experienced sexual innuendo or harassment by faculty members and described an atmosphere where self-disclosure may be difficult for students. As indicated in our survey, one element in the decision to seek consultation involved the atmosphere of safety experienced with the supervisor. When trainees do not feel safe, they tend to inhibit their discussion of sensitive material.

Additionally, the development of training seminars on this topic is prevented when trainers wait for these issues to emerge in supervision rather than acknowledge that trainees need permission to discuss these feelings. The 88% of psychologists who reported feeling attracted to clients need appropriate avenues to explore these feelings.

And what of the 12% who report that they have not

380 experienced sexual attraction? This may be a normal variation of psychologists' reactions to clients, or these psychologists may have suppressed their feelings of attraction. Are these therapists somehow different from the vast majority of psychologists? Future study could

385 investigate and compare these groups of psychologists.

In 1986, Pope et al. called for the integration of this topic into the resources for teaching counseling and therapy skills. Lerman (1990) provides an annotated bibliography of the 3,000 publications on this topic.

390 There is currently an abundance of material, and models exist for training (Brodsky, 1989; Rodolfa et al., 1988; Vasquez, 1988). It is now up to the training program faculty to decide to integrate this material, for the good of their students, for the good of those who seek

395 our psychological services, and for the good of our profession. It is time to train psychologists to accept and understand their sexual feelings and do no harm.

References

Abramowitz, S., Abramowitz, C., Roback, H., Corney, R., McKee, W. (1976). Sex role related countertransference in psychotherapy. *Archives of General Psychiatry, 33,* 71–73.

APA Ethics Committee. (1991). Report of the Ethics Committee, 1989 and 1990. *American Psychologist, 46,* 750–757.

Bates, C., & Brodsky, A. (1989). *Sex in the therapy hour: A professional case of incest.* New York: Guilford Press.

Borys, D., & Pope, K. (1989). Dual relationships between therapist and client: A national study of psychologists, psychiatrists, and social workers. *Professional Psychology: Research and Practice, 20,* 283–293.

Bouhoutsos, J., Holroyd, J., Lerman, H., Forer, B. R., & Greenberg, M. (1983). Sexual intimacy between psychotherapists and patients. *Professional Psychology: Research and Practice, 14.* 185–196.

Brodsky, A. (1989). Sex between patient and therapist: Psychologist's data and response. In G. G. Gabbard (Ed.), *Sexual exploitation in professional relationships* (pp. 15–25). Washington, DC: American Psychiatric Press.

Chesler, P. (1973). *Women and madness.* New York: Avon Books.

Edelwich, J., & Brodsky, A. (1982). *Sexual dilemmas for the helping professional.* New York: Brunner/Mazel.

Edelwich, J., & Brodsky, A. (1991). *Sexual dilemmas for the helping professional: Revised and expanded edition.* New York: Brunner/Mazel.

Feldman-Summers, S., & Jones, G. (1984). Psychological impacts of sexual contacts between therapist or other health care professionals and their clients. *Journal of Consulting and Clinical Psychology, 52,* 1054–1061.

Freeman, L., & Roy, J. (1976). *Betrayal.* New York: Stein and Day.

Gabbard, G. (Ed.). (1989). *Sexual exploitation in professional relationships.* Washington, DC: American Psychiatric Press.

Gartrell, N., Herman, J., Olarte, S., Feldstein, M., & Localio, R. (1987). Reporting practices of psychiatrists who knew of sexual misconduct by colleagues. *American Journal of Orthopsychiatry, 57,* 287–295.

Glaser, R., & Thorpe, J. (1986). Unethical intimacy: A survey of sexual contact and advances between psychology educators and female graduate students. *American Psychologist, 41,* 43–51.

Hall, J. (1987). Gender-related ethical dilemmas and ethics education. *Professional Psychology: Research and Practice, 18,* 573–579.

Holroyd, J., & Brodsky, A. (1977). Psychologists' attitudes and practices regarding erotic and nonerotic contact with patients. *American Psychologist, 32,* 843–849.

Hotelling, K. (1988). Ethical, legal and administrative options to address sexual relationships between counselor and client. *Journal of Counseling and Development, 67,* 233–237.

Kluft, R. (1989). Treating the patient who has been sexually exploited by a previous therapist. *Psychiatric Clinics of North America, 12,* 483–500.

Lerman, H. (1990). *Sexual intimacies between psychotherapists and patients: An annotated bibliography of mental health, legal and public media literature and relevant legal cases.* (2nd ed.). Phoenix, AZ: APA Division of Psychotherapy (Division 12).

Pope, K. (1988). How clients are harmed by sexual contact with mental health professionals: The syndrome and its prevalence. *Journal of Counseling and Development, 67,* 222–226.

Pope, K., & Bouhoutsos, J. (1986). *Sexual intimacy between therapist and patient.* New York: Praeger.

Pope, K., Keith-Speigel, P., & Tabachnik, B. (1986). Sexual attraction to clients: The human therapist and the (sometimes) inhuman training system. *American Psychologist, 41,* 147–158.

Pope, K., Levenson, H., & Shover, L. (1979). Sexual intimacy in psychology training: Results and implications of a national survey. *American Psychologist, 34,* 682–689.

Pope, K., Tabachnick, B., & Keith-Speigel, P. (1987). Ethics of practice: The beliefs and behaviors of psychologists as therapists. *American Psychologist, 35,* 993–1006.

Pope, K., & Vasquez, M. (1991). *Ethics in psychotherapy and counseling: A practical guide for psychologists.* New York: Jossey-Bass.

Robinson, W., & Reid, P. (1985). Sexual intimacies in psychology revisited. *Professional Psychology: Research and Practice, 16,* 512–520.

Rodolfa, E., Kitzrow, M., Vohra, S., & Wilson, B. (1990). Training interns to respond to sexual dilemmas. *Professional Psychology: Research and Practice, 21,* 313–315.

Rodolfa, E., & Reilley, R. (1991). *A model for training psychology interns about sexual dilemmas.* Paper presented at the APA Convention, San Francisco.

Rutter, P. (1989). *Sex in the forbidden zone: When men in power—therapists, doctors, clergy, teachers and others—betray women's trust.* Los Angeles: Tarcher.

Schoener, G., & Gonsiorek, J. (1988). *Assessment and development of rehabilitation plans for counselors who have sexually exploited their clients, 67,* 227–232.

Simon, R. (1989). Sexual exploitation of patients: How it begins before it happens. *Contemporary Psychiatry, 8,* 104–112.

Sonne, J., Meyer, C., Borys, D., & Marshall, V. (1985). Clients' reactions to sexual intimacy in therapy. *American Journal of Orthopsychiatry, 55,* 183–189.

Stake, J., & Oliver, J. (1991). Sexual contact and touching between therapists and clients: A survey of psychologists' attitudes and behavior. *Professional Psychology: Research and Practice, 22,* 297–307.

Vasquez, M. (1988). Counselor-client sexual contact implications for ethics training. *Journal of Counseling and Development, 67,* 238–241.

Vasquez, M. (1991). *Sexuality and gender issues in psychotherapy and counseling: Approaches to education.* Paper presented at the APA Convention, San Francisco.

About the Authors: Emil Rodolfa received his Ph.D. from Texas A&M University. He is a licensed psychologist and Associate Director for Training and Program Development at the University of California, Davis Counseling Center. Tom Hall received his Ph.D. from the California School of Professional Psychology, Fresno. He is a licensed psychologist in private practice. Valerie Holms received her Ph.D. from the University of Manitoba. She is a licensed psychologist and Assistant Professor at the University of Manitoba. Anita Davena, Ph.D., recently received her doctorate in counseling psychology from The Ohio State University. David Komatz received his Psy.D. from the Illinois School of Professional Psychology. He is currently half-time instructor in psychology and half-time counselor at the Counseling Center at St. Norbert College. Malu Antunez, M.A., is licensed as a psychologist in Peru. She is currently a student in the Division of Education at the University of California, Davis, working on her school psychology credential. Anna Hall received her Ph.D. from the University of California, Los Angeles. She is currently a licensed psychologist in private practice.

Acknowledgments: This project was funded by a grant received from the University of California, Davis.

Address correspondence to: Correspondence concerning this article, including requests for a copy of the questionnaire used in this research project, should be addressed to Emil Rodolfa, Associate Director, Counseling Center, University of California, Davis, California 95616.

Exercise for Case 14

Directions: The following questions ask you to compare Article 13, which is *qualitative*, with this *quantitative* article.

1. In Article 13, the authors suggest that there are limitations to using structured closed-ended questions for studying this topic. (See the paragraph beginning with line 49 in Article 13.) Do you agree?

2. Were the authors of Article 13 or Article 14 more articulate in explaining their choice of research methods (qualitative vs. quantitative) in the introduction to their research? Explain.

3. Are the samples used in both articles appropriate? Is one sample more appropriate than the other?

4. Which method of measurement (semistructured interviews in Article 13 or a structured questionnaire in Article 14) seems better suited for investigating the problem? Explain.

5. In your opinion, which method yielded more interesting results? Which method yielded more detailed results? Which method yielded more useful results? Explain.

6. In your opinion, did both studies yield information that is valuable for advancing knowledge in this area?

7. In addition to any points you made in response to questions 1 through 6, are there any other strengths or weaknesses of the methodology used in Article 13? In Article 14?

8. Overall, which method (quantitative or qualitative) seems better suited for exploring the general problem area? Explain.

9. Has your comparison of Articles 13 and 14 changed your opinions on the relative merits of qualitative and quantitative research methodologies? Explain.

Case 15

The Other Side of the Story: Student Narratives on the California Drug, Alcohol, and Tobacco Education Programs

MARIANNE D'EMIDIO-CASTON
University of California, Santa Barbara

JOEL H. BROWN
Center for Educational Research
and Development, Berkeley, California

ABSTRACT. Within the context of a large-scale, comprehensive evaluation of the California Drug Alcohol Tobacco Education (DATE) program, this study sought to extend knowledge of student perceptions of prevention education using a naturalistic approach. The constant comparative method was used to analyze 40 focus group interviews of risk and thriving groups conducted in 11 high, middle, and elementary school districts. This article presents three assertions generated solely from 490 "narrative stories" found in the data set. "At-risk" and "thriving" students at all three levels of schooling (a) use "story" to make sense of prevention education, and (b) distinguish use from abuse. High school students of both groups (c) believe that hearing only one side of the substance use/abuse story and strict expulsion policies further alienate students most in need of help. Implications for the use of story as an assessment tool are discussed, as are implications for substance use prevention policy.

From *Evaluation Review, 22,* 95–117. Copyright © 1998 by Sage Publications, Inc. Reprinted with permission of Sage Publications, Inc.

When social problems capture public imagination, public schools often become the vehicle for social change (Sarason, 1982). With the focus of public attention, efforts are made by politicians to "do something" to solve the problem. The "something" often results in a mandate to public schools. Directly tied to and intricately connected with state and federal government through funding, schools are readily available settings for delivery of the mandated solution. In the last decade, public schools have increasingly been held accountable to teach young people about the dangers of drugs, alcohol and tobacco, AIDS, gangs, and violence. Each of these issues now claims time in the curriculum delivered to students alongside a basic program of academic study. Beginning in the 1980s, "Just Say No!" became the slogan for an ongoing social change effort known as the War on Drugs, aimed at the target of a drug-, alcohol-, and tobacco-free society.

In 1991, the California Drug, Alcohol, and Tobacco Education (DATE) Program was initiated in an effort to consolidate programs to prevent substance use and abuse by children and adolescents. School districts were mandated to provide comprehensive drug, alcohol, and tobacco education for students K through 12th grade. A large-scale evaluation of DATE by the Southwest Regional Laboratory (SWRL) suggests that "at a minimum California schools spent $83.78 per student in 1992–93 to provide students with prevention education curricula, and positive alternative activities, provide personnel with staff development and Alcohol Tobacco or Other Drugs (ATOD) training in curricula, identification and referral services" (Romero et al., 1994, 38). Since 1991, the cost of DATE has been estimated at $1.6 billion (Brown, D'Emidio-Caston, and Pollard, 1997). Such public focus and fiscal priority on a perceived social problem requires comprehensive evaluation and public accountability.

From 1991 to 1994, an evaluation was conducted along three quantitative dimensions: cost, program implementation, and self-reported student substance use knowledge, attitudes, beliefs, and behaviors (Romero et al., 1993, 1994). Another study, using the same school districts included in the Romero evaluation, looked at the social processes of DATE program implementation (Brown et al., 1993, 1995). These two studies present findings that are often contradictory. Romero, for example, leaves the reader with a positive impression of the effects of DATE. Brown and colleagues are not so convinced of the benefits in relation to students who are labeled most at risk for substance abuse. Although both studies are valuable, an explanation for the discrepancy in findings may be that the voices of students are more clearly heard in the Brown et al. study.

DATE programs have been designed and implemented from a "risk orientation" toward prevention (Brown et al., 1993). A risk orientation includes three characteristics. First, the terms substance use and substance abuse are interchangeable. Second, a risk orientation assumes that a majority of children fall into the "at-risk" category. Thus, "at-risk" is not differentiated from "high-risk." Third, with a risk orientation, there is an absence of focus on resilience as a prevention strategy. As it applies to prevention, the risk orientation is an operational definition of a deficit model, where young people are seen as problems to be fixed rather than resources who make contributions to their families, schools, and communities (Blue-Swadner, 1995; Benard, 1993).

There are serious problems associated with the risk-orientation. Using it to inform the solution of one or another perceived social problems masks the underlying social, economic, or environmental conditions that contribute to alienation and hopelessness. Another problem with the risk orientation we argue is that by using broadly defined categories (Hawkins et al., 1987), risk-oriented programs cannot be sufficiently targeted to students most in need of help. Given these limitations, we contend that the risk orientation limits practices in such prevention programs to those that are primarily symbolic (Brown et al., 1997). The appearance of a uniformed officer in classrooms, as in the widely implemented D.A.R.E. (Drug Abuse Resistance Education) program, or Red Ribbons tied around trees during Red Ribbon Week are public displays of something being done about the drug problem. The risk orientation makes it easier to believe that such symbolic public displays are effective programs (Brown and D'Emidio-Caston, 1995; Brown et al., 1997).

It is time to sort out the symbolic from the actual effects of DATE services. The story of DATE from the students' point of view is essential to the comprehensive assessment of DATE. If the alienation and hopelessness that young people feel leads to drug or other substance abuse, it is crucial to know whether the risk orientation that guides program development contributes to reducing the alienation and hopelessness. The primary focus of this article is to illuminate the influence DATE services have on students, through analysis of the unsolicited stories students told.

Results of the 1992–1993 qualitative evaluation are reported in Brown et al. (1993). Student perspectives were not included in the first-year results. The second year (1993–1994) qualitative study recognizes the centrality of the learner in prevention education. What meanings do students make of the programs in which they participate? This article posits that the voices of students can be heard through their narrative attempts to make meaning of prevention education. From the story data, we have a better understanding of the answer to the question, Do students perceive that prevention education makes a positive difference in their lives, or are the effects of these programs primarily symbolic?

Theoretical Framework

"Narrative" is becoming more widely accepted as "a way of knowing" in educational research (Schubert and Ayers, 1992; Witherell and Noddings, 1991; Connelly and Clandinin, 1990; Polkinghorne, 1988; Rosen, 1985; Mitchell, 1980). Mitchell's *On Narrative* brought the study of the role of narrative "out of the realm of the aesthetic into the realm of social and psychological formations," particularly in structures of value and cognition. The study of narrative "has now become a positive source of insight for all the branches of human and natural science" (Mitchell, 1980, ix). Cognitive psychologists have been interested in the study of the general structure and function of narrative (Chomsky, 1966; Rosen, 1985) and the acquisition of narrative skills by children (Bruner, 1990; Kemper, 1984). The role of narrative in curriculum studies has influenced a reconceptualization of curriculum at the macro and micro levels. Curriculum developed from one perspective has been reconceptualized as the collective story made of multiple perspectives. In "narrative inquiry" (Connelly and Clandinin, 1990), researchers seek to understand the ways in which curriculum is constituted in the subjectivity of teachers and other curriculum workers by privileging individual storytelling.

Nevertheless, the role of narrative in evaluation research is in its infancy. Researchers could uncover no work in which narrative as an evaluation tool was applied to substance use and abuse prevention. Researchers did, however, uncover one scientifically sound and germane narrative evaluation. In the "Voices From the Inside" Report (Poplin and Weeres, 1992), a "bottom up" narrative approach was taken to examine the state of public schools. Here, they used context-dependent units to produce an infrastructure that, when compared with the primary target population, explains program effects (Patton, 1990; Manning and Cullum-Swan, 1994). "Voices From the Inside" established the narrative of the target population (presumably the "bottom" in a bottom-up evaluation) in comparison with a given context as an important way to determine program effectiveness. In the Claremont "Voices" study, Poplin and Weeres interviewed teachers, custodians, parents, day-care workers, security guards, cafeteria workers, nurses, and administrators to create a contextual infrastructure for "multiethnic student voices," who formed the centerpiece of their evaluation. By contrasting these contextual voices with the students' voices, they determined that "heretofore identified problems of schooling (lowered achievement, high dropout rates and problems in the teaching profession) are rather consequences of much deeper and more fundamental problems" (p. 11). In both methodology and findings, the "Voices" evaluation represents an important advance in evaluation research.

In conjunction with other methods, in the DATE evaluation, researchers also use the bottom-up narrative evaluation format to help determine program effectiveness. By interviewing nearly 400 educators, administrators, and community members, the Brown and D'Emidio-Caston (1995) publication described the contextual infrastructure of DATE, contrasting it with the student voices. This research showed that 42.5% of 40 student focus groups (Grades 5–12) reported receiving health/science courses delivered by teachers and 95% of student focus groups reported receiving prevention education from specialists such as D.A.R.E. officers. It was also reported that in delivering prevention, the risk orientation as described above was the dominant context. In this article, with primary focus on prevention-related stories, students are once again the evaluation centerpiece.

Because drug, alcohol, and tobacco education is primarily an effort to influence the knowledge, value orientation, and behavior of students, attention to the construction of meanings revealed through narrative "story" is an exciting and valuable approach. Through the methods of narrative inquiry, our data reveal the construction of students' understanding of DATE. In effect, what they tell us is their side of the story of the War on Drugs.

Evaluation Questions

Our evaluation research questions focus on qualitative process and outcome examinations as described by Donabedian (1980), who viewed process as the set of activities that go on within and between practitioners (and in this case service recipients) and the outcome as a change in a service recipient's current and future status that can be attributed to antecedent practices.

This article is based on the assumption that if school programs are effective, such effects will be borne out in extensive student interview data regarding program process (how children construct understanding of the effects of substance use) and outcomes (how students feel these understandings have affected their current status as related to prevention programs).

These specific questions focus attention on the process and product of students' meaning making:

- Process: In the context of focus groups, how do students at different school levels (elementary, middle, high school) share their understanding of the effects of substance use?
- Outcome: How do students perceive the effects of substance use prevention programs?

Methods

Data Collection

The 11 of 12 California districts represented in the second-year follow-up evaluation study of DATE were purposely chosen based on the 1992 evaluation of 50 California districts (Brown et al. 1993; Brown, D'Emidio-Caston, and Pollard, 1997). A balance was sought among districts with respect to socioeconomic status (SES), demographics, and average daily attendance (ADA). Of these, 7 were from Southern and Central California, 2 were from the Bay Area, and 2 were from extreme Northern California. One of the state's largest districts was purposefully selected corresponding to the Romero et al. (1994) study. Two schools from each district were randomly assigned by computer selection. In the largest district only, three were selected. Because a detailed description of the methods used to determine participation in this study has already been presented elsewhere (Brown, D'Emidio-Caston, and Pollard, 1997), methods are presented here in only as much detail as necessary to provide the reader with an understanding of the analyzed data subset.

From 23 randomly selected schools, two focus groups of students from each school were interviewed. The two groups were chosen by their principal or other delegated authority on the basis of perceived characteristics of "at risk for substance abuse" or "thriving." Criteria for selection for each group were found to be consistent with expectations. For example, inclusion criteria for the perceived at-risk students were the risk factors of low academic achievement and low commitment to school. Criteria for inclusion in the perceived thriving group were characterized by leadership in the school community. The sampling process yielded 40 useable focus group interviews: 20 elementary school interviews, 9 middle school interviews, and 11 high school interviews, representing approximately 240 students. This process generated 18 complete pairs (thriving and at-risk), 3 mixed groups, and 1 unpaired thriving and 1 blank interview due to audio tape malfunction. The three mixed interviews, from the largest school district, offered a means of comparing mixed groups with the risk versus thriving groups. The data presented here are representative of the entire sample of thriving and at-risk student groups ($N = 40$). The student focus groups allowed researchers to evaluate DATE programs from the student point of view.

Students were interviewed by four trained interviewers in focus groups using a semistructured, open-ended interview schedule (Brown et al., 1995). Interviews were subsequently transcribed for analysis.

Data Analysis

Using the grounded theoretical approach (Strauss and Corbin, 1990), conceptual categories were developed inductively from the data and systematically related to one another. Among the categories emerging from the data set was a surprising number of unsolicited stories students used to explain or elaborate their ideas, to give examples of what they meant, or to demonstrate their immediate engagement with the content of the interview question. Stories are distinctive from other interview data in that they illuminate the connections students make of the stimulus topic to what they know in an authentic and recognizable discourse form. Restricting the data analysis to the stories students told increased the internal validity of the data (Goetz and LeCompte, 1984).

What "counted" as story? Stein and Policastro (1984) in their studies of what counts as "story" found

285 that no one single structural definition can account for the wide range of compositions people accept as stories. Their work showed that "segments must include at least an animate protagonist and some type of causal sequence before they will be considered a story"
290 (Polkinghorne, 1988, 111). Susan Kemper described the simplest form of story as a dyadic event where something happens and the protagonist responds. A more complete definition of the prototypical story identifies a protagonist and a predicament and attempts
295 to resolve the predicament, the outcomes of such attempts, the reactions of the protagonists to the situation, and the causal relationships among each of the elements in the story (Polkinghorne, 1988). Many student stories fit Polkinghorne's prototypical story, in-
300 cluding all of the required elements. In our analysis, a student statement was considered a story if it had at least one of these characteristics:

1. The statement included at least the elements of a subject and an action related to the use or abuse of
305 substances. For example, R (Respondent): My grandmother is not very old, she's in her 50s and she drinks one beer a day.

2. It was an expression of personal experience or a tale that had been told and passed along to the
310 speaker. For example, R: Deputy J. told us that this one lady sold her baby for crack.

3. The story had a subject who had performed some action or been involved in some event. For example,
315 R: A lot of people who get drunk and stuff and they go out and do something like usually they'll get in accidents or what happened was I had an uncle, I don't remember his name, but—no Uncle Jack, I think his name was Jack. He was drunk and he went
320 fishing and he was fooling around with the fishing and so he got the hook caught in his leg [several voices: ugh] and so he got gangrene.

R: He got what?

R: Gangrene and died.

325 Well-formed stories (Burke, in Bruner, 1990, 50) include the following five elements: actor, action, goal, scene, instrument. Bruner asserts that when there is a disunity between any of the five elements (trouble), the narrative agent uses the pattern of discourse known as
330 narrative to make sense of the trouble. The addition of "trouble," or what Bruner refers to as a "deviation from canonical culture," provides the stimulus for the telling of the tale. Using Burke's dramatism model, the fishing story is the student's attempt to illustrate his statement
335 that "a lot of people who get drunk go out and get in accidents" (deviation from the canonical culture): Uncle Jack (actor), was drunk (trouble), went fishing (scene), was fooling around (action), got the hook stuck in his leg (instrument), got gangrene and died
340 (goal). This exemplar has all of the required elements of a well-formed story. It is, for the student, a schema

for making meaning of the concept "getting drunk." An important caveat for those who find little credibility in the story told above is that the veracity of the story is
345 not as important as the student's use of narrative as a form of communicating his understanding of the concept of getting drunk. Regardless of the truth of the story, it is a recognizable discourse unit that we believe illuminates how this student thinks about the concept.

350 When encountered in the evaluation of substance use prevention education, the students' stories become an authentic assessment tool to illuminate what young people know, believe, and hope. It is through their stories that students tell us how they connect with their
355 world, how they see themselves as members of school communities, and how they see themselves in relation to the use of substances.

Findings

The results of analysis show that in 40 interviews, there were a total of 494 stories told by students. The
360 stories weave together numerous topics including how students understand the no-use message of DATE, the difference between what they hear in school and what they see at home, their understanding of addiction and of harmful consequences to their health, their under-
365 standing of what happens if they get caught using a substance at school, their fears for friends who have substance-related problems, who they think are helping them and who they think are not, and what they think would make a difference. The findings presented in this
370 article, stated as assertions, illuminate the relationships of the various topics, the process of making sense of prevention education, and the outcomes. The findings are organized in the following manner: First, evidence is presented to support the assertion that students at all
375 three levels of schooling use personal narrative to make sense of the information they receive in substance prevention programs. This assertion corresponds to the evaluation question focused on the process of students' meaning making. Second, building on the evidence
380 presented to support the first assertion, evidence is presented to support the related assertion that by connecting and contrasting the information they learn in school about substance use/abuse with their own experience, students at all three levels in contrast to prevention
385 education programs distinguish use from abuse. This assertion corresponds to both the process and outcome questions. Finally, story evidence is presented to support the assertion that the application of sanctions (detention, suspension, and expulsion) provokes further
390 alienation and disconnection of those students who already see themselves on the periphery of the school community. This assertion corresponds to the outcome question guiding this study. The excerpts provided in all cases represent the predominant point of view found
395 throughout the story data. The excerpts chosen are the most articulate exemplars.

Process

In the context of focus groups, how do students at different school levels share their understanding of what they know about the effects of substance use? Students at all three levels of schooling use personal narrative to make sense of the information they receive in drug prevention education. In the following excerpt, a high school student tells his own story about experimentation with marijuana. He contrasts what he has heard in school with his own experience.

Personal Experience in Narrative Form

R: People say you use it once you're gonna get addicted! I don't see that! But, there, I don't even see, some people say that the drug is addictive, like with a little pressure that you could do anything to keep on using it! Any drug is addictive! And I mean, I, myself, I have smoked marijuana before and I believe it's all in the way you look at it.

I: Uh huh.

R: I tried it and it wasn't nothing, there wasn't anything there for me! People say oh, it makes you feel better and all this stuff, I didn't, there was nothing there for me! And I made my choice to say there's what I thought to myself, what compels people to do this? Because there was nothing there for me, and I was thinking what is there for them? (0211, ST.S 593, p. 19)

The preceding excerpt is an example of personal experience in the form of narrative story. It offers insights to the meaning the student makes of the prevention education he received. He has clearly not been convinced to forgo experimentation with marijuana. Rather, the information he received conflicts with what others have said, causing disequilibrium, which in turn has prompted personal experimentation. He is struggling to understand the different choices people make. In the next excerpt during a discussion of the various effects of alcohol on people the students knew, two elementary students were moved to tell their own stories:

R: [first] Like, see my uncle, he can drink and he won't get drunk and then my other uncle he can drink a couple of beers and he will get drunk and get into stuff.

R: [second] Like my dad he can drink like three or four beers and he doesn't really get drunk, he gets kind of weird [said with a kind of laugh], but he doesn't get drunk and if my mom if she drinks anything alcoholic she gets really sick, because he, I mean, my dad used to drink more than he does now. I mean, lately he has maybe one beer a month and my mom doesn't drink. So, it just kind of depends on the attitude of the person they drink, too, because if they're already violent then if they drink they might get even more violent and then if it doesn't bother them, you know.

I: Does the D.A.R.E. officer teach you those things?

R: [third] No, not really.

R: [different respondent] I don't think so.

I: So how did you come to know that? Just by watching?

R: [second] You just kind of know it. [short laugh] [second respondent says "Yes" in the background] You know just by observing your surroundings and you can tell how people act. I mean, all families have different examples of stuff but you can just about get in any family somebody that drinks. (0027, ST.E 567, p. 6–7)

The stories told by these elementary students are typical of both risk and thriving groups. They are aware that alcohol has a negative effect on the behavior of some people. They are also aware that others who drink do not have a problem and can use alcohol occasionally. Most important, the D.A.R.E. officer has not given them this message. As the high school excerpt also illuminated, they have constructed it from their own personal observations and experiences. Through the stories about uncles' and parents' alcohol use, they reveal the understanding they have of use ("he can drink and won't get drunk") and abuse ("he can drink a couple of beers and he will get drunk and get into stuff").

In the following middle school excerpt, during a discussion of what the students think should be in the curriculum they receive, the researcher asked a question that prompted the student to talk about her parents' enjoyment of wine.

I: Well then, what would you guys like to see in the classes that you don't get now?

R: Two sides of the story.

R: Yeah, we…

I: Wait. Can you explain to me what you mean by two sides to the story?

R: Because they give one side, telling you how bad it is, and then they should have another side saying, cause well, they always tell us drinking it really bad and don't drink cause you get drunk and you end up killing people and yourself. But, that's not true cause they tell you that one glass of wine could do that! But, I think they all had another side. That it's okay if you have a little, but not get drunk.

R: Yeah, because everybody is going to drink when they get older! Maybe just, I mean my parents enjoy a glass of wine with dinner and that's just the way it goes! [laughs] It's not like we can stop them from having a…

I: Well, would you want to stop them from having a glass of wine with dinner?

R: No, because I think they enjoy it. They don't get drunk on one glass of wine! [laughs] I think they enjoy having a glass of wine once in a while. They go up to Napa and get some nice aged wine and have some nice wine with dinner or at a party. I wouldn't want to stop them from doing something that they enjoy! (0005, ST.M 507, p. 19)

510   One of California's largest industries is wine making, as many California students are aware. By telling the story of her parents' trip to Napa, this student demonstrates an awareness of the culture that enjoys wine with dinner. She believes that everyone will drink
515   when they get older. She is also able to distinguish use (enjoy a glass of wine with dinner) from abuse (it's OK if you have a little but not get drunk), and she is outspoken in her desire to hear both sides of the story from those who deliver substance use prevention education.
520   More significant, she says clearly that what she has heard in school is not true.

The excerpts presented above are representative of 38 of 40 interviews. In each case, the student uses his or her own personal experience or a significant other's
525   experience with a substance to make a connection with the information he or she has received in school. It is apparent from the above excerpts that the students use narrative to not only link their personal experience to what they have learned in school but also to contrast it.

530   Close examination of the three excerpts above reveals that in each case, what students learned in their substance abuse prevention education is not consistent with other life experiences. In the elementary school excerpt, two students present stories. The first story is
535   about an uncle who is harmed by using alcohol and an uncle who is not. The second student describes the different reactions of his mother and father to the use of alcohol. These students are aware that different people have different reactions to the use of alcohol. The
540   D.A.R.E. officer has not given them this information; they have constructed it from their observations of people in their lives. In the middle school story, the student contrasts her parents' enjoyment of wine with the no-use message she has heard at school. The dis-
545   tinction is not present in the education she receives, and she is clearly aware of the difference labeling the prevention message "untrue." In the high school excerpt, the student contrasts his own experience of using marijuana with the two different ideas he has heard
550   about the use of the substance. He has been taught that "if you use substances you will get addicted." Others in his experience have told him it "will make you feel better." His personal experimentation has not confirmed either of the two predictions. Bruner's assertion
555   that stories are stimulated by the mismatch of an event and the "canonical" would certainly seem to be operating here.

All of the preceding leads to a more developed version of the process assertion. Through the narrative
560   form, students in our study relate the experiences they have in their personal lives to the information they receive at school. By linking and contrasting the two experiences, they construct their own understanding of the effect of using drugs, alcohol, and tobacco.

Outcomes

565   How do students perceive the effects of substance use prevention programs? In the next section, we will make more explicit the contrasts between prevention education and the students' constructed understandings. When students contrast their experiences with
570   what they are taught, a common theme emerges. The theme corresponds to the outcome question guiding this evaluation. Students perceive the effects of prevention education as having little influence on their decision making. We have presented evidence
575   throughout the article to support the assertion that students construct their own understandings of the effects of the use of substances. When students' understandings are different enough from the message they receive in DATE, the credibility of the information they
580   receive and in some cases the students' trust in those who offer the information may be called into question. The following example illustrates a student's blatant distrust of the information he has received.

Student Constructed Understandings

R: No, I don't believe that stuff about one cigarette!
585   No! My mom smokes to calm her, my mom is a really hyper person and she smokes to calm her nerves. She's allowed to do it, she works, she pays her bills, so she's allowed to do it! (0005, ST.M 507, p. 23)

590   The middle school student is certain about his mother's right to smoke when she wants to calm her nerves. He appreciates the fact that she is a responsible adult and can make her own decisions.

Students at all three school levels are able to distin-
595   guish use from abuse. The following representative excerpts at each of the three school levels constitute evidence that students distinguish between use and abuse. The stories students told distinguishing use from abuse often included their personal experiences. Al-
600   though elementary students are legally prohibited from drinking, it must be acknowledged that many of the elementary students have tried alcohol in one form or another under various conditions.

Distinction of Use and Abuse

R: But if you drink like too much alcohol at one time,
605   too fast, it happened to me once, it was an occasion and I had a little shot of wine and I was thirsty and I drank it all at once because I was really thirsty and five minutes later I was sort of snoring.
I: [laughs] Right, right.
610   R: I'm in the seat going [makes snoring noises].
I: So you were out, huh?
R: Yes. I'm not going to do that again. (0072, ST.EH 533, p. 8)

Students at the elementary level are aware that
615   drinking "too much" "too fast" is abuse. The story illustrates the power of personal experience to teach and reinforce lessons that adults would like students to

learn. The middle school students in the following excerpt use story to support their conclusion that not eve-
620 ryone who tries alcohol or drugs "has a problem."

R: I have a friend in high school and she used to do
    alcohol and she quit. She used to do drugs, but she
    quit. It's very easy to quit! If you put your mind to
    it.

625 R: Some people it's easy for, some people it ain't.
I: So, you don't think that everybody that tries it has a
    problem?
R: Right. No. (0005, ST.MH 508, p. 8)

        Stories told throughout the data illuminate stu-
630 dents' understanding of what constitutes a "problem"
or "abuse" of a substance. "Being able to stop" is one
way students identify who does and who does not have
a problem. In the next excerpt, a story of a person who
"can't stop" offers an example of what the high school
635 student sees as the road to alcoholism.

R: My friend's girl has 3 or 4 beers and she'll get real
    buzzed and she has to keep drinking more and
    more! She can't just enjoy it, she has to get loaded.
    She can't stop! I can just walk away from it any-
640 time, or drink several and have a buzz and be al-
    right. And I see her, I don't like people who drink to
    get drunk! You know, just to drink?
R: Yeah!
R: People like that are turning into alcoholics! You can
645 see it coming! (0185, ST.SH 545, p. 14)

    The stories selected to support the notion that stu-
dents distinguish between use and abuse are, again,
typical of those found in the majority of interviews.
The importance of this assertion is understood in the
650 context of the clear message presented to the students
at all grade levels that use of substances equals abuse.
Students typically understand that all use of alcohol is
not abuse, and they clearly identify what is abuse. The
disparity between what they are taught and what they
655 present as story demonstrates that the no-use message
is not being "taken up" (Bruner, 1990, 63).
    From the excerpt presented above, an extension of
the disparity between what is taught in school and what
is understood by students is uncovered. Many students
660 not only differentiate use from abuse, they believe that
a person has to want to stop abusing substances for
counseling or sanctions to have an effect. The idea that
it is easy to quit for some people and more difficult for
others is linked to a story about a high school friend
665 who was successful when she "put her mind to it." This
story illuminates an important issue for students at all
grade levels but most notably at the high school level
when young people are most likely to start using substances. Students believe that it is up to the person to
670 want to stop. Neither counseling nor sanctions levied
against students who are caught using have much preventive influence.

R: Um, no. I don't think that counseling can really, it

675 can help you, but I don't think it's gonna change
    your mind. You have to be willing to change your
    mind! To not to do it, or to not want to do it. If you
    go to counseling and they tell you it's all bad, but
    you still think it's good, then you're gonna do it!
    (0005, ST.SH, p.12)

680 This extension of the assertion will also be discussed.

Inconsistent Message of Home and School

    If what is taught in school is not being accepted by
students, is it because what they learn in school is different from what their parents say and do? As in sev-
685 eral of the prior story examples, dissonance occurs
when students witness their parents' use of substances.
They are forced to deny what they learn in school, "I
don't believe them..." or make a judgment about their
parents, "she had a right to smoke..." The following
690 elementary excerpt is presented in order to make explicit the lack of consistency between what parents are
telling their children and what the school is telling
them.

I: OK, but what I'm asking you guys—this is a very
    personal question—what I'm asking you guys is
695 how do you decide that a little bit is OK and a lot is
    too much? Did someone tell you that?
R: Yes.
I: Or did you just make up your mind on your own?
R: My dad when he was—I don't remember how old—
700 he told me that he was with his friends at a party
    and they told him to try a beer and so he said OK
    and so he drank one and then drank another and he
    started getting sick and he threw up so since he's
    only drank like a half a beer or something so he
705 doesn't get sick any more.
I: So did most of you get that idea—is he right and
    most of you got that idea from your parents?
R: Yes. [several voices] (0072, ST.E 532, p. 19)

    The notion that students use narrative story to con-
710 struct meaning of their diverse experiences with substance use and abuse is very powerful. When there is a
mismatch between home and school, the student is
forced to resolve the dissonance she or he experiences
by making sense of the two worlds. In effect, the stu-
715 dents are being asked to make choices between two
authorities, both of whom lose credibility in the students' eyes in too many cases. Often, the dissonance
results in undermining the students' trust in adults in
general.

Undermining of Students' Trust in Adults

720 Analysis of the stories found in the high school data
revealed a general outcome related to the lack of trust,
but having even more serious consequences in the
"high risk" population (Hawkins et al., 1987) the very
student prevention programs were originally intended
725 to help. The following excerpt is typical of students
who see themselves outside the school community.

R: I mean they always do it like we're all bad people here.

R: I don't think the schools are for like helping it's just for getting the bad kids out and it's just...

R: Yeah.

R: Well, maybe if you could get them to care more then they would do that [a different respondent than the others above].

R: If they suspect you of smoking or having drugs on you or whatever, if they see a kid like that in their school then, instead of suspending them and getting them out of school, why don't they help them? (0072, ST.SH 531, p. 13)

These at-risk students, according to the "risk factor model" (Hawkins et al., 1987), are the most likely to become dropouts, drug addicts, homeless, or criminals. Yet, all too often these young people feel hopeless and disheartened and see no future for themselves in the school or society. Another excerpt gives further insight to the minimal effects of prevention education.

R: It's pretty sad if society puts you in a position where you can't be happy unless you use drugs. I mean if you got school and you got the wrong problem, not a drug user, but about the way society treats kids. (0072, ST.SH 531, p. 10)

These students believe the treatment (prevention education) is for the wrong problem. They see themselves as victims of social pressures, and they are concerned about the lack of care and support they receive from school personnel to cope with these perceived pressures.

If only the voices of at-risk students were raised urging those in authority to help, they would probably not be heard. However, they are not the only voices urging a change in the way students are treated when they have a problem. School personnel recognize the failure of the school system to help these students as well. "We still get rid of too many kids... those are the kids that the state of California and the United States of America have identified as their target population.... The kids that are at risk the most, are the kids that are exited from the system and they do not have access to the resources.... The kids that we need to help in and provide resources to are the kids that we exit from the system" (0027, GF 558, p. 18).

Given the previous data, we come to the final assertion generated in this study: The application of sanctions (detention, suspension, and expulsion) provokes further alienation and disconnection of those students who already see themselves on the periphery of the school community.

The next section of the article will discuss the implications of the preceding assertions.

Discussion

Returning to the first of the two questions that guided this evaluation, it is apparent from the evidence supporting the assertions that the students of both groups, at all three levels of school, use narrative story to display their understandings of substance use and abuse. The ubiquity of this form of discourse in the student data adequately supports the proposition that story provides a way of sorting out our thoughts about the world. The student stories also support Bruner's idea that narrative mediates between the canonical world of culture and the idiosyncratic world of beliefs, desires, and hopes. If stories are the medium by which human beings construct meaning, we argue that the student stories found in the interviews are a key to understanding how students are making sense of the programs they receive. Unsolicited stories were woven throughout all but two of the interviews. Curiously, these two interviews were conducted by the same interviewer whose style of interaction with the students included interrupting them while they were speaking and making references to time during the interview. This interview style undoubtedly contributed to the lack of stories. Excerpts from the interviews have adequately shown how the students, stimulated by the conversation, voluntarily share the stories they associate with the stimulus. This primary assertion supports Polkinghorne's (1988) notion that "experience is constructed when a person assimilates the stimuli and matches them with his or her existing structural representations of events which are judged to be similar to the input given" (p. 108). During the interviews, questions were asked that stimulated the mental representations of similar events (stories) that, in the student's mind, matched the stimuli.

In analyzing the data, we did not view the stories of students uncritically. The DATE evaluation used multiple methods to assess program effectiveness, and narrative story was one of them. Narrative stories were not anticipated in our data collection process. It was the overwhelming number of stories that the students told that focused our attention on the value of narrative. Our primary concern is not the factual basis of these stories. As we have shown, whereas many stories may represent facts, others represent misconceptions or partial truths regarding substances like alcohol. We see, through students' stories, as in the construction of understanding of other types of knowledge, the logic the student uses to make sense of the world. The importance of narrative as an evaluation tool is twofold. It features the voices of the target population at the center of the evaluation of programs, and it helps evaluators gain insight to the construction of meaning students are making. In this study, when students told their stories, we gained insight to what they have learned and how they make sense of prevention education. Viewing these findings critically, we feel reassured by the triangulation of other results from different data sources in the DATE evaluation (Brown, D'Emidio-Caston, and Pollard, 1997; Brown and D'Emidio-Caston, 1995).

Regarding the outcomes of prevention education

840 and what we now understand as the mismatch between prevention education and personal experience, we can begin to sort out the effects. In some cases, the stories told were simple accounts of someone's use of a substance. In other cases, they are elaborate, well-formed

845 stories that illustrate the students' confusion, disequilibrium, or dissatisfaction with the lack of consistency between their personal experience and what the school authorities tell them. Students' ability to distinguish between the use and abuse of substances is an indicator

850 of such lack of consistency. The narrative evidence revealed how the students interpret and connect what they learn in school with what they experience out of school in the popular culture and home environment. When a student's home life includes drinking wine

855 with dinner, for example, or one parent's capacity to drink and another not, there is a problem with telling that student that all drinking is unhealthy or bad. They must resolve their disequilibrium, and often do, at the expense of not believing the information or the person

860 who delivers the inconsistent message. When that person is a teacher or a police officer in the D.A.R.E. program, the unfortunate result is a loss of credibility in those who represent social authority.

For many students, particularly those who are ac-

865 tive, thriving members of the school community, the loss of credible authority in the form of teachers and police officers is not alienating. These students see themselves as members of the school community. They perceive that the reason behind the inconsistent mes-

870 sage is good will and "caring" for their well-being. The unfortunate antithesis of this is true for those who are already on the periphery of the school community. For the students who have "low commitment for school," the loss of credible adult authority pushes them further

875 toward the periphery.

Clearly, the hard line policies called for by the DATE application are successful in reducing the number of students with drug-related problems in the schools. Equally as clear is the unfortunate way this

880 outcome is enacted. The schools do not seem to have the capacity to help or heal. They have only the capacity to punish and expel. Those students who perceive themselves as "bad" have no incentive whatever to comply with the no-use policies (Napier and Gershen-

885 feld, 1993). For them, detention, suspension, and expulsion confirm their perceived non-member status. These implications undermine the position that a risk orientation is a valuable tool to change patterns of substance use or abuse in young people. We argue here

890 that it would seem appropriate and propitious to change the assumptions guiding the substances use prevention programs in California public schools.

Others too have urged a different approach. Benard (1993) and Brown and Horowitz (1993) have clearly

895 stated a different orientation to working with students who see themselves as alienated from the school community. Benard urges schools to become places char-

acterized by caring, participation, and high expectations for all students. Her argument is that when stu-

900 dents feel connected to the school community, they feel cared for and they have better resiliency and healthy responses to challenges. Brown and Horowitz urge a "harm-reduction" model that reduces the actual damage a person might experience from secondary causes

905 related to use of substances. Designated driver programs are one example of a harm-reduction strategy.

What do students say? It is fitting to end this article with some final excerpts from students who have a great deal more knowledge than we often credit them.

910 When asked what the goal of a drug education program should be, this high school student replied:

To know what your limitations are, to make yourself aware enough so that you know—personally, I've never felt very worried that I would ever become a substance

915 abuser. When I was like elementary school it was crammed down my throat, Just Say No, it's the most awful thing in the world, and so when it first came, like in ninth grade, I remember this girl was trying to get me to do pot I'm like, "No, that's evil." It was that kind of a

920 thing, but I think the goal of education should be you're going to be in the situation, you're going to see this, that and the other thing, it's not evil if you've got a good enough sense of self-worth, if you know what your boundaries are, if you know what you feel comfortable

925 with and if you know what it's going to do to you and you know what the consequences may be. (0072, ST.S 530 p. 15)

Her recommendation that students need to have a good sense of self-worth and know what their bounda-

930 ries are resounds the wisdom of the adults cited above. If the school creates a climate where all students experience success and a sense of accomplishment, they will be more resilient when faced with the givens of conflicting authorities or economic hardship. Another

935 student had this recommendation:

I just want to say that I guess the best education would be the education that would allow you to evaluate yourself and allow you to evaluate your own personal beliefs and your morals and your values and take a strong look at

940 what you're feeling and if you might have the possibility to be a substance abuser. (0072, ST.S 530, p. 31)

The figure attached to the DATE Program during the years of this evaluation in the state of California is estimated at more than $1.5 billion. Public account-

945 ability for this large an expenditure is appropriate. Our research has shown that risk-oriented policies and programs like D.A.R.E., Red Ribbon Week, and anti-drug assemblies are highly implemented. Their primary program components are some form of scare tactics, of-

950 fering a reward in exchange for not using substances and enhancing self-esteem through refusal skills. Policies widely in place are intended to enforce the social and legal consequences of substance use (Brown et al., 1997; Brown and D'Emidio-Caston, 1995). The stories

955 presented in this article are representative of hundreds

of stories the students in the DATE evaluation told. It is clear that they do not believe what they are being told and instead construct their own version of the consequences of substance use. The DATE evidence
960 stands with other evidence in suggesting a high level of program implementation and low level of effectiveness (Klitzner, 1987; Moskowitz, 1989; Tobler, 1992; Ennett et al., 1994). We have presented an argument here that demonstrates that prevention programs designed
965 with the risk orientation have a potentially more insidious effect, that of reinforcing the perception of alienated young people that adult authorities are not credible or caring. We suggest we listen to their voices as they tell us we are treating the wrong problem. In examining
970 and observing programs and program records, performing interviews, doing surveys, and performing meta-analyses of other study results, we are left with few alternative explanations in our inability to show positive program effects.
975 The War on Drugs has had many casualties. Our results indicate that students who demonstrate the need for the most support may be unintended victims of that war; not from the use of substances themselves but from the process of substance use prevention education
980 and the policies in place in school districts, which exclude them. Those students who are thriving, although they may experiment, have good reason for not abusing substances. They see themselves in the future, and they have legitimate, school-sanctioned support networks.
985 Those who abuse substances are often those with little vision of themselves in the future. Without a legitimate, sanctioned support system, they may seek in gangs the affiliation and recognition society has withheld. Without condoning the use of substances by
990 young people, a more authentic and realistic orientation to working with students who have problems must be found. Emphasis on resiliency and harm reduction are two possibilities. With each day, as our jails take up more and more of the available resources, an ever
995 greater need is apparent. For prevention programs to be effective, they must support those most at risk to be able to see a future when they close their eyes and dream.

References

Benard, B. (1993). *Turning the corner risk to resiliency.* San Francisco: Western Regional Center.

Blue-Swadner, B., & Lubeck, S. (1995). *Children and families at promise: Reconstructing the discourse of risk.* New York: SUNY Press.

Brown, J. H., & D'Emidio-Caston, M. (1995). On becoming at risk through drug education: How symbolic policies and their practices affect students. *Evaluation Review, 19* (4), 451–492.

Brown, J. H., D'Emidio-Caston, M., Goldsworthy-Hanner, T., & Alioto, M. (1993). *Technical report of 1992 qualitative findings for the drug, alcohol, and tobacco education program evaluation.* Los Alamitos, CA: South West Regional Laboratory.

Brown, J. H., D'Emidio-Caston, M., Kaufman, K., Goldsworthy-Hanner, T., & Alioto, M. (1995). *In their own voices: Students and educators evaluate school based drug alcohol and tobacco education programs.* Prepared for the California Department of Education by Pacific Institute for Research and Evaluation.

Brown, J. H., D'Emidio-Caston, M., & Pollard, J. A. (1997). Students and substances: Social power in drug education. *Educational Evaluation and Policy Analysis, 19* (1), 65–82.

Brown, J. H., & Horowitz, J. E. (1993). Deviance and deviants: Why adolescent substance use prevention programs do not work. *Evaluation Review, 17* (5), 529–555.

Bruner, J. (1990). *Acts of meaning.* Cambridge, MA: Harvard University Press.

Chomsky, N. (1966). *Cartesian linguistics: A chapter in the history of rationalist thought.* New York: Harper and Row.

Connelly, F. M., & Clandinin, D. J. (1990). Stories of experience and narrative inquiry. *Educational Researcher, 19* (5), 2–14.

Donabedian, A. (1980). *Explorations in quality assessment and monitoring: Vol. 1. The definition of quality and approaches to its assessment.* Ann Arbor, MI: Health Administration Press.

Ennett, S. T., Tobler, N. S., Ringwalt, C. L., & Flewelling, R. L. (1994). How effective is drug abuse resistance education? A meta-analysis of project D.A.R.E. outcome evaluations. *American Journal of Public Health, 84* (9), 1394–1401.

Goetz, J. P., & LeCompte, M. (1984). *Ethnography and qualitative design in educational research.* Orlando, FL: Academic Press.

Hawkins, J. D., Kuagbwem, J. M., Jenson, J. M., & Catalano, R. F. (1987). Delinquents and drugs: What the evidence suggests about prevention and treatment programming. In B. S. Brown & A. R. Mills (Eds.), *Youth at high risk for substance abuse* (DHHS Publication No. ADM 87-1537; reprinted 1990 as ADM 90-1537), (pp. 81–131). Washington, DC: U.S. Government Printing Office.

Kemper, S. (1984). The development of narrative skills: Explanations and entertainments. In S. A. Kuczaj (Ed.) *Discourse development: Progress in cognitive development research* (pp. 99–124). New York: Springer-Verlag.

Klitzner, M. D. (1987). *Part 2: An assessment of the research on school-based prevention programs.* Report to Congress and the White House on the nature and effectiveness of federal, state, and local drug prevention/education programs. Washington, DC: U.S. Department of Education.

Manning, P. K., & Cullum-Swan, B. (1994). Narrative, content, and semiotic analysis. In N. K. Denzin & Y. S. Lincoln (Eds.), *Handbook of qualitative research.* Newbury Park, CA: Sage.

Mitchell, W. J. T. (Ed.) (1980). *On narrative.* Chicago: University of Chicago Press.

Moskowitz, J. M. (1989). The primary prevention of alcohol problems: A critical review of the research literature. *Journal of Studies on Alcohol, 50,* 54–88.

Napier, R. W., & Gershenfeld, M. K. (1993). *Groups theory and practice.* Boston: Houghton Mifflin.

Patton, M. Q. (1990). *Qualitative evaluation and research methods* (2d ed). Newbury Park, CA: Sage.

Polkinghorne, D. E. (1988). *Narrative knowing and the human services.* New York: State University of New York Press.

Poplin, M., & Weeres, J. (1992). *Voices from the inside: A report on school from inside the classroom.* Claremont, CA: The Institute for Education in Transformation at The Claremont Graduate School.

Romero, F., Bailey, J., Carr, C., Flaherty, J., Fleming, T., Gaynor, J. R., Houle, D., Karam, R., Lark, M., Martino, T., & Thomas, C. (1994). *1992–93 California programs to prevent and reduce drug, alcohol, and tobacco use among in-school youth: Annual evaluation report.* Prepared for the California Department of Education by Southwest Regional Laboratory. Los Alamitos, NM: The Southwest Regional Laboratory.

Romero, F., Carr, C., Pollard, J., Houle, D., Brown, J., Gaynor, J. R., Fleming, T., Flaherty, J., Martino, T., & Karam, R. (1993). *Drug, alcohol and tobacco education evaluation: Second year interim evaluation report.* Prepared for the California Department of Education by Southwest Regional Library. Los Alamitos, NM: The Southwest Regional Laboratory.

Rosen, H. (1985). The importance of story. *Language Arts, 63* (3), 226–237.

Sarason, S. B. (1982). *The culture of the school and the problem of change* (2d ed.). Boston: Allyn & Bacon.

Schubert, W. H., & Ayers, W. C. (Eds.). (1992). *Teacher lore, learning from our own experience.* New York: Longman.

Stein, N. L., & Policastro, M. (1984). The concept of story: A comparison between children's and teachers' viewpoints. In H. Mandl, N. L. Stein, & T. Trabasso (Eds.), *Learning and comprehension of text* (pp. 113–155). Hillsdale, NJ: Lawrence Erlbaum.

Strauss, A., & Corbin, J. (1990). *Basics for qualitative research: Grounded theory procedures and techniques.* Newbury Park, CA: Sage.

Tobler, N. S. (1992). Drug prevention programs can work: Research findings. *Journal of Addictive Diseases, 11* (3), 1–26.

Witherell, C., & Noddings, N. (Eds.) (1991). *Stories lives tell.* New York: Teachers College Press.

About the Authors: Marianne D'Emidio-Caston is presently the coordinator of the Elementary Teacher Education Program and Lecturer in the Graduate School of Education, University of California at Santa Barbara. She has more than 20 years of field experience as a teacher and administrator and has published articles on the development of practical theory in beginning teachers and the use of the affective domain to enhance teaching and learning. Joel H. Brown is an educational consultant. Currently, he directs the Center for Edu cational Research and Development (CERD), a Berkeley-based educational evaluation, research, and policy development organization focusing on the development and well-being of youth. Among many other studies, he was the principal investigator of the nationally recognized research entitled "In Their Own Voices: Students and Educators Evaluate California School-Based Drug, Alcohol, and Tobacco Education (DATE) Programs." His areas of expertise, all within social welfare, public health, and psychological contexts, include the study of adolescent development, organizational change, school evaluation program/policy development, and the integration of qualitative with quantitative research methods.

Authors' Note: This research was supported by the California State Department of Education, Contract No. 3279. It was originally presented at the Annual Meeting of the American Educational Research Association (AERA), April 1995. The views expressed herein are those of the authors and do not necessarily represent those of the California State Department of Education.

Exercise for Case 15

Note: Article 16 is a *quantitative study* on the same general topic as this one. If you are assigned Article 16, you will find questions asking you to compare the two articles in the exercise for that article.

1. Introduction

A. Is the problem area for the research clearly described? Explain.

B. Have the researchers convinced you that the problem area is important? Explain.

C. To what extent does the literature presented in the introduction help you understand the problem? Is the literature used to put the problem in context? Explain.

D. Do the researchers indicate how this study is different from and/or similar to earlier ones reported in the literature?

E. Do the researchers reveal their personal perspectives on the problem area, including any possible biases? Explain.

2. Methods

A. Are the demographics of the participants (i.e., background characteristics such as age, race, and so on) described in sufficient detail? Explain.

B. Considering the problem area for the research, do you think that appropriate participants were selected? If you had been conducting the study, would you have selected the same type(s) of participants? Would you have used the same number of participants? Explain.

C. Which strategies listed in Table 1 on page 161 of this book were employed by the researchers? Are they described in sufficient detail? Explain.

D. In addition to those you named in response to question 2C, have the researchers used any additional strategies to help assure the validity of the study? If yes, what are they? Are they described in sufficient detail? Explain.

3. Analysis and Results

A. Are the steps taken in the analysis described in sufficient detail? Explain.

B. Are the results clearly organized? Explain.

C. Are the results discussed in terms of a theory or theories (either theories that emerged from this study or previously existing ones)? Explain.

D. Were the direct quotations of the participants' statements, if any, judiciously selected? Do they help you understand the results? Explain.

E. Are there other ways the results could have been organized and interpreted? Explain.

4. Conclusions/Implications

A. Are the researchers' concluding remarks appropriate? Do they flow logically from the material presented earlier?

B. Do the researchers describe any implications? If yes, are they appropriate? Are there other implications that are not discussed by the researchers? Explain.

5. Ethical Considerations

A. In your opinion, could this research have caused physical or psychological harm to the participants? If yes, did the researchers take adequate measures to ameliorate the potential for harm? Explain.

B. If you had conducted this research, would you have obtained written, informed consent from the participants before conducting the study? Explain. Does this research report indicate that the researchers obtained such consent?

6. Overall Evaluation

A. Throughout the article, are all specialized terms and jargon defined to your satisfaction? Explain.

B. Briefly describe your overall evaluation of the research report, noting any special strengths and weaknesses.

C. If you had been a reviewer for the journal in which this report was published, would you have recommended publication of the report? If yes, would you have recommended that it be published "as is" or modified before publication? Explain. If no, what is the primary reason why you would recommend not publishing it?

An Evaluation of a Pre-School Based Prevention Program: Longitudinal Effects on Children's Alcohol-Related Expectancies

KENNETH CORVO
Syracuse University

LINDA PERSSE
Case Western Reserve University

Editor's note: This is a *quantitative* research article on the same general topic as Article 15, which is *qualitative*. The questions at the end of this article ask you to compare and contrast the two articles.

ABSTRACT. Though little evidence of their effectiveness exists, the number and variety of drug abuse prevention programs available for pre-school children have increased greatly. One effort to evaluate a pre-school drug prevention program in Cleveland, Ohio, using alcohol-related expectancies as an outcome measure is described. Alcohol-related expectancies of program participants at three years post-treatment did not differ from those of a comparison group. Theoretical and methodological issues in program development and evaluation are explored.

From *Journal of Alcohol and Drug Education*, *43*, 36–47. Copyright © 1998 by the American Alcohol and Drug Information Foundation. Reprinted with permission.

Introduction

With the growing awareness that even very young children are at risk of socialization into drug and alcohol-using behavior, the number and variety of drug
5 abuse prevention programs available for pre-school children have increased greatly. This growth has occurred with little empirical evidence that such programs are effective. This shortage of sound evidence stems in part from the methodological difficulties encountered when evaluating outcomes for pre-school
10 drug prevention programs. Such difficulties include: How to assess impact on behavior when the onset of those targeted behaviors (drug or alcohol use) are a number of years distant; generally weak predictive power of other indicators; and attrition of samples over
15 time in longitudinal studies. For example, Hall and Zigler's (1997) survey of drug abuse prevention programs for young children found no longitudinal outcome data available on program effectiveness that was linked to impacting drug abuse. Where evaluation data
20 were available, pre-test/post-test intervals typically were only several weeks in duration, leaving the question of longer-term effects unanswered.

The purpose of this paper is to describe an outcome evaluation study which sought to assess if the effects of
25 a pre-school based drug prevention program could be identified at three years post-program. The relevance of this study for pre-school based substance abuse prevention, as well as for prevention evaluation methodology, will be discussed.

Review of the Literature

30 Hall and Zigler (1997) identify the late 1980's – early 1990's as the period when prevention programs began to be directed toward children younger than five years of age. Johnston (1991) found that as the age of first use was lowering, the ages at which prevention
35 and intervention efforts were deemed appropriate were lowering as well. As younger children are seen as being at risk for alcohol or drug abuse, prevention efforts are more likely to be guided by what Glantz (1992) called a "developmental psychopathology model." In
40 this model, deficits or disturbances in mastering developmental tasks are etiologically linked to drug or alcohol abuse. At each developmental stage in childhood and adolescence, certain characteristics or conditions (e.g., poor care-giver attachment during infancy) place
45 the child at risk for future drug or alcohol abuse. Prevention approaches which are ameliorative or promote resilience are to be used in a developmentally relevant way.

Also during this period, social learning theory-
50 based research was exploring how children's cognitive development and exposure to models and information about drug and alcohol use could interact to influence beliefs about alcohol. Much of this research was guided by the constructs of alcohol expectancy theory. Gold-
55 man, Brown, and Christiansen (1987) describe expectancies as the anticipation of a predictable relationship between events: "The relationship is understood to be of an if-then variety: **If** a certain event or object is registered **then** a certain event is expected to follow…" (p.

60 183). Smith and Goldman (1991) stated: "Alcohol expectancies are thought to develop as a function of individual's alcohol-related learning histories. They are
seen as an individual's internal summary representations, in if-then rule form, of their learning histories
65 relating alcohol consumption to various contingen-
cies." (p. 1) (for example, an individual's belief that
drinking alcohol produces an elevation of mood). Expectancies can be seen as memories or cognitive
schemes arising out of early experience (not necessar-
70 ily actual drinking) with alcohol which mediate contemporary behavior (Kraus, Smith, & Ratner, 1994).
Christiansen, Roehling, Smith, and Goldman (1989)
found that alcohol expectancies were present in adoles-
cent/pre-adolescent samples prior to actual drinking
75 experience and that those expectancies could predict
the emergence of problem drinking within a one-year
period. Miller, Smith, and Goldman (1990), measuring
alcohol expectancies in elementary school children,
found them present in children as young as age six.
80 They identified a developmentally linked increase in
alcohol expectancies which correlated with age and
academic grade, with a particularly sharp increase in
the fourth grade at about age nine. Noll, Zucker, and
Greenberg (1990) report that children as young as three
85 to five years could identify alcohol (through smell and
photographs) and could articulate some of the rules
concerning adult-use substances. The ability to successfully identify alcohol was related to heavier parental drinking.

90 To summarize: 1) the average age for first use of
drugs and alcohol appears to be lowering; 2) children
as young as age three are able to identify alcohol; 3)
alcohol expectancies increase "naturally" with age as
well as a result of exposure and experience; 4) expec-
95 tancies are reliably measurable in children and are able
to predict problem drinking **before actual use begins**.
Taken together, the developmental psychopathology
model and the findings being generated by expectan-
cies-guided research have provided ample support to
100 consider initiating substance abuse prevention efforts
aimed at very young children.

*The Use of Alcohol Expectancies as an Outcome
Measure*

Alcohol expectancies were selected as the primary
outcome measure for the current evaluation for the
following reasons:

105 1. The process and type of developmental risks for
both alcohol and drug abuse are similar (Zucker &
Fitzgerald, 1991; Glantz, 1992).
2. These developmental risk factors, taken as a
group, are extremely difficult to disentangle in
110 their etiological influences (consider only the
intergenerational interactions of parental anti-
social personality and alcohol abuse on child adjustment).
3. Measurably altering each of these developmental

115 risk factors in early childhood and validating the
effect size as adequate to impact later drug or alcohol abuse presents enormous methodological
difficulties.
4. Expectancies can predict problematic drinking (at
120 least in adolescence) better than many other risk
factors (including parental drinking behavior)
(Christiansen & Goldman, 1983).
5. Alcohol expectancies can be considered a proxy
variable for a wide range of factors associated with
125 risk.

Overview of the Program

During the academic year periods 1991–1992 and
1992–1993, the Alcohol and Drug Addiction Services
Board of Cuyahoga County (ADASBCC) funded the
130 implementation of a drug abuse prevention demonstration project targeted at pre-school children and their
families. The ADASBCC is the administrative and
funding oversight body for local and state funding of
alcohol and drug prevention and treatment programs in
metropolitan Cleveland, Ohio. This project, the Pre-
135 school Drug Prevention Project (PDPP), provided
services to approximately 1700 children at 20 pre-
school sites in low-income areas of Cleveland and approximately 350 parents in a variety of settings. Five
human service agencies contracted with the
140 ADASBCC to provide services to these children and
families. Each contract agency submitted a proposal
and work plan indicating how they would comply with
the broad objectives of the project. These objectives
required each agency to provide on-site prevention
145 services directly to children in their pre-schools; to
provide education and support to their parents in the
areas of positive parenting styles and the risks of alcohol and abuse; and to train and support the pre-schools'
teachers and administrators in learning how to recog-
150 nize and respond to the presence of alcohol and drug
abuse in families. Service provider teams combined
staff with early childhood experience and staff with
substance abuse prevention experience. Although there
were some differences in approaches (e.g., either more
155 or less emphasis given to self-esteem building) among
the participating agencies, there was general agreement
that providing prevention services to preschool children ages 3, 4, and 5 would be guided broadly by developmental theory. The principals of developmental
160 theory were incorporated into the request for proposals
issued by the ADASBCC in the form of project goals.
As such, all program approaches included a mix of
activities which were intended to raise the children's
self-esteem, to improve decision-making and problem-
165 solving skills, to enhance resiliency, and to provide
health education. Methods used by the staff varied, but
all included at least weekly visits and presentations to
each site by the service-providing team throughout the
school year. Some employed existing packaged curric-
170 ula (Beginning Alcohol and Addiction Basic Education

Studies [B.A.B.E.S.]) and others developed or modified curricular materials to better fit the needs and abilities of young, low-income children. Methods of implementation included arts and play activities, group
175 activities, and instruction.

Although contact was made with approximately 350 parents, services to parents varied greatly across providers and settings. In general, attendance at scheduled activities and meetings was erratic. Efforts to en-
180 gage and retain parents in program activities were, overall, not successful. As a project-wide component, it is not likely that services to parents were able to make a significant impact on outcomes.

Training and support of pre-school staff were ap-
185 proached with a variety of methods, including in-service training and classroom observation and consultation. Sites included Head Start and other pre-school sites with contracts to serve low-income children. Some sites were plagued by high staff turnover
190 and inadequate physical environments, while others provided higher quality and more stable conditions.

In short, there was broad agreement on goals, but less unanimity in implementation.

Evaluation Methods

Context for the Evaluation

An initial evaluation of the PDPP, completed in
195 1993, focused both on process and implementation issues, as well as on program outcomes. Pertinent to the present report was the attempt to use outcome measures derived from the alcohol-expectancies theory. At that time, a sub-sample of the older pre-school
200 children (54 months and older) could not be reliably tested using a simplified version of the Children's Alcohol Related Expectancies (CARE) questionnaire (Miller et al., 1990), without selectively removing cases that were inappropriate. As a group, the children
205 were too young to respond to the instrument in a way that did not compromise the validity of the results (e.g., answering "no" to all items, even those that were reverse scored). Although the resulting report found some evidence of change in the desired direction, the
210 evidence was based on a pattern of findings including other measures (attitudes toward, intentions to drink, and preference, for alcohol). At the conclusion of the demonstration phase, the ADASBCC requested that the first author secure parental permission to re-approach
215 participating children in the future. At the close of the second year, the program census was approximately 900 children and about 242 parents that provided written permission to contact them in the future. Access to the remaining cases was closed to provide maximum
220 confidentiality. Service-providing agencies in the PDPP were assured that, since this was a demonstration project, and therefore to some degree experimental, program outcomes for individual agencies would not be identified nor compared to each other.
225 The present study was designed to assess if the

PDPP had any effect on alcohol expectancies that could be identified at three years post-program.

Design

This study employed a quasi-experimental design, post-test only, comparing a sample of the children who
230 had received PDPP services during the period 1992–1993 (treatment group) to a group of children (comparison group) drawn from second and third grade classes at Almira Elementary School, an urban public school in Cleveland.

Measures

235 The CARE questionnaire is a 39-item, "yes/no" scale, with five factors designed to assess children's expectancies about the effects of alcohol. The five factors are: alcohol can make global positive transformations of experience; alcohol can enhance or impede
240 social behavior; alcohol enhances heterosexual interaction; alcohol increases arousal; and alcohol promotes relaxation. The higher the score the greater the expectancies regarding alcohol's effects, and the stronger the prediction of problem drinking. Adequate internal con-
245 sistency reliability (*alpha* = .88) and construct validity has been established for children the same age as those in the present study (Miller et al., 1990). The internal consistency coefficient of the CARE scale in this study was *alpha* = .76. Other measures were also applied,
250 including attitudes toward alcohol, intentions to drink alcohol, and preference for alcohol as a beverage. These other measures were responded to positively so rarely in either sample that they were dropped from further analysis.

Sampling

255 In the fall of 1996 efforts were made to contact all of the 242 families which returned authorization to contact forms at the close of program year 1993. Graduate student interviewers made multiple attempts to contact parents by telephone and mail. A $10.00
260 stipend was offered for participation. In the intervening three years, many families had moved with no forwarding address, had disconnected or changed telephone service or were otherwise unable to be located. Of approximately 50 families located, forty-two agreed
265 to have their children interviewed.

Efforts to locate children for a comparison group were undertaken when the characteristics of the treatment group became known. Variables of greatest concern were age and academic grade, both linked to
270 variation in expectancy scores. The search for a comparison group was guided by the wish to match samples as much as possible on those variables. The administration of Almira Elementary School facilitated access to second and third graders at the school. Ap-
275 proximately 120 request for permission to participate forms were sent to the parents of these children. Thirty-three returned them authorizing permission to interview. A $10.00 stipend was also provided to these par-

ents. Treatment group children were individually inter-
280 viewed in their homes by trained graduate students in
social work. Comparison group children were individually interviewed by the same students in counselors' offices in the elementary school.

Other than removing two treatment group respon-
285 dents who were in the first and fourth grades, no other
efforts to match the samples were undertaken.

Since data on characteristics for all program participants during the demonstration period was not collected, it is not possible to ascertain with precision the
290 representativeness of the sample for the treatment
group. It is reasonable to conclude, however, that this
sample is somewhat more residentially stable than the
entire program population, in that they either hadn't
moved in the interim, or had left a "trail" which per-
295 mitted them to be located. To the extent that residential
stability among low-income families is an indicator of
other relevant conditions, the sample may differ from
the program population.

Data Analysis

Scores on the CARE questionnaire for each group
300 (treatment and comparison) were compared using independent samples t tests. Post-hoc analyses of the data
were performed to assess if differences in the composition of the samples may have affected CARE scores.

Findings

Characteristics of the Sample

Selected relevant characteristics of the treatment
305 and comparison groups are shown in Table 1: Description of Treatment and Comparison Group Characteristics. Although not matched case-by-case, efforts were
made to select a comparison group that did not differ
greatly in ways that were known to effect expectancy
310 scores. Expectancy scores are positively correlated
with age and academic grade (Miller et al., 1990). In
this study, the treatment group had a higher ratio of
third to second graders, but a lower mean age.

*Expectancies Scores for the Treatment and Compari-
son Groups*

The CARE scores for the treatment group ranged
315 from 1–20, and from 0–14 for the comparison group.
For means, standard deviation and test of significance,
please see Table 2: Treatment and Comparison Group
CARE Scores.

Discussion

The difference found between the samples on
320 CARE expectancy scores approaches, but does not
reach, the generally accepted minimum standard of
statistical significance of $p = .05$. Treatment group
scores are actually numerically greater. Post-hoc examinations of available data from several variables
325 which may be associated with variation in expectancy
scores found no significant differences due to
grade/group interactions, for sex of the child, nor for

pre-school experience within groups (e.g., Head Start
to other pre-schools). The samples were comparable on
330 age (a strong predictor of expectancy scores). We do
not know, however, if the samples differ in degree of
exposure to models of alcohol use. Regardless of other
differences that may exist between these two groups,
their expectancy scores do not greatly differ. Given the
335 compromises inherent in the design, and for samples of
this size, substantially lower CARE scores in the treatment group would have been required to support an
interpretation of positive program effects over time.
Interestingly, expectancy scores for both groups of
340 children in this study are lower than those reported in
some other studies for children of this age, particularly
for the third grade children (Miller et al., 1990; Kraus
et al., 1994).

Table 1
*Description of Treatment Group and Comparison
Group Characteristics*

	Treatment Group ($N = 36$)*	Comparison Group ($N = 33$)
Sex (%)		
Male	58	33
Female	42	67
Age (mean years)	8.3	8.7
Grade (%)		
Second	28	42
Third	72	58
Pre-School (%)		
Head Start	58	21
Other Pre-school	39	33
No pre-school	0	45

*Smaller than original sample due to incomplete inter-
views and removal of two respondents in first and fourth
grades. Some column totals less than 100% due to round-
ing.

Table 2
*Treatment and Comparison Group CARE Scores
(t test)*

	Mean	Standard Deviation	Probability
Treatment Group	6.9	4.1	
Comparison Group	5.0	4.1	.06*

*Not significant

345 The major objective of this study was to explore if
pre-school based prevention could produce a longitudinal change in expectancies. What can we conclude
from the findings of this study? First, whatever other
positive effects may have occurred, we do not have
350 evidence that the level or type of services provided by

157

the PDPP produced a measurable impact on alcohol expectancies at three years post-program. It may be that the complex of influences that effect alcohol expectancies over time (parental behavior; cognitive development; community and media messages) overwhelmed the effects of prevention. The PDPP was not intentionally designed to disconfirm expectancies; specific and theory-driven efforts to modify expectancies had not been part of the project. However, other interventions specifically tailored to modify children's alcohol expectancies have provided mixed results. Kraus et al. (1994) report that a video-taped intervention developed to lower expectancies in children, unexpectedly **raised** them instead. Another video-tape intervention reported by Kraus et al. (1994) did, however, lower expectancies in children; and Darkes and Goldman (1993) report reduced drinking behavior in college students as a result of an intervention intended to challenge alcohol expectancies. Results in both studies were verified at about four weeks post-intervention, leaving open the question of longer-term effects.

In the broader context of establishing longer-term efficacy for primary prevention as a change strategy, the PDPP confirms, perhaps, the difficulty and complexity of confirming program effects. Issues of methodology, theory, ideology, finance, and implementation often compromise our search for clarity. For example, allegiance to various approaches persists in spite of a lack of support for efficacy. A meta-analysis of Project DARE, the most widely used, school-based drug abuse prevention program in the country, found that effects on actual drug use were negligible and smaller than other less popular programs (Ennet, Tobler, Ringwalt, & Flewelling, 1994). Little empirical evidence exists that the extremely popular school-based conflict resolution programs have any impact on violent behavior (Corvo, 1997).

The Perry Preschool Study (Schweinhart & Weikart, 1990) found that an intensive child development enrichment program for low-income three- and four-year old children, with social support for their parents, could enhance social adjustment throughout childhood and adolescence. The cost of this program (in 1988 dollars) was estimated to be $6,500/child for 30 weeks and $12,700 for 60 weeks. This level of expenditure more closely resembles treatment costs than those typically associated with primary prevention. Where longer-term effects are measurable, we find costs which could prohibit wider application.

The opportunity to aim substance abuse prevention at very young children is tempting. These children are more malleable; efforts at prevention can be seen as "inoculations" against problems in the future. Developmental theory and expectancy theory hold out the promise that early interventions can positively alter the trajectory of a child's life. This may be so, but the conditions which make that more likely are not easily achieved. Effective drug prevention programs for young children must incorporate better specification of risk factors linked to drug and alcohol use, as well as the recognition that such use is influenced by a cascade of ecological risk factors which will continue beyond early childhood. Not only must prevention efforts be theory-based and well-implemented, they must be provided at the level of intensity and duration required to measurably alter the targeted behavior(s). Particularly for children at moderate-to-high risk, it is important to consider effective prevention as an undertaking which may require consistent phase appropriate application throughout childhood and adolescence.

The alcohol expectancies of young children (and, perhaps, their likelihood of alcohol or drug abuse) may be longitudinally modifiable to the extent that efforts in that direction incorporate an understanding of the difficulty of the task.

The PDPP, as a demonstration project, has provided a valuable opportunity to test a model of prevention, as well as a model of evaluation.

References

Christiansen, B. A., & Goldman, M. S. (1983). Alcohol-related expectancies versus demographic/background variables in the prediction of adolescent drinking. *Journal of Consulting and Clinical Psychology, 51*(2), 249–257.

Christiansen, B. A., Roehling, P. V., Smith, G. T., & Goldman, M. S. (1989). Using alcohol expectancies to predict adolescent drinking behavior after one year. *Journal of Consulting and Clinical Psychology, 57*(1), 93–99.

Corvo, K. N. (1997). Community-based youth violence prevention: A framework for planners and funders. *Youth and Society, 28*(3), 291–316.

Darkes, J., & Goldman, M. S. (1993). Expectancy challenge and drinking reduction: Experimental evidence for a mediation process. *Journal of Consulting and Clinical Psychology, 61*(2), 344–353.

Ennet, S. T., Tobler, N. S., Ringwalt, C. L., & Flewelling, R. L. (1994). How effective is drug abuse resistance education? A meta-analysis of Project DARE outcome evaluations. *American Journal of Public Health, 84*(9), 1394–1401.

Glantz, M. D. (1992). A developmental psychopathology model of drug abuse vulnerability. In M. Glantz and R. Pickens (Eds.), *Vulnerability to drug abuse* (pp. 389–418). Washington, D.C.: American Psychological Association.

Goldman, M. S., Brown, S. A., & Christiansen, B. A. (1987). Expectancy theory: Thinking about drinking. In H. T. Blane and K. E. Leonard (Eds.), *Psychological theories of drinking and alcoholism* (pp. 181–226). New York: Guilford Press.

Hall, N. W., & Zigler, E. (1997). Drug abuse prevention efforts for young children: A review and critique of existing programs. *American Journal of Orthopsychiatry, 67*(1), 134–143.

Johnston, L. D. (1991). Contributions of drug epidemiology to the field of drug abuse prevention. In C. G. Leukefeld and W. J. Bukoski (Eds.), *Drug abuse prevention intervention research: Methodological issues* (pp. 57–80). National Institute of Drug Abuse Research Monograph 107. DHHS Pub. No. (ADM)91-1761. Washington, D.C.: Supt. of Docs., U.S. Govt. Print. Off.

Kraus, D., Smith, G. T., & Ratner, H. H. (1994). Modifying alcohol-related expectancies in grade-school children. *Journal of Studies on Alcohol, 55*, 535–542.

Miller, P. M., Smith, G. T., & Goldman, M. S. (1990). Emergence of alcohol expectancies in childhood: A possible critical period. *Journal of Studies on Alcohol, 51*(4) 343–349.

Noll, R. B., Zucker, R. A., & Greenberg, G. S. (1990). Identification of alcohol by smell among pre-schoolers: Evidence for early socialization about drugs occurring in the home. *Child Development, 61*, 1520–1527.

Schweinhart, L. J., & Weikart, D. P. (1990). The High/Scope Perry Preschool Study: Implications for early childhood care and education. *Prevention in Human Services, 7*(1), 109–132.

Smith, G. T., & Goldman, M. S. (1991, April). *Expectancy theory and children's acquisition of knowledge about alcohol.* Paper presented at the Society for Research in Child Development symposium: The Socialization of Drinking in Children, Seattle, WA.

Zucker, R. A., & Fitzgerald, H. E. (1991). Early developmental factors and risk for alcohol problems. *Alcohol Health and Research World, 15*(1), 18–24.

Address correspondence to: The first author at: Syracuse University, School of Social Work, Syracuse, NY 13244-1230.

Exercise for Case 16

Directions: The following questions ask you to compare Article 15, which is *qualitative*, with this *quantitative* article.

1. In Article 15, the researchers solicited narratives. In this article, they obtained "yes/no" answers on a structured questionnaire. Which do you think is more appropriate for obtaining information on this particular topic? Do both methods have a place in this type of study? Explain.

2. Were the authors of Article 15 or Article 16 more articulate in explaining their choice of research methods (qualitative or quantitative) in their introduction?

3. Are the samples used in both articles appropriate? Is one sample more appropriate than the other?

4. In your opinion, which method yielded more interesting results? Which method yielded more detailed results? Which method yielded more useful results? Explain.

5. In your opinion, did both studies yield information that is valuable for advancing knowledge in this area?

6. Did one article have any special strengths over the other? Any special weaknesses? Explain.

7. Overall, which method (quantitative or qualitative) seems better suited for exploring the general problem area? Explain.

8. Has your comparison of Articles 15 and 16 changed your opinions on the relative merits of qualitative and quantitative research methodologies? Explain.

Examining the Validity Structure of Qualitative Research

R. BURKE JOHNSON
University of South Alabama

ABSTRACT. Three types of validity in qualitative research are discussed. First, descriptive validity refers to the factual accuracy of the account as reported by the qualitative researcher. Second, interpretive validity is obtained to the degree that the participants' viewpoints, thoughts, intentions, and experiences are accurately understood and reported by the qualitative researcher. Third, theoretical validity is obtained to the degree that a theory or theoretical explanation developed from a research study fits the data and is, therefore, credible and defensible. The two types of validity that are typical of quantitative research, internal and external validity, are also discussed for qualitative research. Twelve strategies used to promote research validity in qualitative research are discussed.

From *Education, 118,* 282–292. Copyright © 1997 by Project Innovation. Reprinted with permission of the publisher and author.

Discussions of the term "validity" have traditionally been attached to the quantitative research tradition. Not surprisingly, reactions by qualitative researchers have been mixed regarding whether or not this concept
5 should be applied to qualitative research. At the extreme, some qualitative researchers have suggested that the traditional quantitative criteria of reliability and validity are not relevant to qualitative research (e.g., Smith, 1984). Smith contends that the basic epistemo-
10 logical and ontological assumptions of quantitative and qualitative research are incompatible, and, therefore, the concepts of reliability and validity should be abandoned. Most qualitative researchers, however, probably hold a more moderate viewpoint. Most qualitative re-
15 searchers argue that some qualitative research studies are better than others, and they frequently use the term validity to refer to this difference. When qualitative researchers speak of research validity, they are usually referring to qualitative research that is plausible, credi-
20 ble, trustworthy, and, therefore, defensible. We believe it is important to think about the issue of validity in qualitative research and to examine some strategies that have been developed to maximize validity (Kirk & Miller, 1986; LeCompte & Preissle, 1993; Lincoln &
25 Guba, 1985; Maxwell, 1996). A list of these strategies is provided in Table 1.

One potential threat to validity that researchers must be careful to watch out for is called *researcher bias.* This problem is summed up in a statement a col-
30 league of mine once made to me. She said, "The problem with qualitative research is that the researchers find what they want to find, and then they write up their results." It is true that the problem of researcher bias is frequently an issue because qualitative research
35 is open-ended and less structured than quantitative research. This is because qualitative research tends to be exploratory. (One would be remiss, however, to think that researcher bias is never a problem in quantitative research!) Researcher bias tends to result from selec-
40 tive observation and selective recording of information, and also from allowing one's personal views and perspectives to affect how data are interpreted and how the research is conducted.

The key strategy used to understand researcher bias
45 is called *reflexivity,* which means that the researcher actively engages in critical self-reflection about his or her potential biases and predispositions (Table 1). Through reflexivity, researchers become more self-aware, and they monitor and attempt to control their
50 biases. Many qualitative researchers include a distinct section in their research proposals titled Researcher Bias. In this section, they discuss their personal background, how it may affect their research, and what strategies they will use to address the potential prob-
55 lem. Another strategy that qualitative researchers use to reduce the effect of researcher bias is called *negative case sampling* (Table 1). This means that they attempt carefully and purposively to search for examples that disconfirm their expectations and explanations about
60 what they are studying. If you use this approach, you will find it more difficult to ignore important information, and you will come up with more credible and defensible results.

We will now examine some types of validity that
65 are important in qualitative research. We will start with three types of validity that are especially relevant to qualitative research (Maxwell, 1992, 1996). These types are called descriptive validity, interpretive validity, and theoretical validity. They are important to
70 qualitative research because description of what is observed and interpretation of participants' thoughts are

Table 1
Strategies Used to Promote Qualitative Research Validity

Strategy	Description
Researcher as "Detective"	A metaphor characterizing the qualitative researcher as he or she searches for evidence about causes and effects. The researcher develops an understanding of the data through careful consideration of potential causes and effects and by systematically eliminating "rival" explanations or hypotheses until the final "case" is made "beyond a reasonable doubt." The "detective" can utilize any of the strategies listed here.
Extended fieldwork	When possible, qualitative researchers should collect data in the field over an extended period of time.
Low inference descriptors	The use of description phrased very close to the participants' accounts and researchers' field notes. Verbatims (i.e., direct quotations) are a commonly used type of low inference descriptors.
Triangulation	"Cross-checking" information and conclusions through the use of multiple procedures or sources. When the different procedures or sources are in agreement, you have "corroboration."
Data triangulation	The use of multiple data sources to help understand a phenomenon.
Methods triangulation	The use of multiple research methods to study a phenomenon.
Investigator triangulation	The use of multiple investigators (i.e., multiple researchers) in collecting and interpreting the data.
Theory triangulation	The use of multiple theories and perspectives to help interpret and explain the data.
Participant feedback	The feedback and discussion of the researcher's interpretations and conclusions with the actual participants and other members of the participant community for verification and insight.
Peer review	Discussion of the researcher's interpretations and conclusions with other people. This includes discussion with a "disinterested peer" (e.g., with another researcher not directly involved). This peer should be skeptical and play the "devil's advocate," challenging the researcher to provide solid evidence for any interpretations or conclusions. Discussion with peers who are familiar with the research can also help provide useful challenges and insights.
Negative case sampling	Locating and examining cases that disconfirm the researcher's expectations and tentative explanation.
Reflexivity	This involves self-awareness and "critical self-reflection" by the researcher on his or her potential biases and predispositions as these may affect the research process and conclusions.
Pattern matching	Predicting a series of results that form a "pattern" and then determining the degree to which the actual results fit the predicted pattern.

two primary qualitative research activities. For example, ethnography produces descriptions and accounts of the lives and experiences of groups of people with a 75 focus on cultural characteristics (Fetterman, 1998; LeCompte & Preissle, 1993). Ethnographers also attempt to understand groups of people, from the insider's perspective (i.e., from the viewpoints of the people in the group; called the *emic* perspective). Developing a theo- 80 retical explanation of the behavior of group members is also of interest to qualitative researchers, especially qualitative researchers using the grounded theory perspective (Glaser & Strauss, 1967; Strauss and Corbin, 1990). After discussing these three forms of validity, 85 the traditional types of validity used in quantitative research, internal and external validity, are discussed. Internal validity is relevant when qualitative researchers explore cause and effect relationships. External validity is relevant when qualitative researchers gener- 90 alize beyond their research studies.

Descriptive Validity

The first type of validity in qualitative research is called *descriptive validity*. Descriptive validity refers to the factual accuracy of the account as reported by the researchers. The key questions addressed in descriptive 95 validity are: Did what was reported as taking place in the group being studied actually happen? and Did the researchers accurately report what they saw and heard? In other words, descriptive validity refers to accuracy in reporting descriptive information (e.g., description 100 of events, objects, behaviors, people, settings, times, and places). This form of validity is important because description is a major objective in nearly all qualitative research.

One effective strategy used to obtain descriptive 105 validity is called *investigator triangulation*. In the case of descriptive validity, investigator triangulation in-

161

volves the use of multiple observers to record and describe the research participants' behavior and the context in which they were located. The use of multiple observers allows cross-checking of observations to make sure the investigators agree about what took place. When corroboration (i.e., agreement) of observations across multiple investigators is obtained, it is less likely that outside reviewers of the research will question whether something occurred. As a result, the research will be more credible and defensible.

Interpretive Validity

While descriptive validity refers to accuracy in reporting the facts, interpretive validity requires developing a window into the minds of the people being studied. *Interpretive validity* refers to accurately portraying the *meaning* attached by participants to what is being studied by the researcher. More specifically, it refers to the degree to which the research participants' viewpoints, thoughts, feelings, intentions, and experiences are accurately understood by the qualitative researcher and portrayed in the research report. An important part of qualitative research is understanding research participants' inner worlds (i.e., their phenomenological worlds), and interpretive validity refers to the degree of accuracy in presenting these inner worlds. Accurate interpretive validity requires that the researcher get inside the heads of the participants, look through the participants' eyes, and see and feel what they see and feel. In this way, the qualitative researcher can understand things from the participants' perspectives and provide a valid account of these perspectives.

Some strategies for achieving interpretive validity are provided in Table 1. *Participant feedback* is perhaps the most important strategy (Table 1). This strategy has also been called "member checking" (Lincoln & Guba, 1985). By sharing your interpretations of participants' viewpoints with the participants and other members of the group, you may clear up areas of miscommunication. Do the people being studied agree with what you have said about them? While this strategy is not perfect, because some participants may attempt to put on a good face, useful information is frequently obtained and inaccuracies are often identified.

When writing the research report, using many low inference descriptors is also helpful so that the reader can experience the participants' actual language, dialect, and personal meanings (Table 1). A verbatim is the lowest inference descriptor of all because the participants' exact words are provided in direct quotations. Here is an example of a verbatim from a high school dropout who was part of an ethnographic study of high school dropouts:

> I wouldn't do the work. I didn't like the teacher and I didn't like my mom and dad. So, even if I did my work, I wouldn't turn it in. I completed it. I just didn't want to turn it in. I was angry with my mom and dad because they were talking about moving out of state at the time

(Okey & Cusick, 1995: p. 257).

This verbatim provides some description (i.e., what the participant did) but it also provides some information about the participant's interpretations and personal meanings (which is the topic of interpretive validity). The participant expresses his frustration and anger toward his parents and teacher, and shares with us what homework meant to him at the time and why he acted as he did. By reading verbatims like this one, readers of a report can experience for themselves the participants' perspectives. Again, getting into the minds of research participants is a common goal in qualitative research, and Maxwell calls our accuracy in portraying this inner content interpretive validity.

Theoretical Validity

The third type of validity in qualitative research is called *theoretical validity*. You have theoretical validity to the degree that a theoretical explanation developed from a research study fits the data and, therefore, is credible and defensible. Theory usually refers to discussions of *how* a phenomenon operates and *why* it operates as it does. Theory is usually more abstract and less concrete than description and interpretation. Theory development moves beyond just the facts and provides an explanation of the phenomenon. In the words of Joseph Maxwell (1992):

> …one could label the student's throwing of the eraser as an act of resistance, and connect this act to the repressive behavior or values of the teacher, the social structure of the school, and class relationships in U.S. society. The identification of the throwing as resistance constitutes the application of a theoretical construct….the connection of this to other aspects of the participants, the school, or the community constitutes the postulation of theoretical relationships among these constructs (p. 291).

In the above example, the theoretical construct called "resistance" is used to explain the student's behavior. Maxwell points out that the construct of resistance may also be related to other theoretical constructs or variables. In fact, theories are often developed by relating theoretical constructs.

A strategy for promoting theoretical validity is *extended fieldwork* (Table 1). This means that you should spend a sufficient amount of time studying your research participants and their setting so that you can have confidence that the patterns of relationships you believe are operating are stable and so that you can understand why these relationships occur. As you spend more time in the field collecting data and generating and testing your inductive hypotheses, your theoretical explanation may become more detailed and intricate. You may also decide to use the strategy called *theory triangulation* (Table 1; Denzin, 1989). This means that you would examine how the phenomenon being studied would be explained by different theories. The various theories might provide you with insights and help you develop a more cogent explanation. In a related way, you might also use investigator triangulation and consider the ideas and explanations generated by additional researchers studying the research participants.

As you develop your theoretical explanation, you should make some predictions based on the theory and test the accuracy of those predictions. When doing this, you can use the *pattern matching* strategy (Table 1). In pattern matching, the strategy is to make several predictions at once; then, if all of the predictions occur as predicted (i.e., if the pattern is found), you have evidence supporting your explanation. As you develop your theoretical explanation you should also use the negative case sampling strategy mentioned earlier (Table 1). That is, you must always search for cases or examples that do not fit your explanation so that you do not simply find the data that support your developing theory. As a general rule, your final explanation should accurately reflect the majority of the people in your research study. Another useful strategy for promoting theoretical validity is called *peer review* (Table 1). This means that you should try to spend some time discussing your explanation with your colleagues so that they can search for problems with it. Each problem must then be resolved. In some cases, you will find that you will need to go back to the field and collect additional data. Finally, when developing a theoretical explanation, you must also think about the issues of internal validity and external validity to which we now turn.

Internal Validity

Internal validity is the fourth type of validity in qualitative research of interest to us. Internal validity refers to the degree to which a researcher is justified in concluding that an observed relationship is causal (Cook and Campbell, 1979). Often qualitative researchers are not interested in cause and effect relationships. Sometimes, however, qualitative researchers are interested in identifying potential causes and effects. In fact, qualitative research can be very helpful in describing how phenomena operate (i.e., studying process) and in developing and testing preliminary causal hypotheses and theories (Campbell, 1979; Johnson, 1994; LeCompte & Preissle, 1993; Strauss, 1995; 1990).

When qualitative researchers identify potential cause and effect relationships, they must think about many of the same issues that quantitative researchers must consider. They should also think about the strategies used for obtaining theoretical validity discussed earlier. The qualitative researcher takes on the role of the detective searching for the true cause(s) of a phenomenon, examining each possible clue, and attempting to rule out each rival explanation generated (see *researcher as detective* in Table 1). When trying to identify a causal relationship, the researcher makes mental comparisons. The comparison might be to a hypothetical control group. Although a control group is rarely used in qualitative research, the researcher can think about what would have happened if the causal factor had not occurred. The researcher can sometimes rely on his or her expert opinion, as well as published research studies when available, in deciding what would have happened. Furthermore, if the event is something that occurs again the researcher can determine if the causal factor precedes the outcome. In other words, when the causal factor occurs again, does the effect follow?

When a researcher believes that an observed relationship is causal, he or she must also attempt to make sure that the observed change in the dependent variable is due to the independent variable and not to something else (e.g., a confounding extraneous variable). The successful researcher will always make a list of rival explanations or rival hypotheses, which are possible or plausible reasons for the relationship other than the originally suspected cause. Be creative and think of as many rival explanations as you can. One way to get started is to be a skeptic and think of reasons why the relationship should not be causal. Each rival explanation must be examined after the list has been developed. Sometimes you will be able to check a rival explanation with the data you have already collected through additional data analysis. At other times you will need to collect additional data. One strategy would be to observe the relationship you believe to be causal under conditions where the confounding variable is not present and compare this outcome with the original outcome. For example, if you concluded that a teacher effectively maintained classroom discipline on a given day but a critic maintained that it was the result of a parent visiting the classroom on that day, then you should try to observe the teacher again when the parent is not present. If the teacher is still successful, you have some evidence that the original finding was not because of the presence of the parent in the classroom.

All of the strategies shown in Table 1 are used to improve the internal validity of qualitative research. Now we will explain the only two strategies not yet discussed (i.e., methods triangulation and data triangulation). When using *methods triangulation*, the researcher uses more than one method of research in a single research study. The word methods should be used broadly here, and it refers to different methods of research (e.g., ethnography, survey, experimental, etc.) as well to different types of data collection procedures (e.g., interviews, questionnaires, and observations). You can intermix any of these (e.g., ethnography and survey research methods, or interviews and observations, or experimental research and interviews). The logic is to combine different methods that have "nonoverlapping weaknesses and strengths" (Brewer & Hunter, 1989). The weaknesses (and strengths) of one method will tend to be different from those of a different method, which means that when you combine two or more methods you will have better evidence! In other words, the "whole" is better than its "parts."

335   Here is an example of methods triangulation. Perhaps you are interested in why students in an elementary classroom stigmatize a certain student named Brian. A stigmatized student would be an individual that is not well liked, has a lower status, and is seen as
340   different from the normal students. Perhaps Brian has a different haircut from the other students, is dressed differently, or doesn't act like the other students. In this case, you might decide to observe how students treat Brian in various situations. In addition to observing the
345   students, you will probably decide to interview Brian and the other students to understand their beliefs and feelings about Brian. A strength of observational data is that you can actually see the students' behaviors. A weakness of interviews is that what the students say
350   and what they actually do may be different. However, using interviews you can delve into the students' thinking and reasoning, whereas you cannot do this using observational data. Therefore, the whole will likely be better than the parts.

355   When using *data triangulation*, the researcher uses multiple data sources in a single research study. "Data sources" does not mean using different methods. Data triangulation refers to the use of multiple data sources using a single method. For example, the use of multiple
360   interviews would provide multiple data sources while using a single method (i.e., the interview method). Likewise, the use of multiple observations would be another example of data triangulation; multiple data sources would be provided while using a single method
365   (i.e., the observational method). Another important part of data triangulation involves collecting data at different times, at different places, and with different people.

Here is an example of data triangulation. Perhaps a researcher is interested in studying why certain stu-
370   dents are apathetic. It would make sense to get the perspectives of several different kinds of people. The researcher might interview teachers, interview students identified by the teachers as being apathetic, and interview peers of apathetic students. Then the researcher
375   could check to see if the information obtained from these different data sources was in agreement. Each data source may provide additional reasons as well as a different perspective on the question of student apathy, resulting in a more complete understanding of the phe-
380   nomenon. The researcher should also interview apathetic students at different class periods during the day and in different types of classes (e.g., math and social studies). Through the rich information gathered (e.g., from different people, at different times, and at differ-
385   ent places) the researcher can develop a better understanding of why students are apathetic than if only one data source is used.

External Validity

External validity is important when you want to generalize from a set of research findings to other peo-
390   ple, settings, and times (Cook and Campbell, 1979). Typically, generalizability is not the major purpose of qualitative research. There are at least two reasons for this. First, the people and settings examined in qualitative research are rarely randomly selected, and, as you
395   know, random selection is the best way to generalize from a sample to a population. As a result, qualitative research is virtually always weak in the form of population validity focused on "generalizing to populations" (i.e., generalizing from a sample to a population).

400   Second, some qualitative researchers are more interested in documenting particularistic findings than universalistic findings. In other words, in certain forms of qualitative research the goal is to show what is unique about a certain group of people, or a certain
405   event, rather than generate findings that are broadly applicable. At a fundamental level, many qualitative researchers do not believe in the presence of general laws or universal laws. General laws are things that apply to many people, and universal laws are things
410   that apply to everyone. As a result, qualitative research is frequently considered weak on the "generalizing across populations" form of population validity (i.e., generalizing to different kinds of people), and on ecological validity (i.e., generalizing across settings) and
415   temporal validity (i.e., generalizing across times).

Other experts argue that rough generalizations can be made from qualitative research. Perhaps the most reasonable stance toward the issue of generalizing is that we can generalize to other people, settings, and
420   times to the degree that they are similar to the people, settings, and times in the original study. Stake (1990) uses the term *naturalistic generalization*[1] to refer to this process of generalizing based on similarity. The bottom line is this: The more similar the people and
425   circumstances in a particular research study are to the ones that you want to generalize to, the more defensible your generalization will be and the more readily you should make such a generalization.

To help readers of a research report know when
430   they can generalize, qualitative researchers should provide the following kinds of information: the number and kinds of people in the study, how they were selected to be in the study, contextual information, the nature of the researcher's relationship with the partici-
435   pants, information about any informants who provided information, the methods of data collection used, and the data analysis techniques used. This information is

---

[1] Donald Campbell (1986) makes a similar point, and he uses the term *proximal similarity* to refer to the degree of similarity between the people and circumstances in the original research study and the people and circumstances to which you wish to apply the findings. Using Campbell's term, your goal is to check for proximal similarity.

usually reported in the Methodology section of the final research report. Using the information included in a well-written methodology section, readers will be able to make informed decisions about to whom the results may be generalized. They will also have the information they will need if they decide to replicate the research study with new participants.

Some experts show another way to generalize from qualitative research (e.g., Yin, 1994). Qualitative researchers can sometimes use *replication logic,* just like the replication logic that is commonly used by experimental researchers when they generalize beyond the people in their studies, even when they do not have random samples. According to replication logic, the more times a research finding is shown to be true with different sets of people, the more confidence we can place in the finding and in the conclusion that the finding generalizes beyond the people in the original research study (Cook and Campbell, 1979). In other words, if the finding is replicated with different kinds of people and in different places, then the evidence may suggest that the finding applies very broadly. Yin's key point is that there is no reason why replication logic cannot be applied to certain kinds of qualitative research.[2]

Here is an example. Over the years you may observe a certain pattern of relations between boys and girls in your third grade classroom. Now assume that you decided to conduct a qualitative research study and you find that the pattern of relation occurred in your classroom and in two other third grade classrooms you studied. Because your research is interesting, you decide to publish it. Then other researchers replicate your study with other people and they find that the same relationship holds in the third grade classrooms they studied. According to replication logic, the more times a theory or a research finding is replicated with other people, the greater the support for the theory or research finding. Now assume further that other researchers find that the relationship holds in classrooms at several other grade levels (e.g., first grade, second grade, fourth grade, and fifth grade). If this happens, the evidence suggests that the finding generalizes to students in other grade levels, adding additional generality to the finding.

We want to make one more comment before concluding. If generalizing through replication and theoretical validity (discussed above) sound similar, that is because they are. Basically, generalizing (i.e., external validity) is frequently part of theoretical validity. In other words, when researchers develop theoretical explanations, they often want to generalize beyond their original research study. Likewise, internal validity is

also important for theoretical validity if cause and effect statements are made.

References

Brewer, J., & Hunter, A. (1989). *Multimethod research: A synthesis of styles.* Newbury Park, CA: Sage.

Campbell, D.T. (1979). Degrees of freedom and the case study. In T.D. Cook & C.S. Reichardt (Eds.), *Qualitative and quantitative methods in evaluation research* (pp. 49–67). Beverly Hills, CA: Sage Publications.

Campbell, D.T. (1986). Relabeling internal and external validity for applied social scientists. In W. Trochim (Ed.), Advances in quasi-experimental design and analysis: *New Directions for Program Evaluation,* 31, San Francisco: Jossey-Bass.

Cook, T.D., & Campbell, D.T. (1979). *Quasi-experimentation: Design and analysis issues for field settings.* Chicago: Rand McNally.

Denzin, N.K. (1989). *The research act: Theoretical introduction to sociological methods.* Englewood Cliffs, NJ: Prentice Hall.

Fetterman, D.M. (1998). Ethnography. In *Handbook of Applied Social Research Methods* by L. Bickman & D.J. Rog (Eds.). Thousand Oaks, CA: Sage.

Glaser, B.G., & Strauss, A.L. (1967). *The discovery of grounded theory: Strategies for qualitative research.* New York: Aldine de Gruyter.

Johnson, R.B. (1994). Qualitative research in education. *SRATE Journal, 4*(1), 3–7.

Kirk, J., & Miller, M.L. (1986). *Reliability and validity in qualitative research.* Newbury Park, CA: Sage.

LeCompte, M.D., & Preissle, J. (1993). *Ethnography and qualitative design in educational research.* San Diego, CA: Academic Press.

Lincoln, Y.S., & Guba, E.G. (1985). *Naturalistic inquiry.* Beverly Hills, CA: Sage.

Maxwell, J.A. (1992). Understanding and validity in qualitative research. *Harvard Educational Review, 62*(3), 279–299.

Maxwell, J.A. (1996). *Qualitative research design.* Newbury Park, CA: Sage.

Okey, T.N., & Cusick, P.A. (1995). Dropping out: Another side of the story. *Educational Administration Quarterly, 31*(2), 244–267.

Smith, J.K. (1984). The problem of criteria for judging interpretive inquiry. *Educational Evaluation and Policy Analysis, 6,* 379–391.

Smith, J.K. (1986). Closing down the conversation: The end of the quantitative-qualitative debate among educational inquirers. *Educational Researcher, 15,* 12–32.

Stake, R.E. (1990). Situational context as influence on evaluation design and use. *Studies in Educational Evaluation, 16,* 231–246.

Strauss, A. (1995). Notes on the nature and development of general theories. *Qualitative Inquiry 1*(1), 7–18.

Strauss, A., & Corbin, J. (1990). *Basics of qualitative research: Grounded theory procedures and techniques.* Newbury Park, CA: Sage.

Yin, R.K. (1994). *Case study research: Design and methods.* Newbury Park: Sage.

---

[2] The late Donald Campbell, perhaps the most important quantitative research methodologist over the past 50 years, approved of Yin's (1994) book. See, for example, his introduction to this book.

Understanding and Evaluating Qualitative Research

ANNE-MARIE AMBERT
York University

PETER ADLER
University of Boulder

PATRICIA A. ADLER
University of Colorado

DANIEL F. DETZNER
University of Minnesota

From *Journal of Marriage and the Family*, 57, 879–893. Copyright © 1995 by the National Council on Family Relations, 3989 Central Ave. NE, Suite 550, Minneapolis, MN 55421. Reprinted by permission. All rights reserved.

Evaluating Qualitative Research

While we do believe that each piece of research should be examined for its individual contribution to family research, we also agree that there are some universals that should apply to all field research, as suggested by the structure of our presentation. Therefore,
5   qualitative research should be evaluated on the same overall basis as other research, that is, according to whether it makes a substantive contribution to empirical knowledge and/or advances theory. Qualitative
10   research can achieve this in a multitude of ways, however: by providing new data or replicating previous studies within a different time and/or space frame; by giving voice to those not heard before; by studying family groups that are difficult to access, and family
15   situations that are emerging; by advancing new theories or amending previously accepted ones; or by correcting biases in previous research, asking questions that have never been asked, presenting new epistemologies, or highlighting the values that are at the foundation of the
20   research questions we ask. Consequently, qualitative research is vastly different from purely quantitative methods and deserves its own set of evaluation guidelines. By its very nature, it can provide data and raise questions that no quantitative methods could generate,
25   in great part because it allows for the emergence of the unexpected (Ambert, 1994; see also Taylor & Bogdan, 1984). All of this implies that evaluators of qualitative research must be able to recognize the limitations of traditional methods and measurement techniques in
30   family studies. Evaluators must allow for the emergence of new or unanticipated data.

Denzin and Lincoln (1994) reviewed four major perspectives on the issue of evaluation, ranging from the positivist argument that all research must be evalu-
35   ated on exactly the same criteria of scientific validity to

the poststructuralist position that qualitative research, and even each qualitative study, should have its own set of evaluative criteria (pp. 479–483). Despite this diversity of opinion, and despite the diverse ways in
40   which the research process is carried out, there are nevertheless certain criteria for quality. Thus, the reviewer's task in assessing qualitative research that focuses on the study of couples or families involves evaluating the theoretical perspective and linkages to
45   the literature, the analysis of the data, matters of reliability and validity, sample adequacy, and, finally, procedures and ethics, including the role of the researcher. We discuss each of these categories in the sections below.

Theory and Linkages to the Literature

50   Marshall and Rossman's (1989) "model of the research cycle" (p. 23) is a useful heuristic device because it places theory at the center of the qualitative research process and suggests a process that revolves around and draws from theory during the various
55   stages of research. This section and the following sections have been influenced by this model; however, we acknowledge that qualitative research does not always take place in the organized stages and sequences presented in the Marshall and Rossman model (see also,
60   Gilgun, 1992; Glaser & Strauss, 1967; Strauss & Corbin, 1990). For instance, sample development may occur to some researchers at the same time as a theoretical framework (Lofland & Lofland, 1984).

Quantitative researchers are often uncomfortable
65   with this interweaving between theory, data, and methods. In ethnography, for instance, fieldworkers do not necessarily need the prior specification of a theory because it may introduce premature closure on the issues to be investigated and also leads researchers away from
70   the views of participants in a social setting. Such qualitative researchers may prefer not to be committed in advance to developing the theoretical implications of their work in any particular direction; they believe this should flow from the emergent data. They may, how-
75   ever, utilize sensitizing concepts (Blumer, 1969) that will help them pinpoint patterns or new processes that

do not fit these predetermined concepts.

Nevertheless, the emerging conceptual and theoretical framework must be clearly stated and linked to the existing empirical literature and, when appropriate, to existing theories (Lincoln & Guba, 1985; Strauss & Corbin, 1990). It is important that the issues, concepts, topics, themes, or dimensions of the study are linked to the roots of the unanswered questions or dilemmas in the existing research literature. When the literature is thin or the qualitative research study is at the cutting edge, it is necessary to link it to related fields of inquiry and to show why this population, issue, or question has not been previously addressed in the extant research. Therefore, the interweaving between theory and empirical research is in no way synonymous with absence of linkages to the existing literature. In fact, as indicated earlier, qualitative research is an ideal instrument to address new issues or to address established issues in a different manner. This implies prior knowledge of the literature—a guiding principle for reviewers—even if the existing literature is inadequate or somewhat peripheral to the concerns of a particular qualitative epistemology. In the latter case, a reviewer should expect a cogent critique of the literature, and a thoughtful discussion of its limitations.

Analysis

Reviewers need to address the multiple issues surrounding analysis. It is imperative that qualitative research be explicit and detailed about strategies so that the rigor is evident. Here, it is important to restate the essentially dynamic process of qualitative research analysis (Schwartz & Jacob, 1979). Along the lines of grounded theory, qualitative research often begins initial analysis even while data are being collected. The process of doing qualitative research is cyclical and evolutionary rather than linear—as is the process typical of quantitative research. In contrast, the latter generally sets forth its type of analysis before data are gathered.

Qualitative researchers should at least briefly explain the approach they used, and the ways in which they interpreted their early data, and how preliminary findings influenced subsequent data gathering and analysis. Qualitative researchers at times follow an analytic induction model, whereby they are guided by general hypotheses before collecting their data (Manning, 1991). These hypotheses are then revised as the data emerge and as the analysis proceeds (Bogdan & Biklen, 1992). There are actually several variants of this procedure (Bogdan & Biklen, 1992; Campbell, 1979), which resembles deductive research based on hypothesis testing.

The results of a qualitative study should contribute to our understanding of an important family issue or an understudied population. They should challenge or enlarge an existing theory or strike out in a new direction with new theory. The results must be presented in ways that allow the reader to see the evidence from which the author is drawing inferences and conclusions (Becker & Geer, 1960). The data may come from multifaceted sources, possibly several different members of a family (each with his or her own perspective). In view of this wealth of information, reviewers should look for a summary of the data. This summary can be expressed in a variety of ways depending both on the topic researched and the author's epistemology—for instance, via typologies, categories, quantifications, charts, or graphic presentations, as well as using the informants' words quoted verbatim (see Miles & Huberman, 1984). Moreover, the results should lead to additional questions and hypotheses for further research that might be conducted, and they should be accompanied by a concluding section that advances the transsituational relevance of the research to a set of generic principles (Prus, 1987).

Above all, the richness of the quotes, the clarity of the examples, and the depth of the illustrations in a qualitative study should serve to highlight the most salient features of the data. Evaluation of what has been included in this respect should be made on the basis of how these data illuminate and give readers a sense of being there, of visualizing the family members, feeling their conflicts and emotions, and absorbing the flavor of the family setting. Qualitative work should vividly color in the meanings, motivations, and details of what quantitative research can convey only in broader aggregates. If the portrait of the family is superficial or the images of the people and their behavior are not vivid and meaningful, then the paper is weak.

Validity and Reliability

Issues of reliability and validity (or authenticity), which are of paramount importance in quantitative research, are not equally important across the various qualitative methodologies. And, when such issues arise, their evaluation is generally quite different (Altheide & Johnson, 1994; Bernard, 1988; Kirk & Miller, 1986). This stems from the fact that qualitative research often relies primarily on the informants' own formulations and constructions of reality checked against those of other similarly situated informants or the observations of an informed observer. Multiple informants and multiple methods of data gathering or triangulation within a same study are themselves recursive checks against the validity of the researchers' interpretations (Brewer & Hunter, 1989). The depth associated with qualitative research, coupled with researchers' efforts to triangulate (Denzin, 1978) and cross-check (Douglas, 1976) their data, gives this methodology strength in the area of validity.

Moreover, the use of some forms of intercoder reliability is also important when applicable (Miles & Huberman, 1984), although many qualitative researchers object to this on epistemological grounds. It is pointless to carry out intercoder reliability when the informants' words are totally explicit. On the other hand, we recently evaluated a manuscript containing a core of 15 quotes representing various phases of the development of a conceptual family model. We would have placed five (or fully one-third) of the quotes in different categories from those chosen by the author— in this case, inevitably pointing to a need for some form of reliability check. The use of what is called "thick" (Geertz, 1973) or adequate descriptions (Silverman, 1985) representing many layers of diverse realities, as well as many observations (Kirk & Miller, 1986), is another important device. Glaser (1978) also suggested a constant comparative method whereby the researcher begins with a theory or a model and checks each case or each datum against it. At the same time, it should be appreciated that qualitative research strategies do not have to be complicated to be reliable and valid, nor does the process have to be laden with justifying references. As Gubrium (1992) pointed out, "The rigor is more analytic than technical, and this may be deceptively captivating for the enthusiastic but untrained" (p. 581).

Sample

An adequate sample depends on the type of questions posed, the complexity of the model studied, the availability of informants or of texts, the number of family members involved, and the purposes of the study. The size and parameters of the sample may be limited by researchers' access to documents in historical studies, for instance, or by researchers' personal relations with respondents or by their ability to obtain sponsorship from people who will help them "snowball" (Biernacki & Waldorf, 1982) their way to other potential informants. If the purpose is to generalize to an entire population, then the sample must be large and representative. We also suggest that, instead of being statistically "representative" in the sense that this word is used in surveys, the sample can be constituted in order to include individuals or families who are as diverse as the general population studied (Bromley, 1986).

If the purpose is to generalize to theory (see Yin, 1989), then the sample may be rather small. The intensive study of a small number of cases can provide an explanation of cause-effect relationships within or between families of a similar type (Yin, 1993). Some of the best examples of small-sample case studies of families include classics such as Hess and Handel's (1959) *Family Worlds* and Oscar Lewis's (1959) *Five Families*. However, theoretical considerations are also important in the selection of a sample for qualitative research, so that, for example, a study of conflict between genders in refugee families should include an approximately equal number of male and female informants (Detzner, 1992).

Evaluators should also consider the fact that qualitative research generally requires a great deal of time and expenditure on the part of the researcher. The problem with qualitative research is not that of limited data generated from a small sample, but rather the sheer quantity of data that must be analyzed and linked to theory or models, either existing or new. Resources, time, depth, and purpose of the research place practical limitations on sample size requirements. Qualitative researchers often reach a saturation point (Glaser & Strauss, 1967); that is, after a certain number of interviews, for instance, major trends begin to recur, and outlying or secondary themes have already emerged. At that point, researchers can stop adding new individuals, couples, or families to their sample.

Reviewers may well examine the suitability of the single-case approach. The single case can be seen as potentially problematic unless there is a highly limited number of persons in a particular category, and unless it presents several realities or perspectives in the ethnographic tradition (Geertz, 1973) or in interviews with several family members. Generally, if the purpose is to generalize, a single case can carry biases in that the person or family studied will obviously be unique in many ways. A great deal of clinical research is done this way and it is especially problematic when conclusions are then drawn and applied to nonclinical populations. Moreover, for the very same reasons of uniqueness, the single-case approach can be problematic for theory development, especially so without considerations of race, gender, or culture.

Other qualitative scholars see the case study as an especially potent method for probing the depth of feelings, context, multifaceted viewpoints, and relationships, making the family an ideal subject for this approach (Bulmer, 1986; Handel, 1992; Jarrett, 1992). Nevertheless, this approach may be more fruitful when it is based on a reasonably large number of case studies. Indeed, one of the techniques used in participant observation and in-depth interviewing involves constructing case studies on each person, couple, or family included in the sample (Spradley, 1979). The collection and analysis of several case studies is thus a fundamental part of doing qualitative research (Bromley, 1986; Yin, 1989), and is to be differentiated from research based on a single case.

Procedures and Ethics

The methods selected should be appropriate to the epistemological orientation, the questions asked, and the population studied. There should be congruence of methods and topic researched. A study of the history of fatherhood will include analysis of documents from a variety of groups, sources, and time periods (Schvaneveldt, Pickett, & Young, 1993). The selected documents must be described and justified so that the evaluator has some context for judging the type and quality of data upon which the author has based the analysis and conclusions.

Another related question is whether the behavior

and interactions of the researcher as participant or observer has led to biases. Two different viewpoints have evolved in this regard. One view regards ethnographic work as particularly complex to evaluate in this respect
305 (on ethnography, see Hammersley, 1990, 1992). Specific issues arise and must be assessed by the reviewers: In what ways does the presence of the observer disturb the regular functioning of the family observed? Do the persons studied respond by altering their be-
310 havior? Do the informants treat the observer as a valued (or devalued) guest and consequently behave as they would when in the presence of a guest rather than when they are alone in the family group? It is the researchers' responsibility to discuss and analyze their
315 own role, behaviors, and impact on the research process and the results. The researchers' limitations or advantages stemming from their own ethnicity, gender, and socioeconomic status should also be addressed when these are relevant to the research process (Steier,
320 1991).

Within this perspective, it is not necessary that the research team include members who are actually experiencing or have lived the situations studied. This requirement would preclude the study of many categories
325 of persons. Nevertheless, research led by persons who have lived through a situation that is being studied has the advantage of providing fresh insight, and it constitutes a way to deconstruct the hierarchy inherent in researcher-researched relationships. But it also carries a
330 danger of blinding researchers to what may perhaps be idiosyncratic to their own group (Douglas, 1985) and would not apply to another social class, for instance.

This matter holds a particular meaning for family research for we are all, as individual researchers, mem-
335 bers of a family or families (see Doherty, 1992). Thus, reviewers have to be particularly alert about the potential of such bias, and authors who are able to express their own "biases" (e.g., Gilgun, Daly, & Handel, 1992) should not be penalized by reviewers for being
340 "unscientific" (see also Gans, 1982). We have argued that researchers' values and perspectives are an important dimension in all types of research (Harding, 1987; Miller, 1993; Scarr, 1985; Smith, 1990a; Thompson, 1992), as may be their biographies (Hankin, 1979;
345 Smith, 1979). On a related level, Daly (1992) presented an interesting discussion of the advantages in data gathering of divulging to the respondents some of the researcher's own experiences, in order to enhance the equality between researcher and researched, allowing
350 the latter to contribute personal information with a feeling of self-empowerment in an egalitarian and meaningful exchange (Ambert, 1982). Reviewers, however, have to be alert to possible suggestibility.

A second set of epistemologies emphasizes that
355 qualitative research should be evaluated according to how close researchers become to the persons and social worlds they study. This is grounded in the belief that the ideal of researchers refraining from influencing

their settings represents a hypothetical rather than a
360 real possibility (Jarvie, 1969), and that the strength of quality research derives from how close researchers get to their data, rather than the extent to which they are able to maintain detachment. They therefore select research foci where they can more easily bridge the gap
365 between subjects and themselves, and seek relationships with respondents that will enable them to experience empathy, and therefore communication, at more intimate levels. Qualitative researchers' meaningful ties to their respondents enhance their ability to gain
370 information about hidden behavior, intimacy, and interpersonal feelings and emotions, which are critical components of family research. A host of methodological treatises have appeared recently, advocating closer relationships between researchers and the per-
375 sons they study, including those discussing "membership roles" (Adler & Adler, 1987), "auto-ethnography" (Hayano, 1979), "opportunistic" research (Riemer, 1977), and "systematic introspection" (Ellis, 1991). Authors in this vein, influenced by the existential,
380 subjectivist, and postmodern movements, have also suggested exploring the development of new written and rhetorical genres for the exposition of qualitative research (Atkinson, 1990; Ellis & Flaherty, 1992; Krieger, 1991; Richardson, 1994; Ronai, in press).

385 On the other hand, researchers who emphasize the need to acknowledge the observer's complex role in ethnographic work may see potential biases in such a close researcher involvement with respondents (Miller, 1952). The potential exists for researchers to become
390 advocates, abandoning the research role altogether. Or close friendship may blind the researcher to unpleasant facts. Giddens's (1976) concept of the "double hermeneutic" is useful here in that it clarifies the fact that researchers (re)construct what the actors they are
395 studying have said or done. In this vein, researchers must be aware of the effect of their understanding—that is, knowledge production—on the social world. This concept is embedded in the notion of the reflexive nature of modernity (Giddens, 1990). Allen and Farns-
400 worth (1993) discussed reflexivity as "the main process by which the self is transformed in relation to knowledge" (p. 351). Qualitative researchers may be especially well located to discuss the impact of their data and emergent theories on themselves as researchers and
405 the impact of their epistemologies on the research process (Thompson, 1992)—concerns that are sadly neglected in research.

It is important to note that the specter of ethical problems lurks in close research relations, when re-
410 searchers have access to sensitive data or participate in the intimacy of a family's or a couple's life. Researchers have to be careful not to invade the respondents' privacy so much that they reveal more than intended, in what has been termed "unanticipated self-exposure"
415 (LaRossa, Bennett, & Gelles, 1985). Moreover, when friendships with respondents are ended, the latter may

feel particularly betrayed after they have divulged so much about themselves. In addition, there is definitely the potential for disrupting certain personal and familial patterns, at a cost to the respondents. Finally, when participant observation is utilized, the individuals' informed consent may be a recurring rather than a one-time process (Germain, 1986; Thorne, 1980; Wax, 1980)—an issue that is quite specific to qualitative research. This being said, we also suggest that reviewers should be honest enough to differentiate between an unethical procedure and a procedure they would not like to be subjected to because of their own personalities or because of the vested interests of their epistemological preferences or clinical profession, for instance.

Problems Created by Authors

There are researchers who do qualitative research without any guiding idea or knowledge of the literature. This is often mistakenly called "exploratory" research. One has to distinguish between exploratory research and totally unguided research. The work must have a clear relation to the extant data-based literature. Authors should show throughout the paper, as well as in the introduction, that they are aware of the major works in their substantive area and how they compare and contrast to the current questions asked. The research should build on these works, fitting itself within a line of empirical research.

Because qualitative data are often so rich, one has to be cautious not to ramble on to the point where the reader has no idea where the presentation is going or how it got there. A focused introduction can alleviate this problem. For this same reason, it is often compelling to include every interesting quote, observation, or conceptualization available in the data, instead of presenting a focused article. It is also often tempting to become anecdotal and rely on snippets of conversation, writing, or other forms of qualitative data gathered in a completely unsystematic manner. We meet authors who have a life experience that strikes them as sociologically or psychologically meaningful; they then decide that they can just write this autobiography "qualitatively" and get it published. Indeed, there can be a perception that qualitative research is "easy." By this we do not intend to demean the important contributions to family research that draw on deep and rigorous autobiographical or instrospective data (see Dilworth-Anderson, Burton, & Johnson, 1993; Ellis, 1991, 1993; Sollie & Leslie, 1994). Rather, we refer to the use of unsystematic, anecdotal data to ground simplistic, weak analyses.

A separate issue is the use of shorthand terms that may be understood by other researchers in the author's subdiscipline or epistemology but not by the evaluators or by the educated reader. It is not enough to say that a thematic content analysis was chosen. The author has to tell the reader what specific techniques were used to do the content analysis and how the categories emerged or were constructed from the data. Again, we should point out that these techniques do not have to be elaborate to be rigorous. Then there is the matter of excessive jargon, perhaps in an attempt to appear scientific, rigorous, or theoretically sophisticated (see Chafetz, 1993). This is no more acceptable in qualitative research than in quantitative research where, in the latter case, the statistical jargon is too often left unexplained. Authors who wish to publish in mainstream journals should use a language that will be understandable to the reviewers and the readers. For instance, when introducing new language, effort should be made to explain the terminology in more widespread terms or to include a more accessible synonym upon first mention.

References

Adler, P. A., & Adler, P. (1987) *Membership roles in field research.* Newbury Park, CA: Sage.

Adler, P. A., & Adler, P. (1994). Observational techniques. In N. K. Denzin & Y. S. Lincoln (Eds.) *Handbook of qualitative research* (pp. 377–392). Thousand Oaks, CA: Sage.

Adler, P. A., Adler, P., & Fontana, A. (1987). Everyday life sociology. *Annual Review of Sociology, 13,* 217–235.

Alexander, J. C., & Colomy, P. (1990). Neofunctionalism: Reconstructing a theoretical tradition. In G. Ritzer (Ed.), *Frontiers of social theory: The new syntheses* (pp. 33–67). New York: Columbia University Press.

Alexander, J. C., Giesen, B., Munch, R., & Smelser, N. J. (Eds.). (1987). *The micro-macro link.* Berkeley: University of California Press.

Allen, K. R., & Baber, K. M. (1992). Ethical and epistemological tensions in applying a postmodern perspective to feminist research. *Psychology of Women Quarterly, 16,* 1–15.

Allen, K. R., & Farnsworth, E. B. (1993). Reflexivity in teaching about families. *Family Relations, 42,* 351–356.

Altheide, D. L., & Johnson, J. M. (1994). Criteria for assessing interpretive validity in qualitative research. In N. K. Denzin & Y. S. Lincoln (Eds.), *Handbook of qualitative research* (pp. 485–499).

Ambert, A. M. (1982). Differences in children's behavior toward custodial mothers and custodial fathers. *Journal of Marriage and the Family, 44,* 73–86.

Ambert, A. M. (1994). A qualitative study of peer abuse and its effects: Theoretical and empirical implications. *Journal of Marriage and the Family, 56,* 19–130.

Archer, M. S. (1982). Morphogenesis versus structuralism: On combining structure and action. *British Journal of Sociology, 33,* 455–483.

Archer, M. S. (1988). *Culture and agency: The place of culture in social theory.* Cambridge: Cambridge University Press.

Atkinson, P. A. (1990). *The ethnographic imagination: Textual constructions of reality.* London: Routledge.

Becker, H. S., & Geer, B. (1960). Participant observation: The analysis of qualitative field data. In R. N. Adams & J. J. Preiss (Eds.), *Human organization research: Field relations and techniques* (pp. 267–289). Homewood, IL: Dorsey Press.

Bernard, R. H. (1988). *Research methods in cultural anthropology.* Newbury Park, CA: Sage.

Bernstein, R. J. (1989). Social theory as critique. In D. Held & J. B. Thompson (Eds.), *Social theory of modern societies: Anthony Giddens and his critics* (pp. 19–33). Cambridge: Cambridge University Press.

Biernacki, P., & Waldorf, D. (1982). Snowball sampling. *Sociological Methods and Research, 10,* 141–163.

Blumer, H. (1969). *Symbolic interactionism: Perspective and method.* Englewood Cliffs, NJ: Prentice-Hall.

Boden, D. (1990). The world as it happens: Ethnomethodology and conversation analysis. In G. Ritzer (Ed.), *Frontiers of social theory: The new syntheses* (pp. 185–213). New York: Columbia University Press.

Bogdan, R., & Biklen, S. K. (1992). *Qualitative research for education* (2nd ed.). Boston: Allyn & Bacon.

Brewer, J., & Hunter, A. (1989). *Multimethod research: A synthesis of styles.* Newbury Park, CA: Sage.

Bromley, D. B. (1986). *The case-study method in psychology and related disciplines.* New York: John Wiley.

Bryant, C. G. A. (1985). *Positivism in social theory and research.* New York: St. Martin's Press.

Bryman, A. (1988). *Quantity and quality in social research.* London: Unwin Hyman.

Bulmer, M. (1986). The value of qualitative methods. In M. Bulmer, K. G.

Banting, S. Blume, M. Carley, & C. Weiss (Eds.), *Social science and social policy* (pp. 180–204). Boston: Allen & Unwin.

Burns, N. (1989). Standards for qualitative research. *Nursing Science Quarterly, 2*, 44–52.

Campbell, D. T. (1979). Degrees of freedom and the case study. In T. D. Cook & C. R. Reichardt (Eds.), *Qualitative and quantitative methods in evaluation research* (pp. 49–67). Beverly Hills, CA: Sage.

Chafetz, D. S. (1993). Sociological theory: A case of multiple personality disorder. *American Sociologist, 24*, 60–62.

Clifford, J. (1988). *The predicament of culture: Twentieth-century ethnography, literature, and art.* Cambridge, MA: Harvard University Press.

Clifford, J., & Marcus, G. E. (Eds.). (1986). *Writing culture: The poetics and politics of ethnography.* Berkeley: University of California Press.

Cook, J. A., & Fonow, M. M. (1986). Knowledge and women's interests: Issues of epistemology and methodology in feminist sociological research. *Sociological Inquiry, 56*, 2–29.

Daly, K. (1992). Parenthood as problematic: Insider interviews with couples seeking to adopt. In J. F. Gilgun, K. Daly, & G. Handel (Eds.), *Qualitative methods in family research* (pp. 103–125). Newbury Park, CA: Sage.

Denzin, N. K. (1978). *The research act.* New York: Aldine.

Denzin, N. K. (1992). *Symbolic interactionism and cultural studies: The politics of interpretation.* Cambridge, MA: Blackwell.

Denzin, N. K., & Lincoln, Y. S. (1994). Introduction: Entering the field of qualitative research. In N. K. Denzin & Y. S. Lincoln (Eds.), *Handbook of qualitative research* (pp. 1–17). Thousand Oaks, CA: Sage.

Detzner, D. F. (1992). Life histories: Conflict in Southeast Asian refugee families. In J. F. Gilgun, K. Daly, & G. Handel (Eds.), *Qualitative methods in family research* (pp. 85–102). Newbury Park, CA: Sage.

Dilworth-Anderson, P., Burton, L., & Johnson, I. B. (1993). Reframing theories for understanding race, ethnicity, and families. In P. G. Boss, W. J. Doherty, R. LaRossa, W. R. Schumm, & S. K. Steinmetz (Eds.), *Sourcebook of family theories and methods: A contextual approach* (pp. 627–649). New York: Plenum.

Doherty, W. J. (1992). Private lives, public values. *Psychology Today, 25*, 32–37.

Douglas, J. D. (1976). *Investigative social research.* Beverly Hills, CA: Sage.

Douglas, J. D. (1985). *Creative interviewing.* Beverly Hills, CA: Sage.

Douglas, J. D. & Johnson, J. M. (Eds.). (1977). *Existential sociology.* New York: Cambridge University Press.

Ellis, C. (1991). Sociological introspection and emotional experience. *Symbolic Interaction, 14*, 23–50.

Ellis, C. (1993). Telling a story of sudden death. *Sociological Quarterly, 34*, 711–730.

Ellis, C., & Flaherty, M. G. (Eds.). (1992). *Investigating subjectivity.* Newbury Park, CA: Sage.

Ferree, M. M. (1990). Beyond separate spheres: Feminism and family research. *Journal of Marriage and the Family, 52*, 866–884.

Fine, G. A. (1990). Symbolic interactionism in the post-Blumerian age. In G. Ritzer (Ed.), *Frontiers of social theory: The new syntheses* (pp. 117–157). New York: Columbia University Press.

Fonow, M. M., & Cook, J. A. (Eds.). (1991). Back to the future. A look at the second wave of feminist epistemology and methodology. In M. M. Fonow & J. A. Cook (Eds.), *Beyond methodology: Feminist scholarship as lived experience* (pp. 1–15). Bloomington: Indiana University Press.

Gans, H. J. (1982). The participant observer as human being: Observations on the personal aspects of fieldwork. In R. G. Burgess (Ed.), *Field research: A sourcebook and field manual* (pp. 53–61). London: George Allen & Unwin.

Geertz, C. (1973). *The interpretation of culture.* New York: Basic Books.

Geertz, C. (1988). *Works and lives: The anthropologist as author.* Stanford, CA: Stanford University Press.

Germain, C. (1986). Ethnography: The method. In P. L. Munhall & C. J. Oiler (Eds.), *Nursing research. A qualitative perspective* (pp. 147–162). Norwalk, CT: Appleton-Century-Crofts.

Giddens, A. (1976). *New rules of sociological methods: A positive critique of interpretive sociologies.* New York: Basic Books.

Giddens, A. (1984). *The constitution of society: Outline of the theory of structuration.* Berkeley, CA: University of California Press.

Giddens, A. (1990). *The consequences of modernity.* Stanford, CA: Stanford University Press.

Gilgun, J. F. (1992). Definitions, methodologies, and methods in qualitative family research. In J. F. Gilgun, K. Daly, & G. Handel (Eds.), *Qualitative methods in family research* (pp. 22–39). Newbury Park, CA: Sage.

Gilgun, J. F., Daly, K., & Handel, G. (Eds.). (1992). *Qualitative methods in family research.* Newbury Park, CA: Sage.

Glaser, B. G. (1978). *Theoretical sensitivity: Advances in the methodology of grounded theory.* Mill Valley, CA: Sociology Press.

Glaser, B. G. (1992). *Basics of grounded theory analysis: Emergence vs. forcing.* Mill Valley, CA: Sociology Press.

Glaser, B. G., & Strauss. A. (1967). *The discovery of grounded theory.* New York: Aldine.

Gross, E. (1986). Conclusion. What is feminist theory? In C. Pateman & E. Gross (Eds.), *Feminist challenges: Social and political theory* (pp. 190–204). Boston: Northeastern University Press.

Guba, E. G., & Lincoln. Y. S. (1994). Competing paradigms in qualitative research. In N. K. Denzin & Y. S. Lincoln (Eds.). *Handbook of qualitative research* (pp. 105–117). Thousand Oaks, CA: Sage.

Gubrium, J. F. (1992). Qualitative research comes of age in gerontology. *The Gerontologist, 32*, 581–582.

Habermas, J. (1984). *The theory of communicative action: Reason and the rationalization of society* (Vol. 1, T. McCarthy, Trans.). Boston: Beacon Press.

Habermas, J. (1987). *The theory of communicative action: Lifeworld and system: A critique of functionalist reason* (Vol. 2, T. McCarthy, Trans.). Boston: Beacon Press.

Hammersley, M. (1990). *Reading ethnographic research: A critical guide.* London: Longman.

Hammersley, M. (1992). *What's wrong with ethnography? Methodological explorations.* London: Routledge.

Handel, G. (1992). *Qualitative methods in family research.* Newbury Park, CA: Sage.

Hankin, T. L. (1979). In defense of biography: The use of biography in the history of science. *History of Science, 17*, 1–16.

Haraway, D. (1988). Situated knowledges: The science question in feminism and the privilege of partial perspective. *Feminist Studies, 14*, 575–599.

Harding, S. (Ed.). (1987). *Feminism and methodology.* Bloomington: Indiana University Press.

Hayano, D. M. (1979). Auto-ethnography: Paradigms, problems, and prospects. *Human Organization 38*, 99–104.

Heritage, J. C. (1984). *Garfinkel and ethnomethodology.* Cambridge, England: Polity.

Heritage, J. C. (1985). Recent developments in conversation analysis. *Sociolinguistics, 15*, 1–18.

Heritage, J. C. (1992). Ethnomethodology. In *Encyclopedia of sociology* (Vol. 2, pp. 588–594). New York: Macmillan.

Hess, R. D., & Handel, G. (1959). *Family worlds.* Chicago: University of Chicago Press.

Holstein, J. A., & Gubrium, J. F. (1994). Phenomenology, ethnomethodology, and interpretive practice. In N. K. Denzin & Y. S. Lincoln (Eds.), *Handbook of qualitative research* (pp. 262–272). Thousand Oaks, CA: Sage.

Jarrett, R. L. (1992). A family case study. An examination of the underclass debate. In J. F. Gilgun, K. Daly, & G. Handel (Eds.), *Qualitative methods in family research* (pp. 172–197). Newbury Park, CA: Sage.

Jarvie, I. C. (1969). The problem of ethical integrity in participant-observation. *Current Anthropology, 10*, 505–508.

Jayaratne, T. E., & Stewart, A. J. (1991). Quantitative and qualitative methods in the social sciences. Current feminist issues and practical strategies. In M. G. Fonow & J. A. Cook (Eds.), *Beyond methodology. Feminist scholarship as lived research* (pp. 85–106). Bloomington, IN: Indiana University Press.

Jick, T. D. (1979). Mixing qualitative and quantitative methods: Triangulation in action. *Administrative Science Quarterly, 24*, 602–610.

Jorgensen, D. L. (1989) *Participant observation: A methodology for human studies.* Newbury Park, CA: Sage.

Kirk, J., & Miller, M. L. (1986). *Reliability and validity in qualitative research.* Beverly Hills, CA: Sage.

Kotarba, J. A. (1979). Existential sociology. In S. McNoll (Ed.), *Theoretical perspectives in sociology* (pp 348–368). New York: St. Martin's Press.

Kotarba, J. A., & Fontana, A. (1984) (Eds.). *The existential self in society.* Chicago: University of Chicago Press.

Krieger, S. (1991). *Social science and the self: Personal essays on an art form.* New Brunswick, NJ: Rutgers University Press.

LaRossa, R., Bennett, L. A., & Gelles, R. (1985). Ethical dilemmas in qualitative family research. In G. Handel (Ed.), *The psychosocial interior of the family* (pp. 95–111). New York: Aldine.

LaRossa, R., & Reitzes, D. C. (1993). Symbolic interactionism and family studies. In P. G. Boss, W. J. Doherty, R. LaRossa, W. R. Schumm, & S. K. Steinmetz (Eds.), *Sourcebook of family theories and methods: A contextual approach* (pp. 135–166). New York: Plenum.

LaRossa, R., & Wolf, J. H. (1985). On qualitative family research. *Journal of Marriage and the Family, 47*, 531 –542.

Lewis, O. (1959). *Five families.* New York: Basic Books.

Lincoln, Y. S., & Guba, E. G. (1985). *Naturalistic inquiry.* Beverly Hills, CA: Sage.

Lindesmith, A. L. (1947). *Addiction and opiates.* Chicago: Aldine.

Lofland, J., & Lofland, L. H. (1984). *Analyzing social settings: A guide to qualitative observation and analysis* (2nd ed.). Belmont, CA: Wadsworth.

Maines, D. (1977). Social organization and social structure in symbolic interactionist thought. *Annual Review of Sociology, 3*, 75–95.

Maines, D. (1983). In search of the mesostructure: Studies in the negotiated order. *Urban Life, 11*, 267–279.

Manning, P. K. (1991). Analytic induction. In K. Plummer (Ed.), *Symbolic interactionism: Vol. II. Contemporary issues* (pp. 401–430). Brookfield, VT: Elgar.

Marcus, G. E., & Fischer, M. (1986). *Anthropology as cultural critique: An experimental moment in the human sciences.* Chicago: University of Chicago Press.

Marshall, C., & Rossman, G. B. (1989). *Designing qualitative research.* Newbury Park, CA: Sage.

Mehan, H., & Wood, H. (1975). *The reality of ethnomethodology*. New York: John Wiley.

Merton, R. K, Fiske, M., & Kendall, P. L. (1990). *The focused interview: A manual of problems and procedures* (2nd ed.). New York: Free Press.

Mies, M. (1983). Towards a methodology for feminist research. In G. Bowles & R. Duelli-Klein (Eds.), *Theories of women's studies* (pp. 117–139). London: Routledge & Kegan Paul.

Miles, M. B., & Huberman, A. M. (1984). *Qualitative data analysis: A sourcebook of new methods*. Beverly Hills, CA: Sage.

Miller, B. C. (1993). Families, science, and values: Alternative views of parenting effects and adolescent pregnancy. *Journal of Marriage and the Family, 55*, 7–22.

Miller, S. M. (1952). The participant observer and over-rapport. *American Sociological Review, 17*, 97–99.

Nye, F. I. (1988). Fifty years of family research, 1937–1987. *Journal of Marriage and the Family, 50*, 569–584.

Osmond, M. (1984). Feminist research and scientific criteria. *Journal of Family Issues, 5*, 571–576.

Osmond, M., & Thorne, B. (1994). Feminist theories: The social construction of gender in families and societies. In P. G. Boss, W. J. Doherty, R. LaRossa, W. R. Schumm, & S. K. Steinmetz (Eds.), *Sourcebook of family theories and methods: A contextual approach* (pp. 651–675). New York: Plenum.

Peplau, L. A., & Conrad, A. (1989). Beyond nonsexist research: The perils of feminist methods in psychology. *Psychology of Women Quarterly, 13*, 379–400.

Prus, R. (1987). Generic social processes: Maximizing conceptual development in ethnographic research. *Journal of Contemporary Ethnography, 16*, 250–293.

Rank, M. R. (1992). The blending of qualitative and quantitative methods in understanding childbearing among welfare recipients. In J. F. Gilgun, K. Daly, & G. Handel (Eds.), *Qualitative methods in family research* (pp. 281–300). Newbury Park, CA: Sage.

Richardson, L. (1994). Writing: A method of inquiry. In N. K. Denzin & Y. S. Lincoln (Eds.), *Handbook of qualitative research* (pp. 516–529). Newbury Park, CA: Sage.

Riemer, J. (1977). Varieties of opportunistic research. *Urban Life, 5*, 467–477.

Rist, R. C. (1977). On the relations among educational research paradigms: From disdain to detente. *Anthropology and Education Quarterly, 8*, 42–49.

Ritzer, G. (1992). *Contemporary sociological theory* (3rd ed.). New York: McGraw-Hill.

Ronai, C. R. (in press). Multiple reflections of child sex abuse: An argument for a layered account. *Journal of Contemporary Ethnography*.

Rosaldo, R. (1989). *Culture and truth: The remaking of social analysis*. Boston: Beacon.

Rosenblatt, P. C., & Fischer, L. R. (1993). Qualitative family research. In P. G. Boss, W. J. Doherty, R. LaRossa, W. R. Schumm, & S. K. Steinmetz (Eds.), *Sourcebook of family theories and methods: A contextual approach* (pp. 167–177). New York: Plenum.

Scarr, S. (1985). Constructing psychology: Making facts and fables for our times. *American Psychologist, 40*, 499–512.

Schvaneveldt, J. D., Pickett, R. S., & Young, M. H. (1993). Historical methods in family research. In P. G. Boss, W. J. Doherty, R. LaRossa, W. R. Schumm, & S. K. Steinmetz (Eds.), *Sourcebook of family theories and methods: A contextual approach* (pp. 99–116). New York: Plenum.

Schwartz, H., & Jacob, J. (1979). *Qualitative sociology. A method in the madness*. New York: Free Press.

Silverman, D. (1985). *Qualitative methodology and sociology: Describing the social world*. Hants, England: Gower.

Smith, D. E. (1979). A sociology for women. In J. A. Sherman & E. T. Beck (Eds.), *The prism of sex: Essays in the sociology of knowledge* (pp. 135–187). Madison: University of Wisconsin Press.

Smith, D. E. (1987). *The everyday world as problematic*. Boston: Northeastern University Press.

Smith, D. E. (1990a). *Texts, facts, and femininity*. London: Routledge & Kegan Paul.

Smith, D. E. (1990b). *The conceptual practices of power*. Boston: Northeastern University Press.

Snizek, W. E. (1976). An empirical assessment of "Sociology: A multiple paradigm science." *American Sociologist, 11*, 217–219.

Sollie, D. L., & Leslie, L. A. (1994). (Eds.). *Gender, families and close relationships: Feminist journeys*. Thousand Oaks, CA: Sage.

Spradley, J. P. (1979). *The ethnographic interview*. New York: Rinehart & Winston.

Spradley, J. P. (1980). *Participant observation*. Fort Worth, TX: Holt, Rinehart & Winston.

Steier, D. M. (1991). *Research and reflexivity*. Newbury Park, CA: Sage.

Stevens, P. (1989). A critical social reconceptualization of environment in nursing: Implications for methodology. *Advances in Nursing Science, 11*, 56–68.

Strauss, A., & Corbin, J. (1990). *Basics of qualitative research: Grounded theory, procedures, and techniques*. Newbury Park, CA: Sage.

Taylor, S. J., & Bogdan, R. (1984). *Introduction to qualitatiive methods: The search for meanings* (2nd ed.). New York: Plenum.

Thompson, J. B., & Held, D. (Eds.). (1982). *Habermas: Critical debates*. Cambridge, MA: MIT Press.

Thompson, J. L., Allen, D. G., & Rodrigues-Fischer, L. (1992). (Eds.). *Critique, resistance, and action: Working papers in the politics of nursing*. New York: National League for Nursing Press.

Thompson, L. (1992). Feminist methodology for family studies. *Journal of Marriage and the Family, 54*, 3–18.

Thorne, B. (1980). "You still takin' notes?": Fieldwork and problems of informed consent. *Social Problems, 27*, 284–297.

Turner, J. B. (1985). In defense of positivism. *Sociological Theory, 3*, 24–30.

Turner, J. B. (1990). The past, present, and future of theory in American sociology. In G. Ritzer (Ed.), *Frontiers of social theory: The new synthesis* (pp. 371–391). New York: Columbia University Press.

Van Maanen, J. (1988). *Tales of the field: On writing ethnography*. Chicago: University of Chicago Press.

Wax, M. L. (1980). Paradoxes of "consent" to the practice of fieldwork. *Social Problems, 27*, 272–283.

Wells, D. L. (1994). *On the process of discharge decision making for elderly parents: A critical ethnography*. Unpublished doctoral dissertation, York University, Toronto.

Wiley, N. (1990). The history and politics of recent sociological theory. In G. Ritzer (Ed.), *Frontiers of social theory: The new synthesis* (pp. 392–415). New York: Columbia University Press.

Yin, R. K. (1989). *Case study research: Design and methods* (2nd ed.). Newbury Park, CA: Sage.

Yin, R. K. (1993). *Applications of case study research*. Newbury Park, CA: Sage.

About the Authors: Anne-Marie Ambert, Department of Sociology, York University, North York (Toronto), Ontario, Canada M3J 1P3. Patricia A. Adler, Department of Sociology, University of Colorado, Boulder, CO 80304. Peter Adler, Department of Sociology, University of Denver, Denver, CO 80208. Daniel F. Detzner, Department of Family Social Science, University of Minnesota, St. Paul, MN 55108.

Rigor in Qualitative Research: The Assessment of Trustworthiness

LAURA KREFTING

Queen's University

ABSTRACT. Despite a growing interest in qualitative research in occupational therapy, little attention has been placed on establishing its rigor. This article presents one model that can be used for the assessment of trustworthiness or merit of qualitative inquiry. Guba's (1981) model describes four general criteria for evaluation of research and then defines each from both a quantitative and a qualitative perspective. Several strategies for the achievement of rigor in qualitative research useful for both researchers and consumers of research are described.

From *The American Journal of Occupational Therapy, 45,* 214–222. Copyright © 1991 by the American Occupational Therapy Association, Inc. Reprinted with permission.

The worth of any research endeavor, regardless of the approach taken, is evaluated by peers, grant reviewers, and readers. Most quantitative researchers recognize and document the worth of a project by as-
5 sessing the reliability and validity of the work (Payton, 1979). This same attention to the merit of a research project, however, is much less common in qualitative research.

Schmid (1981) described qualitative research as the
10 study of the empirical world from the viewpoint of the person under study. She identified two underlying principles. The first is that behavior is influenced by the physical, sociocultural, and psychological environment—this is the basis for *naturalistic* inquiry. The
15 second assumption is that behavior goes beyond what is observed by the investigator. Subjective meanings and perceptions of the subject are critical in qualitative research, and it is the researcher's responsibility to access these.
20 Kirk and Miller (1986) suggested a working definition of qualitative research that reflects these two principles. They defined it as "a particular tradition in social science that fundamentally depends on watching people in their own territory and interacting with them
25 in their own language, on their own terms" (p. 9). Qualitative research is pluralistic, consisting of a variety of approaches, including phenomenology, semiotics, ethnography, life history, and historical research. Detailed definitions of the epistemological and philo-

30 sophical bases of qualitative research reviews can be found in Duffy (1985), Guba (1981), and Kielhofner (1982).

The purpose of this paper is to describe one conceptual model that may be used to evaluate the trust-
35 worthiness of qualitative research. Four concepts basic to the model are described, followed by strategies that researchers can use to enhance the worth of their qualitative studies.

Two issues need to be acknowledged in a discus-
40 sion of the assessment of qualitative research. The first is that models used to evaluate quantitative research are seldom relevant to qualitative research. The second is that not all qualitative research can be assessed with the same strategies. These two issues will be addressed
45 briefly before the model is presented.

Criteria for Assessment of Qualitative Versus Quantitative Research

Too frequently, qualitative research is evaluated against criteria appropriate to quantitative research and is found to be lacking. Qualitative researchers contend that because the nature and purpose of the quantitative
50 and qualitative traditions are different, it is erroneous to apply the same criteria of worthiness or merit. Agar (1986) suggested that terms like *reliability* and *validity* are relative to the quantitative view and do not fit the details of qualitative research. For example, the notion
55 of external validity, which is concerned with the ability to generalize from the research sample to the population (Payton, 1979), is one of the key criteria of good quantitative research. In some qualitative approaches, however, the major purpose is to generate hypotheses
60 for further investigation rather than to test them (Sandelowski, 1986). In such situations, external validity is not relevant.

Agar (1986) suggested that a different language is needed to fit the qualitative view, one that would re-
65 place reliability and validity with such terms as *credibility, accuracy of representation,* and *authority of the writer.* Similarly, Leininger (1985) claimed that the issue is not whether the data are reliable or valid but how the terms reliability and validity are defined. She
70 recast the term validity in a qualitative sense to mean gaining knowledge and understanding of the nature (i.e., the meaning, attributes, and characteristics) of the

phenomenon under study. She contrasted this to the common usage of validity in a quantitative sense, in which it refers to the degree to which an instrument measures what it is designed to measure.

Just as there is a need to look at the accuracy and trustworthiness of various kinds of quantitative data in different ways, there is also a need to look at qualitative methods for the different ways in which to ensure the quality of the findings. It is important not to fall into the trap of assuming that all qualitative studies should be evaluated with the same criteria. As Sandelowski (1986) noted, the term *qualitative research* is imprecise and refers to many dissimilar research methods. These approaches have different purposes and methods and therefore different ways of determining whether they are trustworthy. For example, the phenomenological approach asks what it is like to have a certain experience. The goal is to describe accurately the experience of the phenomenon under study, not to generalize to theories or models (Field & Morse, 1985). Because the goal of ethnographic research, however, is to describe social complexities, it often involves development of theoretical constructs. Although some principles are basic to all qualitative research, the incorrect application of the qualitative criteria of trustworthiness to studies is as problematic as the application of inappropriate quantitative criteria.

The issues of the inappropriateness of quantitative criteria in the assessment of qualitative research and the plurality of qualitative research are important to the understanding of any model of trustworthiness of qualitative research.

Guba's Model of Trustworthiness of Qualitative Research

Researchers need alternative models appropriate to qualitative designs that ensure rigor without sacrificing the relevance of the qualitative research. Guba (1981) proposed such a model for assessing the trustworthiness of qualitative data. Although there are other models (e.g., Kirk & Miller, 1986; Leininger, 1985), this presentation will be based on Guba's model because it is comparatively well developed conceptually and has been used by qualitative researchers, particularly nurses and educators, for a number of years.

What follows is my summary and interpretation of Guba's (1981) model following several qualitative research projects. I urge occupational therapists who intend to make use of the model in designing research projects or in the critical assessment of the projects of others to refer to the original sources cited in the references.

Guba's (1981) model is based on the identification of four aspects of trustworthiness that are relevant to both quantitative and qualitative studies: (a) truth value, (b) applicability, (c) consistency, and (d) neutrality. Based on the philosophical differences between qualitative and quantitative approaches, the model de-fines different strategies of assessing these criteria in each type of research. These strategies are important to researchers in designing ways of increasing the rigor of their qualitative studies and also for readers to use as a means of assessing the value of the findings of qualitative research.

Truth Value

Truth value asks whether the researcher has established confidence in the truth of the findings for the subjects or informants and the context in which the study was undertaken (Lincoln & Guba, 1985). It establishes how confident the researcher is with the truth of the findings based on the research design, informants, and context. In quantitative studies, truth is often assessed by how well threats to the internal validity of the study have been managed as well as the validity of the instruments as a measure of the phenomenon under study (Sandelowski, 1986). Internal validity is supported when changes in the dependent variable are accounted for by changes in the independent variable, that is, when the design minimizes the effects of competing confounding variables by control or randomization. (For a detailed discussion of the threats to internal validity, see Campbell and Stanley, 1966).

In qualitative research, truth value is usually obtained from the discovery of human experiences as they are lived and perceived by informants. Truth value is subject-oriented, not defined a priori by the researcher (Sandelowski, 1986). Lincoln and Guba (1985) termed this *credibility*. They argued that internal validity is based on the assumption that there is a single tangible reality to be measured. If this assumption is replaced by the idea of multiple realities, the researcher's job becomes one of representing those multiple realities revealed by informants as adequately as possible. Researchers, then, need to focus on testing their findings against various groups from which the data were drawn or persons who are familiar with the phenomenon being studied. Sandelowski suggested that a qualitative study is credible when it presents such accurate descriptions or interpretation of human experience that people who also share that experience would immediately recognize the descriptions. Truth value is perhaps the most important criterion for the assessment of qualitative research. A number of methodological strategies are required to ensure strong credibility.

Applicability

Applicability refers to the degree to which the findings can be applied to other contexts and settings or with other groups; it is the ability to generalize from the findings to larger populations. In the quantitative perspective, applicability refers to how well the threats to external validity have been managed (Sandelowski, 1986). Payton (1979) defined external validity as the ability to generalize from the study sample to the larger population and noted the importance of sampling technique in its establishment.

Two perspectives to applicability are appropriate for qualitative research. The first perspective suggests that the ability to generalize is not relevant in many qualitative research projects. A strength of the qualitative method is that it is conducted in naturalistic settings with few controlling variables. Each situation is defined as unique and thus is less amenable to generalization. Consequently, as Sandelowski (1986) explained, generalization is somewhat of an illusion because every research situation is made up of a particular researcher in a particular interaction with particular informants. Applicability, then, is not seen as relevant to qualitative research because its purpose is to describe a particular phenomenon or experience, not to generalize to others.

Guba (1981) presented the second perspective on applicability in qualitative research by referring to *fittingness*, or *transferability*, as the criterion against which applicability of qualitative data is assessed. Research meets this criterion when the findings fit into contexts outside the study situation that are determined by the degree of similarity or goodness of fit between the two contexts. Lincoln and Guba (1985) noted that transferability is more the responsibility of the person wanting to transfer the findings to another situation or population than that of the researcher of the original study. They argued that as long as the original researcher presents sufficient descriptive data to allow comparison, he or she has addressed the problem of applicability.

Consistency

The third criterion of trustworthiness considers the consistency of the data, that is, whether the findings would be consistent if the inquiry were replicated with the same subjects or in a similar context. In quantitative research, reliability is the criterion concerned with the stability, consistency, and equivalence in the study (Sandelowski, 1986). It is the extent to which repeated administration of a measure will provide the same data or the extent to which a measure administered once, but by different people, produces equivalent results. Inherent in the goal of reliability is the value of repeatability, that replication of the testing procedures does not alter the findings. The restricted methods of observation and tight designs common in quantitative research are intended to pass this replication test. The quantitative perspective on consistency is also based on the assumption of a single reality, that there is something out there to be studied that is unchanging and can be used as a benchmark (Lincoln & Guba, 1985). If one assumes there are multiple realities, the notion of reliability is no longer as relevant.

Unlike the relatively controlled experimental environment, the qualitative field setting may be complicated by extraneous and unexpected variables. As Duffy (1985) noted, the structure of the experimental design is the antithesis of the unstructured and often spontaneous strategies of qualitative research. The key to qualitative work is to learn from the informants rather than control for them. Moreover, instruments that are assessed for consistency in qualitative research are the researcher and the informants, both of whom vary greatly within the research project. Qualitative research emphasizes the uniqueness of the human situation, so that variation in experience rather than identical repetition is sought (Field & Morse, 1985).

Thus, variability is expected in qualitative research, and consistency is defined in terms of dependability. Guba's (1981) concept of dependability implies trackable variability, that is, variability that can be ascribed to identified sources. Explainable sources of variability might include increasing insight on the part of the researcher, informant fatigue, or changes in the informant's life situation. Another source of variability stems from the fact that qualitative research looks at the range of experience rather than the average experience, so that atypical or non-normative situations are important to include in the findings. In quantitative terms, the outlying data need to be identified to describe the boundaries of the experience or phenomenon. Although the person might not be completely representative of a group, his or her experience is considered important.

Neutrality

The fourth criterion of trustworthiness is neutrality, the freedom from bias in the research procedures and results (Sandelowski, 1986). Neutrality refers to the degree to which the findings are a function solely of the informants and conditions of the research and not of other biases, motivations, and perspectives (Guba, 1981). In quantitative research, objectivity is the criterion of neutrality and is achieved through rigor of methodology through which reliability and validity are established. Objectivity also refers to the proper distance between researcher and subjects that minimizes bias and is achieved through such procedures as instrumentation and randomization. Thus, the objective researcher is seen as scientifically distant, that is, as someone who is not influenced by, and does not influence, the study.

Qualitative researchers, on the other hand, try to increase the worth of the findings by decreasing the distance between the researcher and the informants, for example, by prolonged contact with informants or lengthy periods of observation. Lincoln and Guba (1985) shifted the emphasis of neutrality in qualitative research from the researcher to the data, so that rather than looking at the neutrality of the investigator, the neutrality of the data was considered. They suggested that confirmability be the criterion of neutrality. This is achieved when truth value and applicability are established.

Summary of Guba's Model

Guba's (1981) model identified truth value, applicability, consistency, and neutrality as four criteria applicable to the assessment of research of any type. Guba argued that these criteria must be defined differently for qualitative and quantitative research based on the philosophical and conceptual divergence of the two approaches. (For a summary of the criteria, their common quantitative definitions, and Guba's qualitative definitions, see Table 1.)

Table 1
Comparison of Criteria by Research Approach

Criterion	Qualitative Approach	Quantitative Approach
Truth value	Credibility	Internal Validity
Applicability	Transferability	External Validity
Consistency	Dependability	Reliability
Neutrality	Confirmability	Objectivity

Strategies to Increase the Trustworthiness of Qualitative Work

Specific strategies can be used throughout the research process to increase the worth of qualitative projects. Some strategies need to be addressed in the study design stage, while others are applied during data collection and after data are interpreted. A small number of these strategies will be discussed in detail, such as reflexivity and triangulation, because they are critical to the quality of the research, while other, more straightforward strategies will be described briefly. The strategies are described under one of the four qualitative criteria for trustworthiness. Although some strategies are useful for establishing more than one criterion (e.g., triangulation and reflexivity), the strategies are defined under the criterion to which they are most frequently applied. Many of these strategies are outlined in Guba's (1981) and Lincoln and Guba's (1985) studies. I learned about other strategies, however, from working with experienced researchers, and a few were developed to strengthen my own work. (See Table 2 for a summary of the strategies according to the relevant criteria.) In reviewing these strategies, it is important to remember that although a number of techniques are available, not all are appropriate to every qualitative study.

Credibility Strategies

Leininger (1985) noted the importance of identifying and documenting recurrent features such as patterns, themes, and values in qualitative research. The emphasis on recurrence suggests the need to spend sufficient time with informants to identify reappearing patterns. Credibility requires adequate submersion in the research setting to enable recurrent patterns to be identified and verified. Thus, an important strategy is to spend an extended period of time with informants (Lincoln and Guba [1985] termed this *prolonged en-*

gagement), which allows the researcher to check perspectives and allows the informants to become accustomed to the researcher. Kielhofner (1982) supported the importance of intense participation, suggesting that it enhances research findings through intimate familiarity and discovery of hidden fact. This extended time period is important because as rapport increases, informants may volunteer different and often more sensitive information than they do at the beginning of a research project.

Table 2
Summary of Strategies With Which to Establish Trustworthiness

Strategy	Criteria
Credibility	Prolonged and varied field experience
	Time sampling
	Reflexivity (field journal)
	Triangulation
	Member checking
	Peer examination
	Interview technique
	Establishing authority of researcher
	Structural coherence
	Referential adequacy
Transferability	Nominated sample
	Comparison of sample to demographic data
	Time sample
	Dense description
Dependability	Dependability audit
	Dense description of research methods
	Stepwise replication
	Triangulation
	Peer examination
	Code-recode procedure
Confirmability	Confirmability audit
	Triangulation
	Reflexivity

There are no rules regulating the length of time one should be involved in data collection. It depends on the design and the particular purpose of the study. With the use of my experience as a guide, my disability ethnography (Krefting, 1989) consisted of more than eighty 90-min interviews and 20 to 30 periods of participant observations with 22 persons with brain injury and their families. A life history, which is in progress, consists of more than 20 hr of interviews plus 50 pages of autobiographical writing.

A study's credibility is threatened by errors in which research subjects respond with what they think is the preferred social response—that is, data are based on social desirability rather than on personal experience (Kirk & Miller, 1986). Use of prolonged engagement can assist in detecting response sets where informants consistently either agree or disagree with the questions. Use of numerous interviews and observation periods allows the researcher to identify the occurrence of this problem. The use of hypothetical cases or a reframing of the questions may help elicit more personal responses.

Related is the issue of persistent observation of a phenomenon under various natural situations. The time-sampling strategy makes use of a flowchart to systematize informant contacts and observation to determine if the researcher is sampling all possible situations, including different social settings; times of day, week, and season; and interactions among different social groupings (Knafl & Breitmayer, 1989). For example, in studying the lives of children with disabilities, the researcher would want to observe the children interacting with peers, family, and teachers in a number of contexts at different times of the day and on weekends and weekdays. This strategy emphasizes the importance of the environment in which the data are collected and establishes credibility.

Paradoxically, a major threat to the truth value of a qualitative study lies in the closeness of the relationship between the investigator and the informants that can develop during the prolonged contact required to establish credibility. The researcher can become so enmeshed with the informants that he or she may have difficulty separating his or her own experience from that of the informants (Marcus & Fischer, 1986). Although close researcher-informant relationships are critical to the research enterprise, it is possible to lose the ability to interpret the findings. To help ensure that this extreme overinvolvement does not occur, a strategy called *reflexive analysis*, or *reflexivity*, is useful (Good, Herrera, Good, & Cooper, 1985).

Reflexivity refers to assessment of the influence of the investigator's own background, perceptions, and interests on the qualitative research process (Ruby, 1980). It includes the effect of the researcher's personal history on qualitative research. In the past, many qualitative researchers have claimed neutrality and even invisibility in their fieldwork, much as the objective scientist does in the quantitative approach to research. The focus on reflexivity is a recent trend in cultural anthropology, as evidenced in the work of Crapanzano (1980) in Morocco and Shostak (1981) with the !Kung tribe. Agar (1986) noted that the researcher's background dictates the framework from which he or she will organize, study, and analyze the findings. This background is made up of all of the resources available to make sense out of the experience and is often reflected in multiple roles the researcher plays while engaged in the research. For example, in my ethnographic study of persons with traumatic brain injury (Krefting, 1989), I maintained a double role as a clinical anthropology student and as an experienced health care professional. As an anthropologist, I wanted to do pure ethnography, that is, see community life after brain injury only from the viewpoint of the informants, without the influence of my rehabilitation training. But as a health care provider, I was trained to help, which motivated me to look for specific and practical implications in what I saw and heard. I spent most of the study juggling the influences of the two roles. It was important for me to be aware of and to reflect on the influence of these two roles on the study.

Aamodt (1982) noted that the qualitative approach is reflexive in that the researcher is part of the research, not separate from it. Research situations are dynamic, and the researcher is a participant, not merely an observer. The investigator, then, must analyze himself or herself in the context of the research. On entering a new culture, the researcher must continuously reflect on his or her own characteristics and examine how they influence data gathering and analysis.

One of the ways that researchers can describe and interpret their own behavior and experiences within the research context is to make use of a field journal. This journal is kept throughout the research process and includes three types of information (Lincoln & Guba, 1985). The daily schedule and logistics of the study and a methods log (in which decisions about methods and their rationale are described) are two components of the field journal that are important for auditability, a strategy that will be discussed in a later section. The third, and most important, type of information in the field journal is analogous to that found in a personal diary and reflects the researcher's thoughts, feelings, ideas, and hypotheses generated by contact with informants. It also contains questions, problems, and frustrations concerning the overall research process. In writing these personal thoughts and feelings about the research process, the researcher may become aware of biases and preconceived assumptions. Once aware of these biases, the researcher may alter the way that he or she collects the data or approaches the analysis to enhance the credibility of the research.

Triangulation is a powerful strategy for enhancing the quality of the research, particularly credibility. It is based on the idea of convergence of multiple perspectives for mutual confirmation of data to ensure that all aspects of a phenomenon have been investigated (Knafl & Breitmayer, 1989). The triangulated data sources are assessed against one another to cross-check data and interpretation. This strategy of providing a number of different slices of data also minimizes distortion from a single data source or from a biased researcher, as may be the case in data based on a single application of one measure, a single client interview for example (Field & Morse, 1985). Researchers and readers need to consider how the triangulation either contributed to confirmation of certain aspects of the study or to the completeness with which the phenomenon of interest was addressed.

A number of types of triangulation exist, four of which were identified by Knafl and Breitmayer (1989). The most common is *triangulation of data methods*, in which data collected by various means are compared (e.g., data from structured interviews, participant observation, life histories). A second type, *triangulation of data sources*, maximizes the range of data that might contribute to complete understanding of the concept. It is based on the importance of variety in time, space, and person in observation and interviewing. Examples of triangulated sources include different seasons or days, different settings, and different groupings of people. In a hospital setting, one might observe different shifts on different wards and focus on family, patients, and professionals, either alone or in small groups. *Theoretical triangulation* means that ideas from diverse or competing theories can be tested. For example, triangulation of theory may occur in considering a number of concepts from anthropology, rehabilitation, sociology, and psychology in the conceptual interpretation of the experience of a disability. *Triangulation of investigators* occurs in a study in which a research team, rather than a single researcher, is used. Team members often have a diversity of approaches, for example, a team investigating the costs of home care for patients with arthritis may be made up of a physician, a therapist, an anthropologist, and an economist.

Central to the credibility of qualitative research is the ability of informants to recognize their experiences in the research findings. Member checking is a technique that consists of continually testing with informants the researcher's data, analytic categories, interpretations, and conclusions (Lincoln & Guba, 1985). This strategy of revealing research materials to the informants ensures that the researcher has accurately translated the informants' viewpoints into data. Assessment to see if the data make sense through member checking decreases the chances of misrepresentation.

Member checking can be done through an interweaving of the informant contact hours so that information from one interview is checked with another informant before a subsequent interview with the first. In addition, summaries of taped interviews can be played to informants for their responses, or more formalized work sessions can be held, in which a number of informants are gathered to react to a draft of the analytical codes or report of results, for example. To test the overall interpretation, near the conclusion of the study, one must do a terminal or final member check with key informants to ensure that the final presentation of the data reflects the experience accurately (Lincoln & Guba, 1985). Member checks are more difficult for informants to carry out at the latter stages of the research process, when higher conceptual analysis is necessary, than in the data gathering phase, in which descriptive data are reviewed by informants. The selection criteria for informants for a terminal member check, therefore, are critical.

Despite the usefulness of member checking in enhancing credibility, one must consider the ethical aspect of this strategy. Researchers must be selective about which informants are involved in member checking. Often, informants are not conscious of the information discovered by the researcher and may become troubled if made aware of it. For example, during participant observation, the researcher may have noted that the spouses of persons with disabilities treat them like children. The person who is involved in member checking these data should be carefully selected to ensure that he or she would not be harmed by reading the data. The researcher should not provide insight that might, in fact, be harmful to the well-being of informants. Another difficulty with member checks is that informants may have a tendency to internalize the information they have read, which could affect their subsequent responses. To minimize this, it is best not to reinterview or observe an informant on an aspect of the project for which he or she has conducted a member check.

Peer examination is based on the same principle as member checks but involves the researcher's discussing the research process and findings with impartial colleagues who have experience with qualitative methods. Insights are discussed and problems presented as a form of debriefing. Lincoln and Guba (1985) suggested that this is one way of keeping the researcher honest, and the searching questions may contribute to deeper reflexive analysis by the researcher. Colleagues can also increase credibility by checking categories developed out of data and by looking for disconfirming or negative cases. Peer examination also presents an opportunity for the researcher to present working hypotheses for reaction and to discuss the evolving design of the study (Lincoln & Guba, 1985). The availability of the informants' verbatim accounts (tape recordings or transcripts of interviews) is helpful so that the examiner can critically assess the interpretations from direct quotes.

Credibility can also be enhanced within the interviewing process. The reframing of questions, repetition of questions, or expansion of questions on different occasions are ways in which to increase credibility (May, 1989). Credibility is also supported when interviews or observations are internally consistent, that is, when there is a logical rationale about the same topic in the same interview or observation. In addition, indirect questions about the informants' experiences (questions such as "Do you know others who have this experience?") and structured hypothetical situations are methods that can be used to verify observations and meanings.

The credibility of any argument is enhanced by the establishment of structural coherence, that is, the ensurance that there are no unexplained inconsistencies between the data and their interpretations (Guba, 1981). Although data may conflict, credibility is increased if the interpretation can explain the apparent contradictions. Accounting for rival explanations or deviant cases here is important. For example, in my disability ethnography (Krefting, 1989), informants disagreed over whether peers with brain injury were sought for friends. Rather than looking for consistency, I focused on the heterogeneity of persons with brain

600 injury living in the community and the problems associated with grouping them together because of a shared diagnosis. As was mentioned, a range of experience or phenomena is sought in qualitative research, so that the data are not necessarily consistent but are in fact credi-
605 ble if described and interpreted correctly. Structural coherence is also influenced by the way that the researcher integrates in the research report the masses of loosely connected data into a logical, holistic picture.

The essence of the credibility issue is the unique
610 authority of the researcher, the "I was there" element (Miles & Huberman, 1984). To strengthen the idea of authority, viewing the researcher as a measurement tool has been proposed. Miles and Huberman identified four characteristics that are necessary to assess the
615 trustworthiness of the human instrument: (a) the degree of familiarity with the phenomenon and the setting under study, (b) a strong interest in conceptual or theoretical knowledge and the ability to conceptualize large amounts of qualitative data, (c) the ability to take a
620 multidisciplinary approach, that is, to look at the subject under investigation from a number of different theoretical perspectives, and (d) good investigative skills, which are developed through literature review, course work, and experience in qualitative research
625 methods.

One way of assessing these investigative skills or technical competence is to examine the researcher's background for any special training he or she has received that is relevant to the project, for example, expe-
630 rience in interviewing or observational technique. In addition, those steps that are undertaken to enhance the skills of the researcher in the specific project should be documented, for example, mock interviews, the videotaping and analysis of the researcher's interviewing
635 skills, and pilot interviews (Field & Morse, 1985). Researchers can bolster the credibility of a project by supporting their authority in these four areas.

In summary, the strategies described above are based on the concept of the researcher gathering data
640 about, and interpreting the multiple realities of, informants. They are used to establish the truth value or credibility of the research and are critical to the accurate representation of subjective human experience. The strategies described here are not exhaustive, but
645 represent those techniques most applicable to the types of problems studied by occupational therapists.

Transferability Strategies

As noted, there are two perspectives on applicability or transferability, and depending on one's orientation to qualitative research, transferability may or may
650 not be an issue. If the assumption is made at the beginning of the study that the findings are descriptive in nature, representing one life perspective, as in some life histories, for example, the applicability criterion may not be relevant (Sandelowski, 1986). In such a
655 case, data are of descriptive worth in and of them-

selves. If, however, the researcher means to make generalizations about the subject of the research, as is common in disability ethnography, then strategies to enhance transferability are important.

660 From this latter perspective, the difficulty with qualitative research is situational uniqueness; the particular group studied may not relate to others and hence conclusions may not be transferable. A key factor in the transferability of the data, then, is the representa-
665 tiveness of the informants for that particular group.

One strategy used to address transferability in sample selection is the use of a panel of judges to help in the selection of informants representative of the phenomenon under study. An example of this type of sam-
670 ple, which is also referred to as a *nominated sample*, is the use of one or two longtime members of a family support group to identify persons who are typical of the membership (Field & Morse, 1985). Another means of ensuring transferability is the use of a comparison of
675 the characteristics of the informants to the demographic information available on that group being studied. As fieldwork continues, informants are selected to fill in gaps in the profile.

It is critical that researchers provide dense back-
680 ground information about the informants and the research context and setting to allow others to assess how transferable the findings are. As Lincoln and Guba (1985) noted, it is not the researcher's job to provide an index of transferability; it is his or her responsibility to
685 provide an adequate database to allow transferability judgments to be made by others. The adequacy of the database is especially important in describing informants with disabilities, because persons with similar conditions may be entirely different in terms of, for
690 example, functional ability or severity of symptoms.

Another way to look at transferability is to consider the data rather than the subjects. Specifically, the researcher must determine if the content of the interviews, the behaviors, and observed events are typical
695 or atypical of the lives of the informants. The time sampling and member checking strategies are useful in identifying whether data are typical.

Dependability Strategies

Guba (1981) proposed that the dependability criterion relates to the consistency of findings. Because
700 many qualitative methods are tailored to the research situation, there are no methodological shorthand descriptions, such as interrater reliability, commonly used in quantitative studies. The exact methods of data gathering, analysis, and interpretation in qualitative re-
705 search must be described. Such dense description of methods provides information as to how repeatable the study might be or how unique the situation (Kielhofner, 1982). Guba used the term *auditable* to describe the situation in which another researcher can clearly follow
710 the decision trail used by the investigator in the study. Lincoln and Guba (1985) suggested that a single audit

of the research can enhance both the dependability and confirmability of the project. This strategy, which Lincoln and Guba described in detail, will be discussed below under the confirmability criterion.

Guba (1981) also suggested that a stepwise replication technique be built into the design of a qualitative study to enhance dependability. This strategy is similar to split-half reliability in quantitative studies. Two researchers or research teams deal separately with data that have been divided, and the results are compared. An important consideration in carrying out stepwise replication is that communication between teams and team members is critical. Lincoln and Guba (1985) suggested that provision for communication on a daily basis and at preset points in the research process must be made.

Another means that the researcher can use to increase the dependability of the study is to conduct a code-recode procedure on his or her data during the analysis phase of the study. After coding a segment of data, the researcher should wait at least 2 weeks and then return and recode the same data and compare the results.

Dependability can also be enhanced through triangulation to ensure that the weaknesses of one method of data collection are compensated by the use of alternative data-gathering methods. The use of colleagues and methodological experts (peer examination) to check the research plan and implementation is another means of ensuring dependability. One can enhance stability over time by repeated observation of the same event and requestioning informants about major issues; these are similar strategies to those that enhance credibility (Lincoln & Guba, 1985).

Confirmability Strategies

Guba (1981) viewed neutrality not as researcher objectivity but as data and interpretational confirmability and described the audit strategy as the major technique for establishing confirmability. This strategy involves an external auditor attempting to follow through the natural history or progression of events in a project to try to understand how and why decisions were made. In addition, auditability suggests that another researcher could arrive at comparable conclusions given the same data and research context. The auditor considers the process of research as well as the product, data, findings, interpretations, and recommendations (Lincoln & Guba, 1985).

Lincoln and Guba (1985) identified six categories of records that can be included in the audit: (a) raw data (field notes, video and audio recordings), (b) data reduction and analysis products (quantitative summaries, condensed notes, working hypotheses), (c) data reconstruction and synthesis products (thematic categories, interpretations, inferences), (d) process notes (procedures and design strategies, trustworthiness notes), (e) materials related to intentions and dispositions

(study proposal, field journal), and (f) instrument development information (pilot forms, survey format, schedules). They noted that inspection and verification often are not considered until the completion of the project. In contrast, they emphasized the importance of including an auditor at the beginning of a project so that the nature of the audit trail can be determined. Ideally, the audit should be ongoing throughout the research process; the limitation in this is that the auditor could be co-opted into the project and thus lose his or her objectivity.

A number of other strategies are useful in the establishment of confirmability. Triangulation of multiple methods, data sources, and theoretical perspectives tests the strength of the researcher's ideas. Guba (1981) noted that an investigator should provide documentation for every claim or interpretation from at least two sources to ensure that the data support the researcher's analysis and interpretation of the findings. Another way that one can enhance neutrality is to use a team of researchers familiar with qualitative methods rather than a single researcher. Reflexive analysis is also useful to ensure that the researcher is aware of his or her influence on the data.

Summary and Conclusions

Growing interest in qualitative investigation as a legitimate approach to research questions in occupational therapy has created a need for models to assess the trustworthiness or rigor of qualitative projects. This paper has presented one such model useful both for researchers designing and conducting qualitative inquiry and for consumers of the research. Truth value, applicability, consistency, and neutrality were described as critical to the evaluation of the worth of research. These four criteria were then defined within both the quantitative and qualitative research perspectives. Several practical strategies for enhancing rigor were presented as a way for researchers to address the trustworthiness criteria.

The importance of applying such models as Guba's (1981) cannot be overstated. Occupational therapists conduct research in a climate dominated by quantitative perspectives. Grant reviewers, hospital research review committees, and journal editorial boards typically evaluate research proposals and research findings from the familiar quantitative perspective. The inclusion of a clear definition of the criteria used to assess the research and a description of how these qualitative criteria relate to quantitative criteria will help reviewers assess the value of the work. Until occupational therapists accept the principle that every qualitative research proposal and report must establish its trustworthiness, this important approach to inquiry will be considered the poor cousin of quantitative research perspectives. The knowledge base of the profession will certainly suffer without the valuable contribution of qualitative research approaches.

References

Aamodt, A. M. (1982). Examining ethnography for nurse researchers. *Western Journal of Nursing Research, 4*, 209–220.

Agar, M. (1986). *Speaking of ethnography*. Beverly Hills, CA: Sage.

Campbell, D. T., & Stanley, J. C. (1966). *Experimental and quasi-experimental designs for research*. Chicago: Rand McNally.

Crapanzano, V. (1980). *Tuhami: Portrait of a Moroccan*. Chicago: University of Chicago Press.

Duffy, M. E. (1985). Designing nursing research: The qualitative-quantitative debate. *Journal of Advanced Nursing, 10*, 225–232.

Field, P. A., & Morse, J. (1985). *Nursing research: The application of qualitative approaches*. London: Croom & Helm.

Good, B. J., Herrera, H., Good, M., & Cooper, J. (1985). Reflexivity: Counter-transference and clinical ethnography. A case from a psychiatric cultural consultation clinic. In R. Hahn & A. Gaines (Eds.), *Physicians of Western medicine* (pp. 193–221). Boston: D. Reidel.

Guba, E. G. (1981). Criteria for assessing the trustworthiness of naturalistic inquiries. *Educational Resources Information Center Annual Review Paper, 29*, 75–91.

Kielhofner, G. (1982). Qualitative research: Part one. Paradigmatic grounds and issues of reliability and validity. *Occupational Therapy Journal of Research, 2*, 67–79.

Kirk, J., & Miller, M. (1986). *Reliability and validity in qualitative research*. Beverly Hills, CA: Sage.

Knafl, K., & Breitmayer, B. J. (1989). Triangulation in qualitative research: Issues of conceptual clarity and purpose. In J. Morse (Ed.), *Qualitative nursing research: A contemporary dialogue* (pp. 193–203). Rockville, MD: Aspen.

Krefting, L. M. (1989). Reintegration into the community after head injury: The results of an ethnographic study. *Occupational Therapy Journal of Research, 9*, 67–83.

Leininger, M. M. (1985). Nature, rationale and importance of qualitative research methods in nursing. In M. M. Leininger (Ed.), *Qualitative research methods in nursing* (pp. 1–28). New York: Grune & Stratton.

Lincoln, Y. S., & Guba, E. A. (1985). *Naturalistic inquiry*. Beverly Hills, CA: Sage.

Marcus, G. E., & Fischer, M. J. (1986). *Anthropology as cultural critique: An experimental movement in the human sciences*. Chicago: University of Chicago Press.

May, K. A. (1989). Interview techniques in qualitative research: Concerns and challenges. In J. Morse (Ed.), *Qualitative nursing research: A contemporary dialogue* (pp. 57–166). Rockville, MD: Aspen.

Miles, M. B., & Huberman, A. M. (1984). *Qualitative data analysis: A sourcebook of new methods*. Beverly Hills, CA: Sage.

Payton, O. D. (1979). *Research: The validation of clinical practice*. Philadelphia: F. A. Davis.

Ruby, D. (1980). Exposing yourself: Reflexivity, anthropology and film. *Semiotica, 30*, 153–179.

Sandelowski, M. (1986). The problem of rigor in qualitative research. *Advances in Nursing Science, 8*, 27–37.

Schmid, H. (1981). American Occupational Therapy Foundation—Qualitative research and occupational therapy. *American Journal of Occupational Therapy, 35*, 105–106.

Shostak, M. (1981). *Nisa: The life and words of a !Kung woman*. Cambridge, MA: Harvard University Press.

About the Author: Laura Krefting, PhD, is Associate Professor in Occupational Therapy and Career Scientist in Community-Based Rehabilitation, School of Rehabilitation Therapy, Queen's University, Kingston, Ontario, Canada K7L 3N6.

Acknowledgments: I would like to acknowledge Jan Morse, PhD, for her inspirational commitment to, and scholarly mastery of, qualitative research in the health care field and the skillful editorial work of Betty Yerxa, PhD, and two anonymous reviewers.